Imprisoned Intellectuals

Imprisoned Intellectuals

America's Political Prisoners Write on Life, Liberation, and Rebellion

Edited by Joy James

ROWMAN & LITTLEFIELD PUBLISHERS, INC.
Lanham • Boulder • New York • Oxford

ROWMAN & LITTLEFIELD PUBLISHERS, INC.

Published in the United States of America
by Rowman & Littlefield Publishers, Inc.
A Member of the Rowman & Littlefield Publishing Group
4501 Forbes Boulevard, Suite 200, Lanham, Maryland 20706
www.rowmanlittlefield.com

P.O. Box 317, Oxford OX2 9RU, United Kingdom

British Library Cataloguing in Publication Information Available

Library of Congress Cataloging-in-Publication Data

Imprisoned intellectuals : America's political prisoners write on life, liberation, and rebellion / edited by Joy James.
    p.   cm.—(Transformative politics series)
  Includes bibliographical references and index.
  ISBN 0-7425-2026-9 (cloth : alk. paper)—ISBN 0-7425-2027-7 (pbk. : alk. paper)
    1. Prisoners—United States—Biography. 2. Political prisoners—United States—Biography. 3. Intellectuals—United States—Biography. 4. Government, Resistance to—United States. 5. Political crimes and offenses—United States. I. James, Joy, [date] II. Series.
HV9468 .I49   2003
323'.044'092273—dc21   2002014813

Printed in the United States of America

♾ ™ The paper used in this publication meets the minimum requirements of American National Standard for Information Sciences—Permanence of Paper for Printed Library Materials, ANSI/NISO Z39.48-1992.

This work is dedicated to those ancestors, elders, and
youths who seek, struggle, and suffer for freedom;
and to all who filter their desire to abolish
slavery and social death through compassion
for the fragility of life and love.

Contents

Preface

Divisive debates over who "qualifies" as a U.S. political prisoner, and what means should be used for liberation, have been raging for decades; obviously, they will not be resolved here. Still, deeply held views influenced my shaping of this project and the editing of many of the essays presented here. First, I find that definitions commonly used to discuss U.S. "political prisoners" tend to be overly inclusive and simplistic. Therefore, I reject the following as inherently limited designations for "political prisoner": any incarcerated individual who self-defines as such; anyone the state labels as a "criminal" or "terrorist"; and anyone the state politically discriminates against through differential enforcement of laws, racially and economically driven sentencing regimes, and prison treatment. Of course, the above categories apply to many of the writers in this volume. Yet that in itself is not what qualifies them as progressive "political prisoners"—for the question of political agency for a greater democracy remains to be addressed.

The refusal to politically romanticize criminals reflects narrow self-interest and broader communal goals. Regarding self-interest, the criminal for profit or entertainment (your neighbor, nephew, stockbroker, or statesman)—with less fervor than the white supremacists who engineered the 1995 Oklahoma City bombing or the religious extremists who executed the 1993 and 2001 World Trade Center bombings—furthers the demise of me and my kin. Black women demanding political, economic, intellectual, and sexual freedoms are considered legitimate "targets" by various insurrectionists of varied ideologies. Personal interests are compatible with political goals: Any group or individual seeking domination—whether racial, religious, and sexual or economic, political, and international—is the enemy of a liberated society.

Unlike progressive radicals and revolutionaries (politically, "radical" is not synonymous with "extremist"), reactionaries are restorers—rather than transform the current order, they seek to reimpose or reinvigorate old orders of supremacy. Reactionary political prisoners or prisoners of war (apprehended by the state, they can also be classified as "unlawful combatants" and so denied the protection of international or national norms) are not the subject of this volume. In fact, the volume's contributors are designated not only "enemies of the state"[1] but also enemies of the reactionaries at war with the state.

As progressive political prisoners or prisoners of war, revolutionary "enemies of the state" differ from reactionary "enemies of the state." The former expand, while the latter oppose, democratic freedoms. (Centralizing power with corporate and military elites and violating human rights, the state has also proven itself an adversary to democracy.) Progressive "combatants" who resisted state repression in self-defensive or offensive acts that inadvertently caused the loss of life cannot be easily dismissed as "terrorists" by confining them—conceptually or physically—with racial, ideological, or religious supremacists.

One need not argue that the "enemy of my enemy is my friend." It is reasonable to refuse friendship to a "protective" imperialist state expanding police and war powers, a fearful society with slight regard for civilian losses or "collateral damage" that are not "white" or "American." Likewise, it is more than reasonable to condemn an insurrectionary terrorist (alter ego to a state terrorist?) who targets civilians in asymmetrical warfare.

The following writings by progressive political prisoners as intellectuals function as documentary history/political manifesto/theoretical treatises. This work chronicles the turbulent liberation struggles in the United States beginning and ending with spiritual prophets: respectively, Reverend Martin Luther King, Jr., and Lakota warrior and artist Leonard Peltier. The discussion (debate) of what constitutes a U.S. political prisoner is best understood within a larger historical context of repression and resistance. That context, unfortunately, cannot be adequately developed within the confines of this book. However, we can note four key aspects about the historical trajectory of rebellion from oppressed peoples within the United States.

First, throughout American history, "criminals" are racially invented in the public mind; thus, entire communities or peoples are "criminalized."[2] Criminality is considered to be nonconformity; nonconformity is often determined not merely by behavior but also by biology or appearance. Bodies that fail to conform to "whiteness" are treated differently under state or police gaze. Greater obedience is demanded from—and greater violence is used against—those whose physical difference marks them as offensive or threatening. Racially driven policing and sentencing for both social crime and political rebellion mean that African Americans don't do "white time." Compared to their European American counterparts, they disproportionately serve longer sentences under more severe conditions.

Second, the tradition of armed slave insurrections and maroon societies of indigenous and African fugitives in the Americas established a historical consciousness that would, a century later, infuse the women and men in the Black Panther Party, the Black Liberation Army, and the white anti-imperialist movements.[3] Likewise, the military resistance of indigenous peoples and leaders such as Chief Joseph, Sitting Bull, and Geronimo imprinted the American Indian Movement.

Third, as did the nineteenth-century slave and indigenous rebellions, twentieth-century anticolonial struggles tempered both pacifists and armed combatants. During the post–World War II era, traditional imperialism unraveled as the oppressed in Africa, Asia, and Latin America waged insurrections in national liberation movements that reverberated into the United States. Consequently, India's Mohandas Gandhi influenced Martin Luther King, Jr., while the Congo's freedom fighter and president Patrice Lumumba influenced Malcolm X. U.S. domestic rebellions were international in scope and effect as well. The U.S. government understood this as it developed its response through infamous and assassination-prone "intelligence programs" such as the Federal Bureau of Investigation's COINTELPRO[4] and the Central Intelligence Agency; both police institutions were used to destabilize domestic dissent.

Fourth, some readers might tend to overemphasize the discussions of armed struggle that appear prominently in the first half of this anthology. However, a careful reading of contemporary U.S. history reveals that radical organizations garnered wide support based on their ability to address the material needs and aspirations, as well as ideals, of their communities. For example, reservation, barrio, or urban youths were (and are) disaffected by and overwhelmed with frustration at dead-end jobs, poverty, inferior and disciplinary schooling, and police violence. It is logical then that the Black Panther Party, Brown Berets, Young Lords, Young Patriots, and American Indian Movement would have mass appeal among the young. While the majority media focused on the armed aspect of such groups, it was their free breakfast programs, free medical clinics, freedom schools, and social services that elicited wide support. They offered an alternative to the state; and by their massive appeal in oppressed communities, they presented the government with the real threat of popular insurrection guided by revolutionaries. Hence, the governmental fear which produced COINTELPRO's illegal, outrageous, and murderous acts also became a "rational choice" for maintaining dominance. Likewise when New York governor Nelson Rockefeller used the National Guard to brutally suppress the 1971 Attica prison rebellion, it was not just the physical assault (with makeshift knives and clubs) on state and police authority that was repelled, but the political agency of prisoners collectively organizing to demand safe and sanitary living conditions, decent food, and reasonable rather than "slave" wages for their labor. (The *Attica Manifesto* as well as other writings can be found on the *Imprisoned Intellectuals* website: www.rowmanlittlefield.com.)

When not waged as merely episodic raging against injustice, civil disobedience and rebellion inevitably raise the question, "What is revolutionary?" Of course, that question cannot be adequately addressed within the limited context of this collection (or likely any other). However, a few observations can be made. Revolutionaries are distinct from radicals and insurrectionists even when they share the same progressive desires to end military, racial, economic, or sexual domination. Revolution encompasses and surpasses radicalism and rebellion to pursue a greater objective: freedoms safeguarded by institutions. Rather than merely revolt against repressive hierarchies or disobey unjust laws and customs, revolutionary politics seeks to build new structures and norms. Hence, revolutionaries are more feared than radicals or even insurrectionists (who tend to have little allegiance to the state) by governing structures and elites.

It is worth noting that neither crime nor violence is inherently revolutionary. (Capitalism in the Americas is predicated on the theft of land and labor and the mass murder of indigenous and African peoples.) Yet caged in penal sites because of criminal or violent acts, prisoners can be transformed into revolutionaries. Just as in civil society, state criminality and violence can transform law-abiding citizens into revolutionaries.

Not all rebels favor insurrection or revolution. Demands for a total transformation of the state are rarely sustained even among progressives, although such demands flare periodically with public outrage at government excess. What historian Vincent Harding notes of nineteenth-century slave-turned-abolitionist Frederick Douglass applies to twenty-first-century radicals and prison abolitionists:

> He could not—or would not—sharpen and maintain those occasional radical insights which at times had led him to see the involvement of the American people, the American institutions, and the American government in the steel-like web of racism, exploitative economics, and fear which formed the basic undergirding of slavery. For it was not the call to armed insurrection which was the hallmark of antebellum black radicalism, but a careful capacity to see the entire American government, and the institutions and population which it represented, as the basic foe of any serious black struggle, whatever its form might take. It was America, not simply slaveholders, which needed to be transformed, and above all the government and its institutions.[5]

 This volume is based on the conviction—disturbing to many—that the United States and its governing institutions, not just its penal sites rife with human rights abuses, need to be transformed. Here, activists incarcerated for deeds criminalized by the United States appeal to the U.S. constitution, international law, morality, and religious faith to transform life on both sides of the razor wire. Insights into insurrection, rebellion, and liberation require that we engage with their works, both their contributions and contradictions. Refusing to position imprisoned intellectuals as icons, this collection presents them as gateways to avenues that bypass a pantheon in a difficult journey toward liberation movements.

NOTES

1. See the pamphlet by European American, anti-imperialist political prisoners Marilyn Buck, David Gilbert, and Laura Whitehorn, *Enemies of the State* (Brooklyn: Resistance in Brooklyn, 1999, 2d printing), editor's papers.

2. For analyses of how people are criminalized based on race, see Jerome G. Miller, *Search and Destroy: African American Males in the Criminal Justice System* (Cambridge: Cambridge University Press, 1996); Luana Ross, *Inventing the Savage: The Social Construction of Native*

American Criminality (Austin: University of Texas Press, 1998); and Beth Richie, *Compelled to Crime* (New York: Routledge, 1995).

3. For scholarly works on the history of armed struggle against enslavement, see Vincent Harding, *There Is a River: The Black Struggle for Freedom in America* (New York: Vintage Books, 1983); Thomas Higginson, *Black Rebellion: A Selection from Travellers and Outlaws* (New York: Arno Press, 1969, rprt.; New York: Lee and Shepard Publishers, 1889); Herbert Aptheker, *American Negro Slave Revolts* (New York: Columbia University Press, 1944, 2d printing). For works on resistance to the criminalization of African Americans or "blackness," see Ida B. Wells, *Southern Horrors and Other Writings* (Boston: Bedford, 1997); Herbert Shapiro, *White Violence and Black Response: From Reconstruction to Montgomery* (Amherst: University of Massachusetts Press, 1988). For an analysis exploring both nonviolence and armed struggle see Bill Sutherland and Matt Meyer, *Guns and Gandhi in Africa: Pan African Insights on Nonviolence, Armed Struggle and Liberation in Africa* (Trenton, N.J.: Africa World Press, 2000).

4. See Athan Theoharis, *The FBI: An Annotated Bibliography and Research Guide* (New York: Garland Publishing, 1994); and John Stockwell, *In Search of Enemies: A CIA Story* (New York: W. W. Norton, 1978).

5. Harding, *There Is a River*, 200.

Acknowledgments

This book has taken its own bittersweet time. Over the last several years, it has gained in depth and range, benefiting from the growing works on and by imprisoned progressive authors.

First, acknowledgment to the incarcerated readers who, upon receiving copies of *States of Confinement: Policing, Detention, and Prisons* in 2000, politely thanked me for sending the anthology and then proceeded to critique me and the work for the omission of voices of imprisoned writers and an overemphasis on academic interpretations of policing and imprisonment.

In responding to the challenge to collect and edit the writings of progressive political prisoners, who speak for themselves and whose voices are not easily appropriated, many lent assistance. To those who helped in bringing this work to print and whose names I forget to mention, my apologies, and my thanks.

Dean Birkenkamp, Alison Sullenberger, and Jehanne Schweitzer of Rowman & Littlefield supported this collection. Robert Allen of *The Black Scholar*, Andrew McNeillie of Blackwell Publishers, Mathias Bolton of the Anarchist Black Cross, and Jeffrey Parish of the Radical Philosophy Association newsletter, *RPN*, helpfully provided electronic versions of materials for reprint. Mumia Abu-Jamal provided important editorial comments for earlier drafts of the anthology.

This book also grew with university resources for student researchers that I received from various academic institutions over the last five years. Sabrina Hodges was one of the first students to help in gathering materials when we began this project in 1998–1999 at the University of Colorado-Boulder with funding from UTROP (the University Teaching Research Opportunity Program). While Distinguished Visiting Professor in The Institute for Research in African American Studies (IRAAS) at Columbia University, IRAAS graciously provided me with the opportunity to work with Danyel Peña–Shaw who gave valuable assistance in 1999–2000. From 2000 to 2002, Brown University's UTRA (University Teaching Research Assistance) program enabled Liz Appel, Sharon Luk, Marguerite Graham, Amit Sarin, Brady Heiner, Tiffany Bradley, Christopher Muller, Hana Tauber, and

Elizabeth Walsh, and Manuella Meyer to play instrumental roles in pulling this volume together. Students in the spring 2002 advanced seminar on prison intellectuals researched and drafted biographies for a number of contributors to this collection. In addition, Liz, Brady, Hana, and Chris were invaluable in organizing the spring 2002 conference, *Imprisoned Intellectuals: A Dialogue with Academics, Activists, and (Former) U.S. Political Prisoners on War, Dissent, and Social Justice*, held at Brown University. That gathering (with proceedings published in the journal *Social Justice*) provided an opportunity to reflect on this project and to make new friendships dedicated to justice.

Within and beyond the academic carceral, Beatrice Adderley, Elizabeth Amelia Hadley, Emily Blumenfeld, T. Denean Sharpley-Whiting, Claude Marks, Donna Willmott, Rob McBride, Laura Whitehorn, Susie Day, Dylan Rodriguez, Frank Wilderson, Susan Rosenberg, Mecke Nagel, and Bettina Aptheker assisted in the shaping of this work. My deepest appreciation to Laura Whitehorn, Frank Wilderson, Dylan Rodriguez, and Michael Hames-Garcia for their insightful contributions to the development of the introduction; also "thank you" to Susan Rosenberg and Bettina Aptheker for inspiration to write the preface. Obviously, I am solely responsible for whatever shortcomings appear in the preface and the introduction.

Laura Whitehorn and Susie Day, with tireless energy and vision, lent their considerable knowledge and editing skills toward strengthening this anthology. They, with Madrina and my other kin, sustained me through the long haul of gathering documents and essays, editing, worrying, and wondering about this collection as it evolved toward publication.

Working with patience, insight, and humor—and more patience—radical imprisoned intellectuals have offered and taught me much about critique, commitment, and courage, as well as pain and beauty, discipline and grace. Reading and rereading this collection, I encounter the generosity, frailties and strengths, contradictions and contributions of "disappeared" rebels and heretics, of prophets and soldiers and healers. I am reminded of the noncanonical Gnostic Gospels suppressed by state religion; the heart of this work seems to pulse with the Gospel of Thomas (113):

The disciples said to Him, "When will the Kingdom come?" [Jesus said,] "It will not come by waiting for it."

Prologue

A New Declaration
of Independence

Emma Goldman
July 1909

When, in the course of human development, existing institutions prove inadequate to the needs of man, when they serve merely to enslave, rob, and oppress mankind, the people have the eternal right to rebel against, and overthrow, these institutions.

The mere fact that these forces—inimical to life, liberty, and the pursuit of happiness—are legalized by statute laws, sanctified by divine rights, and enforced by political power in no way justifies their continued existence.

We hold these truths to be self-evident: that all human beings, irrespective of race, color, or sex, are born with the equal right to share at the table of life; that to secure this right, there must be established among men economic, social, and political freedom; we hold further that government exists but to maintain special privilege and property rights; that it coerces man into submission and therefore robs him of dignity, self-respect, and life.

The history of the American kings of capital and authority is the history of repeated crimes, injustice, oppression, outrage, and abuse, all aiming at the suppression of individual liberties and the exploitation of the people. A vast country, rich enough to supply all her children with all possible comforts, and insure well-being to all, is in the hands of a few, while the nameless millions are at the mercy of ruthless wealth gatherers, unscrupulous lawmakers, and corrupt politicians. Sturdy sons of America are forced to tramp the country in a fruitless search for bread, and many of her daughters are driven into the street, while thousands of tender children are daily sacrificed on the altar of Mammon. The reign of these kings is holding mankind in slavery, perpetuating poverty and disease, maintaining crime and corruption; it is fettering the spirit of liberty, throttling the voice of justice, and degrading and oppressing humanity. It is engaged in continual war and slaughter,

1

devastating the country and destroying the best and finest qualities of man; it nurtures superstition and ignorance, sows prejudice and strife, and turns the human
family into a camp of Ishmaelites.

We, therefore, the liberty-loving men and women, realizing the great injustice
and brutality of this state of affairs, earnestly and boldly do hereby declare that each
and every individual is and ought to be free to own himself and to enjoy the full
fruit of his labor; that man is absolved from all allegiance to the kings of authority
and capital; that he has, by the very fact of his being, free access to the land and all
means of production, and entire liberty of disposing of the fruits of his efforts; that
each and every individual has the unquestionable and unabridgeable right of free
and voluntary association with other equally sovereign individuals for economic,
political, social, and all other purposes, and that to achieve this end man must
emancipate himself from the sacredness of property, the respect for man-made law,
the fear of the Church, the cowardice of public opinion, the stupid arrogance of
national, racial, religious, and sex superiority, and from the narrow puritanical con-
ception of human life. And for the support of this declaration, and with a firm reli-
ance on the harmonious blending of man's social and individual tendencies, the
lovers of liberty joyfully consecrate their uncompromising devotion, their energy
and intelligence, their solidarity and their lives.

REFERENCES

Falk, Candace Serena. *Love, Anarchy, and Emma Goldman*. New Brunswick, N.J.: Rutgers
    University Press, 1984.
Goldman, Emma. *Anarchism and Other Essays*. New York: Mother Earth Publishing Associa-
    tion, 1911.
———. *Living My Life*. New York: Knopf, 1931.
Wexler, Alice. *Emma Goldman: An Intimate Life*. New York: Pantheon, 1984.

NOTE

Originally published in *Mother Earth* 4, no. 5 (July 1909).

Born on June 27, 1869, in Kovno Province, Russia, into a Jewish family that suffered
under the anti-Semitic laws of that era, Emma Goldman immigrated to the United States
with her sister Helena in 1886. There she adopted anarchist and radical feminist analyses,
eventually becoming a powerful organizer, and leading the 1889 Cloak Maker Strike and the
1891 New York May Day demonstration. For "inciting a riot" that never materialized, Goldman served one year at Blackwell's Island Penitentiary in New York City. Soon after her
release in 1894, Goldman voluntarily left the country. Upon returning to the United States,
she embarked on an extensive national lecture tour between 1896 and 1899. Arrested frequently, she gained sympathizers at each engagement. Toward the end of her life, Goldman
joined the Spanish struggle against fascism and Generalissimo Francisco Franco in 1936;
while lecturing in support of the Spanish freedom movement, she suffered a stroke and died
in Canada in 1940.

Introduction

Joy James

Under a government which imprisons any unjustly, the true place for a just man is also a prison.

—Henry David Thoreau

It is the action, not the fruit of the action, that's important. You have to do the right thing. It may not be in your time that there will be any fruit, but that doesn't mean you stop doing the right thing. You may never know what results come from your action. But if you do nothing, there will be no result.

—Mahatma Mohandas Gandhi

AMERICAN "PRISON NOTEBOOKS"

Antonio Gramsci, while imprisoned in Mussolini's Italy for his political beliefs and socialist activism, wrote in his *Prison Notebooks* that, "Every social group . . . creates together with itself, organically, one or more strata of intellectuals which give it homogeneity and an awareness of its own function not only in the economic but also in the social and political fields." For Gramsci, because everyone thinks critically and philosophically, everyone is an intellectual; but not everyone officially functions as such in society.[1]

In a stratified culture, one may superficially assume that only professional intellectuals, recognized writers and pundits in the public realm, academics, and policymakers constitute an intellectual formation. However, every group has an "organic" intellectual caste, one that functions as a vehicle to articulate, shape, and further the aspirations of its constituency.

Hence, the "public intellectual" encompasses the oft-forgotten "prison intellectual." That is, the imprisoned intellectual is a public intellectual who, like his or her highly visible and celebrated counterparts, reflects upon social meaning, dis-

3

cord, development, ethics, and justice. Prisons function as intellectual and political sites unauthorized by the state. Yet, when and where the imprisoned intellectual gives voice to the incarcerated or captive, those denied social justice and full democratic power on both sides of the concertina wire, then and there our stories of war and love shaping visions of freedom and fulfillment take on a new life—often a quite disturbing one.

In editing this volume of writings by imprisoned intellectuals, political prisoners in the contemporary United States, I gradually realized the impossibilities of filtering language in harrying and prophetic narratives. One cannot bring some definitive "academic" meaning to this collection, a gathering of words in resistance, words written by revolutionaries captured and detained—for days or years, decades or life—by the leviathan against which they rebelled. This is the leviathan to which most readers of this volume pledge their allegiance in some fashion or another—tithing to domestic and foreign policies that increase military and police powers, and concentrations of wealth and poverty. The rebels went to prison; and, passing through or surviving incarceration, they wrote as outlaw intellectuals with unique and controversial insights into idealism, warfare, and social justice.

When writing is a painful endeavor, marked by political struggle and despair as well as determination and courage, it is potentially transformative. Reading may also share (in an attenuated fashion) the impetus and ethos of the writing. Yet it will not necessarily compel the reader to moral and political acts. Author and academic Barbara Harlow cautions, "Reading prison writing must . . . demand a correspondingly activist counterapproach to that of passivity, aesthetic gratification, and the pleasures of consumption that are traditionally sanctioned by the academic disciplining of literature."[2] An "activist counterapproach" to the consumptive indifference is infrequent, but it does occur. If the circulation of rarely referenced or vilified "resistance literature" reflects the growing public interest in incarceration sites, intellectual and political dissent for social justice, and the possibilities of democratic transformations, then collections such as this should spark new debates about "reading" and activism and political theory.

Reading and editing, from the bipolar lens of academic and radical intellectual, I see that the purpose of this work was to foster or force an encounter between those in the so-called free world seeking personal and collective freedoms and those in captivity seeking liberation from economic, military, racial/sexual systems. Like all good and necessary encounters, this one between writers and readers is provocative and elicits more questions than can be answered within the confines of a book—even an anthology of critique, confrontation, and radical risk taking.

DEBATES, DISOBEDIENCE, AND DISSENT

Amid the debates about "political prisoners" in the United States, one can distinguish between those engaged in civil disobedience who identify as "loyal opposition"—and by their very dissent affirm the institutions of American democracy—and those so alienated by state violence and government betrayals of humanitarian and democratic ideals that their dissent chronicles their disaffection, and at times insurrection.[3] Such insurrection may also at times become (proto-)revolutionary.[4]

"Law abiding dissent" represents a political risk taking with broader social acceptance. This is largely due to its adherence to principles of nonviolent civil disobedience, widely shared moral values, and, sometimes, proximity to the very "corridors of (institutional) power" closed to the disenfranchised; such adherence spares dissenters the harshest of sentences. Although not emphasized in this volume, the narratives of influential political detainees offer important insights. For example, after being imprisoned for engaging in civil disobedience to protest U.S. military bombing practices on Vieques Island, Puerto Rico, Robert F. Kennedy, Jr. wrote:

> I arrived at my difficult decision to join the invasion of Vieques only after I was convinced that its people had exhausted every legal and political avenue to secure their rights. In my 18 years as a lawyer and environmental advocate for the Natural Resources Defense Council and the Riverkeeper movement, I had never engaged in an act of civil disobedience. As an attorney, I have a duty to uphold the law. But I also had a countervailing duty in this case. The bombardment of Vieques is bad military policy and disastrous for public health and the environment. But the most toxic residue of the Navy's history on Vieques is its impact on our democracy. The people I met there are United States citizens, but the Navy's abusive exercise of power on the island has left them demoralized, alienated and feeling that they are neither part of a democracy nor the beneficiaries of the American system of justice.[5]

Kennedy narrates that upon returning for trial, he encountered Reverend Jesse Jackson who was in Puerto Rico to support his wife, Jacqueline, while she served a ten-day jail sentence for protesting against military violations. Upon informing the civil rights leader of Kennedy's expectant wife Mary's insistence that her husband not take a deal to delay his sentencing, Kennedy recalls that Jackson responded, "Suffering is often the most powerful tool against injustice and oppression. If Jesus had plea-bargained the crucifixion, we wouldn't have the faith."

Unlike Kennedy, Jesse Jackson is a veteran of civil rights protest and civil disobedience. Leading demonstrations against domestic infractions such as "driving while black/brown" or "voting while black/brown," the former aide to Martin Luther King, Jr., has for decades vocally criticized U.S. foreign policy and vocally supported Palestinian self-determination and the abolition of apartheid states. In the 1980s, in solidarity with Nelson Mandela[6] and other South African political prisoners, Jackson encouraged U.S. citizens to trespass at the offices of South African government agencies. This civil disobedience, often by middle-class Americans, usually resulted in several hours of detention in city jails, and became seen as a "badge of honor" or rite of (political) passage. Such short-term (symbolic?) jailings prompt several observations. First, it is likely that it is not political incarceration per se that is stigmatized but incarceration based on a refusal to suffer violence without resorting to armed self-defense; the choice of the latter surely leads to one's "disappearance" from conventional society and "respectable" politics. Second, even nonviolent conscientious objectors (COs) during World War II—who sought to "redeem" themselves as patriots by risking their lives as human guinea pigs in U.S. military medical experiments—and religious pacifists in the civil rights and antiwar movements that followed were disavowed once designated as "unpatriotic."

Consider that despite his adherence to Christian faith and Gandhian principles of nonviolent civil disobedience, Martin Luther King, Jr., lost considerable support and organizational funding from both white and black liberals after he publicly criticized imperialism (and capitalism) and the U.S. war against Vietnam.[7] What is largely condemned in American political culture is not the risk taking that leads to incarceration but the radicalism that rejects the validity of the nation-state itself and the legitimacy of its legal and moral standing. How does one reconcile the proximity and distance between the law-abiding loyalist and the pacifist or militarist radical who appear in the same courts, often using similar legal arguments, but with very different political intentions and consequences seem to stand a world apart in their dissent?

Diverse worlds or parallel universes hover about this volume. Contributors disagree about strategy and morality ("nonviolence or violence") and politics ("loyal or revolutionary"). Toward a work such as this, one intended to raise queries, eyebrows, and passions, there appear many questions and debates—particularly for those informed about and disaffected by the criminalization of dissidents amid state criminality and abuse of (police and war) powers. Many debates seem to center on the question of what constitutes shared community, one in struggle for commonly held ideals of justice, individual freedom, collective liberation, and material well-being in civil society marked by growing state control.

Radical philosophers have argued that street and prison gangs are forms of "civil society" conditioned by the state and government apparatuses' manipulation of the drug trade, control of territory, and deployment of police repression. Philosopher Michael Hames-Garcia raises cogent questions about the relationships between the incarcerated and those in the "free world," asking, "how might one situate the specifically intellectual activity of organic prison intellectuals in relation to the state? To what kind of 'civil society' or 'counterpublic' are prison intellectuals directing their writings and how is this audience [readership] positioned in relationship to the state?"[8]

State conditioning is not the only force destabilizing progressive politics. The prison movement has grown immensely over the last decades. Yet, it still has its own internal demons to fight concerning coalitions and efficacy. Activists as "official representatives" can invoke the political prisoner-as-icon in order to derail external and internal criticisms of their strategies, and wield surrogate iconic powers in an uncritical fashion. This raises the question of whether the imprisoned—as political "dependents" relying upon those outside to garner support—might engage in self-censorship concerning the limitations of their allies. Such "self-censorship" and self-conditioning work both ways. The privileged academic might hesitate to criticize a progressive "folk hero" sentenced to life or death in prison, although, in a culture that widely disparages prisoners, the repercussions of academic criticisms seem to be fairly limited. This suggests additional queries about the nature of "parity" between political prisoners and their political allies: In theory and practice, the imprisoned intellectual can be ideologically "frozen" in or physically "freed" by the work of non-incarcerated academics and activists.

Scholar Dylan Rodriguez questions whether, given the constraints, an imprisoned intellectual can truly become a "public intellectual." Arguing that while in prison such writers are "disabled from meaningful participation in the interpretation and 'translation' of their works," Rodriguez references "radical/revolutionary intellectuals whose praxis is in irreconcilable opposition to the very historical and political logic of the 'public' (civil society) as it exists for the endorsement of their virtual (and biological) death." I both agree and disagree with this assessment. True, the general or mainstream public constitutes a mostly hostile or indifferent readership and respondent. Yet, there are multiple "publics" and varied "civil societies"; the "public sphere" is shaped, to varying degrees, by whoever enter as engagees. The intent of imprisoned intellectuals to influence "the public" in its multiple formations is a complicated proposition but a real endeavor. No monolithic "radical political prisoner" exists. Despite shared antiracist and anti-imperialist politics, U.S. political prisoners differ in identity, ideology, and strategy. Rodriguez, though, makes an essential point about how imprisoned intellectuals are "read": "[T]here is a rather widespread, normalized *disavowal* of the political and theoretical substance of the work generated by imprisoned radical intellectuals."[9]

This "abolitionist" assertion is further complicated if we consider how contemporary racism and penal captivity likely evolved from within a historical colonial–settler state built upon, and enriched by, anti-Indigenous genocide and African enslavement. Some contributors to this volume argue in their respective chapters that there is a "normalized disavowal" of the presence of (radical or independent) blacks or Indians in conventional "civil society." Hence, they call for some form(s) of independence or autonomy from what they view as an enveloping and destructive formation (what some have called an "empire"). The racially marked political prisoner tends to be most forgotten, and to serve the longest sentences. Some of the longest sentences and most violent punishments have been meted out to African and Native Americans in the Black Panther Party or American Indian Movement and their allies, and Puerto Rican *independentistas*. To rationalize the sentences and punishments by pointing to the advocacy or use of armed struggle or armed self-defense by some of the incarcerated ignores the fact that a number of those slain or incarcerated (for decades) were innocent of charges. Their innocence is attested to, as in the cases of Fred Hampton and Mark Clark, who were slain, and Dhoruba Bin Wahad and Geronimo ji-Jaga (Pratt), who were finally released in the 1990s, by imillion-dollar settlements paid out by the U.S. government, ostensibly for wrongful deaths and incarcerations.

It is assumed that some readers of this volume will be critical of the "prison industrial complex," and so, to varying degrees, self-identify as "abolitionists." The most militant wing of the twenty-first-century abolitionist movement will likely be that antiracist minority who argues that the abolition of the death penalty, and of (human rights abuses in) prisons and Immigration and Naturalization Services (INS) detention centers, and of the widespread racial bias in sentencing, merely addresses the *symptoms* of a pervasive disease. Revolutionary abolitionists offer their own readings, drawing insights from contemporary battles and historical lessons (following the Civil War, Congress abolished slavery to sanction the convict prison lease system and sharecropping, new forms of legal servitude to be endured and fought by African Americans for one hundred years).

In the wake of the New York Police Department's brutality against people of African descent—viscerally recorded in the 1997 beating-rape of Abner Louima, and the 1999 firing of forty-one shots at Amadou Diallo—theorist Frank Wilderson, III, writes:

[I]f we are to follow [Frantz] Fanon's analysis [in *The Wretched of the Earth*], and the gestures toward this understanding in some of the work of imprisoned intellectuals, then we have to come to grips with the fact that, for Black people, civil society *itself*—rather than its abuses or shortcomings—is a state of emergency. . . . In "The Avant-Garde of White Supremacy," [Steve] Martinot and [Jared] Sexton assert the primacy of Fanon's Manichean zones (without the promise of higher unity) even in the face of American integration. . . . this Manichean delirium manifests itself by way of the US paradigm of policing which (re)produces, repetitively, the inside/outside, the civil society/black world, by virtue of the difference between those bodies that don't magnetize bullets and those bodies that do. "Police impunity serves to distinguish between . . . those whose human being is put permanently in question and those for whom it goes without saying" (Martinot and Sexton, 8). . . . Whiteness then, and by extension civil society . . . must be first understood as a social formation of contemporaries who do not magnetize bullets.[10]

Whether pacifist or militarist, responding to violence and racism in domestic or foreign policy, these works will remain suspect and heatedly debated by many in the public realm. Fine. Our goal here was to ensure that they not remain largely overlooked or erased. Paradoxically, those most passionately seeking collective liberation—from racial or economic or military dominance—are those most likely to lose their individual freedoms. The captive/free dichotomy is a paradox rich in irony: imprisoned intellectuals, the most intensely monitored and repressed by the state's police apparatus, might in fact be those most free of state conditioning. Existing not merely as the output of "victims" of state responses to radical opposition, the analyses of imprisoned intellectuals both deconstruct dominant ideologies and reconstruct new strategies for humanity. Their writings proffer reactive and proactive readings of struggle and freedom.

So the questions and answers continue. "How do you make the 'disappeared' (the captive rebel, the impoverished, the racialized, the addicted, the 'queer') reappear?" "When is a democracy not a democracy?" "Have slavery, surrogate forms of captivity, and social death[11] been reinstated through the Thirteenth Amendment?"[12] "To what degree does self-critique in liberation movements prevent radical responses to state and racial violence from becoming self-inflicted wounds?" This collection raises and addresses queries and explores the implications of responses.

TRACING A HISTORICAL TRAJECTORY

The United States has a long and terrible history of confinement and disappearance of those it racially and politically targets. Include those captives in slavery and on reservations, and it becomes a longer narrative of torture and resistance. W. E. B. Du Bois notes in *Black Reconstruction in America* how over 200,000 African Americans served in combat during the Civil War.[13] Their ancestral line included Denmark Vesey, Nat Turner, and Harriet Tubman and their political lineage, John Brown. With the rise of lynching after the aborted Reconstruction era, investigative journalist Ida B. Wells, armed with a pistol, vigorously organized against racial terror in which as many as ten thousand whites attended "parties" that roasted and dismembered black victims. There has always been resistance. The colonized, subaltern, and subjugated have continuously fought genocide and social death, and in battle called upon progenitors for guidance, and, in failure, for forgiveness.[14] Contemporary incarcerated writers and political theorists are no different. Housed in San Quentin, Vietnamese activist and author Mike Ngo writes of prisoners' forced complicity with authorities and his own shame in participating in the disciplinary machinery, alleviated when he finds comfort in conversation with slain prison writer, revolutionary strategist-turned-icon, George Jackson. For Ngo, if it does not destroy, imprisonment teaches power and political theorizing that emanate from intimacy with death: social, physical, sexual, emotional.[15] Intimacy with death, whether one's own or those prematurely engineered by the voracious appetites of expanding military-corporate power, is written all throughout the following pages: death in resistance to the Klan; death through assassination; death in battles with the police; death in opposition to U.S. military incursions and interventions; death in execution chambers; death on street corners; and death to the very concept of blind civic obedience and patriotic fervor. This intimacy is accompanied by death's companion, life, and, if not the inevitability of political and military victory for the rebels (who, in the phrase of Black Panther Party [BPP] cofounder Huey P. Newton, seemed to court "revolutionary suicide"), the possibility of liberation and freedom, and the certainty of striving for it.

The endemic flight from death in American culture (via its fetishism of youth,

technology, and immortality tied to materiality and science) indicates a marathon
of avoidance politics and censorship. The disappearance of the incarcerated and
the inhumane punishment for rebels suggest that intimacy with the imprisoned,
particularly political prisoners, will be embraced and known by only a few. For
many "law-abiding Americans" are (or socially seem) embarrassed by a family member's incarceration and the realities of political incarceration in their democracy.
With some 2.5 million imprisoned or detained by the state, 70 percent of whom
are African, Latino, Native, or Asian American, many families could claim this
intimacy. Like families in denial, U.S. government officials fervently deny the existence of U.S. political prisoners. State employees do so by defining political militants as "criminals." Yet, who is the "criminal" whose crime is his or her physical
opposition to state criminality (as determined by United Nations conventions,
human rights law, and non-apartheid-based morality)—crimes against humanity in
warfare and profiteering, crimes against the poor, against the racially subordinate,
crimes against children, against women?[16] To address the issue of incarcerated intellectuals, one would have to examine the reasons for their incarceration; examine
not just the acts of which they were accused and convicted (at times with court
malfeasance), but their commitments. Perhaps discussions of political incarceration
in the United States fail to register in conventional speech and education because
of political ignorance and a moral reluctance to attain intimacy with life-and-death
confrontations.

This volume, largely by writers incarcerated because of their legal or illegal, pacifist or violent resistance to repression, constantly references antiracism. African
Americans constitute the greatest percentage not only of those incarcerated for
crimes against private property, drug violations, and social violence, but also of
those incarcerated for political acts (including armed struggle) in opposition to
repression. As the largest contingent of (social and) political prisoners, African
Americans tend to draw the longest sentences with fewer possibilities for clemency
or parole. There is a specificity and temerity about black liberation struggles that
relate to and infuse political prisoners in the United States. From enslaved insurrectionists to their multiethnic progeny, antiracism defines but does not dominate this
collection. There remains the question(s) of gender, community, culture, art, spirituality. I read the connection of white anti-imperialists and peace activists, Puerto
Rican *independentistas*, and Native American resistors through the black gaze.
Hence, there are two sections to this volume, the first on black liberation, the second on internationalism and anti-imperialism. The importance of various struggles
is not reduced to but is framed by the context of racial dynamics of state repression.
Such a context raises another series of questions that also have no easy answers,
ones that, hopefully, will be pursued in continuous, painstaking dialogue: "How and
why do repressive conditions create a certain brand of intellectualism?" "What roles
do the voices of incarcerated intellectuals play in moral and political thought and
action, and social consciousness?" "What makes someone a political prisoner?" The

last question, being the "easiest" to answer, reveals the varied debates waged among those who acknowledge the existence of political prisoners in the United States.

POLITICAL PRISONERS

There is a continuum of debate on who or what constitutes a political prisoner. The debate wages among prisoners themselves and among the non-incarcerated. A political prisoner can be someone who was put in prison for nonpolitical reasons but who became politicized in his or her thought and action while incarcerated. Incarceration is inherently political, but ideology plays a role. If everyone is a political prisoner then no one is. Although the meaning of who is a political prisoner appears to be expanding to include more structural critiques of the state at large, I reserve the use of (a somewhat awkward term) "political-econ" prisoners for those convicted of social crimes tied to property and drug-related crimes and whose disproportionate sentencing to prison rather than rehabilitation or community service is shaped by the political economy of racial and economic privilege and disenfranchisement. As a caste, political-econ prisoners can and do develop and refine their political critiques while incarcerated. (For example, of the contributors to this volume, Malcolm X, George Jackson, and Standing Deer were incarcerated for social crimes against property or people, and politicized as radicals within the penal site; also, paradoxically, youths who renounced their gang memberships and social crime, in order to bring about social change through the Black Panther Party, would find themselves later targeted and imprisoned for their political affiliations.) Those whose thoughts of social justice lead to commitments and acts in political confrontation with oppression acquire the standing of political prisoners. For those who (continue to) prey on others in physical and sexual assaults on children, women, and men, "political prisoners" would be an obscene register; for they do not manifest as liberatory agents but exist as merely one of many sources of danger to be confronted and quelled in a violent culture.

Victimization by a dominant culture and aggrandizing state is not sufficient to qualify one as a "political prisoner." Although the strategies vary concerning violence in resistance politics, if agency and morality are prerequisites shaping the political being, then we speak of a fragment of the incarcerated population, just as we would speak of a fragment of the non-incarcerated population. Here, our discussion centers on revolutionary and radical activists who also constitute intellectual formations influencing political contemporary culture. Some progressives assert that to construct an entity called "political prisoners" creates a dichotomy between a select group and the vast majority of prisoners, and thus in fact promotes a new form of elitism—the iconic prisoner. Yet, these men and women are different. They were different before their incarceration, marked by their critical thinking and confrontations with authoritarian structures and policies and violence. Also, they were and are treated differently by the state, often receiving the harshest of sentences,

relegated to solitary confinement or "lockdown" in control units so that they cannot "infect"—really infuse—other prisoners with their radical politics and aspirations for freedom.

Mondo we Langa (David Rice), incarcerated in Nebraska prisons for decades for
a crime that he states he did not commit, one for which his attorneys argue that
there is no physical evidence implicating him, writes in "Letter from the Inside":

> I know what I mean by "political prisoner": someone who, in the context of U.S. laws
> and court system, has been falsely tried and convicted of a criminal offense as a means
> of ending his or her political activities and making an example of the person for others
> who are espousing, or might espouse, ideas that those in power would find offensive. By
> this definition, I might be the only political prisoner in this joint. But in a broader
> sense, most people behind bars could be considered "political prisoners," inasmuch as
> the process of lawmaking, law-enforcing, and the criminal "justice" system are all
> driven by a political apparatus that is anti-people of color and anti-people of little eco-
> nomic means. At the same time though, many, if not most of the people who are locked
> up have acted in the interests of the very system that oppresses them and victimized
> people who, like themselves, are oppressed.[17]

Attorneys Michael E. Deutsch and Jan Susler describe in "Political Prisoners in
the United States: The Hidden Reality" (1990) three types of political prisoners.
For Deutsch and Susler U.S. political prisoners are

1. Foreign nationals whose political status or political activities against allies of
   U.S. imperialism (e.g., Israel, Great Britain, El Salvador) result in detention
   or imprisonment;
2. Members of U.S. oppressed nationalities (African Americans, Puerto Ricans,
   Chicano/Mexicanos, and Native Americans) who are prosecuted and imprisoned for political activities in furtherance of their [liberation] movements. . . .
   Included in these groups are anticolonial combatants or prisoners of war
   (POWs)—members of national liberation movements who as part of clandestine organizations have employed armed struggle as a means to achieve self-
   determination and independence for their nation and upon capture have the
   right, under the Additional Protocols of the Geneva Convention and the UN
   General Assembly Resolutions, to POW status and not to be tried as domestic
   criminals; and
3. White people who have acted in solidarity with the liberation movements of
   oppressed nationalities or against U.S. foreign or domestic policies.[18]

Deutsch and Susler offer a useful categorization of political prisoners; however, the
first category could be expanded to include nonresident or immigrant detainees
awaiting deportation. Following September 11, 2001, the sweeps of noncitizens
legally organizing for workers' rights in Florida, mostly young people of South Asian
origin, construct a new category—that of political prisoner awaiting deportation.

Although the United States has a history of deporting militants—Emma Goldman, Marcus Garvey, Claudia Jones, C. L. R. James—there appears a schism in alignment with "foreign" political prisoners housed in the United States and awaiting deportation to hostile nations and U.S. citizens who are political prisoners in other countries, as in the case of Lori Berenson, who has been incarcerated in Peru for years.[19] In radical politics around incarceration and the "prison-industrial-complex" most of the strategies regarding political prisoners have focused on the release campaigns of those incarcerated for decades, and rightly so. However, preventive measures and strategies to counter the increasing ability of the government to "disappear" political prisoners (as was the case following September 11 when Attorney General John Ashcroft held Sundiata Acoli, Philip Berrigan (who died of cancer in December 2002), and Marilyn Buck as well as other political prisoners incommunicado) do not appear clearly defined by advocates of prisoners' rights.[20]

In its 2002 letter to Governor George Pataki and the New York State Parole Board, the New York Task Force on Political Prisoners states that in Europe, Africa, and the United States,

> prisoners long incarcerated for their political beliefs and actions have been set free—and in their freedom, have given the world back some hope and dignity. The release, for example, of Nelson Mandela, who spent twenty-seven years in prison for revolutionary actions against [the apartheid government] . . . has proved a catalyst for healing and justice in South Africa.

Signatories, attorneys who work pro bono for the release campaign for political prisoners attest:

> These prisoners' convictions reflect as yet unresolved issues of civil, racial, and economic justice of the 1960s and 1970s, a time when thousands of people of all races, young and old, women and men, formed militant movements to demand fundamental social change. Their trials occurred during a time when their juries and the general public did not know that, in response to these movements, the government was engaging in illegal and unconstitutional acts—acts of infiltration and surveillance which, according to the government's own documents, carried over into the legal arena. Foremost in the government's campaign was the FBI's now-infamous Counter-Intelligence Program [COINTELPRO], condemned by a 1975 United States Senate Committee which became known as the "Church Committee" [named after Senator Frank Church (D-Idaho), the committee's proceedings were published in 1976].[21]

The legal challenges brought by the prisoners referenced in this letter have been denied, primarily due to the 1996 federal law drastically limiting prisoners' access to *habeas corpus*. Heartbreakingly for their families and communities, some of these prisoners have repeatedly been denied parole because of their political views or offenses—despite the fact that they more than meet current parole standards. . . . Some of the actions for which these men were convicted were taken in response to severe social repression and government misconduct. Some convictions, for example, arose directly from the targeting of activists by COINTELPRO. Others sought to defend themselves and their communities from police violence [or drug dealers]. All of them devoted their hearts, their minds, and their lives to working for a world of justice, peace, and human equality. Whatever one's opinion of their political beliefs or alleged actions, not one of these men was motivated by personal gain. All have served enough time and all would be a credit to their communities if released.[22]

The imprisonment of those seeking social and political change in the United States is as old as its elite-based democracy rooted in slavery, anti-Indian genocidal wars, and "manifest destiny." Yet the attempts to bring the voices of imprisoned intellectuals to the general society and petition for their release remain a constant (re)invention of strategic interventions, using the language of "rehabilitation" commingled with the language of rebellious resistance.

ANTHOLOGIZING IMPRISONED INTELLECTUALS

Prisons constitute one of the most controversial and contested sites in a democratic society. The United States has the highest incarceration rate in the industrialized world, with over two million people in jails, prisons, and detention centers; with over three thousand on death row, it is also one of the few developed countries that continues to deploy the death penalty. Examining intellectuals whose analyses of U.S. society, politics, culture, and social justice are rarely referenced in conventional political speech or academic discourse, this anthology takes shape along the contours of a body of outlawed "public intellectuals" offering incisive critiques of our society and shared (in)humanity. The brief biographies introducing each chapter contextualize these writings in opposition to state policies that support racism, war, imperialism, corporate capitalism, and globalization. Like the accompanying biographies, a number of these essays by writer-activists incarcerated because of their political beliefs and acts (some released by President Bill Clinton on his last day of office, others working as educators and activists behind bars) are far too brief to fully detail and explore the conditions of their political radicalism and imprisonment. However, references are provided to help the reader further explore controversial liberation praxes from the civil rights/black power, women's, gay/lesbian, American Indian, Puerto Rican Independence, and antiwar movements based on radical democracy and revolutionary struggle.

We begin with European anarchist Emma Goldman's "A New Declaration of Independence" as a contrast to calls for "patriotism" as unquestioning obedience to the state. We end with the poem "Incommunicado" by Marilyn Buck, written after September 11, 2001, during and following her weeks of detention in solitary confinement without access to attorneys or family on the orders of Attorney General John Ashcroft.[23] Buck, imprisoned in the 1980s for her work with the militant sectors of the black liberation movement, of course, has no actual or ideological connections with reactionary al-Qaeda forces. Yet, the foreign war on terrorism provided an excellent opportunity for expanding repressive measures in the United States.

Confrontations combating state censorship of dissent and critical voices reached their apex in the mass movements of the 1950s, 1960s, and early 1970s. In the post-enslavement era of the mid-twentieth century, the civil rights movements, referred to by some activists and academics as the "second Reconstruction" and by their more radical counterparts as the "second civil war," brought the new wave of protests and dissent. Arrested while organizing a bus boycott, Rosa Parks became briefly a political detainee. The young man whom she and the organizers of the bus boycott chose as their titular leader, largely because of his status as formally educated clergy and middle-class, was the Reverend Martin Luther King, Jr. His missive opens the first section of our collection of writings by imprisoned intellectuals.

Part I, Black Liberationists, begins with "Letter from Birmingham Jail," which was written the same year as the 1963 March on Washington where King gave his famous "I Have a Dream" speech-sermon; the same year that the Ku Klux Klan bombed a Birmingham, Alabama, church, killing four African American girls—Carole Robertson, Cynthia Wesley, Addie Mae Collins, Denise McNair—and the year of John F. Kennedy's assassination in Dallas, Texas.[24] In his open letter to clergy, King set forth an eloquent plea for support of an antiracist movement in which he had been active since 1955.[25] This anthology juxtaposes with King his peer and symbolic nemesis, Malik El-Shabazz, or Malcolm X. In chapter two, "The Ballot or the Bullet" (abridged), Malcolm X offers a critique of King's nonviolent activism. Although Malcolm X was not a "political prisoner" in the restrictive sense in which we use the term in this work, incarcerated as Malcolm Little for social crimes (including the "crimes" of burglary and of consorting with white women), he transformed or "reinvented" himself as a political agent while imprisoned. Politicized through his association (and later confrontation) with the Nation of Islam and his pilgrimage to Mecca, he influenced the growing militancy of the civil rights movement. Through his life, speeches, and writings—most notably, *The Autobiography of Malcolm X*—he achieved an iconic stature for many, including (political) prisoners. Constant police and FBI surveillance after he served his prison sentence likely increased his radical political and moral presence and inspired activists who would eventually become incarcerated, and in reflecting on his life, spirit, and death struggle to "reinvent" themselves as political agents, formulating a liberation praxis "by any means necessary." One year after Malcolm X's assassination, the Black Panther Party (for Self-Defense) was founded in 1966 in Oakland, California, by Huey P. Newton and Bobby Seale; armed resistance to police brutality became the most noted and "inflammatory" position of their emancipatory "10-Point Platform."

Angela Y. Davis would work with the Panthers but become better known as a communist and leader in the Soledad Brothers Defense Committee, a prisoners' rights organization cofounded by imprisoned Black Panther Field Marshall George Jackson. Davis was incarcerated in the early 1970s on charges related to George Jackson's younger brother Jonathan's attempt, using weapons registered in Davis's name, to liberate African American prisoners from the Marin County Courthouse, a failed endeavor that Newton would describe later at the seventeen-year-old's funeral as "revolutionary suicide."

One year before her 1972 acquittal of all charges, Davis wrote from her prison cell "Political Prisoners, Prisons, and Black Liberation," which is published here as chapter three; this essay would appear in the volume she coedited with Bettina Aptheker, *If They Come in the Morning*. Also in that anthology, which has been out of print for some time, was first published this volume's chapters four and five, respectively by Huey P. Newton and George Jackson. In chapter four, "Prison, Where Is Thy Victory?" Newton distinguishes between types or classes of prisoners, reserving his highest consideration for the imprisoned who rebel against rather than acquiesce to domination and (racial) control. In "Towards the United Front," chapter five, George Jackson, self-identified militarist for liberation and a key theorist and proponent of armed struggle, argues for a multiracial formation, new relations of unity that transcend common divisions. The Black Panthers became the most confrontational of the antiracist radical groups of the late 1960s and early 1970s (following the disintegration of the Student Nonviolent Coordinating Committee [SNCC]). Among the black militant formations, the Panthers developed some of the strongest allegiances with other racialized peoples, and the strongest ties with white radicals and revolutionaries.

The Panthers would also become the lightning rod for some of the government's most horrific forms of violent repression used against dissidents in the post–World War II era. In chapter six, former Panther Dhoruba Bin Wahad describes the deadly counterinsurgency program, COINTELPRO, initiated by J. Edgar Hoover and the Federal Bureau of Investigation (FBI). Decades before the BPP emerged, the FBI had destabilized progressives with violent means; but its violence would operate with virtually no restraint until the Black Panther Party and the American Indian Movement (AIM) were destroyed. "COINTELPRO and the Destruction of Black Leaders and Organizations" (abridged) presents the scenario in which state violence against the Black Panther Party and its membership had become routine. Bin Wahad argues that any revolutionary movement coincides with a cultural movement, but a cultural movement will not empower its people unless it is politicized. COINTELPRO succeeded because it halted the political consciousness of the Black Panther Party that coincided with the cultural awareness of "Black Power." Through violence, manipulation of the media, and disinformation campaigns, the FBI engaged in a twofold attack on the dissemination of information by black revolutionaries, destabilizing the public support base of the movement and then removing its leaders from public discourse through imprisonment, exile, or death.

State malfeasance and criminality in which the FBI participated included anonymous letters to Martin Luther King, Jr., urging that he commit suicide before his marital infidelities were publicized; the extra-judicial killings or assassinations of Chicago Panther leaders Fred Hampton and Mark Clark in December 1969; and the many killings during 1973–1976 of indigenous activists at the Pine Ridge reservation who aligned themselves with AIM. Such state violence provides a context and background for chapter seven, the excerpted "On the Black Liberation Army" (BLA) by Jalil Muntaqim. Muntaqim offers a brief historical snapshot of an underground military formation in battle with U.S. law enforcement, primarily on the East Coast. Although no theoretical justification for armed struggle appears in this succinct account of BLA activities, the historical trajectory of the COINTELPRO era of the early 1970s shapes the reasoning. Muntaqim's view stems from a different template than most, that of the slave insurrectionist, and so it shapes a unique worldview, one gazed upon, interacted with, but not fully experienced by the non-rebel or nonslave.

In chapter eight, "July 4th Address," a statement issued by former Black Panther and Black Liberation Army member Assata Shakur while she was in prison and on trial, evokes slave-turned-fugitive then abolitionist Frederick Douglass's 1852 "What to the Slave Is the Fourth of July" address. One of the few women leaders of the Black Panther Party (whose leadership was not tied to an influential male partner), Shakur would also become active in the military underground via the Black Liberation Army. Her memoir, *Assata: An Autobiography*, functions in a manner similar to the memoirs of King, Malcolm X, Davis, Newton, and Jackson: it highlights turbulent and dangerous times and personalizes the struggles and failings of revolutionaries and revolutionaries-in-waiting. For example, Shakur writes in her memoir:

> Some of the groups thought they could just pick up arms and struggle and that, somehow, people would see what they were doing and begin to struggle themselves. They wanted to engage in a do-or-die battle with power structure in amerika, even though they were weak and ill prepared for such a fight. But the most important factor is that armed struggle, by itself, can never bring about a revolution. Revolutionary war is a people's war.[26]

Unlike Shakur, Safiya Bukhari-Alston has (to date) not written a full-length memoir; yet, like Shakur, she was one of the few women leaders in the Black Liberation Army. Her autobiographical narrative, "Coming of Age: A Black Revolutionary," chapter nine, describes conditions unique to women political prisoners. A unit leader while underground, Bukhari-Alston encountered sexism in the party (as did Assata Shakur).

In chapter ten, "An Updated History of the New Afrikan Prison Struggle" (abridged), former Black Panther Sundiata Acoli provides a continuum of African American resistance to captivity and incarceration (the unabridged text places the enslavement era as foundational in this resistance). Acoli presents the Black Liberation Army as a "New Afrikan guerrilla organization" with mobile strike teams. Guerrilla warfare was seen as an inevitable counterresponse to U.S. "low-intensity warfare" against militants and radicals. Some members of the BLA identify as "prisoners of war" or POWs, viewing themselves as captive liberation fighters. The

Republic of New Afrika (RNA) stated its independence from the United States in 1968. BLA combatants subsequently declared that the U.S. courts had no jurisdiction over them. Acoli's historical discussions of "gang" formations in prisons as part of the prison struggles provide insight into their political nature and functions both in and outside of prison.

The idea of resisting all oppressive constraints—whether racism, sexism, heterosexism, or class/corporate privilege—is not uniformly shared in these essays. Women contributors tend to note sexism and heterosexism more so than the men (in this volume, white women are more vocal about the rights of gays and lesbians than black women are, perhaps because the former are writing at a later date when gay, lesbian, and bisexual rights are more publicly espoused). Although they fought for a more inclusive democracy, centralized, nondemocratic decision making— steeped in either patriarchal politics or a Leninist model of democratic centralism— was routinely practiced by Martin Luther King, Jr.'s Southern Christian Leadership Conference (SCLC), Malcolm X's Nation of Islam (from which he was expelled in 1963–1964), Angela Davis's Communist Party USA (CPUSA) (from which she was expelled in 1991), and Huey P. Newton's faction of the Black Panther Party. A discussion of forgoing vanguard or elite formations and rigid fixations on a line of leadership is found in chapter eleven, "Anarchism and the Black Revolution" (abridged), by Lorenzo Komboa Ervin. In this chapter, Ervin, who organized with the BPP among other groups, is highly critical of what he perceives as its "Marxist-Leninist" rigidity and repressive authoritarianism. It is difficult at times to distinguish which Black Panther Party critics are referencing—East Coast or West Coast? Cleaver or Newton faction? Newton prior to or during drug addiction and criminal intrigues? Nonetheless, the BPP in general (as did political organizations such as the SCLC and CPUSA) embraced a wealth of contradictions that limited the agency and efficacy of its "rank and file."

What, then, constitutes leadership that can face and function against repressive state policies? Such issues are explored in chapter twelve, an essay by journalist Mumia Abu-Jamal, "Intellectuals and the Gallows." This essay was written while Abu-Jamal was facing a sentence of death. It is one of the few pieces in this anthology that directly confronts readers as non-incarcerated intellectuals, exploring their confines in a Foucauldian carceral that restricts their own resistance to a state that oversees life and death.

Part II, Internationalists and Anti-Imperialists, begins with chapter thirteen, "Genocide against the Black Nation in the U.S. Penal System" (abridged) by Mutulu Shakur, Anthony X. Bradshaw, Malik Dinguswa, Terry Long, Mark Cook, Adolfo Matos, and James Haskins. The chapter focuses on African American emancipation, yet appeals to the international community; and so, it provides a bridge between the two sections of this anthology, emphasizing historical links between African American activism and the interplay of domestic and foreign policies. This essay's argument follows in a tradition established by African American radicals in the post–World War II era: William Patterson and the Civil Rights Congress in

1951 presented to the United Nations their antilynching petition "We Charge Genocide," and Malcolm X in the 1960s appealed to the United Nations for redress from lynching and white supremacist policies in the United States.[27] Chapter fourteen, "The Struggle for Status under International Law" by Marilyn Buck, revisits themes raised by chapter thirteen in its reflections on the use of international law to address U.S. domestic human rights violations. Situating Buck within the tradition of radical white antiracism and armed resistance, a tradition that dates back to and precedes John Brown's antislavery militancy, lesbian activist Rita Bo Brown describes the parameters of white activism in the 1970s and 1980s in chapter fifteen, "White North American Political Prisoners." In chapter fifteen, Brown provides a comprehensive view that encompasses a number of political formations. Chapter sixteen, "On Trial" (abridged), by former Vietnam veteran Raymond Luc Levasseur, chronicles the militancy of another white anti-imperialist who invokes international law and human rights conventions in antiracist struggles. Levasseur argued in his opening trial statement for the dismissal of criminal charges under International Law; he was acquitted of charges at the conclusion of his trial. Rejecting the domestic criminal charges brought by the government, he asserted a morality based on human rights and freedom fighters criminalized for their oppositional politics. Maintaining that the U.S. government/corporations committed crimes against humanity, Levasseur catalogues the acts that led to his organizational response through the UFF (United Freedom Front) and Sam Melville/Jonathan Jackson Unit. The series of bombings against military targets attributed to these formations occurred a number of years after the bombings attributed to the Weather Underground, the militant splinter group from the Students for a Democratic Society (SDS).

"Letter to the Weathermen," chapter seventeen, is a response by a Christian pacifist militant, Catholic priest Daniel Berrigan. Berrigan and his brother Philip, also a Catholic priest involved in activist resistance during the 1970s and 1980s and beyond, were heavily influenced by Martin Luther King, Jr., and the "peaceful" confrontation of state repression by the civil rights movement. Philip Berrigan would go on to cofound the Plowshares community where Michele Naar-Obed would become radicalized and, as a mother and peace activist, write the pamphlet excerpted here as chapter eighteen, "Maternal Convictions: A Mother Beats a Missile into a Plowshare." In "Maternal Convictions," Naar-Obed recounts her growing spiritual and political awareness for peace activism that entailed civil disobedience and illegal actions, and her multiple "short-term" incarcerations.

Women have varied responses in their resistance to U.S. militarism and warfare; not all of course are gendered as pacifist. "Dykes and Fags Want to Know: Interview with Lesbian Political Prisoners," chapter nineteen, was conducted in 1990–1991 by QUISP (Queer women and men United in Support of Political Prisoners). This interview focuses on Linda Evans, Susan Rosenberg, and Laura Whitehorn, women who spent years incarcerated because of their political beliefs and acts. Whitehorn completed her sentence and was released in 1999. Evans and Rosenberg were granted presidential clemency by President Bill Clinton in 2001. In 1999, Clinton had granted clemency to eleven of fifteen Puerto Rican *independentistas* or nationalists who had been imprisoned for years (included in those receiving clemency was Elizam Escobar). Clinton's release of *independentistas* did not signal the end of imprisonment for advocates and agitators for freeing Puerto Rico from its status as a colonial possession of the United States. In chapter twenty, "This Is Enough!" educator José Solís Jordan, incarcerated in Florida and later placed under detention in Puerto Rico, writes of the historical struggle for Puerto Rican independence and autonomy and his own connections to this struggle.

The following essays speak of the nonmaterial, of the spiritual and transcendent, of autonomy from the political formation and from purely political identification and identity. Chapter twenty-one, "Art of Liberation: A Vision of Freedom" by artist Elizam Escobar, offers one of the more creative and imaginative discussions of roles, conflicts, and contradictions of the revolutionary who maintains an independence from the struggle itself via his or her connection through art. In chapter twenty-two, "Violence and the State" (abridged), Standing Deer recounts an attempt on the part of prison authorities to get him to assault AIM activist and political prisoner Leonard Peltier. Standing Deer's "conversion" is both political and spiritual, both rational and suprarational. It provides an introduction to the final essay by Leonard Peltier who offers new meanings for freedom and resistance in our final chapter, twenty-three, "Inipi: Sweat Lodge." Peltier's excerpt from his autobiography, *Prison Writings: My Life Is My Sundance*,[28] reminds us of the nonmaterial aspects of struggle and the spiritual dimensions of freedom.

CONCLUSION

So much of what is controversial in this collection will center on the issue of violence: the use of violence by the state to squash dissent and destroy dissenters; the use of violence by dissidents either in immediate self-defense, in military strategies for "nation-building," or to promote a political stance and commitment. Obviously state violence is not synonymous with the violence of the subaltern or oppressed or imprisoned. Most Americans are more familiar with (inured to?) state violence, particularly when it is directed against disenfranchised or racially or politically suspect minorities. Therefore, police or military violence against the "racially suspect," against the poor and immigrants, against prisoners, is not as unsettling as counterviolence against the police or military by the subaltern and incarcerated. Thus, George Jackson's militarist stance in *Blood in My Eye*[29] is more terrifying for the conventional reader than the Central Intelligence Agency (CIA) torture manual for the School of the Americas.[30] Perhaps this is because the conventional reader assumes (*knows*) that state violence is never earmarked for the obedient and the law-abiding.[31]

No essay in this volume makes a sustained theoretical argument for armed resistance to state violence—although several essays offer theoretical and religious justifications for nonviolent civil disobedience and dissent. The book that heavily influenced many of the activists whose writings appear here is Frantz Fanon's *The Wretched of the Earth*. Fanon argues that the "native" (the colonized and racialized, here, the imprisoned) does not have to theorize or articulate the truth; she or he *is* the truth—the breathing, living embodiment of the contradictions, debasement, rage, and resentment and rebellion that mark the very conditions of oppression.[32] Yet the "truth," or some approximation of it, can be spoken in critical encounters and dialogues with rebels seeking social justice.

The non-incarcerated's sense of security and our real and imagined distance from political prisoners shape the expanse between the law-abiding (reader) and the outlaw (writer). Yet, what if the issues of political prisoners are in fact the touchstones to what ails us: structural impoverishment, racial–sexual discrimination and violence, political disenfranchisement, war profiteering? In degrees of (imagined) separation, amnesic fatigue about state violence couples with outrage at extralegal challenges to domination. Despite stolid dichotomies, if liberation struggles for human rights—and against war and captivity—intersect, radical imprisoned rebels may in fact stand at Elegba's crossroads; if so, then the writings that follow illuminate bridges that span or buckle under the intimacies of death and life struggles.

NOTES

1. Antonio Gramsci, *Selections from the Prison Notebooks*, edited and translated by Quintin Hoare and Geoffrey Nowell Smith (New York: International Publishers, 1985), 5. Gramsci writes: "When one distinguishes between intellectuals and non-intellectuals, one is referring in reality only to the immediate social function of the professional category of the intellectuals. . . . although one can speak of intellectuals, one cannot speak of non-intellectuals, because non-intellectuals do not exist" (9).

2. Barbara Harlow, *Barred: Women, Writing, and Political Detention* (Middletown, Conn.: Wesleyan University Press, 1992).

3. For descriptions and analyses of U.S. domestic and foreign policies that (violently) destabilized democracies, independence, and liberation movements see: Ward Churchill, *From a Native Son: Selected Essays in Indigenism, 1985–1995* (Boston: South End Press, 1997); Noam Chomsky, *The Culture of Terrorism* (Boston: South End Press, 1988); Manning Marable, *How Capitalism Underdeveloped Black America* (Boston: South End Press, 1983); Howard Zinn, *A People's History of the United States* (New York: HarperCollins, 1999); Joy James, *Resisting State Violence* (Minneapolis: University of Minnesota Press, 1996); Joy James, ed., *States of Confinement: Policing, Detention & Prisons* (New York: St. Martin's, 2002, revised paperback edition); Jerome G. Miller, *Search and Destroy: African American Males in the Criminal Justice System* (Cambridge: Cambridge University Press, 1976).

Also see: David J. Brown and Robert Merrill, eds., *Violent Persuasions: The Politics and Imagery of Terrorism* (Seattle: Bay Press, 1993); Ward Churchill and Jim Vander Wall, *Agents of Repression: The FBI's Secret Wars against the Black Panther Party and American Indian Movement* (Boston: South End Press, 2002, revised edition); Troy Johnson et al., eds., *American*

Indian Activism: Alcatraz to the Longest Walk (Urbana: University of Illinois Press, 1997); W. E. B. Du Bois, *Black Reconstruction in America* (New York: Harcourt, Brace, and Company, 1935); and, Matthew Mancini, *One Dies, Get Another: Convict Leasing in the American South, 1866–1928* (Columbia: University of South Carolina Press, 1996).

4. In its desires for freedoms guarded by institutions, revolutionary politics encompass and surpass insurrectionary politics. Rather than merely revolt against repressive hierarchies, laws, and customs, revolutionary politics seeks to build new structures and norms. Hence, revolutionaries are more feared than are insurrectionists by governing structures and elites. Just as insurrection is not inherently revolutionary, neither is crime or violence intrinsically proto-revolutionary: consider that capitalism in the Americas is rooted in the theft of land and labor and the mass murder of indigenous and African peoples.

5. Page 80. The nephew of President John F. Kennedy and son of Senator Robert Kennedy, Robert F. Kennedy, Jr., a senior attorney for the Natural Resources Defense Council, engaged in civil disobedience at Vieques, Puerto Rico, in 2001. Joined by actor Edward James Olmos and union leader Dennis Rivera, Kennedy protested the U.S. Navy having "saturated Vieques with thousands of pounds of ordinance—a total that eventually exceeded the explosive power of the Hiroshima bomb." Arrested after illegally trespassing on the military site, the *disobedientes* were eventually sentenced to thirty days in Guaynabo prison. After citing the Navy's civil and criminal violations of federal laws such as the Clean Water Act and the Resource Conservation and Recovery Act, Kennedy writes: "Our defense was based on the doctrine of necessity; a defendant cannot be convicted of trespassing if he shows he entered the land to prevent a greater crime from being committed. . . . we had engaged in civil disobedience for a single purpose: to prevent a criminal violation of the Endangered Species Act by the Navy that the federal court had refused to redress" (115). The presiding judge, admonishing that he was not interested in philosophy, dismissed the necessity defense.

As Kennedy's attorney (and his sister's father-in-law), former New York governor Mario Cuomo made the following argument at trial:

> We ask the court to recall that this nation was conceived in the civil disobedience that preceded the Revolutionary War, the acts of civil disobedience that were precipitated by the Fugitive Slave Act of 1793, in the famous Sit-Down Strikes of 1936 and 1937, all through the valiant struggle for civil rights in the 1960s, and the movement against the Vietnam War. Always they were treated by the courts one way: not like crimes committed for personal gain or out of pure malice, but as technical violations designed to achieve a good purpose. (115)

See Robert Kennedy's essay in *Outside*, October 2001, 80–84 and 114–16.

Of course, Cuomo and Kennedy would see violations that resulted in the loss of life (and liberty) as tragedies rather than as technicalities. Years prior to Kennedy's trial, Mutulu Shakur and Marilyn Buck also unsuccessfully argued the "necessity defense," appealing to international instead of U.S. standards.

6. There is insufficient space to address the ways in which political prisoners are at times burdened with the characteristics of prophets; hence their limitations in efficacy in the "free world" once they are released resonate so much more intensely. Activists, such as the slain leader Chris Hani, attempted to prevent the "marriage of Mandela-ism with liberalism." With the African National Congress (ANC)'s acceptance of the apartheid government's debt and its failure to nationalize and redistribute key resources and wealth, the observation

by some local South African activists that Mandela had "sold out the bush" resonated with the intense frustrations of an economically subjugated people.

7. Some accounts of the southern civil rights movement argue that pacifists were often provided protection from Klan and police violence by armed and organized African American men and women, such as those who formed the Deacons for Defense and Justice in North Carolina. See: Anne Moody, *The Coming of Age in Mississippi* (Laureleaf, 1997, reprint); Robert Franklin Williams, *Negroes with Guns* (Detroit: Wayne State University Press, 1998, reprint); and Timothy B. Tyson, *Radio Free Dixie: Robert F. Williams and the Roots of Black Power* (Chapel Hill: University of North Carolina Press, 1999).

8. November 7, 2002, e-mail correspondence from Michael Hames-Garcia, editor's papers. For further discussions analyzing incarceration politics, see: Michael Hames-Garcia, *Crucibles of Freedom* (Minneapolis: University of Minnesota Press, 2003).

9. Dylan Rodriguez maintains:

"Free" activists (scholars, etc.) often appropriate the iconography of captive radicals/ revolutionaries . . . and may even do so in critical and radical ways (for example, to introduce the discourse of "political prisoners/POW's" to a public that cannot assimilate such a possibility in their midst). Yet, it is far more difficult for free people to engage the political work of radical prisoners in a manner that seriously informs their praxis. Of course, to do so would necessitate a far more urgent, even desperate attempt to trans-late the political dream (vision) of prison/police abolition into an antagonistic and accessible political-cultural practice. . . . 50 activists and critically informed students could read the anthology *through* this structure of . . . disavowal, such that the mundane pro-state progressivism (inherently white supremacist) of the CBO, non-profit, and aca-demic sectors remains sacrosanct. To refuse the urgency of principled hostility and oppo-sition to this civic and state formation is a virtual religious fiat of the current (post–civil rights) era of the alleged Left. (Dylan Rodriguez, September 2002 e-mail correspon-dence, editor's papers.)

For another critical perspective on the "prison writer," see Paul St. John, "Behind the Mirror's Face," in *Doing Time: Twenty-Five Years of Prison Writing*, ed. Bell Gale Chevigny (New York: Arcade, 1999).

10. Using historian Eugene Genovese's statement "The Black experience in this country has been a phenomenon without analog" as the epigraph for his essay, Frank Wilderson, III, quotes from Steve Martinot and Jared Sexton, "The Avant-Garde of White Supremacy," April 2002, www.ocf.berkeley.edu/~marto/paradigm/. Genovese's citation is given as: *Boston Review* October/November 1993. See: Frank Wilderson, III, "The Prison Slave as Hegemo-ny's (Silent) Scandal," in *Social Justice* (forthcoming).

11. For a discussion of the concept "social death" in a global and historical context, see: Orlando Patterson, *Slavery and Social Death: A Comparative Study* (Cambridge, Mass.: Har-vard University Press, 1982). For contemporary analyses of "social death" within the context of U.S. racial and incarceration politics, see: Frank Wilderson, III, "The Prison Slave as Hegemony's (Silent) Scandal" and Dylan Rodriguez, " 'Social Truth' and Imprisoned Radical Intellectuals" in the forthcoming issue of the journal *Social Justice*.

12. The Thirteenth Amendment to the U.S. Constitution legalizes slavery for those duly convicted of a crime. In the convict prison lease system following the Civil War, African Americans, criminalized for their "blackness," were worked to death in mines, fields, and forests in joint ventures between the state and private industries. For an analysis of the his-

tory of the convict lease system in the United States, see Matthew Mancini, *One Dies, Get Another: Convict Leasing in the American South, 1866–1928* (Columbia: University of South Carolina Press, 1996).

13. W. E. B. Du Bois, *Black Reconstruction in America* (New York: Harcourt, Brace, and Company, 1935).

14. See Vincent Harding, *There Is a River: The Black Struggle for Freedom in America* (New York: Harcourt Brace, 1981).

15. See Mike Ngo, under pseudonym "An Unknown Soldier," "A Day in the Life," prisoners' zine, untitled, January 13, 2000; also see Dylan Rodriguez, "Interview with Mike Ngo," in *Abolitionists: Imprisoned Writers on Incarceration, Enslavement and Emancipation*, ed. Joy James (forthcoming).

16. For details of U.S. foreign and domestic policies that instigated considerable warfare, destabilization, and death in the post–World War II era, see: Noam Chomsky, *The Culture of Terrorism* (Boston: South End Press, 1988); Ward Churchill and Jim Vander Wall, *Agents of Repression: The FBI's Secret War against the Black Panther Party and the American Indian Movement* (Boston: South End Press, revised 2002 edition); Joy James, *Resisting State Violence: Radicalism, Gender, and Race in U.S. Culture* (Minneapolis: University of Minnesota Press, 1996).

17. See Mondo we Langa, "Letter from Inside," *Nebraska Report*, May/June 1999, 9. For information on Wopashitwe Mondo Eyen we Langa (David Rice), see *Can't Jail the Spirit* (Chicago: Committee to End the Marion Lockdown, 2002, 5th edition). Mondo we Langa was deputy minister of information for the Omaha, Nebraska, chapter of the National Committees to Combat Fascism, an organization affiliated with the Black Panther Party, and is serving a life sentence for the first-degree murder of a policeman. He was active in protesting police brutality against African American residents in Omaha. According to the Center for Constitutional Rights, we Langa was targeted by COINTELPRO and his conviction "was based on the testimony of a frightened teenager and on explosives allegedly found in [we Langa's] house." A Federal Court of Appeals declared the search illegal yet the Supreme Court "sustained the conviction holding that the Federal courts should not have reviewed the state court decision." See Center for Constitutional Rights, "Political Prisoners in the United States," September 1988.

18. This article was first published in the International Association of *Democratic Lawyers Bulletin*, January 1990, and reprinted in *Social Justice*, vol. 18, no. 3.

19. For information on Lori Berenson, see Rhoda Berenson, *Lori: My Daughter, Wrongfully Imprisoned in Peru* (New York: Context Books, 2000). For discussions of prisoners with the status of "illegal [non]combatants" following September 11, 2001, see: Amnesty International, "USA: Detainees from Afghan Conflict Should Be Released or Tried," AI Index: AMR 51/164/2002, 1 November 2002; and Joseph Lelyveld, "In Guantánamo," *The New York Review of Books*, November 7, 2002.

20. See Anne-Marie Cusac, "You're in the Hole: A Crackdown on Dissident Prisoners," *The Progressive*, December 2001. *The Progressive* reports that on October 26, 2001, John Ashcroft signed the "National Security: Prevention of Acts of Violence and Terrorism," which was subsequently published in the Federal Register. Cusac writes: "Under the new rules, the Department of Justice, 'based on information from the head of a federal law enforcement or intelligence agency,' will select certain prisoners for 'special administrative measures' . . . [including isolation, denials of correspondence, telephone communication, visitations, and media interviews]."

21. Targets of FBI repression have been fairly varied, including Albert Einstein, because of his socialism and antiracist activism (Einstein worked with W. E. B. Du Bois and Paul Robeson; with the latter he cofounded an anti-lying organization), and John Lennon, targeted because of his antiwar activism. See, respectively, Frank Jerome, *The Einstein F.B.I. File* (New York: St. Martin's, 2002) and Jon Wiener, *Come Together: John Lennon in His Time* (New York: Random House, 1984) and "John Lennon versus the F.B.I.," *The New Republic*, vol. 188.

On October 10, 2001, Laura W. Murphy, director of the American Civil Liberties Union (ACLU) Washington National Office, issued "Trust Us, We're the Government"; the statement details government malfeasance and illegal surveillance and harassment tied to COINTELPRO, in which "few members of any of the groups targeted by COINTELPRO were ever charged with a crime." It also makes reference to the 1976 Church Committee Senate report that concluded: "The Government has often undertaken the secret surveillance of citizens on the basis of their political beliefs, even when those beliefs posed no threat of violence or illegal acts on behalf of a hostile foreign power. . . . Groups and individuals have been harassed and disrupted because of their political views and their lifestyles." In 1986, a federal court determined that COINTELPRO was responsible for at least 204 burglaries by FBI agents, the use of 1,300 informants, the theft of 12,600 documents, 20,000 illegal wiretap days, and 12,000 bug days.

Alongside COINTELPRO, the ACLU notes the "STOP INDEX," where FBI computerized databases monitored antiwar activists; "CONUS" (Continental United States), which in the 1950s and 1960s "collected and maintained files on upwards of 100,000 political activists and used undercover operatives recruited from the Army to infiltrate these activist groups and steal confidential information and files for distribution to federal, state and local governments"; "OPERATION CHAOS" in the 1960s, where the Central Intelligence Agency engaged in domestic spying to destabilize the American peace movement; and "CISPES" harassment, in which the Committee in Solidarity with the People of El Salvador (CISPES) was targeted because of its opposition to President Ronald Reagan's support of paramilitary death squads in El Salvador. Murphy asserts that "the Bush Administration's defense of its new, and frighteningly broad, anti-terrorism bill is also being couched in exactly these terms [of trust for the government's use of police powers]. Unfortunately, history has also shown us that, more often than not, these expansions of domestic surveillance powers are used to violate the freedoms guaranteed to the American public by the Constitution and the Bill of Rights."

22. Writing for clemency for Anthony Jalil Bottom (#77A4283), Herman Bell (#79C0262), Abdul Majid (#83A0483), Bashir Hameed (#82A6313), Robert Seth Hayes (#74A2280), Sekou Odinga (#05228-054), and David Gilbert (#83A6158) in the petition were attorneys Robert Boyle, Robert Bloom, William Goodman, Kathleen Cleaver, Jill Soffiyah Elijah, Elizabeth Fink, Karl Franklin, Daniel Meyers, Charles Ogletree, Michael Tarif Warren, Nkechi Taifa, and Susan Tipograph. *New York Task Force for Political Prisoners 2002 Report/Petition*, editor's papers.

23. The USA PATRIOT (Provide Appropriate Tools Required to Intercept and Obstruct Terrorism) Act of 2001 permits the U.S. government to detain noncitizens indefinitely with little or no process at the discretion of the Attorney General; permits the government to conduct searches, seizures, and surveillance with lower levels of judicial review; and potentially criminalizes otherwise lawful contacts with groups engaging in politically motivated

(violent and nonviolent) illegal acts. See Nancy Chang, *Silencing Political Dissent: How Post–September 11 Anti-Terrorism Measures Threaten Our Civil Liberties* (New York: Seven Stories, 2002); *The USA PATRIOT Act: A Legal Analysis* (Washington, D.C.: Congressional Research Service, Library of Congress, 2002).

24. See Spike Lee's documentary *Four Little Girls* (New York: Forty Acres and a Mule/ HBO Home Video, 1998).

25. Former Black Panther and Black Liberation Army member Jalil Abdul Muntaqim's "Religion and Revolution" offers an interesting perspective on the role of liberation theology and Christianity in the injunction for freedom; see Jalil Muntaqim, "Religion and Revolution"; and Jalil Muntaqim, *We Are Our Own Liberators* (Montreal: Abraham Guillen Press, 2002).

26. Assata Shakur, *Assata: An Autobiography* (Westport, Conn.: Lawrence Hill & Co.), 242–43.

27. See William Patterson, ed., *We Charge Genocide: The Crime of Government against the Negro People, A Petition to the United Nations* (New York: Civil Rights Congress, 1951).

28. Leonard Peltier, *Prison Writings: My Life Is My Sundance*, edited by Harvey Arden (New York: St. Martin's, 1999).

29. In September 1971, responding to George Jackson's killing by San Quentin prison guards and administrators and to dehumanizing and racist prison conditions, 1,500 African American, Puerto Rican, and white prisoners seized control of Attica, a maximum-security prison in New York. In 2001, the California-based media organization Freedom Archives produced *Prisons on Fire*, a CD of two audio documentaries commemorating the thirtieth anniversaries of the death of George Jackson and the Attica Rebellion. The CD consists of archival and contemporary interviews, music, and narration. Featured in part one of the narrative are: George Jackson; his seventeen-year-old brother, Jonathan, who was killed in the Marin County "takeover," and his mother, Georgia Jackson; former Soledad Brother Defense Committee leader Angela Davis; former Black Panther Party leader David Hilliard; writer James Baldwin; actor Harry Belafonte; and current or former prisoners David Johnson, Hugo Pinell, Luis Talamantez, and Sundiata Tate—the latter three were charged with the San Quentin rebellion following the death of George Jackson. Part two of the CD features the voices of former Attica prison leader Frank "Big Black" Smith; Attica activists' attorneys William Kunstler, Elizabeth Fink, and Michael Deutsch; L. D. Barkley (killed in the retaking of the prison, Barkley read the Attica Manifesto to the media); and Ruchell Magee (prison activist and participant in the 1971 Marin County escape in which Jonathan Jackson and prisoners James McClain and William Christmas and Judge Harold Haley were killed by guards). The *Prisons on Fire* audio documentary is available through Rowman and Littlefield and from Freedom Archives: cd@freedomarchives.org, www.freedomarchives.org.

30. For a critique of the School of the Americas, which officially closed in 2000 (but which human rights advocates say has simply been renamed and reorganized), see Jack Nelson-Pallmeyer, *School of Assassins: The Case for Closing the School of the Americas and for Fundamentally Changing U.S. Foreign Policy* (New York: Orbis Books, 1997).

31. Ralph Miliband writes in *The State in Capitalist Society* that in the United States people "live in the shadow of the state," as political actors attempt to influence or represent "the state's power and purpose" in order to obtain its support. A comprehensive theory of the state requires that we address economic, racial, and sexual as well as political, repression and disenfranchisement. Here, I use "state violence" as a descriptive term that denotes political–

economic and police violence based on nationality, ethnicity, gender, sexuality, class, and political ideology. The primary instruments and controlling interests in state violence are largely determined by corporate and police (para)military elites. Although Miliband distinguishes the state system from the political system of electoral parties and seemingly nonpolitical organizations such as religious and educational institutions, media, businesses and civic groups, it is not realistic to maintain a sharp division between the state and civil society, particularly in a racially driven or constructed culture. Without formally sharing in state power, social and ethnic groups can contribute to the erasure or validation of state violence and government misconduct. Frequently in the United States, where racial fears and hostilities are manipulated, state and civil society seem to speak in one voice regarding policing, punishment, and violence as the media, educational institutions, and private citizens are organized to further state hegemony in spite of their autonomy from state apparatuses. See: Ralph Miliband, *The State in Capitalist Society* (New York: Basic, 1969); and Joy James, *Resisting State Violence* (Minneapolis: University of Minnesota Press, 1996), 6.

32. Fanon writes: "[T]he *fellah*, the unemployed man, the starving native do not lay a claim to the truth; they do not *say* that they represent the truth, for they *are* the truth." See Frantz Fanon, *The Wretched of the Earth* (New York: Grove Press, 1963), 49.

Part One

BLACK LIBERATIONISTS

Chapter One

Martin Luther King, Jr.

Born in Atlanta, Georgia, on January 15, 1929, Martin Luther King, Jr. was the eldest son of Alberta Williams King, a schoolteacher, and Martin Luther King, Sr., a Baptist minister. At age fifteen, King entered Morehouse College, where he first read Henry David Thoreau's *On Civil Disobedience* and began to work with organizations dedicated to racial justice. After graduating from Morehouse in 1948 with a bachelor's degree in sociology, King entered Crozer Theological Seminary. In 1951, he enrolled in Boston University, where, studying Reinhold Niebuhr and G. W. Hegel, he earned a doctorate in systematic theology in 1955. King synthesized the divergent influences of his studies into a "realistic pacifism" and a theology that considered both "souls" and "societal change."[1] In Boston he met and married Coretta Scott, then a music student; they would have four children: Martin Luther III, Dexter Scott, Yolanda Denise, and Bernice Albertine.

King accepted his first pastorate at the Dexter Avenue Baptist Church in Montgomery, Alabama, in 1954. In Montgomery, he began simultaneous work with the National Association for the Advancement of Colored People (NAACP) and the interracial Alabama Council on Human Relations. When NAACP leader Rosa Parks was arrested on December 1, 1955, for refusing to give up her seat to a white passenger on a public bus, Joanne Robinson's Montgomery Women's Political Caucus, with trade unionist E. D. Nixon, organized a bus boycott. The originators of the boycott chose the politically inexperienced King as its titular leader for appearances of respectability and authority tied to middle-class male clergy, and with their assistance King was elected president of the ad hoc Montgomery Improvement Association (MIA).

The Montgomery bus boycott lasted more than a year. During that struggle for civil rights, King had his first experience of being jailed. Arrested for "speeding" by Montgomery police, he was taken to the Montgomery city jail. Violence and police harassment and brutality against black protesters, including the bombing of King's home, punctuated the long boycott. By the time the U.S. Supreme Court declared segregation of public transportation unconstitutional in November of 1956, and the

MIA triumphed through its civil disobedience, Martin Luther King, Jr., had been catapulted into the national spotlight.

In 1957, King helped found and became the president of what would eventually become the Southern Christian Leadership Conference (SCLC).[2] The SCLC, first headed by Ella Baker, protested racial injustice and racism through marches, boycotts, and demonstrations. King was arrested and jailed for his involvement in such activity.

In 1960, King accepted a position as co-pastor of the Ebenezer Baptist Church in Atlanta. The SCLC's offices in Atlanta became the organizational base for most of King's civil rights activity after 1960. In the early 1960s, the SCLC began a series of protest campaigns triggered by student sit-ins and the Freedom Ride movement. The de facto head of SCLC, Ella Baker, would prove instrumental in the founding of the Student Nonviolent Coordinating Committee (SNCC), which would work with, and at times critique and radicalize, the SCLC.

After unsuccessful organizing initiatives in Albany, Georgia, the SCLC turned its focus to Birmingham, Alabama. In 1963, King stated, "Birmingham is so segregated, we're within a cab ride of being in Johannesburg, South Africa."[3] Birmingham city officials had declared the NAACP a "foreign corporation" and criminalized its activities. The head of Birmingham's police was Commissioner of Public Safety Eugene "Bull" Connor, who prided himself "on knowing how to handle the Negro and keep him in his 'place.'"[4]

In the ensuing confrontation with racist police and city administration, King was arrested on April 12, and "charged with violation of a city ordinance in parading without a permit and also with defying a state court injunction against demonstrations."[5] While being held for over twenty-four hours in solitary confinement, he woke in the morning to find in his cell a newspaper with an advertisement taken out by eight clergymen of the major denominations who condemned the demonstrations and criticized the civil rights activists as "extremists."[6]

"Letter from Birmingham Jail," Reverend King's response, was first published in *Christian Century*, *Liberation*, and *Christianity and Crisis*, three progressive journals. In his "Letter," King set forth an incisive critique of the "white moderate," who, he claimed, was "more devoted to 'order' than justice." The recipient of the Nobel Peace Prize, Martin Luther King, Jr., was assassinated in Memphis, Tennessee, in April 1968.

REFERENCES

Dyson, Michael Eric. *I May Not Get There with You: The True Martin Luther King, Jr.* New York: Free Press, 2000.

Fairclough, Adam. *Martin Luther King, Jr.* Athens: University of Georgia Press, 1995.

Hailey, Foster. "Dr. King Arrested at Birmingham." *New York Times*, 13 April 1963, late ed., A1.

King, Martin Luther, Jr. *The Autobiography of Martin Luther King, Jr.* Edited by Clayborne Carson. New York: Time Warner, 1998.

———. *Where Do We Go from Here: Chaos or Community?* Boston: Beacon, 1967.

———. *Why We Can't Wait.* New York: New American Library, 1964.

Schulke, Flip, and Penelope Ortner McPhee, *King Remembered.* New York: Norton, 1986.

NOTES

Research and draft for this biography were provided by Christopher Muller.

1. Martin Luther King, Jr. *The Autobiography of Martin Luther King, Jr.* (New York: Warner, 1998).

2. *Autobiography*, 102.

3. Flip Schulke and Penelope Ortner McPhee, *King Remembered* (New York: Norton, 1986), 118.

4. Adam Fairclough, *Martin Luther King, Jr.* (Athens: University of Georgia, 1995), 72; *Autobiography*, 172.

5. Foster Hailey, "Dr. King Arrested at Birmingham," *New York Times*, 13 April 1963, A1.

6. *Autobiography*, 187.

Letter from Birmingham Jail

April 16, 1963

AUTHOR'S NOTE: This response to a published statement by eight fellow clergymen from Alabama (Bishop C. C. J. Carpenter, Bishop Joseph A. Durick, Rabbi Hilton L. Grafman, Bishop Paul Hardin, Bishop Holan B. Harmon, the Reverend George M. Murray, the Reverend Edward V. Ramage and the Reverend Earl Stallings) was composed under somewhat constricting circumstance. Begun on the margins of the newspaper in which the statement appeared while I was in jail, the letter was continued on scraps of writing paper supplied by a friendly Negro trusty, and concluded on a pad my attorneys were eventually permitted to leave me. Although the text remains in substance unaltered, I have indulged in the author's prerogative of polishing it for publication.

April 16, 1963

MY DEAR FELLOW CLERGYMEN:

While confined here in the Birmingham city jail, I came across your recent statement calling my present activities "unwise and untimely." Seldom do I pause to answer criticism of my work and ideas. If I sought to answer all the criticisms that cross my desk, my secretaries would have little time for anything other than such correspondence in the course of the day, and I would have no time for constructive work. But since I feel that you are men of genuine good will and that your criticisms are sincerely set forth, I want to try to answer your statements in what I hope will be patient and reasonable terms.

I think I should indicate why I am here in Birmingham, since you have been influenced by the view which argues against "outsiders coming in." I have the honor of serving as president of the Southern Christian Leadership Conference, an organization operating in every southern state, with headquarters in Atlanta, Georgia. We have some eighty-five affiliated organizations across the South, and one of them is the Alabama Christian Movement for Human Rights. Frequently we share staff, educational and financial resources with our affiliates. Several months ago the affiliate here in Birmingham asked us to be on call to engage in a nonviolent direct-action program if such were deemed necessary. We readily consented, and when the hour came we lived up to our promise. So I, along with several members of my staff, am here because I was invited here. I am here because I have organizational ties here.

But more basically, I am in Birmingham because injustice is here. Just as the prophets of the eighth century b.c. left their villages and carried their "thus saith the Lord" far beyond the boundaries of their home towns, and just as the Apostle Paul left his village of Tarsus and carried the gospel of Jesus Christ to the far corners of the Greco-Roman world, so am I compelled to carry the gospel of freedom beyond my own home town. Like Paul, I must constantly respond to the Macedonian call for aid.

Moreover, I am cognizant of the interrelatedness of all communities and states. I cannot sit idly by in Atlanta and not be concerned about what happens in Birmingham. Injustice anywhere is a threat to justice everywhere. We are caught in an inescapable network of mutuality, tied in a single garment of destiny. Whatever affects one directly, affects all indirectly. Never again can we afford to live with the narrow, provincial "outside agitator" idea. Anyone who lives inside the United States can never be considered an outsider anywhere within its bounds.

You deplore the demonstrations taking place in Birmingham. But your statement, I am sorry to say, fails to express a similar concern for the conditions that brought about the demonstrations. I am sure that none of you would want to rest content with the superficial kind of social analysis that deals merely with effects and does not grapple with underlying causes. It is unfortunate that demonstrations are taking place in Birmingham, but it is even more unfortunate that the city's white power structure left the Negro community with no alternative.

In any nonviolent campaign there are four basic steps: collection of the facts to determine whether injustices exist; negotiation; self-purification; and direct action. We have gone through all these steps in Birmingham. There can be no gainsaying the fact that racial injustice engulfs this community. Birmingham is probably the most thoroughly segregated city in the United States. Its ugly record of brutality is widely known. Negroes have experienced grossly unjust treatment in the courts. There have been more unsolved bombings of Negro homes and churches in Birmingham than in any other city in the nation. These are the hard, brutal facts of the case. On the basis of these conditions, Negro leaders sought to negotiate with the city fathers. But the latter consistently refused to engage in good-faith negotiation.

Then, last September, came the opportunity to talk with leaders of Birmingham's economic community. In the course of the negotiations, certain promises were made by the merchants—for example, to remove the stores' humiliating racial signs. On the basis of these promises, the Reverend Fred Shuttlesworth and the leaders of the Alabama Christian Movement for Human Rights agreed to a moratorium on all demonstrations. As the weeks and months went by, we realized that we were the victims of a broken promise. A few signs, briefly removed, returned; the others remained.

As in so many past experiences, our hopes had been blasted, and the shadow of deep disappointment settled upon us. We had no alternative except to prepare for direct action, whereby we would present our very bodies as a means of laying our case before the conscience of the local and the national community. Mindful of the difficulties involved, we decided to undertake a process of self-purification. We began a series of workshops on nonviolence, and we repeatedly asked ourselves: "Are you able to accept blows without retaliating?" "Are you able to endure the ordeal of jail?" We decided to schedule our direct-action program for the Easter season, realizing that except for Christmas, this is the main shopping period of the year. Knowing that a strong economic withdrawal program would be the by-product of direct action, we felt that this would be the best time to bring pressure to bear on the merchants for the needed change.

Then it occurred to us that Birmingham's mayoralty election was coming up in March, and we speedily decided to postpone action until after election day. When we discovered that the Commissioner of Public Safety, Eugene "Bull" Connor, had piled up enough votes to be in the run-off we decided again to postpone action until the day after the run-off so that the demonstrations could not be used to cloud the issues. Like many others, we waited to see Mr. Connor defeated, and to this end we endured postponement after postponement. Having aided in this community need, we felt that our direct-action program could be delayed no longer.

You may well ask: "Why direct action? Why sit-ins, marches and so forth? Isn't negotiation a better path?" You are quite right in calling for negotiation. Indeed, this is the very purpose of direct action. Nonviolent direct action seeks to create such a crisis and foster such a tension that a community which has constantly refused to negotiate is forced to confront the issue. It seeks so to dramatize the issue that it can no longer be ignored. My citing the creation of tension as part of the work of the nonviolent-resister may sound rather shocking. But I must confess that I am not afraid of the word "tension." I have earnestly opposed violent tension, but there is a type of constructive, nonviolent tension which is necessary for growth. Just as Socrates felt that it was necessary to create a tension in the mind so that individuals could rise from the bondage of myths and half-truths to the unfettered realm of creative analysis and objective appraisal, we must see the need for nonviolent gadflies to create the kind of tension in society that will help men rise from the dark depths of prejudice and racism to the majestic heights of understanding and brotherhood.

The purpose of our direct-action program is to create a situation so crisis-packed that it will inevitably open the door to negotiation. I therefore concur with you in our call for negotiation. Too long has our beloved Southland been bogged down in a tragic effort to live in monologue rather than dialogue.

One of the basic points in your statement is that the action that I and my associates have taken in Birmingham is untimely. Some have asked: "Why didn't you give the new city administration time to act?" The only answer that I can give to this query is that the new Birmingham administration must be prodded about as much as the outgoing one, before it will act. We are sadly mistaken if we feel that the election of Albert Boutwell as mayor will bring the millennium to Birmingham. While Mr. Boutwell is a much more gentle person than Mr. Connor, they are both segregationists, dedicated to maintenance of the status quo. I have hope that Mr. Boutwell will be reasonable enough to see the futility of massive resistance to desegregation. But he will not see this without pressure from devotees of civil rights. My friends, I must say to you that we have not made a single gain in civil rights without determined legal and nonviolent pressure. Lamentably, it is an historical fact that privileged groups seldom give up their privileges voluntarily. Individuals may see the moral light and voluntarily give up their unjust posture; but, as Reinhold Niebuhr has reminded us, groups tend to be more immoral than individuals.[1] *fanton conn.*

We know through painful experience that freedom is never voluntarily given by the oppressor; it must be demanded by the oppressed. Frankly, I have yet to engage in a direct-action campaign that was "well timed" in the view of those who have not suffered unduly from the disease of segregation. For years now I have heard the word "Wait!" It rings in the ear of every Negro with piercing familiarity. This "Wait" has almost always meant "Never." We must come to see, with one of our distinguished jurists, that "justice too long delayed is justice denied."

We have waited for more than 340 years for our constitutional and God-given rights. The nations of Asia and Africa are moving with jetlike speed toward gaining political independence, but we still creep at horse-and-buggy pace toward gaining a cup of coffee at a lunch counter. Perhaps it is easy for those who have never felt the stinging dark of segregation to say, "Wait." But when you have seen vicious mobs lynch your mothers and fathers at will and drown your sisters and brothers at whim; when you have seen hate-filled policemen curse, kick and even kill your black brothers and sisters; when you see the vast majority of your twenty million Negro brothers smothering in an airtight cage of poverty in the midst of an affluent society; when you suddenly find your tongue twisted and your speech stammering as you seek to explain to your six-year-old daughter why she can't go to the public amusement park that has just been advertised on television, and see tears welling up in her eyes when she is told that Funtown is closed to colored children, and see ominous clouds of inferiority beginning to form in her little mental sky, and see her beginning to distort her personality by developing an unconscious bitterness toward white people; when you have to concoct an answer for a five-year-old son who is asking: "Daddy, why do white people treat colored people so mean?"; when you take a cross-country drive and find it necessary to sleep night after night in the uncomfortable corners of your automobile because no motel will accept you; when you are humiliated day in and day out by nagging signs reading "white" and "colored"; when your first name becomes "nigger," your middle name becomes "boy" (however old you are) and your last name becomes "John," and your wife and mother are never given the respected title "Mrs."; when you are harried by day and haunted by night by the fact that you are a Negro, living constantly at tiptoe stance, never quite knowing what to expect next, and are plagued with inner fears and outer resentments; when you are forever fighting a degenerating sense of "nobodiness" then you will understand why we find it difficult to wait. There comes a time when the cup of endurance runs over, and men are no longer willing to be plunged into the abyss of despair. I hope, sirs, you can understand our legitimate and unavoidable impatience.

You express a great deal of anxiety over our willingness to break laws. This is certainly a legitimate concern. Since we so diligently urge people to obey the

Supreme Court's decision of 1954 outlawing segregation in the public schools, at first glance it may seem rather paradoxical for us consciously to break laws. One may well ask: "How can you advocate breaking some laws and obeying others?" The answer lies in the fact that there are two types of laws: just and unjust. I would be the first to advocate obeying just laws. One has not only a legal but a moral responsibility to obey just laws. Conversely, one has a moral responsibility to disobey unjust laws. I would agree with St. Augustine that "an unjust law is no law at all."

Now, what is the difference between the two? How does one determine whether a law is just or unjust? A just law is a man-made code that squares with the moral law or the law of God. An unjust law is a code that is out of harmony with the moral law. To put it in the terms of St. Thomas Aquinas: An unjust law is a human law that is not rooted in eternal law and natural law. Any law that uplifts human personality is just. Any law that degrades human personality is unjust. All segregation statutes are unjust because segregation distorts the soul and damages the personality. It gives the segregator a false sense of superiority and the segregated a false sense of inferiority. Segregation, to use the terminology of the Jewish philosopher Martin Buber, substitutes an "I-it" relationship for an "I-thou" relationship and ends up relegating persons to the status of things. Hence segregation is not only politically, economically and sociologically unsound, it is morally wrong and awful. Paul Tillich said that sin is separation. Is not segregation an existential expression "of man's tragic separation, his awful estrangement, his terrible sinfulness?" Thus it is that I can urge men to obey the 1954 decision of the Supreme Court, for it is morally right; and I can urge them to disobey segregation ordinances, for they are morally wrong.

Let us consider a more concrete example of just and unjust laws. An unjust law is a code that a numerical or power majority group compels a minority group to obey but does not make binding on itself. This is difference made legal. By the same token, a just law is a code that a majority compels a minority to follow and that it is willing to follow itself. This is sameness made legal.

Let me give another explanation. A law is unjust if it is inflicted on a minority that, as a result of being denied the right to vote, had no part in enacting or devising the law. Who can say that the legislature of Alabama which set up that state's segregation laws was democratically elected? Throughout Alabama all sorts of devious methods are used to prevent Negroes from becoming registered voters, and there are some counties in which, even though Negroes constitute a majority of the population, not a single Negro is registered. Can any law enacted under such circumstances be considered democratically structured?

Sometimes a law is just on its face and unjust in its application. For instance, I have been arrested on a charge of parading without a permit. Now, there is nothing wrong in having an ordinance which requires a permit for a parade. But such an ordinance becomes unjust when it is used to maintain segregation and to deny citizens the First Amendment privilege of peaceful assembly and protest.

I hope you are able to face the distinction I am trying to point out. In no sense do I advocate evading or defying the law, as would the rabid segregationist. That would lead to anarchy. One who breaks an unjust law must do so openly, lovingly, and with a willingness to accept the penalty. I submit that an individual who breaks a law that conscience tells him is unjust and who willingly accepts the penalty of imprisonment in order to arouse the conscience of the community over its injustice, is in reality expressing the highest respect for law.

Of course, there is nothing new about this kind of civil disobedience. It was evidenced sublimely in the refusal of Shadrach, Meshach and Abednego to obey the laws of Nebuchadnezzar, on the ground that a higher moral law was at stake. It was practiced superbly by the early Christians, who were willing to face hungry lions and the excruciating pain of chopping blocks rather than submit to certain unjust laws of the Roman Empire. To a degree, academic freedom is a reality today because Socrates practiced civil disobedience. In our own nation, the Boston Tea Party represented a massive act of civil disobedience.

We should never forget that everything Adolf Hitler did in Germany was "legal" and everything the Hungarian freedom fighters did in Hungary was "illegal." It was "illegal" to aid and comfort a Jew in Hitler's Germany. Even so, I am sure that, had I lived in Germany at the time, I would have aided and comforted my Jewish brothers. If today I lived in a Communist country where certain principles dear to the Christian faith are suppressed, I would openly advocate disobeying that country's antireligious laws.

I must make two honest confessions to you, my Christian and Jewish brothers. First, I must confess that over the past few years I have been gravely disappointed with the white moderate. I have almost reached the regrettable conclusion that the Negro's great stumbling block in his stride toward freedom is not the White Citizen's Counciler[2] or the Ku Klux Klanner, but the white moderate, who is more devoted to "order" than to justice; who prefers a negative peace which is the absence of tension to a positive peace which is the presence of justice; who constantly says: "I agree with you in the goal you seek, but I cannot agree with your methods of direct action"; who paternalistically believes he can set the timetable for another man's freedom; who lives by a mythical concept of time and who constantly advises the Negro to wait for a "more convenient season." Shallow understanding from people of good will is more frustrating than absolute misunderstanding from people of ill will. Lukewarm acceptance is much more bewildering than outright rejection.

I had hoped that the white moderate would understand that law and order exist for the purpose of establishing justice and that when they fail in this purpose they become the dangerously structured dams that block the flow of social progress. I had hoped that the white moderate would understand that the present tension in the South is a necessary phase of the transition from an obnoxious negative peace, in which the Negro passively accepted his unjust plight, to a substantive and positive peace, in which all men will respect the dignity and worth of human personality. Actually, we who engage in nonviolent direct action are not the creators of tension.

We merely bring to the surface the hidden tension that is already alive. We bring it out in the open, where it can be seen and dealt with. Like a boil that can never be cured so long as it is covered up but must be opened with all its ugliness to the natural medicines of air and light, injustice must be exposed, with all the tension its exposure creates, to the light of human conscience and the air of national opinion before it can be cured.

In your statement you assert that our actions, even though peaceful, must be condemned because they precipitate violence. But is this a logical assertion? Isn't this like condemning a robbed man because his possession of money precipitated the evil act of robbery? Isn't this like condemning Socrates because his unswerving commitment to truth and his philosophical inquiries precipitated the act by the misguided populace in which they made him drink hemlock? Isn't this like condemning Jesus because his unique God-consciousness and never-ceasing devotion to God's will precipitated the evil act of crucifixion? We must come to see that, as the federal courts have consistently affirmed, it is wrong to urge an individual to cease his efforts to gain his basic constitutional rights because the quest may precipitate violence. Society must protect the robbed and punish the robber.

I had also hoped that the white moderate would reject the myth concerning time in relation to the struggle for freedom. I have just received a letter from a white brother in Texas. He writes: "All Christians know that the colored people will receive equal rights eventually, but it is possible that you are in too great a religious hurry. It has taken Christianity almost two thousand years to accomplish what it has. The teachings of Christ take time to come to earth." Such an attitude stems from a tragic misconception of time, from the strangely rational notion that there is something in the very flow of time that will inevitably cure all ills. Actually, time itself is neutral; it can be used either destructively or constructively. More and more I feel that the people of ill will have used time much more effectively than have the people of good will. We will have to repent in this generation not merely for the hateful words and actions of the bad people but for the appalling silence of the good people. Human progress never rolls in on wheels of inevitability; it comes through the tireless efforts of men willing to be co-workers with God, and without this hard work, time itself becomes an ally of the forces of social stagnation. We must use time creatively, in the knowledge that the time is always ripe to do right. Now is the time to make real the promise of democracy and transform our pending national elegy into a creative psalm of brotherhood. Now is the time to lift our national policy from the quicksand of racial injustice to the solid rock of human dignity.

You speak of our activity in Birmingham as extreme. At first I was rather disappointed that fellow clergymen would see my nonviolent efforts as those of an extremist. I began thinking about the fact that we stand in the middle of two opposing forces in the Negro community. One is a force of complacency, made up in part of Negroes who, as a result of long years of oppression, are so drained of self-respect and a sense of "somebodiness" that they have adjusted to segregation; and in part of a few middle class Negroes who, because of a degree of academic and economic security and because in some ways they profit by segregation, have become insensitive to the problems of the masses. The other force is one of bitterness and hatred, and it comes perilously close to advocating violence. It is expressed in the various black nationalist groups that are springing up across the nation, the largest and best-known being Elijah Muhammad's Muslim movement.[3] Nourished by the Negro's frustration over the continued existence of racial discrimination, this movement is made up of people who have lost faith in America, who have absolutely repudiated Christianity, and who have concluded that the white man is an incorrigible "devil."

I have tried to stand between these two forces, saying that we need emulate neither the "do-nothingism" of the complacent nor the hatred and despair of the black nationalist. For there is the more excellent way of love and nonviolent protest. I am grateful to God that, through the influence of the Negro church, the way of nonviolence became an integral part of our struggle.

If this philosophy had not emerged, by now many streets of the South would, I am convinced, be flowing with blood. And I am further convinced that if our white brothers dismiss as "rabble-rousers" and "outside agitators" those of us who employ nonviolent direct action, and if they refuse to support our nonviolent efforts, millions of Negroes will, out of frustration and despair, seek solace and security in black-nationalist ideologies—a development that would inevitably lead to a frightening racial nightmare.

Oppressed people cannot remain oppressed forever. The yearning for freedom eventually manifests itself, and that is what has happened to the American Negro. Something within has reminded him of his birthright of freedom, and something without has reminded him that it can be gained. Consciously or unconsciously, he has been caught up by the Zeitgeist, and with his black brothers of Africa and his brown and yellow brothers of Asia, South America and the Caribbean, the United States Negro is moving with a sense of great urgency toward the promised land of racial justice. If one recognizes this vital urge that has engulfed the Negro community, one should readily understand why public demonstrations are taking place. The Negro has many pent-up resentments and latent frustrations, and he must release them. So let him march; let him make prayer pilgrimages to the city hall; let him go on freedom rides—and try to understand why he must do so. If his repressed emotions are not released in nonviolent ways, they will seek expression through violence; this is not a threat but a fact of history. So I have not said to my people: "Get rid of your discontent." Rather, I have tried to say that this normal and healthy discontent can be channeled into the creative outlet of nonviolent direct action. And now this approach is being termed extremist.

But though I was initially disappointed at being categorized as an extremist, as I continued to think about the matter I gradually gained a measure of satisfaction from the label. Was not Jesus an extremist for love: "Love your enemies, bless them that curse you, do good to them that hate you, and pray for them which despitefully use you, and persecute you." Was not Amos an extremist for justice: "Let justice roll down like waters and righteousness like an ever-flowing stream." Was not Paul an extremist for the Christian gospel: "I bear in my body the marks of the Lord Jesus." Was not Martin Luther an extremist: "Here I stand; I cannot do otherwise, so help me God." And John Bunyan: "I will stay in jail to the end of my days before I make a butchery of my conscience." And Abraham Lincoln: "This nation cannot survive half slave and half free." And Thomas Jefferson: "We hold these truths to be self-evident, that all men are created equal. . . ." So the question is not whether we will be extremists, but what kind of extremists will we be. Will we be extremists for hate or for love? Will we be extremists for the preservation of injustice or for the extension of justice? In that dramatic scene on Calvary's hill three men were crucified. We must never forget that all three were crucified for the same crime—the crime of extremism. Two were extremists for immorality, and thus fell below their environment. The other, Jesus Christ, was an extremist for love, truth and goodness, and thereby rose above his environment. Perhaps the South, the nation and the world are in dire need of creative extremists.

I had hoped that the white moderate would see this need. Perhaps I was too optimistic; perhaps I expected too much. I suppose I should have realized that few members of the oppressor race can understand the deep groans and passionate yearnings of the oppressed race, and still fewer have the vision to see that injustice must be rooted out by strong, persistent and determined action. I am thankful, however, that some of our white brothers in the South have grasped the meaning of this social revolution and committed themselves to it. They are still too few in quantity, but they are big in quality. Some—such as Ralph McGill, Lillian Smith, Harry Golden, James McBride Dabbs, Ann Braden and Sarah Patton Boyle—have written about our struggle in eloquent and prophetic terms.[4] Others have marched with us down nameless streets of the South. They have languished in filthy, roach-infested jails, suffering the abuse and brutality of policemen who view them as "dirty nigger lovers." Unlike so many of their moderate brothers and sisters, they have recognized the urgency of the moment and sensed the need for powerful "action" antidotes to combat the disease of segregation.

Let me take note of my other major disappointment. I have been so greatly disappointed with the white church and its leadership. Of course, there are some notable exceptions. I am not unmindful of the fact that each of you has taken some significant stands on this issue. I commend you, Reverend Stallings, for your Christian stand on this past Sunday, in welcoming Negroes to your worship service on a nonsegregated basis. I commend the Catholic leaders of this state for integrating Spring Hill College several years ago.[5]

But despite these notable exceptions, I must honestly reiterate that I have been disappointed with the church. I do not say this as one of those negative critics who can always find something wrong with the church. I say this as a minister of the gospel, who loves the church; who was nurtured in its bosom; who has been sustained by its spiritual blessings and who will remain true to it as long as the cord of Rio shall lengthen.

When I was suddenly catapulted into the leadership of the bus protest in Montgomery, Alabama, a few years ago, I felt we would be supported by the white church; I felt that the white ministers, priests and rabbis of the South would be among our strongest allies. Instead, some have been outright opponents, refusing to understand the freedom movement and misrepresenting its leadership; and too many others have been more cautious than courageous and have remained silent behind the anesthetizing security of stained-glass windows.

In spite of my shattered dreams, I came to Birmingham with the hope that the white religious leadership of this community would see the justice of our cause and, with deep moral concern, would serve as the channel through which our just grievances could reach the power structure. I had hoped that each of you would understand. But again I have been disappointed.

I have heard numerous southern religious leaders admonish their worshipers to comply with a desegregation decision because it is the law, but I have longed to hear white ministers declare: "Follow this decree because integration is morally right and because the Negro is your brother." In the midst of blatant injustices inflicted upon the Negro, I have watched white churchmen stand on the sideline and mouth pious irrelevancies and sanctimonious trivialities. In the midst of a mighty struggle to rid our nation of racial and economic injustice, I have heard many ministers say: "Those are social issues, with which the gospel has no real concern." And I have watched many churches commit themselves to a completely otherworldly religion which makes a strange, non-Biblical distinction between body and soul, between the sacred and the secular.

I have traveled the length and breadth of Alabama, Mississippi and all the other southern states. On sweltering summer days and crisp autumn mornings I have looked at the South's beautiful churches with their lofty spires pointing heavenward. I have beheld the impressive outlines of her massive religious-education buildings. Over and over I have found myself asking: "What kind of people worship here? Who is their God? Where were their voices when the lips of Governor [Ross] Barnett dripped with words of interposition and nullification? Where were they when Governor [George] Wallace gave a clarion call for defiance and hatred? Where were their voices of support when bruised and weary Negro men and women decided to rise from the dark dungeons of complacency to the bright hills of creative protest?"

Yes, these questions are still in my mind. In deep disappointment I have wept over the laxity of the church. But be assured that my tears have been tears of love. There can be no deep disappointment where there is not deep love. Yes, I love the church. How could I do otherwise? I am in the rather unique position of being the son, the grandson and the great-grandson of preachers. Yes, I see the church as the body of Christ. But, oh! How we have blemished and scarred that body through social neglect and through fear of being nonconformists.

There was a time when the church was very powerful in the time when the early Christians rejoiced at being deemed worthy to suffer for what they believed. In those days the church was not merely a thermometer that recorded the ideas and principles of popular opinion; it was a thermostat that transformed the mores of society. Whenever the early Christians entered a town, the people in power became disturbed and immediately sought to convict the Christians for being "disturbers of the peace" and "outside agitators." But the Christians pressed on, in the conviction that they were "a colony of heaven," called to obey God rather than man. Small in number, they were big in commitment. They were too God-intoxicated to be "astronomically intimidated." By their effort and example they brought an end to such ancient evils as infanticide and gladiatorial contests.

Things are different now. So often the contemporary church is a weak, ineffectual voice with an uncertain sound. So often it is an arch defender of the status quo. Far from being disturbed by the presence of the church, the power structure of the average community is consoled by the church's silent and often even vocal sanction of things as they are.

But the judgment of God is upon the church as never before. If today's church does not recapture the sacrificial spirit of the early church, it will lose its authenticity, forfeit the loyalty of millions, and be dismissed as an irrelevant social club with no meaning for the twentieth century. Every day I meet young people whose disappointment with the church has turned into outright disgust.

Perhaps I have once again been too optimistic. Is organized religion too inextricably bound to the status quo to save our nation and the world? Perhaps I must turn my faith to the inner spiritual church, the church within the church, as the true ecclesia and the hope of the world. But again I am thankful to God that some noble souls from the ranks of organized religion have broken loose from the paralyzing chains of conformity and joined us as active partners in the struggle for freedom. They have left their secure congregations and walked the streets of Albany, Georgia, with us. They have gone down the highways of the South on tortuous rides for freedom. Yes, they have gone to jail with us. Some have been dismissed from their churches, have lost the support of their bishops and fellow ministers. But they have acted in the faith that right defeated is stronger than evil triumphant. Their witness has been the spiritual salt that has preserved the true meaning of the gospel in these troubled times. They have carved a tunnel of hope through the dark mountain of disappointment.

I hope the church as a whole will meet the challenge of this decisive hour. But even if the church does not come to the aid of justice, I have no despair about the future. I have no fear about the outcome of our struggle in Birmingham, even if our motives are at present misunderstood. We will reach the goal of freedom in Birmingham, and all over the nation, because the goal of America is freedom. Abused and scorned though we may be, our destiny is tied up with America's destiny. Before the pilgrims landed at Plymouth, we were here. Before the pen of Jefferson etched the majestic words of the Declaration of Independence across the pages of history, we were here. For more than two centuries our forbears labored in this country without wages; they made cotton king; they built the homes of their masters while suffering gross injustice and shameful humiliation—and yet out of a bottomless vitality they continued to thrive and develop. If the inexpressible cruelties of slavery could not stop us, the opposition we now face will surely fail. We will win our freedom because the sacred heritage of our nation and the eternal will of God are embodied in our echoing demands.

Before closing I feel impelled to mention one other point in your statement that has troubled me profoundly. You warmly commended the Birmingham police force for keeping "order" and "preventing violence." I doubt that you would have so warmly commended the police force if you had seen its dogs sinking their teeth into unarmed, nonviolent Negroes. I doubt that you would so quickly commend the policemen if you were to observe their ugly and inhumane treatment of Negroes here in the city jail; if you were to watch them push and curse old Negro women and young Negro girls; if you were to see them slap and kick old Negro men and young boys; if you were to observe them, as they did on two occasions, refuse to give us food because we wanted to sing our grace together. I cannot join you in your praise of the Birmingham police department.

It is true that the police have exercised a degree of discipline in handling the demonstrators. In this sense they have conducted themselves rather "nonviolently" in public. But for what purpose? To preserve the evil system of segregation. Over the past few years I have consistently preached that nonviolence demands that the means we use must be as pure as the ends we seek. I have tried to make clear that it is wrong to use immoral means to attain moral ends. But now I must affirm that it is just as wrong, or perhaps even more so, to use moral means to preserve immoral ends. Perhaps Mr. [Eugene] Connor and his policemen have been rather nonviolent in public, as was Chief Pritchett in Albany, Georgia but they have used the moral means of nonviolence to maintain the immoral end of racial injustice. As T. S. Eliot has said: "The last temptation is the greatest treason: To do the right deed for the wrong reason."

I wish you had commended the Negro sit-inners and demonstrators of Birmingham for their sublime courage, their willingness to suffer and their amazing discipline in the midst of great provocation. One day the South will recognize its real heroes. They will be the James Merediths, with the noble sense of purpose that enables them to face jeering and hostile mobs, and with the agonizing loneliness that characterizes the life of the pioneer.[6] They will be old, oppressed, battered Negro women, symbolized in a seventy-two-year-old woman in Montgomery, Alabama, who rose up with a sense of dignity and with her people decided not to ride segregated buses, and who responded with ungrammatical profundity to one who inquired about her weariness: "My feets is tired, but my soul is at rest." They will be the young high school and college students, the young ministers of the gospel and a host of their elders, courageously and nonviolently sitting in at lunch counters and willingly going to jail for conscience's sake. One day the South will know that when these disinherited children of God sat down at lunch counters, they were in reality standing up for what is best in the American dream and for the most sacred values in our Judaeo-Christian heritage, thereby bringing our nation back to those great wells of democracy which were dug deep by the founding fathers in their formulation of the Constitution and the Declaration of Independence.

Never before have I written so long a letter. I'm afraid it is much too long to take your precious time. I can assure you that it would have been much shorter if I had been writing from a comfortable desk, but what else can one do when he is alone in a narrow jail cell, other than write long letters, think long thoughts and pray long prayers?

If I have said anything in this letter that overstates the truth and indicates an unreasonable impatience, I beg you to forgive me. If I have said anything that understates the truth and indicates my having a patience that allows me to settle for anything less than brotherhood, I beg God to forgive me.

I hope this letter finds you strong in the faith. I also hope that circumstances will soon make it possible for me to meet each of you, not as an integrationist or a civil rights leader but as a fellow clergyman and a Christian brother. Let us all hope that the dark clouds of racial prejudice will soon pass away and the deep fog of misunderstanding will be lifted from our fear-drenched communities, and in some not too distant tomorrow the radiant stars of love and brotherhood will shine over our great nation with all their scintillating beauty.

> Yours for the cause of Peace and
> Brotherhood,
> Martin Luther King, Jr.

NOTES

Originally published as "Letter from Birmingham Jail: A Vigorous, Eloquent Reply to Criticism Expressed by a Group of Eight Clergymen," in *The Christian Century: An Ecumenical Weekly* LXXX, no. 24 (12 June 1963): 767–73.

1. *Editor's note:* Karl Paul Reinhold Niebuhr, theologian and author of *Moral Man and Immoral Society* (New York: Scribner, 1960) and *The Irony of American History* (New York: Scribner, 1952).

2. *Editor's note:* The White Citizen's Council (renamed the "Conservative Citizen's Council") was a white supremacist group similar to the Ku Klux Klan in both its support for discriminatory legislation and its acts of physical brutality against African American people.

3. *Editor's note:* The Nation of Islam (NOI) was established in Detroit by Wallace D. Fard at the beginning of the Great Depression. In 1933, Elijah Muhammad, who expelled Malcolm X from the NOI in 1963–1964, assumed leadership of the organization, which is today headed by Louis Farrakhan.

4. *Editor's note:* Ralph McGill, "A Church, A School," in *Pulitzer Prize Editorials: America's Best Editorial Writing, 1917–1993,* ed. Wm. David Sloan and Laird B. Anderson (Ames: Iowa State University Press, 1994); *No Place to Hide: The South and Human Rights* (Macon, Ga.: Mercer University Press, 1984); *The South and the Southerner* (Boston: Little, Brown, 1964). Lillian Smith, *Killers of the Dream* (New York: Norton, 1949); *Now Is the Time* (New York: Viking, 1955); *One Hour* (New York: Harcourt, Brace and Co., 1959); *Our Faces, Our*

Words (New York: Norton, 1964); *Strange Fruit* (New York: New American Library, 1944); *The Winner Names the Age: A Collection of Writings* (New York: Norton, 1978). Harry Golden, *Mr. Kennedy and the Negroes* (Cleveland: World Pub. Co., 1964); "From Negro and Jew: An Encounter in America" in *Strangers & Neighbors: Relations between Blacks & Jews in the United States*, ed. Maurianne Adams and John Bracey (Amherst: University of Massachusetts Press, 1999). James McBride Dabbs, *Haunted by God* (Richmond, Va.: John Knox Press, 1972); *The Southern Heritage* (New York: Knopf, 1958); *Who Speaks for the South* (New York: Funk & Wagnalls, 1964). Anne Braden, *House Un-American Activities Committee, Bulwark of Segregation* (Los Angeles: National Committee to Abolish the House Un-American Activities Committee, 1964); *The Wall Between* (New York: Monthly Review Press, 1958). Sarah Patton Boyle, *The Desegregated Heart: A Virginian's Stand in Time of Transition* (New York: Morrow, 1962).

   5. *Editor's note:* Spring Hill College is a Jesuit college in Mobile, Alabama.

   6. *Editor's note:* James Meredith was the first African American student to attend the University of Mississippi. His 1962 admission was met by deadly riots eventually quelled by the National Guards. Despite constant threats and intimidation, Meredith graduated from "Ole Miss," and went on to a career of social activism.

Chapter Two

Malcolm X

Born Malcolm Little on May 19, 1925, in Omaha, Nebraska, to Louisa Little, from the West Indies, and Earl Little, a Baptist preacher and a member of Marcus Garvey's Universal Negro Improvement Association (UNIA), as a child Malcolm X faced racist terror and isolation. The Ku Klux Klan burned down his family's home and were suspected in his father's murder. Upon his mother's institutionalization, welfare agencies separated him and his siblings, placing them into various white foster homes. Young Malcolm's aspirations to become a lawyer were ridiculed and discouraged by racist teachers and schooling.

As black militancy rose with World War II, Malcolm Little, the young adult, became part of hipster and gangster culture, zoot suiting, "conking" his hair, and avoiding formal wage labor whenever possible. In 1943, he worked a train between Boston and New York City, engaging in petty hustling, drug dealing, pimping, and gambling. In 1946, apprehended in Boston for burglary, he surrendered without violence. In his autobiography, he reflects, "I believe that Allah was with me even then. I didn't try to shoot him [the arresting officer] and that saved my life."[1] He was tried and convicted with his friends, "Shorty" and two upper-middle-class white women, the latter of whom received lesser bail and shorter sentences. Both men were sentenced to ten years in the Charlestown State Prison. According to Little, the prosecution seemed more concerned with two black men's association with affluent white women than with the criminal charges.[2]

Prison transformed Little. He began studying the teachings of Elijah Muhammad and the Nation of Islam (NOI) and adopted the discipline and practices of Islam. Reading whatever books were available to him, writing letters regularly, and leading the debate team, he trained as an orator and rhetorician and began developing his political ideology and praxis. In 1952, the NOI gave him the surname "X" to reflect the fact that his African name remained unknown. The political and intellectual changes that Malcolm X underwent in prison suggest that the attraction to the NOI was both religious and political: the Nation of Islam provided a vehicle for spirituality while providing a mechanism for addressing black repression and humiliation under white supremacy.

Released from prison in 1954, the year of the Supreme Court school desegregation ruling, *Brown v Board of Education*, Malcolm X worked as a furniture salesman and auto-assemblyman, and immediately began speaking as a minister in temples across the country. He founded *Muhammad Speaks*, the NOI newspaper, and led or participated in rallies confronting local police brutality and racism. He married Betty Sanders (Betty Shabazz) in 1958, and fathered four daughters. In the 1960s, his stature as a national NOI leader grew as he offered public support for the civil rights movement and militancy, with sit-ins and the 1960 formation of the Student Nonviolent Coordinating Committee (SNCC). Malcolm X frequently criticized Martin Luther King, Jr.'s pacifism, and offered support to SNCC radicals. He also supported the independence movements and revolutionary liberation struggles to decolonize Africa.

His growing leadership soon posed a threat to Elijah Muhammad. When Malcolm X learned that the NOI's spiritual and moral leader had fathered multiple children by former secretaries and young women, tensions grew between the two men and within the organization. In 1963 Elijah Muhammad silenced him for his public comment describing the assassination of John F. Kennedy as "chickens coming home to roost"—referencing Kennedy's support for assassinations of socialist leaders such as Cuba's Fidel Castro and the Congo's Patrice Lumumba. On March 8, 1964, Malcolm X announced his resignation from the Nation of Islam and formed the Muslim Mosque, Inc., a new Islamic movement, seeking to build a broader base by working with civil rights leaders. Also in 1964, he made Hajj and took the name El-Hajj Malik El-Shabazz. On the trip to Mecca, he visited Beirut and several African nations, meeting with anticolonialist leaders (including Kwame Nkrumah, Ghana's first president). Attempting to foster support for the unity of national liberation struggles of African and "Afro-American" peoples, he founded the Organization of Afro-American Unity (OAAU). These international travels and political meetings likely exposed him to the attention of the Central Intelligence Agency (CIA). Upon returning to the United States, for the following months, Malik El-Shabazz worked with SNCC and Fannie Lou Hamer; visited Martin Luther King, Jr., when King was jailed in Selma, Alabama; and spoke tirelessly against racist injustice, as well as capitalism and imperialism. Malcolm X was assassinated in February 1965, by men associated with the Nation of Islam, after months of death threats, surveillance by the Federal Bureau of Investigation (FBI), and the firebombing of his home (allegedly by members of the Nation of Islam).

REFERENCES

Appiah, Kwame Anthony, and Henry Louis Gates, Jr., eds. *Africana: Encyclopedia of African and African-American Experience*. New York: Civitas, 1999.

Cone, James. *Martin and Malcolm: A Dream or a Nightmare?* Maryknoll, N.Y.: Orbis Books, 1991.

Davis, Thulani, and Howard Chapnick. *Malcolm X: The Great Photographs.* New York: Stewart, Tabori, & Chang, 1993.

Dyson, Michael Eric. *The Myth and Meaning of Malcolm X.* New York: Oxford University Press, 1995.

Malcolm X. *The Autobiography of Malcolm X.* New York: Ballantine, 1964.

―――. *By Any Means Necessary,* edited by George Breitman. New York: Pathfinder Press, 1970.

―――. *Malcolm X Speaks: Selected Speeches and Statements,* edited by George Breitman. New York: Grove Weidenfeld, 1990.

NOTES

Research and draft for this biography were provided by Martha Oatis.

1. Malcolm X, *The Autobiography of Malcolm X* (New York: Ballantine, 1964), 152.

2. *Autobiography,* 153.

The Ballot or the Bullet (*Abridged*)

April 3, 1964

Mr. Moderator, Brother [Louis E.] Lomax, brothers and sisters, friends and enemies: I just can't believe everyone in here is a friend and I don't want to leave anybody out. The question tonight, as I understand it, is "The Negro Revolt, and Where Do We Go From Here?" or "What Next?" In my little humble way of understanding it, it points toward either the ballot or the bullet.

Before we try and explain what is meant by the ballot or the bullet, I would like to clarify something concerning myself. I'm still a Muslim, my religion is still Islam. That's my personal belief. Just as Adam Clayton Powell is a Christian minister who heads the Abyssinian Baptist Church in New York, but at the same time takes part in the political struggles to try and bring about rights to the black people in this country; and Dr. Martin Luther King is a Christian minister down in Atlanta, Georgia, who heads another organization fighting for the civil rights of black people in this country; and Rev. [Milton] Galamison, I guess you've heard of him, is another Christian minister in New York who has been deeply involved in the school boycotts to eliminate segregated education; well, I myself am a minister, not a Christian minister, but a Muslim minister; and I believe in action on all fronts by whatever means necessary.

Although I'm still a Muslim, I'm not here tonight to discuss my religion. I'm not here to try and change your religion. I'm not here to argue or discuss anything that we differ about, because it's time for us to submerge our differences and realize that it is best for us to first see that we have the same problem, a common problem, a problem that will make you catch hell whether you're a Baptist, or a Methodist, or a Muslim, or a nationalist. Whether you're educated or illiterate, whether you live on the boulevard or in the alley, you're going to catch hell just like I am. We're all in the same boat and we all are going to catch the same hell from the same man. He just happens to be a white man. All of us have suffered here, in this country, political oppression at the hands of the white man, economic exploitation at the hands of the white man, and social degradation at the hands of the white man.

Now in speaking like this, it doesn't mean that we're anti-white, but it does mean we're anti-exploitation, we're anti-degradation, we're anti-oppression. And if the white man doesn't want us to be anti-him, let him stop oppressing and exploiting and degrading us. Whether we are Christians or Muslims or nationalists or agnostics or atheists, we must first learn to forget our differences. If we have differences, let us differ in the closet; when we come out in front, let us not have anything to argue about until we get finished arguing with the man. If the late President [John F.] Kennedy could get together with [Nikita] Khrushchev and exchange some wheat, we certainly have more in common with each other than Kennedy and Khrushchev had with each other.

If we don't do something real soon, I think you'll have to agree that we're going to be forced either to use the ballot or the bullet. It's one or the other in 1964. It isn't that time is running out—time has run out! 1964 threatens to be the most explosive year America has ever witnessed. The most explosive year. Why? It's also a political year. It's the year when all of the white politicians will be back in the so-called Negro community jiving you and me for some votes. The year when all of the white political crooks will be right back in your and my community with their false promises, building up our hopes for a letdown, with their trickery and their treachery, with their false promises which they don't intend to keep. As they nourish these dissatisfactions, it can only lead to one thing, an explosion; and now we have the type of black man on the scene in America today—I'm sorry, Brother Lomax—who just doesn't intend to turn the other cheek any longer.

Don't let anybody tell you anything about "the odds are against you." If they draft you, they send you to Korea and make you face 800 million Chinese. If you can be brave over there, you can be brave right here. These odds aren't as great as those odds. And if you fight here, you will at least know what you're fighting for.

I'm not a politician, not even a student of politics; in fact, I'm not a student of much of anything. I'm not a Democrat, I'm not a Republican, and I don't even consider myself an American. If you and I were Americans, there'd be no problem. Those Hunkies that just got off the boat, they're already Americans; Polacks are already Americans; the Italian refugees are already Americans. Everything that came out of Europe, every blue-eyed thing, is already an American. And as long as you and I have been over here, we aren't Americans yet.

Well, I am one who doesn't believe in deluding myself. I'm not going to sit at your table and watch you eat, with nothing on my plate, and call myself a diner. Sitting at the table doesn't make you a diner, unless you eat some of what's on that plate. Being here in America doesn't make you an American. Being born here in America doesn't make you an American. Why, if birth made you American, you wouldn't need any legislation, you wouldn't need any amendments to the Constitution, you wouldn't be faced with civil-rights filibustering in Washington, D.C., right now. They don't have to pass civil-rights legislation to make a Polack an American.

No, I'm not an American. I'm one of the 22 million black people who are the victims of Americanism. One of the 22 million black people who are the victims of democracy, nothing but disguised hypocrisy. So, I'm not standing here speaking to you as an American, or a patriot, or a flag-saluter, or a flag-waver—no, not I. I'm speaking as a victim of this American system. And I see America through the eyes of the victim. I don't see any American dream; I see an American nightmare.

These 22 million victims are waking up. Their eyes are coming open. They're beginning to see what they used to only look at. They're becoming politically mature. They are realizing that there are new political trends from coast to coast. As they see these new political trends, it's possible for them to see that every time there's an election the races are so close that they have to have a recount. They had to recount in Massachusetts to see who was going to be governor, it was so close. It was the same way in Rhode Island, in Minnesota, and in many other parts of the country. And the same with [John] Kennedy and [Richard] Nixon when they ran for president. It was so close they had to count all over again.[1] Well, what does this mean? It means that when white people are evenly divided, and black people have a bloc of votes of their own, it is left up to them to determine who's going to sit in the White House and who's going to be in the dog house.

It was the black man's vote that put the present administration [of Lyndon Baines Johnson] in Washington, D.C. Your vote, your dumb vote, your ignorant vote, your wasted vote put in an administration in Washington, D.C., that has seen fit to pass every kind of legislation imaginable, saving you until last, then filibustering on top of that. And your and my leaders have the audacity to run around clapping their hands and talk about how much progress we're making. And what a good president we have. If he wasn't good in Texas, he sure can't be good in Washington, D.C. Because Texas is a lynch state. It is in the same breath as Mississippi, no different; only they lynch you in Texas with a Texas accent and lynch you in Mississippi with a Mississippi accent. And these Negro leaders have the audacity to go and have some coffee in the White House with a Texan, a Southern cracker—that's all he is—and then come out and tell you and me that he's going to be better for us because, since he's from the South, he knows how to deal with the Southerners. What kind of logic is that? Let [Senator James O.] Eastland [D-Mississippi] be president, he's from the South too. He should be better able to deal with them than Johnson.

In this present administration they have in the House of Representatives 257 Democrats to only 177 Republicans. They control two-thirds of the House vote. Why can't they pass something that will help you and me? In the Senate, there are sixty-seven senators who are of the Democratic Party. Only thirty-three of them are Republicans. Why, the Democrats have got the government sewed up, and you're the one who sewed it up for them. And what have they given you for it? Four years in office, and just now getting around to some civil-rights legislation. Just now, after everything else is gone, out of the way, they're going to sit down now and play with you all summer long—the same old giant con game that they call filibuster. All those are in cahoots together. Don't you ever think they're not in cahoots together, for the man that is heading the civil-rights filibuster is a man from Georgia named Richard Russell. When Johnson became president, the first man he asked for when he got back to Washington, D.C., was "Dicky"—that's how tight they are. That's his boy, that's his pal, that's his buddy. But they're playing that old con game. One of them makes believe he's for you, and he's got it fixed where the other one is so tight against you, he never has to keep his promise.

So it's time in 1964 to wake up. And when you see them coming up with that kind of conspiracy, let them know your eyes are open. And let them know you got something else that's wide open too. It's got to be the ballot or the bullet. The ballot or the bullet. If you're afraid to use an expression like that, you should get on out of the country, you should get back in the cotton patch, you should get back in the alley. They get all the Negro vote, and after they get it, the Negro gets nothing in return. All they did when they got to Washington was give a few big Negroes big jobs. Those big Negroes didn't need big jobs, they already had jobs. That's camouflage, that's trickery, that's treachery, window-dressing. I'm not trying to knock out the Democrats for the Republicans, we'll get to them in a minute. But it is true— you put the Democrats first and the Democrats put you last.

Look at it the way it is. What alibis do they use, since they control Congress and the Senate? What alibi do they use when you and I ask, "Well, when are you going to keep your promise?" They blame the Dixiecrats. What is a Dixiecrat? A Democrat. A Dixiecrat is nothing but a Democrat in disguise. The titular head of the Democrats is also the head of the Dixiecrats, because the Dixiecrats are a part of the Democratic Party. The Democrats have never kicked the Dixiecrats out of the party. The Dixiecrats bolted themselves once, but the Democrats didn't put them out. Imagine, these lowdown Southern segregationists put the Northern Democrats down. But the Northern Democrats have never put the Dixiecrats down. No, look at that thing the way it is. They have got a con game going on, a political con game, and you and I are in the middle. It's time for you and me to wake up and start looking at it like it is, and trying to understand it like it is; and then we can deal with it like it is.

The Dixiecrats in Washington, D.C., control the key committees that run the government. The only reason the Dixiecrats control these committees is because they have seniority. The only reason they have seniority is because they come from states where Negroes can't vote. This is not even a government that's based on democracy. It is not a government that is made up of representatives of the people. Half of the people in the South can't even vote. Eastland is not even supposed to be in Washington. Half of the senators and congressmen who occupy these key positions in Washington, D.C., are there illegally, are there unconstitutionally.

I was in Washington, D.C., a week ago Thursday, when they were debating whether or not they should let the bill come onto the floor. And in the back of the room where the Senate meets, there's a huge map of the United States, and on that map it shows the location of Negroes throughout the country. And it shows that the Southern section of the country, the states that are most heavily concentrated with Negroes, are the ones that have senators and congressmen standing up filibustering and doing all other kinds of trickery to keep the Negro from being able to vote. This is pitiful. But it's not pitiful for us any longer; it's actually pitiful for the white man, because soon now, as the Negro awakens a little more and sees the vise that he's in, sees the bag that he's in, sees the real game that he's in, then the Negro's going to develop a new tactic.

These senators and congressmen actually violate the constitutional amendments that guarantee the people of that particular state or county the right to vote. And the Constitution itself has within it the machinery to expel any representative from a state where the voting rights of the people are violated. You don't even need new legislation. Any person in Congress right now, who is there from a state or a district where the voting rights of the people are violated, that particular person should be expelled from Congress. And when you expel him, you've removed one of the obstacles in the path of any real meaningful legislation in this country. In fact, when you expel them, you don't need new legislation, because they will be replaced by black representatives from counties and districts where the black man is in the majority, not in the minority.

If the black man in these Southern states had his full voting rights, the key Dixie-crats in Washington, D.C., which means the key Democrats in Washington, D.C., would lose their seats. The Democratic Party itself would lose its power. It would cease to be powerful as a party. When you see the amount of power that would be lost by the Democratic Party if it were to lose the Dixiecrat wing, or branch, or element, you can see where it's against the interests of the Democrats to give voting rights to Negroes in states where the Democrats have been in complete power and authority ever since the Civil War. You just can't belong to that Party without ana-lyzing it.

I say again, I'm not anti-Democrat, I'm not anti-Republican, I'm not anti-any-thing. I'm just questioning their sincerity, and some of the strategy that they've been using on our people by promising them promises that they don't intend to keep. When you keep the Democrats in power, you're keeping the Dixiecrats in power. I doubt that my good Brother Lomax will deny that. A vote for a Democrat is a vote for a Dixiecrat. That's why, in 1964, it's time now for you and me to become more politically mature and realize what the ballot is for; what we're sup-posed to get when we cast a ballot; and that if we don't cast a ballot, it's going to end up in a situation where we're going to have to cast a bullet. It's either a ballot or a bullet.

In the North, they do it a different way. They have a system that's known as gerrymandering, whatever that means. It means when Negroes become too heavily concentrated in a certain area, and begin to gain too much political power, the white man comes along and changes the district lines. You may say, "Why do you keep saying white man?" Because it's the white man who does it. I haven't ever seen any Negro changing any lines. They don't let him get near the line. It's the white man who does this. And usually, it's the white man who grins at you the most, and pats you on the back, and is supposed to be your friend. He may be friendly, but he's not your friend.

So, what I'm trying to impress upon you, in essence, is this: You and I in America are faced not with a segregationist conspiracy, we're faced with a government con-spiracy. Everyone who's filibustering is a senator—that's the government. Everyone who's finagling in Washington, D.C., is a congressman—that's the government. You don't have anybody putting blocks in your path but people who are a part of the government. The same government that you go abroad to fight for and die for is the government that is in a conspiracy to deprive you of your voting rights, deprive you of your economic opportunities, deprive you of decent housing, deprive you of decent education. You don't need to go to the employer alone, it is the government

itself, the government of America, that is responsible for the oppression and exploitation and degradation of black people in this country. And you should drop it in
their lap. This government has failed the Negro. This so-called democracy has failed
the Negro. And all these white liberals have definitely failed the Negro.

So, where do we go from here? First, we need some friends. We need some new
allies. The entire civil-rights struggle needs a new interpretation, a broader interpretation. We need to look at this civil-rights thing from another angle—from the
inside as well as from the outside. To those of us whose philosophy is black nationalism, the only way you can get involved in the civil-rights struggle is to give it a new
interpretation. That old interpretation excluded us. It kept us out. So, we're giving
a new interpretation to the civil-rights struggle, an interpretation that will enable
us to come into it, take part in it. And these handkerchief-heads who have been
dillydallying and pussyfooting and compromising—we don't intend to let them
pussyfoot and dillydally and compromise any longer.

How can you thank a man for giving you what's already yours? How then can
you thank him for giving you only part of what's already yours? You haven't even
made progress if what's being given to you, you should have had already. That's not
progress. And I love my Brother Lomax, the way he pointed out we're right back
where we were in 1954. We're not even as far up as we were in 1954. We're behind
where we were in 1954. There's more segregation now than there was in 1954.
There's more racial animosity, more racial hatred, more racial violence today in
1964, than there was in 1954. Where is the progress?

And now you're facing a situation where the young Negro's coming up. They
don't want to hear that "turn-the-other-cheek" stuff, no. In Jacksonville, those were
teenagers, they were throwing Molotov cocktails.[2] Negroes have never done that
before. But it shows you there's a new deal coming in. There's new thinking coming
in. There's new strategy coming in. It'll be Molotov cocktails this month, hand
grenades next month, and something else next month. It'll be ballots, or it'll be
bullets. It'll be liberty, or it will be death. The only difference about this kind of
death—it'll be reciprocal. You know what is meant by "reciprocal"? That's one of
Brother Lomax's words, I stole it from him. I don't usually deal with those big words
because I don't usually deal with big people. I deal with small people. I find you can
get a whole lot of small people and whip hell out of a whole lot of big people. They
haven't got anything to lose, and they've got every thing to gain. And they'll let
you know in a minute: "It takes two to tango; when I go, you go."

The black nationalists, those whose philosophy is black nationalism, in bringing
about this new interpretation of the entire meaning of civil rights, look upon it as
meaning, as Brother Lomax has pointed out, equality of opportunity. Well, we're
justified in seeking civil rights, if it means equality of opportunity, because all we're
doing there is trying to collect for our investment. Our mothers and fathers invested
sweat and blood. Three hundred and ten years we worked in this country without a
dime in return—I mean without a dime in return. You let the white man walk

around here talking about how rich this country is, but you never stop to think how it got rich so quick. It got rich because you made it rich.

You take the people who are in this audience right now. They're poor, we're all poor as individuals. Our weekly salary individually amounts to hardly anything. But if you take the salary of everyone in here collectively it'll fill up a whole lot of baskets. It's a lot of wealth. If you can collect the wages of just these people right here for a year, you'll be rich—richer than rich. When you look at it like that, think how rich Uncle Sam had to become, not with this handful, but millions of black people. Your and my mother and father, who didn't work an eight-hour shift, but worked from "can't see" in the morning until "can't see" at night, and worked for nothing, making the white man rich, making Uncle Sam rich.

This is our investment. This is our contribution—our blood. Not only did we give of our free labor, we gave of our blood. Every time he had a call to arms, we were the first ones in uniform. We died on every battlefield the white man had. We have made a greater sacrifice than anybody who's standing up in America today. We have made a greater contribution and have collected less. Civil rights, for those of us whose philosophy is black nationalism, means: "Give it to us now. Don't wait for next year. Give it to us yesterday, and that's not fast enough."

I might stop right here to point out one thing. Whenever you're going after something that belongs to you, anyone who's depriving you of the right to have it is a criminal. Understand that. Whenever you are going after something that is yours, you are within your legal rights to lay claim to it. And anyone who puts forth any effort to deprive you of that which is yours, is breaking the law, is a criminal. And this was pointed out by the Supreme Court decision. It outlawed segregation. Which means segregation is against the law. Which means a segregationist is breaking the law. A segregationist is a criminal. You can't label him as anything other than that. And when you demonstrate against segregation, the law is on your side. The Supreme Court is on your side.

Now, who is it that opposes you in carrying out the law? The police department itself. With police dogs and clubs. Whenever you demonstrate against segregation, whether it is segregated education, segregated housing, or anything else, the law is on your side, and anyone who stands in the way is not the law any longer. They are breaking the law, they are not representatives of the law. Any time you demonstrate against segregation and a man has the audacity to put a police dog on you, kill that dog, kill him, I'm telling you, kill that dog. I say it, if they put me in jail tomorrow, kill that dog. Then you'll put a stop to it. Now, if these white people in here don't want to see that kind of action, get down and tell the mayor to tell the police department to pull the dogs in. That's all you have to do. If you don't do it, someone else will.

If you don't take this kind of stand, your little children will grow up and look at you and think "shame." If you don't take an uncompromising stand—I don't mean go out and get violent; but at the same time you should never be nonviolent unless you run into some nonviolence. I'm nonviolent with those who are nonviolent with me. But when you drop that violence on me, then you've made me go insane, and I'm not responsible for what I do. And that's the way every Negro should get. Any time you know you're within the law, within your legal rights, within your moral rights, in accord with justice, then die for what you believe in. But don't die alone. Let your dying be reciprocal. This is what is meant by equality. What's good for the goose is good for the gander.

When we begin to get in this area, we need new friends, we need new allies. We need to expand the civil-rights struggle to a higher level—to the level of human rights. Whenever you are in a civil-rights struggle, whether you know it or not, you are confining yourself to the jurisdiction of Uncle Sam. No one from the outside world can speak out in your behalf as long as your struggle is a civil-rights struggle. Civil rights comes within the domestic affairs of this country. All of our African brothers and our Asian brothers and our Latin-American brothers cannot open their mouths and interfere in the domestic affairs of the United States. And as long as it's civil rights, this comes under the jurisdiction of Uncle Sam.

But the United Nations [UN] has what's known as the charter of human rights, it has a committee that deals in human rights. You may wonder why all of the atrocities that have been committed in Africa and in Hungary and in Asia and in Latin America are brought before the UN, and the Negro problem is never brought before the UN. This is part of the conspiracy. This old, tricky, blue-eyed liberal who is supposed to be your and my friend, supposed to be in our corner, supposed to be subsidizing our struggle, and supposed to be acting in the capacity of an adviser, never tells you anything about human rights. They keep you wrapped up in civil rights. And you spend so much time barking up the civil-rights tree, you don't even know there's a human-rights tree on the same floor.

When you expand the civil-rights struggle to the level of human rights, you can then take the case of the black man in this country before the nations in the UN. You can take it before the General Assembly.[3] You can take Uncle Sam before a world court. But the only level you can do it on is the level of human rights. Civil rights keeps you under his restrictions, under his jurisdiction. Civil rights keeps you in his pocket. Civil rights means you're asking Uncle Sam to treat you right. Human rights are some thing you were born with. Human rights are your God given rights. Human rights are the rights that are recognized by all nations of this earth. And any time any one violates your human rights, you can take them to the world court. Uncle Sam's hands are dripping with blood, dripping with the blood of the black man in this country. He's the earth's number-one hypocrite. He has the audacity— yes, he has—imagine him posing as the leader of the free world. The free world! And you over here singing "We Shall Overcome." Expand the civil-rights struggle to the level of human rights, take it into the United Nations, where our African brothers can throw their weight on our side, where our Asian brothers can throw their weight on our side, where our Latin-American brothers can throw their weight on our side, and where 800 million Chinamen are sitting there waiting to throw their weight on our side.

Let the world know how bloody his hands are. Let the world know the hypocrisy that's practiced over here. Let it be the ballot or the bullet. Let him know that it must be the ballot or the bullet.

When you take your case to Washington, D.C., you're taking it to the criminal who's responsible; it's like running from the wolf to the fox. They're all in cahoots together. They all work political chicanery and make you look like a chump before the eyes of the world. Here you are walking around in America, getting ready to be drafted and sent abroad, like a tin soldier, and when you get over there, people ask you what are you fighting for, and you have to stick your tongue in your cheek. No, take Uncle Sam to court, take him before the world.

By ballot I only mean freedom. Don't you know—I disagree with Lomax on this issue—that the ballot is more important than the dollar? Can I prove it? Yes. Look in the UN. There are poor nations in the UN; yet those poor nations can get together with their voting power and keep the rich nations from making a move. They have one nation—one vote, everyone has an equal vote. And when those brothers from Asia and Africa and the darker parts of this earth get together, their voting power is sufficient to hold Sam in check. Or Russia in check. Or some other section of the earth in check. So, the ballot is most important.

Right now, in this country, if you and I, 22 million African-Americans—that's what we are—Africans who are in America. You're nothing but Africans. Nothing but Africans. In fact, you'd get farther calling yourself African instead of Negro. Africans don't catch hell. You're the only one catching hell. They don't have to pass civil-rights bills for Africans. An African can go anywhere he wants right now. All you've got to do is tie your head up. That's right, go anywhere you want. Just stop being a Negro. Change your name to Hoogagagooba. That'll show you how silly the white man is. You're dealing with a silly man. A friend of mine who's very dark put a turban on his head and went into a restaurant in Atlanta before they called themselves desegregated. He went into a white restaurant, he sat down, they served him, and he said, "What would happen if a Negro came in here?" And there he's sitting, black as night, but because he had his head wrapped up the waitress looked back at him and says, "Why, there wouldn't no nigger dare come in here."

So, you're dealing with a man whose bias and prejudice are making him lose his mind, his intelligence, every day. He's frightened. He looks around and sees what's taking place on this earth, and he sees that the pendulum of time is swinging in your direction. The dark people are waking up. They're losing their fear of the white man. No place where he's fighting right now is he winning. Everywhere he's fighting, he's fighting someone your and my complexion. And they're beating him. He can't win any more. He's won his last battle. He failed to win the Korean War. He couldn't win it. He had to sign a truce. That's a loss. Any time Uncle Sam, with all his machinery for warfare, is held to a draw by some rice eaters, he's lost the battle. He had to sign a truce. America's not supposed to sign a truce. She's supposed to be bad. But she's not bad any more. She's bad as long as she can use her hydrogen bomb, but she can't use hers for fear Russia might use hers. Russia can't use hers, for fear that Sam might use his. So, both of them are weaponless. They can't use the weapon because each's weapon nullifies the other's. So the only place where action can take place is on the ground. And the white man can't win another war fighting on the ground. Those days are over. The black man knows it, the brown man knows it, the red man knows it, and the yellow man knows it. So they engage him in guerrilla warfare. That's not his style. You've got to have heart to be a guerrilla warrior, and he hasn't got any heart. I'm telling you now.

I just want to give you a little briefing on guerrilla warfare. It takes heart to be a guerrilla warrior because you're on your own. In conventional warfare you have tanks and a whole lot of other people with you to back you up, planes over your head and all that kind of stuff. But a guerrilla is on his own. All you have is a rifle, some sneakers and a bowl of rice, and that's all you need—and a lot of heart. The Japanese on some of those islands in the Pacific [during World War II], when the American soldiers landed, one Japanese sometimes could hold the whole army off. He'd just wait until the sun went down, and when the sun went down they were all equal. He would take his little blade and slip from bush to bush, and from American to American. The white soldiers couldn't cope with that. Whenever you see a white soldier that fought in the Pacific, he has the shakes, he has a nervous condition, because they scared him to death.

The same thing happened to the French up in French Indochina [Vietnam]. People who just a few years previously were rice farmers got together and ran the heavily-mechanized French army out of Indochina. You don't need it—modern warfare today won't work. This is the day of the guerrilla. They did the same thing in Algeria. Algerians, who were nothing but Bedouins, took a knife and sneaked off to the hills, and [Charles] de Gaulle and all of his highfalutin' war machinery couldn't defeat those guerrillas. Nowhere on this earth does the white man win in guerrilla warfare. It's not his speed. Just as guerrilla warfare is prevailing in Asia and in parts of Africa and in parts of Latin America, you've got to be mighty naive, or you've got to play the black man cheap, if you don't think some day he's going to wake up and find that it's got to be the ballot or the bullet.

I would like to say, in closing, a few things concerning the Muslim Mosque, Inc., which we established recently in New York City. It's true we're Muslims and our religion is Islam, but we don't mix our religion with our politics and our economics and our social and civil activities—not any more. We keep our religion in our mosque. After our religious services are over, then as Muslims we become involved in political action, economic action and social and civic action. We become involved with anybody, anywhere, any time and in any manner that's designed to eliminate the evils, the political, economic and social evils that are afflicting the people of our community.

The political philosophy of black nationalism means that the black man should control the politics and the politicians in his own community; no more. The black man in the black community has to be re-educated into the science of politics so he will know what politics is supposed to bring him in return. Don't be throwing out any ballots. A ballot is like a bullet. You don't throw your ballots until you see a target, and if that target is not within your reach, keep your ballot in your pocket. The political philosophy of black nationalism is being taught in the Christian church. It's being taught in the NAACP. It's being taught in CORE meetings. It's being taught in SNCC—Student Nonviolent Coordinating Committee—meetings. It's being taught in Muslim meetings. It's being taught where nothing but atheists and agnostics come together. It's being taught everywhere. Black people are fed up with the dillydallying, pussyfooting, compromising approach that we've been using toward getting our freedom. We want freedom now, but we're not going to get it saying "We Shall Overcome." We've got to fight until we overcome.

NOTES

Originally published in *Malcolm X Speaks: Selected Speeches and Statements*, ed. George Breitman (New York: Merit, 1965), 23–44.

1. *Editor's note*: In the 1960 presidential election between John F. Kennedy and Richard Nixon, Kennedy won the popular vote by a 49.7 to 49.5 percent margin and the electoral vote 303 to 219. Nixon did not demand a recount, but in his next campaign, as protection against fraud, he organized 100,000 poll watchers, headed by a former FBI official. Richard Nixon was elected president in 1968 and 1972 and resigned under threat of impeachment in 1974. Melvin Small, *The Presidency of Richard Nixon* (Lawrence: University Press of Kansas, 1999), 21.

2. *Editor's note*: During the Jacksonville, Florida, uprisings of 1960 and 1964, the African American community used tactics of heightened militancy in order to protest the continual discrimination and segregation of their community. On August 27, 1960, an African American youth was attacked by a Ku Klux Klan member, and the police did not intervene. When the Klansmen continued to chase teens into the African American neighborhood, the Boomerang gang, armed with guns, sticks, and Molotov cocktails, retaliated until the Klansmen retreated. In 1964, the African American community again protested against racial oppression and violence. A civil rights worker's home was bombed by Klansmen on February 16. The urban uprisings that followed that March used such tactics as the hit-and-run strategy: protesting in a location and then leaving before the police arrived. Youth armed with rocks and firebombs directed at buildings were also involved in the protests. Abel A. Bartley, *Keeping the Faith: Race, Politics, and Social Development in Jacksonville, Florida* (Westport, Conn.: Greenwood, 2000), 101, 105–11.

3. *Editor's note*: In 1964, Malcolm X spoke before the Organization of African Unity charging the United States with genocide against African American people. Genocide was first charged to the United Nations on December 17, 1951, by William L. Patterson and Paul Robeson, who originated and delivered a petition entitled "We Charge Genocide!"

Chapter Three

Angela Y. Davis

Angela Y. Davis was born in Birmingham, Alabama, in 1944. She grew up in the southern United States under Jim Crow segregation and codified racial discrimination. During the late 1940s, her family integrated a neighborhood that subsequently became known as "Dynamite Hill" because of Ku Klux Klan terrorism against African American families integrating the previously all-white community. Davis left the South in 1959 for Manhattan where, under the auspices of a Quaker educational program, she lived with a white family and attended a progressive private high school. At age fifteen, she became active in a youth organization associated with the Communist Party USA. Attending Brandeis University as an undergraduate, Davis studied with Marxist philosopher Herbert Marcuse, and took her junior year in France at the Sorbonne. Terrorist acts against civil rights activists, particularly the Birmingham church bombing in 1963 where playmates of Davis's younger sister Fania were murdered, provided the radicalizing impetus to eventually end her European studies. Torn between the desire to learn from different national cultures and political systems and the need to join "the movement," Davis decided not to pursue a doctorate at Goethe University in Frankfurt, Germany, choosing instead to return to the United States to work with Marcuse at the University of California-San Diego.

The search for human rights, more far-reaching than the civil and electoral rights supposedly guaranteed under the U.S. Constitution and in its amendments, led Davis to the Black Panther Party. After a period of involvement with the Student Nonviolent Coordinating Committee, Davis simultaneously joined the Black Panther Party and the Communist Party USA. Her relationship with the former was always much more problematic. She describes her affiliation with the Panther organization as a permanently ambiguous status that fluctuated between member and fellow-traveler. In 1969, she came to national attention after being removed from her teaching position in the Philosophy Department at the University of California-Los Angeles because of her social activism and membership in the Communist Party.

Davis's long-standing commitment to prisoners' rights dates back to her involvement in the campaign to free the California prisoners known as the Soledad Brothers, which led to her own arrest and imprisonment. In 1970 she was placed on the FBI's Ten Most Wanted List on false charges connected to the attempt by seventeen-year-old Jonathan Jackson to secure the release of his elder brother, George Jackson, and the other Soledad Brothers by taking hostages at the Marin County courthouse, using guns registered in the name of Angela Davis. The Marin County confrontation resulted in the deaths of Jonathan Jackson, Judge Harold Haley, and prisoners James McClain and William Christmas by guards following official policy to prevent escapes regardless of casualties. Davis became the subject of an intense police and Federal Bureau of Investigation search that drove her underground and culminated in one of the most famous trials in recent U.S. history. During her sixteen months of incarceration, a massive international "Free Angela Davis" campaign was organized; she was acquitted of all charges in 1972.

An advocate of human rights and a critic of repression, racism, and sexism in the criminal justice system, in 1997, Angela Davis cofounded Critical Resistance, an organization for prison abolition. A professor in the History of Consciousness Program at the University of California-Santa Cruz, her publications include: *Women, Race & Class; Women, Culture & Politics; Blues Legacies and Black Feminisms;* and *If They Come in the Morning: Voices of Resistance* (coedited with Bettina Aptheker). Her essays, spanning thirty years of activism and writing, are collected in *The Angela Y. Davis Reader.*

REFERENCES

Aptheker, Bettina. *The Morning Breaks: The Trial of Angela Davis.* New York: International Publishers, 1975 (reprint, Ithaca, N.Y.: Cornell University Press, 1999).

Davis, Angela Y. *Angela Davis: An Autobiography.* New York: Random House, 1974.

———. *The Angela Y. Davis Reader,* edited by Joy James. Malden, Mass.: Blackwell, 1998.

———. *Violence against Women and the Ongoing Challenge to Racism.* Latham, N.Y.: Kitchen Table, 1985.

———. *Women, Culture & Politics.* New York: Vintage, 1990.

———. *Women, Race & Class.* New York: Vintage, 1983.

———, and Bettina Aptheker, eds. *If They Come in the Morning: Voices of Resistance.* New York: Third Press, 1971.

James, Joy. "Revolutionary Icons and NeoSlave Narratives." *Shadowboxing: Representations of Black Feminist Politics.* New York: St. Martin's, 1999.

Perkins, Margo V. *Autobiography as Activism: Three Black Women of the Sixties.* Jackson: University Press of Mississippi, 2000.

Political Prisoners, Prisons, and Black Liberation

May 1971

Despite a long history of exalted appeals to man's inherent right to resistance, there has seldom been agreement on how to relate in practice to unjust immoral laws and the oppressive social order from which they emanate. The conservative, who does not dispute the validity of revolutions deeply buried in history, invokes visions of impending anarchy in order to legitimize his demand for absolute obedience. Law and order, with the major emphasis on order, is his watchword. The liberal articulates his sensitivity to certain of society's intolerable details, but will almost never prescribe methods of resistance that exceed the limits of legality—redress through electoral channels is the liberal's panacea.

In the heat of our pursuit of fundamental human rights, black people have been continually cautioned to be patient. We are advised that as long as we remain faithful to the existing democratic order, the glorious moment will eventually arrive when we will come into our own as full-fledged human beings.

But having been taught by bitter experience, we know that there is a glaring incongruity between democracy and the capitalist economy which is the source of our ills. Regardless of all rhetoric to the contrary, the people are not the ultimate matrix of the laws and the system which govern them—certainly not black people and other nationally oppressed people, but not even the mass of whites. The people do not exercise decisive control over the determining factors of their lives.

Officials' assertions that meaningful dissent is always welcome, provided it falls within the boundaries of legality, are frequently a smokescreen obscuring the invitation to acquiesce in oppression. Slavery may have been un-righteous, the constitutional precision for the enslavement of blacks may have been unjust, but conditions were not to be considered so unbearable (especially since they were profitable to a small circle) as to justify escape and other acts proscribed by law. This was the import of the fugitive slave laws.[1]

Needless to say, the history of the Unites States has been marred from its inception by an enormous quantity of unjust laws, far too many expressly bolstering the oppression of black people. Particularized reflections of existing social inequities, these laws have repeatedly borne witness to the exploitative and racist core of the society itself. For blacks, Chicanos, for all nationally oppressed people, the problem of opposing unjust laws and the social conditions which nourish their growth has always had immediate practical implications. Our very survival has frequently been a direct function of our skill in forging effective channels of resistance. In resisting we as societies have been compelled to openly violate those laws which directly or indirectly buttress our oppression. But even containing our resistance within the

64

orbit of legality, we have been labeled criminals and have been methodically perse-cuted by a racist legal apparatus.

Under the ruthless conditions of slavery, the underground railroad provided the framework for extra-legal anti-slavery activity pursued by vast numbers of people, both black and white. Its functioning was in flagrant violation of the fugitive slave law; those who were apprehended were subjected to severe penalties. Of the innu-merable recorded attempts to rescue fugitive slaves from the clutches of slave catch-ers, one of the most striking is the case of Anthony Burns, a slave from Virginia, captured in Boston in 1853. A team of his supporters, in attempting to rescue him by force during the course of his trial, engaged the police in a fierce courtroom battle. During the gun-fight, a prominent Abolitionist, Thomas Wentworth Higgin-son, was wounded. Although the rescuers were unsuccessful in their efforts, the impact of this incident ". . . did more to crystallize Northern sentiment against slavery than any other except the exploit of John Brown, 'and this was the last time a fugitive slave was taken from Boston. It took twenty-two companies of state mili-tia, four platoons of marines, a battalion of United States artillerymen, and the city's police force . . . to ensure the performance of this shameful act, the cost of which, the Federal government alone, came to forty thousand dollars.' "[2]

Throughout the era of slavery, blacks, as well as progressive whites, repeatedly discovered that their commitment to the anti-slavery cause frequently entailed the overt violation of the laws of the land. Even as slavery faded away into a more subtle yet equally pernicious apparatus to dominate black people, "illegal" resistance was still on the agenda. After the Civil War, Black Codes, successors to the old Slave Codes, legalized convict labor, prohibited social intercourse between blacks and whites, gave white employers an excessive degree of control over the private lives of black workers, and generally codified racism and terror. Naturally, numerous indi-vidual as well as collective acts of resistance prevailed. On many occasions, blacks formed armed teams to protect themselves from white terrorists who were, in turn, protected by law enforcement agencies, if not actually identified with them.

By the second decade of the twentieth century, the mass movement, headed by Marcus Garvey, proclaimed in its Declaration of Rights that black people should not hesitate to disobey all discriminatory laws. Moreover, the Declaration announced, they should utilize all means available to them, legal or illegal, to defend themselves from legalized terror as well as Ku Klux Klan violence. During the era of intense activity around civil rights issues, systematic disobedience of oppressive laws was a primary tactic. The sit-ins were organized transgressions of racist legislation.

All these historical instances involving the overt violation of the laws of the land converge around an unmistakable common denominator. At stake has been the col-lective welfare and survival of a people. There is a distinct and qualitative difference between one breaking a law for one's own individual self-interest and violating it in the interests of a class of people whose oppression is expressed either directly or indirectly through that particular law. The former might be called criminal (though in many instances he is a victim), but the latter, as a reformist or revolutionary, is interested in universal social change. Captured, he or she is a political prisoner.

The political prisoner's words or deed have in one form or another embodied political protests against the established order and have consequently brought him into acute conflict with the state. In light of the political content of his act, the "crime" (which may or may not have been committed) assumes a minor importance. In this country, however, where the special category of political prisoners is not officially acknowledged, the political prisoner inevitably stands trial for a specific criminal offense, not for a political act. Often the so-called crime does not even have a nominal existence. As in the 1914 murder frame-up of the IWW [Industrial Workers of the World] organizer, Joe Hill, it is a blatant fabrication, a mere excuse for silencing a militant crusader against oppression. In all instances, however, the political prisoner has violated the unwritten law which prohibits disturbances and upheavals in the status quo of exploitation and racism. This unwritten law has been contested by actually and explicitly breaking a law or by utilizing constitutionally protected channels to educate, agitate, and organize masses to resist.

A deep-seated ambivalence has always characterized the official response to the political prisoner. Charged and tried for the criminal act, his guilt is always political in nature. This ambivalence is perhaps best captured by Judge Webster Thayer's comment upon sentencing Bartolomeo Vanzetti to fifteen years for an attempted payroll robbery: "This man, although he may not have actually committed the crime attributed to him, is nevertheless morally culpable, because he is an enemy of our existing institutions." (The very same judge incidentally, sentences Sacco and Vanzetti[3] to death for a robbery and murder of which they were manifestly innocent.)[4] It is not surprising that Nazi Germany's foremost constitutional lawyer, Carl Schmitt, advanced the theory which generalized this a priori culpability. A thief, for example, was not necessarily one who had committed an overt act of theft, but rather one whose character renders him a thief (*wer nach seinem wesen ein Dieb ist*). [President Richard] Nixon's and [FBI Director] J. Edgar Hoover's pronouncements lead one to believe that they would readily accept Schmitt's fascist legal theory. Anyone who seeks to overthrow oppressive institutions, whether or not he has engaged in an overt act, is a priori a criminal who must be buried away in one of America's dungeons.

Even in all of Martin Luther King's numerous arrests, he was not so much charged with the nominal crimes of trespassing, and disturbance of the peace, as with being an enemy of the southern society, an inveterate foe of racism. When Robert Williams[5] was accused of kidnapping, this charge never managed to conceal his real offense—the advocacy of black people's incontestable right to bear arms in their own defense.

The offense of the political prisoner is political boldness, the persistent challenging—legally or extra-legally—of fundamental social wrongs fostered and reinforced by the state. The political prisoner has opposed unjust laws and exploitative, racist social conditions in general, with the ultimate aim of transforming these laws and this society into an order harmonious with the material and spiritual needs and interests of the vast majority of its members.

Nat Turner and John Brown were political prisoners in their time. The acts for which they were charged and subsequently hanged, were the practical extensions of their profound commitment to the abolition of slavery. They fearlessly bore the responsibility for their actions. The significance of their executions and the accompanying widespread repression did not lie so much in the fact that they were being punished for specific crimes, nor even in the effort to use their punishment as an implicit threat to deter others from similar *armed* acts of resistance. These executions, and the surrounding repression of slaves, were intended to terrorize the anti-slavery movement in general; to discourage and diminish both legal and illegal forms of abolitionist activity. As usual, the effect of repression was miscalculated and in both instances, anti-slavery activity was accelerated and intensified as a result.

Nat Turner and John Brown can be viewed as examples of the political prisoner who has actually committed an act which is defined by the state as "criminal." They killed and were consequently tried for murder. But did they commit murder? This raises the question of whether American revolutionaries had *murdered* the British in their struggle for liberation. Nat Turner and his followers killed some sixty-five white people, yet shortly before the revolt had begun, Nat is reputed to have said to the other rebelling slaves: "Remember that ours is not war for robbery nor to satisfy our passions, it is a *struggle for freedom*. Ours must be deeds and not words."[6]

The very institutions which condemned Nat Turner and reduced his struggle for freedom to a simpler criminal case of murder, owed their existence to the decision, made a half-century earlier, to take up arms against the British oppressor.

The battle for the liquidation of slavery had no legitimate existence in the eyes of the government and therefore the special quality of deeds carried out in the interests of freedom was deliberately ignored. There were no political prisoners, there were only criminals; just as the movement out of which these deeds flowed was largely considered criminal.

Likewise, the significance of activities which are pursued in the interests of liberation today is minimized not so much because officials are unable to *see* the collective surge against oppression, but because they have consciously set out to subvert such movements. In the Spring of 1970, Los Angeles Panthers took up arms to defend themselves from an assault initiated by the local police force on their office and on their persons. They were charged with criminal assault. If one believed the official propaganda, they were bandits and rogues who pathologically found pleasure in attacking policemen. It was not mentioned that their community activities—educational work, services such as free breakfast and free medical programs—which had legitimized them in the black community, were the immediate reason for which the wrath of the police had fallen upon them. In defending themselves from the attack waged by some 600 policemen (there were only eleven Panthers in the office)

double standard

they were defending not only their lives, but even more importantly their accomplishments in the black community surrounding them, and in the broader thrust for black liberation. Whenever blacks in struggle have recourse to self-defense, particularly armed self-defense, it is twisted and distorted on official levels and ultimately rendered synonymous with criminal aggression. On the other hand, when policemen are clearly indulging in acts of criminal aggression, officially they are defending themselves through "justifiable assault" or "justifiable homicide."

The ideological acrobatics characteristic of official attempts to explain away the existence of the political prisoner do not end with the equation of the individual political act with the individual criminal act. The political act is defined as criminal in order to discredit radical and revolutionary movements. A political event is reduced to a criminal event in order to affirm the absolute invulnerability of the existing order. In a revealing contradiction, the court resisted the description of the New York Panther 21[7] trial as "political," yet the prosecutor entered as evidence of criminal intent, literature which represented, so he purported, the political ideology of the Black Panther Party.

The legal apparatus designates the black liberation fighter a criminal, prompting Nixon, [Vice President Spiro] Agnew, [California Governor Ronald] Reagan et al. to proceed to mystify with their demagogy millions of Americans whose senses have been dulled and whose critical powers have been eroded by the continual onslaught of racist ideology.

As the black liberation movement and other progressive struggles increase in magnitude and intensity, the judicial system and its extension, the penal system, consequently become key weapons in the state's fight to preserve the existing conditions of class domination, and therefore racism, poverty and war.

In 1951, W. E. B. Du Bois, as Chairman of the Peace Information Center, was indicted by the federal government for "failure to register as an agent of a foreign principal." In assessing this ordeal, which occurred in the ninth decade of his life, he turned his attention to the inhabitants of the nation's jails and prisons:

> What turns me cold in all this experience is the certainty that thousands of innocent victims are in jail today because they had neither money nor friends to help them. The eyes of the world were on our trial despite the desperate efforts of press and radio to suppress the facts and cloud the real issues; the courage and money of friends and of strangers who dared stand for a principle freed me; but God only knows how many who were as innocent as I and my colleagues are today in hell. They daily stagger out of prison doors embittered, vengeful, hopeless, ruined. And of this army of the wronged, the proportion of Negroes is frightful. We protect and defend sensational cases where Negroes are involved. But the great mass of arrested or accused black folk have no defense. There is desperate need of nationwide organizations to oppose this national racket of railroading to jails and chain gangs the poor, friendless and black.[8]

Almost two decades passed before the realization attained by Du Bois on the occasion of his own encounter with the judicial system achieved extensive acceptance. A number of factors have combined to transform the penal system into a prominent terrain of struggle, both for the captives inside and the masses outside. The impact of large numbers of political prisoners both on prison populations and on the mass movement has been decisive. The vast majority of political prisoners have not allowed the fact of imprisonment to curtail their educational, agitational, and organizing activities, which they continue behind prison walls. And in the course of developing mass movements around political prisoners, a great deal of attention has inevitably been focused on the institutions in which they are imprisoned. Furthermore the political receptivity of prisoners—especially black and brown captives—has been increased and sharpened by the surge of aggressive political activity rising out of black, Chicano, and other oppressed communities. Finally, a major catalyst for intensified political action in and around prisons has emerged out of the transformation of convicts, originally found guilty of criminal offenses, into exemplary political militants. Their patient educational efforts in the realm of exposing the specific oppressive structures of the penal system in their relation to the larger oppression of the social system have had a profound effect on their fellow captives.

The prison is a key component of the state's coercive apparatus, the overriding function of which is to ensure social control. The etymology of the term "penitentiary" furnishes a clue to the controlling idea behind the "prison system" at its inception. The penitentiary was projected as the locale for doing penitence for an offense against society, the physical and spiritual purging of proclivities to challenge rules and regulations which command total obedience. While cloaking itself with the bourgeois aura of universality—imprisonment was supposed to cut across all class lines, as crimes were to be defined by the act, not the perpetrator—the prison has actually operated as an instrument of class domination, a means of prohibiting the have-nots from encroaching upon the haves. *purpose of prisons*

The occurrence of crime is inevitable in a society in which wealth is unequally distributed, as one of the constant reminders that society's productive forces are being channeled in the wrong direction. The majority of criminal offenses bear a direct relationship to property. Contained in the very concept of property, crimes are profound but suppressed social needs which express themselves in anti-social modes of action. Spontaneously produced by a capitalist organization of society, this type of crime is at once a protest against society and a desire to partake of its exploitative content. It challenges the symptoms of capitalism, but not its essence.

Some Marxists in recent years have tended to banish "criminals" and the lumpenproletariat as a whole from the arena of revolutionary struggle. Apart from the absence of any link binding the criminal to the means of production, underlying this exclusion has been the assumption that individuals who have recourse to anti-social acts are incapable of developing the discipline and collective orientation required by revolutionary struggle.

With the declassed character of lumpenproletarians in mind, Marx had stated that they are as capable of "the most heroic deeds and the most exalted sacrifices, as of the basest banditry and the dirtiest corruption."⁹ He emphasized the fact that the provisional government's mobile guards under the Paris Commune—some 24,000 troops—were largely formed out of young lumpenproletarians from fifteen to twenty years of age. Too many Marxists have been inclined to overvalue the second part of Marx's observation—that the lumpenproletariat is capable of the basest banditry and the dirtiest corruption—while minimizing or indeed totally disregarding his first remark, applauding the lumpen for their heroic deeds and exalted sacrifices.

Especially today when so many black, Chicano, and Puerto Rican men and women are jobless as a consequence of the internal dynamic of the capitalist system, the role of the unemployed, which includes the lumpenproletariat, in revolutionary struggle must be given serious thought. Increased unemployment, particularly for the nationally oppressed, will continue to be an inevitable by-product of technological development. At least thirty percent of black youth are presently without jobs.¹⁰ In the context of class exploitation and national oppression it should be clear that numerous individuals are compelled to resort to criminal acts, not as a result of conscious choice—implying other alternatives—but because society has objectively reduced their possibilities of subsistence and survival to this level. This recognition should signal the urgent need to organize the unemployed and lumpenproletariat, as indeed the Black Panther Party as well as activists in prison have already begun to do.

In evaluating the susceptibility of the black and brown unemployed to organizing efforts, the peculiar historical features of the US, specifically racism and national oppression, must be taken into account. There already exists in the black and brown communities, the lumpenproletariat included, a long tradition of collective resistance to national oppression.

Moreover, in assessing the revolutionary potential of prisoners in America as a group, it should be borne in mind that not all prisoners have actually committed crimes. The built-in racism of the judicial system expresses itself, as Du Bois has suggested, in the railroading of countless innocent blacks and other national minorities into the country's coercive institutions.

One must also appreciate the effects of disproportionately long prison terms on black and brown inmates. The typical criminal mentality sees imprisonment as a calculated risk for a particular criminal act. One's prison term is more or less rationally predictable. The function of racism in the judicial-penal complex is to shatter that predictability. The black burglar, anticipating a two-to-four-year term, may end up doing ten to fifteen years, while the white burglar leaves after two years.

Within the contained, coercive universe of the prison, the captive is confronted with the realities of racism, not simply as individual acts dictated by attitudinal bias; rather he is compelled to come to grips with racism as an institutional phenomenon collectively experienced by the victims. The disproportionate representation of the black and brown communities, the manifest racism of parole boards, the intense brutality inherent in the relationship between prison guards and black and brown inmates—all this and more causes the prisoner to be confronted daily, hourly, with the concentrated systematic existence of racism.

For the innocent prisoner, the process of radicalization should come easy; for the "guilty" victim, the insight into the nature of racism as it manifests itself in the judicial-penal complex can lead to a questioning of his own past criminal activity and a re-evaluation of the methods he has used to survive in a racist and exploitative society. Needless to say, this process is not automatic, it does not occur spontaneously. The persistent educational work carried out by the prison's political activists plays a key role in developing the political potential of captive men and women.

Prisoners—especially blacks, Chicanos and Puerto Ricans—are increasingly advancing the proposition that they are *political* prisoners. They contend that they are political prisoners in the sense that they are largely the victims of an oppressive politico-economic order, swiftly becoming conscious of the causes underlying their victimization. The *Folsom Prisoners' Manifesto of Demands and Anti-Oppression Platform*[11] attests to a lucid understanding of the structures of oppression within the prison—structures which contradict even the avowed function of the penal institution: "The program we are submitted to, under the ridiculous title of rehabilitation, is relative to the ancient stupidity of pouring water on the drowning man, in as much as we are treated for our hostilities by our program administrators with their hostility for medication." The *Manifesto* also reflects an awareness that the severe social crisis taking place in this country, predicated in part on the ever-increasing mass consciousness of deepening social contradictions, is forcing the political function of the prisons to surface in all its brutality. Their contention that prisons are being transformed into the "fascist concentration camps of modern America," should not be taken lightly, although it would be erroneous as well as defeatist in a practical sense, to maintain that fascism has irremediably established itself.

The point is this, and this is the truth which is apparent in the *Manifesto*: the ruling circles of America are expanding and intensifying repressive measures designed to nip revolutionary movements in the bud as well as to curtail radical-democratic tendencies, such as the movement to end the war in Indochina. The government is not hesitating to utilize an entire network of fascist tactics, including the monitoring of congressmen's telephone calls, a system of "preventive fascism," as [Herbert] Marcuse has termed it, in which the role of the judicial-penal systems looms large. The sharp edge of political repression, cutting through the heightened militancy of the masses, and bringing growing numbers of activists behind prison walls, must necessarily pour over into the contained world of the prison where it understandably acquires far more ruthless forms.

It is a relatively easy matter to persecute the captive whose life is already dominated by a network of authoritarian mechanisms. This is especially facilitated by the indeterminate sentence policies of many states, for politically conscious prisoners will incur inordinately long sentences on the original conviction. According to Louis S. Nelson, warden of the San Quentin Prison, "if the prisons of California become known as schools for violent revolution, the Adult Authority would be remiss in their duty not to keep the inmates longer" (*San Francisco Chronicle*, May 2, 1971). Where this is deemed inadequate, authorities have recourse to the whole spectrum of brutal corporal punishment, including out and out murder. At San Quentin, Fred Billingslea was teargassed to death in February 1970. W. L. Nolen, Alvin Miller, and Cleveland Edwards were assassinated by a prison guard in January 1970, at Soledad Prison. Unusual and inexplicable "suicides" have occurred with incredible regularity in jails and prisons throughout the country.

It should be self-evident that the frame-up becomes a powerful weapon within the spectrum of prison repression, particularly because of the availability of inform-ers, the broken prisoners who will do anything for a price. The Soledad Brothers and the Soledad Three are leading examples of frame-up victims. Both cases involve militant activists who have been charged with killing Soledad prison guards. In both cases, widespread support has been kindled within the California prison sys-tem. They have served as occasions to link the immediate needs of the black com-munity with a forceful fight to break the fascist stronghold in the prisons and therefore to abolish the prison system in its present form.

Racist oppression invades the lives of black people on an infinite variety of levels. Blacks are imprisoned in a world where our labor and toil hardly allow us to eke out a decent existence, if we are able to find jobs at all. When the economy begins to falter, we are forever the first victims, always the most deeply wounded. When the economy is on its feet, we continue to live in a depressed state. Unemployment is generally twice as high in the ghettos as it is in the country as a whole and even higher among black women and youth. The unemployment rate among black youth has presently skyrocketed to thirty percent. If one-third of America's white youths were without a means of livelihood, we would either be in the thick of revolution or else under the iron rule of fascism. Substandard schools, medical care hardly fit for animals, over-priced, dilapidated housing, a welfare system based on a policy of skimpy concessions, designed to degrade and divide (and even this may soon be canceled)—this is only the beginning of the list of props in the overall scenery of oppression which, for the mass of blacks, is the universe.

In black communities, wherever they are located, there exists an ever-present reminder that our universe must remain stable in its drabness, its poverty, its brutal-ity. From Birmingham to Harlem to Watts, black ghettos are occupied, patrolled and often attacked by massive deployments of police. The police, domestic caretak-ers of violence, are the oppressor's emissaries, charged with the task of containing us within the boundaries of our oppression.

The announced function of the police, "to protect and serve the people," becomes the grotesque caricature of protecting and preserving the interests of our oppressors and serving us nothing but injustice. They are there to intimidate blacks, to persuade us with their violence that we are powerless to alter the conditions of our lives. Arrests are frequently based on whims. Bullets from their guns murder human beings with little or no pretext, aside from the universal intimidation they are charged with carrying out. Protection for drug-pushers, and Mafia-style exploiters, support for the most reactionary ideological elements of the black community (especially those who cry out for more police), are among the many functions of forces of law and order. They encircle the community with a shield of violence, too often forcing the natural aggression of the black community inwards. [Frantz] Fanon's analysis of the role of colonial police is an appropriate description of the function of the police in America's ghettos.[12]

It goes without saying that the police would be unable to set into motion their racist machinery were they not sanctioned and supported by the judicial system. The courts not only consistently abstain from prosecuting criminal behavior on the part of the police, but they convict, on the basis of biased police testimony, countless black men and women. Court-appointed attorneys, acting in the twisted interests of overcrowded courts, convince eighty-five percent of the defendants to plead guilty. Even the manifestly innocent are advised to cop a plea so that the lengthy and expensive process of jury trials is avoided. This is the structure of the apparatus which summarily railroads black people into jails and prisons. (During my imprisonment in the New York Women's House of Detention, I encountered numerous cases involving innocent black women who had been advised to plead guilty. One sister had entered her white landlord's apartment for the purpose of paying rent. He attempted to rape her and in the course of the ensuing struggle, a lit candle toppled over, burning a tablecloth. The landlord ordered her arrested for arson. Following the advice of her court-appointed attorney, she entered a guilty plea, having been deceived by the attorney's insistence that the court would be more lenient. The sister was sentenced to three years.)

The vicious circle linking poverty, police courts, and prison is an integral element of ghetto existence. Unlike the mass of whites, the path which leads to jails and prisons is deeply rooted in the imposed patterns of black existence. For this very reason, an almost instinctive affinity binds the mass of black people to the political prisoners. The vast majority of blacks harbor a deep hatred of the police and are not deluded by official proclamations of justice through the courts.

For the black individual, contact with the law-enforcement-judicial-penal network, directly or through relatives and friends, is inevitable because he or she is black. For the activist become political prisoner, the contact has occurred because he has lodged a protest, in one form or another, against the conditions which nail blacks to this orbit of oppression.

Historically, black people as a group have exhibited a greater potential for resistance than any other part of the population. The iron-clad rule over our communities, the institutional practice of genocide, the ideology of racism have performed a strictly political as well as an economic function. The capitalists have not only extracted super profits from the underpaid labor of over 15 percent of the American population with the aid of a superstructure of terror. This terror and more subtle forms of racism have further served to thwart the flowering of a resistance—even a revolution that would spread to the working class as a whole.

In the interests of the capitalist class, the consent to racism and terror has been demagogically elicited from the white population, workers included, in order to more efficiently stave off resistance. Today, Nixon, [Attorney General John] Mitchell and J. Edgar Hoover are desperately attempting to persuade the population that dissidents, particularly blacks, Chicanos, Puerto Ricans, must be punished for being members of revolutionary organizations; for advocating the overthrow of the government; for agitating and educating in the streets and behind prison walls. The political function of racist domination is surfacing with accelerated intensity. Whites who have professed their solidarity with the black liberation movement and have moved in a distinctly revolutionary direction find themselves targets of the same repression. Even the anti-war movement, rapidly exhibiting an anti-imperialist consciousness, is falling victim to government repression.

Black people are rushing full speed ahead towards an understanding of the circumstances that give rise to exaggerated forms of political repression and thus an overabundance of political prisoners. This understanding is being forged out of the raw material of their own immediate experiences with racism. Hence, the black masses are growing conscious of their responsibility to defend those who are being persecuted for attempting to bring about the alleviation of the most injurious immediate problems facing black communities and ultimately to bring about total liberation through armed revolution, if it must come to this.

The black liberation movement is presently at a critical juncture. Fascist methods of repression threaten to physically decapitate and obliterate the movement. More subtle, yet no less dangerous ideological tendencies from within threaten to isolate the black movement and diminish its revolutionary impact. Both menaces must be counteracted in order to ensure our survival. Revolutionary blacks must spearhead and provide leadership for a broad anti-fascist movement.

Fascism is a process, its growth and development are cancerous in nature. While today, the threat of fascism may be primarily restricted to the use of the law-enforcement-judicial-penal apparatus to arrest the overt and latent revolutionary trends among nationally oppressed people, tomorrow it may attack the working class *en masse* and eventually even moderate democrats. Even in this period, however, the cancer has already commenced to spread. In addition to the prison army of thousands and thousands of nameless Third World victims of political revenge, there are increasing numbers of white political prisoners—draft resisters, anti-war activists such as the Harrisburg Eight,[13] men and women who have involved themselves on all levels of revolutionary activity.

Among the further symptoms of the fascist threat are official efforts to curtail the power of organized labor, such as the attack on the manifestly conservative construction workers and the trends towards reduced welfare aid. Moreover, court decisions and repressive legislation augmenting police powers—such as the Washington no-knock law, permitting police to enter private dwellings without warning, and Nixon's "Crime Bill" in general—can eventually be used against any citizen. Indeed congressmen are already protesting the use of police-state wire-tapping to survey their activities. The fascist content of the ruthless aggression in Indo-China should be self-evident.

One of the fundamental historical lessons to be learned from past failures to prevent the rise of fascism is the decisive and indispensable character of the fight against fascism in its incipient phases. Once allowed to conquer ground, its growth is facilitated in geometric proportion. Although the most unbridled expressions of the fascist menace are still tied to the racist domination of blacks, Chicanos, Puerto Ricans, Indians, it lurks under the surface wherever there is potential resistance to the power of monopoly capital, the parasitic interests which control this society. Potentially it can profoundly worsen the conditions of existence for the average American citizen. Consequently, the masses of people in this country have a real, direct, and material stake in the struggle to free political prisoners, the struggle to abolish the prison system in its present form, the struggle against all dimensions of racism.

No one should fail to take heed of Georgi Dimitrov's warning: "Whoever does not fight the growth of fascism at these preparatory stages is not in a position to prevent the victory of fascism, but, on the contrary, facilitates that victory" (Report to the VIIth Congress of the Communist International, 1935). The only effective guarantee against the victory of fascism is an indivisible mass movement which refuses to conduct business as usual as long as repression rages on. It is only natural that blacks and other Third World peoples must lead this movement, for we are the first and most deeply injured victims of fascism. But it must embrace all potential victims and most important, all working-class people, for the key to the triumph of fascism is its ideological victory over the entire working class. Given the eruption of a severe economic crisis, the door to such an ideological victory can be opened by the active approval or passive toleration of racism. It is essential that white workers become conscious that historically through their acquiescence in the capitalist-inspired oppression of blacks they have only rendered themselves more vulnerable to attack.

The pivotal struggle which must be waged in the ranks of the working class is consequently the open, unreserved battle against entrenched racism. The white worker must become conscious of the threads which bind him to a James Johnson, a black auto worker, member of UAW [United Auto Workers], and a political prisoner presently facing charges for the killings of two foremen and a job setter.[14] The merciless proliferation of the power of monopoly capital may ultimately push him inexorably down the very same path of desperation. No potential victim [of the fascist terror] should be without the knowledge that the greatest menace to racism and fascism is unity!

—Marin County Jail

NOTES

Originally published in Angela Y. Davis and Bettina Aptheker, eds., *If They Come in the Morning: Voices of Resistance* (New York: The Third Press, 1971), 19–36.

1. *Editor's note:* The Fugitive Slave Act of 1850, signed into law by President Millard Fillmore, greatly facilitated the recapture of escaped slaves and the capture of free African Americans who could be claimed as "runaways" by slave owners. The act served largely as a concession to southern slaveholding states in return for admission to the Union of territories won during the Mexican-American War as nonslave states. See Howard Zinn, *A People's History of the United States 1492–Present* (New York: HarperPerennial, 1995), 176.

2. William Z. Foster, *The Negro People in American History* (New York: International Publishers, 1954), 169–70 (quoting Herbert Aptheker).

3. *Editor's note:* Nicola Sacco and Bartolomeo Vanzetti were convicted, on July 14, 1921, of first-degree murder for their alleged involvement in the holdup of a shoe factory in South Braintree, Massachusetts, on April 15 of the previous year. As Italian anarchists and activists, their case drew international attention and support for the defendants. Despite numerous protests and appeals, Sacco and Vanzetti were sentenced to death in August of 1927, a sentence that was most likely due to their political involvement and ideals. *A People's History*, 366–67; Felix Frankfurter, "The Case of Sacco and Vanzetti," *The Atlantic Monthly*, March 1927.

4. Louis Adamic, *Dynamite: The Story of Class Violence in America* (Gloucester, Mass.: Peter Smith, 1963), 312.

5. *Editor's note:* Robert Williams, former National Association for the Advancement of Colored People (NAACP) official, cofounder of the Revolutionary Action Movement (RAM), former head of the Republic of New Afrika (RNA), and author of *Negroes with Guns*, was charged with the kidnapping of Mr. and Mrs. Stegall, a white couple, in Monroe, N.C., on August 21, 1971. Williams fled to Cuba and China to avoid charges, successfully fighting extradition until the charges were dropped in 1975. Hollie West, "Notes of a Traveler: From China to Cuba and Home Again," *Washington Post*, 28 January 1978, D1; "Kidnapping Charges against Black Activist," *New York Times*, 17 January 1976, 26. For a biography of Williams, see Timothy B. Tyson, *Radio Free Dixie: Robert F. Williams and the Roots of Black Power* (Chapel Hill: University of North Carolina Press, 1999).

6. Herbert Aptheker, *Nat Turner's Slave Rebellion* (New York: Grove Press, 1968), 45. According to Aptheker these are not Nat Turner's exact words.

7. *Editor's note:* See trial statement: "To Judge Murtagh: From the Panther 21," in *The Black Panthers Speak*, ed. Philip S. Foner (New York: Lippincott, 1970), 196.

8. W. E. B. Du Bois, *Autobiography of W. E. B. Du Bois* (New York: International Publishers, 1968), 390.

9. Karl Marx, "The Class Struggle in France," in *Handbook of Marxism* (New York: International Publishers, 1935), 109.

10. *Editor's note:* According to the Sentencing Project's midyear 2001 statistics, one in every eight African American males in the twenty-five to thirty-four age range is incarcerated in prison or jail on any given day. See *New Inmate Population Figures Show Continued Growth, Prospects for Change in Policy Unclear*, www.sentencingproject.org/news/inmatepop-apr02.pdf.

11. *Editor's note:* The Folsom Prisoners' Manifesto of Demands and Anti-Oppression Platform can be found in Angela Davis and Bettina Aptheker, eds., *If They Come in the Morning: Voices of Resistance* (New York: Third Press, 1971), 57.

12. *Editor's note:* See Frantz Fanon, *The Wretched of the Earth* (New York: Grove Press, 1968).

13. *Editor's note:* The Harrisburg Eight, including Philip Berrigan, were charged in 1971 with plotting to bomb utilities beneath federal buildings; kidnap Henry Kissinger, Richard Nixon's national security advisor; and destroy the East Coast section of the Selective Service System. It is widely believed that the "conspirators" were targeted by J. Edgar Hoover for their antiwar activities. The defendants were acquitted in 1972. See Philip Berrigan and Fred A. Wilcox, *Fighting the Lamb's War: Skirmishes with the American Empire: The Autobiography of Philip Berrigan* (Monroe, Maine: Common Courage Press, 1996), 125.

14. See Angela Davis and Bettina Aptheker, eds., *If They Come in the Morning: Voices of Resistance* (New York: Third Press, 1971); see chapter five on political prisoners for the details of James Johnson's case.

Chapter Four

Huey P. Newton

Named for populist Louisiana governor Huey P. Long, Huey Percy Newton was born the youngest of seven children in Monroe, Louisiana, in 1942. Three years later, his family moved to Oakland, California. His was a difficult childhood, one filled with conflict. Expelled from a number of public high schools, Newton later claimed that he did not know how to read until the age of sixteen. As a high school sophomore, he brought a hammer to school for self-defense and in a confrontation assaulted another student. This led to his first arrest. Graduating from Berkeley High School, Newton attended Merritt College, where in 1962 he met Bobby Seale, an older student, at an Afro-American Association meeting.

In 1966, Newton and Seale wrote a ten-point political platform, "What We Believe" and "What We Want," that would become the foundation for the Black Panther Party for Self-Defense, later renamed the Black Panther Party (BPP). The BPP grew after its public rallies against police brutality; armed Panther patrols of police in black neighborhoods; highly visible protection offered Betty Shabazz, the widow of Malcolm X, when she visited the Bay Area; and a May 1967 rally in which Bobby Seale and other Panthers walked into a session of the California legislature while carrying guns to protest the Mumford Bill, gun-control legislation. With such activities, the Black Panthers gained national and international attention and notoriety.[1]

The BPP was still a relatively small organization on October 28, 1967, when Huey P. Newton was pulled over by Oakland police and subsequently involved in a shootout. Newton and police officer Herbert Heanes were seriously wounded, and Officer John Frey was killed. Charged with murder, kidnapping, assault, and attempted murder, Newton was found guilty of manslaughter on September 28, 1968, by an Alameda County jury. His imprisonment led to the "Free Huey" campaigns, which mobilized hundreds of thousands of supporters worldwide. Bobby Seale, Eldridge and Kathleen Cleaver, and other Panthers focused on raising money for his legal defense through speeches and rallies, as Newton evolved into a national icon of antiracist and antistate resistance, and a black "folk hero,"[2] one with a transracial appeal. The "Free Huey" mobilization sparked a dramatic growth in party membership. By the time his conviction was overturned on August 5, 1970, the BPP had chapters in most urban areas in the United States, as well as international support committees.

The Federal Bureau of Investigation (FBI) COINTELPRO, along with actions by local police departments, fueled internal tensions in the organization. Subsequently, in early 1971, Newton expelled several members (including Eldridge Cleaver, who was in Algeria in flight from a U.S. warrant, and East Coast Panther leaders). This would be the first of many expulsions and violent internal conflicts that would cripple the party. Newton became increasingly isolated in his changing philosophy, focusing on electoral politics and "survival programs" and his extravagant lifestyle and addictions. The "movement" that had grown around his release from prison had continued to do so without him; and in order to control it, he would help to eviscerate the Panther party.

After his release from prison, as he struggled to convince the masses of his theory of "Revolutionary Intercommunalism"—the belief that communities, not nations, constitute a borderless world shaped by international capital—and attempted to cope with an organization moving out of his control, Newton descended again into substance abuse. A series of violent incidents by Newton culminated in the beating of his tailor and the street-corner shooting of Kathleen Smith during the summer of 1974.³ Newton fled to Cuba after his indictment on murder charges, and three years after his return to the United States in 1977, the Black Panther Party was formally disbanded.

Despite struggles with substance addiction, Newton received his doctorate from the University of California-Santa Cruz in 1980. However, on August 22, 1989, he was shot and killed by Tyrone Robinson, an alleged member of the Black Guerilla Family (an organization originally cofounded by George Jackson), in a drug deal gone awry.

REFERENCES

Black Panthers. *Up against the Wall*. London: Ellipsis, 2000. Compact disc.

Booker, Chris. "Lumpenization: A Critical Error of the Black Panther Party." In *The Black Panther Party [Reconsidered]*, edited by Charles E. Jones. Baltimore: Black Classic Press, 1998.

Newton, Huey P. *Revolutionary Suicide*. New York: Harcourt and Brace, 1973.

———. *To Die for the People*. New York: Random House, 1972.

Newton, Michael. *Bitter Grain: Huey P. Newton and the Black Panther Party*. Los Angeles: Holloway House Publishing Company, 1980.

Umoja, Akinyele Omowale. "Set Our Warriors Free: The Legacy of the Black Panther Party and Political Prisoners." In *The Black Panther Party [Reconsidered]*, edited by Charles E. Jones. Baltimore: Black Classic Press, 1998.

NOTES

Research and draft for this biography were provided by Will Tucker.

1. Chris Booker, "Lumpenization: A Critical Error of the Black Panther Party," in *The Black Panther Party [Reconsidered]*, ed. Charles E. Jones (Baltimore: Black Classic Press, 1998), 343.

2. See: Akinyele Omowale Umoja, "Set Our Warriors Free: The Legacy of the Black Panther Party and Political Prisoners," in *The Black Panther Party [Reconsidered]*, 419.

3. Michael Newton, *Bitter Grain: Huey P. Newton and the Black Panther Party* (Los Angeles: Holloway House Publishing Company, 1980), 211.

Prison, Where Is Thy Victory?

July 12, 1969

When a person studies mathematics he learns that there are many mathematical laws which determine the approach he must take to solving the problems presented to him. In the study of geometry one of the first laws a person learns is that "the whole is not greater than the sum of its parts." This means simply that one cannot have a geometrical figure such as a circle or a square which contains more than it does when broken down into smaller parts. Therefore, if all the smaller parts add up to a certain amount the entire figure cannot add up to a larger amount. The prison cannot have a victory over the prisoner because those in charge take the same kind of approach and assume if they have the whole body in a cell that they have contained all that makes up the person. But a prisoner is not a geometrical figure, and an approach which is successful in mathematics is wholly unsuccessful when dealing with human beings.

In the case of the human we are not dealing only with the single individual, we are also dealing with the ideas and beliefs which have motivated him and which sustain him, even when his body is confined. In the case of humanity the whole is much greater than its parts because the whole includes the body, which is measurable and confinable, and the ideas, which cannot be measured or confined.

The ideas which can and will sustain our movement for total freedom and dignity of the people cannot be imprisoned, for they are to be found in the people, all the people, wherever they are. As long as the people live by the ideas of freedom and dignity, there will be no prison which can hold our movement down. Ideas move from one person to another by the association of brothers and sisters who recognize that a most evil system of capitalism has set us against each other, although our real enemy is the exploiter who profits from our poverty. When we realize such an idea, then we come to love and appreciate our brothers and sisters who we may have seen as enemies, and those exploiters who we may have seen as friends are revealed for what they truly are to all oppressed people. The people are the idea. The respect and dignity of the people, as they move toward their freedom, are the sustaining force which reaches into and out of the prison. The walls, the bars, the guns and the guards can never encircle or hold down the idea of the people. And the people must always carry forward the idea which is their dignity and beauty.

The prison operates with the concept that since it has a person's body it has his entire being, because the whole cannot be greater than the sum of the parts. They put the body in a cell and seem to get some sense of relief and security from that fact. The idea of prison victory, then is that when the person in jail begins to act, think, and believe the way they want him to, they have won the battle and the person is then "rehabilitated." But this cannot be the case because those who operate the prisons have failed to examine their own beliefs thoroughly, and they fail to

81

understand the types of people they attempt to control. Therefore, even when the prison thinks it has won, there is no victory.

There are two types of prisoners. The largest number are those who accept the legitimacy of the assumptions upon which the society is based. They wish to acquire the same goals as everybody else: money, power, and conspicuous consumption. In order to do so, however, they adopt techniques and methods which the society has defined as illegitimate. When this is discovered such people are put in jail. They may be called "illegitimate capitalists" since their aim is to acquire everything capitalist society defines as legitimate. The second type of prisoner is the one who rejects the legitimacy of the assumptions upon which the society is based. He argues that the people at the bottom of the society are exploited for the profit and advantage of those at the top. Thus, the oppressed exist and will always be used to maintain the privileged status of the exploiters. There is no sacredness, there is no dignity in either exploiting or being exploited. Although this system may make the society function at a high level of technological efficiency, it is an illegitimate system, since it rests upon the suffering of humans who are as worthy and as dignified of those who do not suffer. Thus, the second type of prisoner says that the society is corrupt and illegitimate and must be overthrown. This second type of prisoner is the "political prisoner." They do not accept the legitimacy of the society and cannot participate in its corruption and exploitation, whether they are in the prison or on the block.

The prison cannot gain a victory over either type of prisoner no matter how hard it tries. The "illegitimate capitalist" recognizes that if he plays the game the prison wants him to play he will have his time reduced and be released to continue his activities. Therefore, he is willing to go through the prison programs and say the things the prison authorities want to hear. The prison assumes he is "rehabilitated" and ready for the society. The prisoner has really played the prison's game so that he can be released to resume pursuit of his capitalist goals. There is no victory, for the prisoner from the "git-go" accepted the idea of the society. He pretends to accept the idea of the prison as a part of the game he has always played.

The prison cannot gain a victory over the political prisoner because he has nothing to be rehabilitated from or to. He refuses to accept the legitimacy of the system and refuses to participate. To participate is to admit that the society is legitimate because of its exploitation of the oppressed. This is the idea which the political prisoner does not accept for which he has been imprisoned, and this is the reason why he cannot cooperate with the system. The political prisoner will, in fact, serve his time just as will the "illegitimate capitalist." Yet the idea which motivated and sustained the political prisoner rests in the people. All the prison has is the body.

The dignity and beauty of man rests in the human spirit which makes him more than simply a physical being. This spirit must never be suppressed for exploitation by others. As long as the people recognize the beauty of their human spirits and move against suppression and exploitation, they will be carrying out one of the most beautiful ideas of all time. Because the human whole is much greater than the sum of its parts. The ideas will always be among the people. The prison cannot be victorious because walls, bars and guards cannot conquer or hold down an idea.

parallels with sartre's "radical freedom" philosophy

NOTE

Originally published in Angela Y. Davis and Bettina Aptheker, eds., *If They Come in the Morning* (New York: Third Press, 1971), 50–56.

Chapter Five

George Jackson

George Lester Jackson was born on September 23, 1941, on the West Side of Chicago, the second of Georgia and Lester Jackson's five children. Georgia Jackson, George's namesake, was very protective, and forbade George and his sister from going outside alone except for school and errands. Her son nevertheless demonstrated a mind of his own. In his prison letters, Jackson at times harshly criticizes his parents, castigating his mother for teaching him "obedience" and his father for his "neo-slave" mentality.

The family moved among Chicago's urban neighborhoods, ultimately settling in the Troop Street Projects, where for George Jackson truancy and conflicts with the police became routine. In 1956, seeking to protect his son, Lester Jackson transferred his post office job to Los Angeles. Yet, soon after settling in Los Angeles, George began to have serious confrontations with the law. After an attempted burglary and possession of a stolen motorcycle (which he claimed to have purchased), he was sent to the Paso Robles School for Boys, an institution of the California Youth Authority. In Paso Robles, he avoided disciplinary attention for the duration of his seven-month sentence by reading the work of Rafael Sabatini and Jack London.[1]

In 1958, a few months after his parole, Jackson and several friends were arrested for robberies to which he pled guilty. He escaped from the Bakersfield jail and was recaptured to serve the rest of his sentence. After his release, on September 18, 1960, Jackson allegedly drove the getaway car after his friend robbed a gas station of seventy-one dollars. He agreed to confess in return for a light sentence; the judge gave him one-to-life, a sentence designed to allow judicial flexibility, but which ultimately put sentencing in the hands of prison administrators. Jackson's one year became life imprisonment. Initially sent to Soledad Prison, he was transferred at least four times during his incarceration. During his first years, he and his close friend, James Carr, gained power and respect within prison as the leaders of a gang called the "Wolf Pack." Each year, Jackson was denied parole because of infractions.

George Jackson entered prison during a time when prisoners like Eldridge

Cleaver, who would author *Soul on Ice* and become a national leader of the Black Panther Party, were beginning to undertake serious study of their conditions of incarceration. W. L. Nolen, a major figure in this movement, was the first to introduce Jackson to radical philosophy. As Jackson's disciplinary record grew, he was forced to spend up to twenty-three hours a day in solitary confinement. There he read Karl Marx, V. I. Lenin, Leon Trotsky, Friedrich Engels, Mao Tse-tung (Zedong), and other political theorists. In 1968, Jackson, Nolen, David Johnson, Carr, and other revolutionary convicts began leading "ethnic awareness classes"—study groups on radical philosophy. These meetings led to the formation of the Black Guerilla Family, a revolutionary organization (described by authorities as a "gang") that proclaimed black prisoners' rights to self-defense.

In January of 1969, Jackson and Nolen were transferred to Soledad Prison, a notoriously racist penal site among racist prisons. In the O Wing, which housed Soledad's most dangerous captives, racial tension led to the closing of the exercise yard. Nolen and five other black inmates were preparing civil suits against the O Wing guards for their complicity in creating a dangerously racially divisive atmosphere.

On January 13, 1970, guards reopened the O Wing exercise yard, and released a racially mixed group of prisoners, fully aware of the potential for violence.[2] The fight that began immediately was quickly ended by guard Opie Miller, a sharpshooter who fired four shots, killing African American inmates Nolen (Jackson's mentor), Cleveland Edwards, and Alvin Miller, and wounding a white prisoner.[3] Three days later, a Monterey County grand jury ruled the deaths "justifiable homicide." Following the publicizing of the ruling, guard John V. Mills was thrown to his death from the third tier of Y Wing—George Jackson's cellblock.

One month later, with no physical evidence, Jackson, Fleeta Drumgo, and John Cluchette were indicted for killing Mills. Huey P. Newton requested that his attorney, Fay Stender, meet with Jackson. After doing so, Stender subsequently formed the Soledad Brothers Defense Committee, which eventually was headed by Angela Davis.[4]

Stender also arranged for the publication of the influential *Soledad Brother: The Prison Letters of George Jackson*. Two months before its publication, Jackson's seventeen-year-old brother, Jonathan, entered the Marin County Courthouse—with weapons registered in the name of Angela Davis—during the trial of prisoner James McClain, who was charged with the attempted stabbing of a Soledad guard. Jonathan Jackson armed McClain and, with prisoner witnesses Ruchell Magee and William Christmas, herded the assistant district attorney, Judge Harold Haley, and three jurors into a van parked outside. Law enforcement officers fired upon the parked van without regard for the hostages, as was prison policy, killing Christmas, McClain, and Jackson; wounding Magee; and killing Haley and wounding other hostages.

The following version of events is pieced together from a variety of (sometimes contradictory) sources. On August 21, 1971, Stephen Bingham (who had replaced

Stender as Jackson's attorney) visited George Jackson at San Quentin. Inside Bingham's tape recorder were hidden a 9mm pistol and an Afro wig. During their meeting in a private attorney room, Bingham allegedly gave Jackson the gun, which he placed on his head and covered with the wig. A guard later noticed something protruding from Jackson's hair and asked to see it.[5] Discovered, Jackson loaded and fired the gun, subduing the guard(s) and freeing most of the prisoners in the Adjustment Center. Three guards and two white inmate trusties were executed in the takeover. When Jackson rushed out of the Adjustment Center into the yard, he was shot in the back. Stephen Bingham, who eventually emerged from underground to stand trial, was acquitted in 1986.

REFERENCES

Durden-Smith, Jo. *Who Killed George Jackson?* New York: Knopf, 1976.
Jackson, George. *Blood in My Eye*. Baltimore: Black Classic Press, 1990.
———. "Letters to Jonathan Jackson." In *If They Come in the Morning: Voices of Resistance*, edited by Angela Y. Davis and Bettina Aptheker, 148–51. San Francisco: National United Committee to Free Angela Davis, 1971.
———. *Soledad Brother: The Prison Letters of George Jackson*. Chicago: Lawrence Hill Books, 1994.
———. "A Talk with George Jackson." Interview with Jessica Mitford. *New York Times*, 13 June 1971, sec. 7, 30.
———. "Toward the United Front." In *If They Come in the Morning: Voices of Resistance*, edited by Angela Y. Davis and Bettina Aptheker, 141–47. San Francisco: National United Committee to Free Angela Davis, 1971.
Mann, Eric. *Comrade George: An Investigation into the Life, Political Thought, and Assassination of George Jackson*. New York: Harper & Row, 1974.

NOTES

Research and draft for this biography were provided by Daniel Schleifer.

1. *Soledad Brother: The Prison Letters of George Jackson* (Chicago: Lawrence Hill Books, 1994), 14. Also see: Rafael Sabatini, *The Writings of Rafael Sabatini* (Boston: Houghton Mifflin, 1924); Jack London, "'Pinched': A Prison Experience" and "The Pen: Long Days in a County Penitentiary" in *Prison Writing in 20th-Century America*, edited by H. Bruce Franklin (New York: Penguin, 1998); Jack London, *The Call of the Wild* (New York: The Daily Worker, 1915); Philip S. Foner, ed., *Jack London, American Rebel* (New York: Citadel Press, 1947).

2. Jo Durden-Smith, *Who Killed George Jackson?* (New York: Knopf, 1976), 177.

3. *Who Killed George Jackson?* 177.

4. Eight years after George Jackson's death, Fay Stender was shot in 1979, allegedly by a member of the Black Guerilla Family for not supporting Jackson's militarist politics. She suffered severe injuries that led to her paralysis. Stender committed suicide in May 1980. See

Paul Liberatore, *The Road to Hell: The True Story of George Jackson, Stephen Bingham, and the San Quentin Massacre* (New York: Atlantic Monthly Press, 1996), 199.

5. "Pistol and Wig Experiment," *San Francisco Chronicle*, 28 August 1971. Quoted in Eric Mann, *Comrade George: An Investigation into the Life, Political Thought and Assassination of George Jackson* (New York: Harper & Row, 1974).

Towards the United Front

1971

There exists already a new unitarian and progressive current in the movement centering around political prisoners. The question at this point, I feel, is how to develop unitarian conduct further—against the natural resistance of establishment machinations—through the creation of new initiatives and a dialectic so clear in its argumentation, presentation and implementation that it will of its own weight force the isolation of reactionary elements. Both individual-attitudinized and organized reaction must be isolated.

Unitary conduct implies a "search" for that something in common, a conscious reaching for the relevant, the entente, and in our case especially the reconcilable. Throughout the centralizing-authoritarian process of American history, the ruling classes have found it expedient, actually necessary to insinuate upon the people instrumentalities designed to discourage and punish any genuine opposition to hierarchy. There have always been individuals and groups who rejected the ideal of society above society. The men who placed themselves above society through guile, fortuitous outcome of circumstance and sheer brutality have developed two principal institutions to deal with any and all serious disobedience—the prison and institutionalized racism. There are more prisons of all categories in the United States than in all other countries of the world combined. There are at all times two-thirds of a million people or more confined to these prisons. Hundreds are destined to be executed outright legally and thousands quasi-legally. Other thousands will never again have any freedom of movement barring a revolutionary change in all the institutions that combine to make up the order of things. Two thirds of a million people may not seem like a great number compared against the total population of nearly two hundred and five million.[1] However compared to the one million who are responsible for all the affairs of men within the extended state, it constitutes a striking contrast not at all coincidental, and perhaps deserving of careful analysis. What I want to explore now are a few of the subtle elements that I have observed to be standing in the path of a much needed united front (nonsectarian) to effectively reverse the legitimatized rip-off.

I will emphasize again that prisons were not institutionalized on so massive a scale by the people. Though all crime can be considered a manifestation of antithesis, some crime does work out to the well understood detriment of the people. Most crime, however, is clearly the simple effect of a grossly disproportionate distribution of wealth and privilege, a reflection of the state of present property relations. There are no wealthy men on death row, and so very few in the general prison population that we can discount them altogether—imprisonment is an aspect of class struggle from the outset. A closed society intended to isolate those who quite healthfully disregard the structures of a hypocritical establishment with their individual actions, and those who would organize a mass basis for such action. U.S. history is replete with examples of both types, the latter extending from the early Working Men's Benevolent Association through the events surrounding the Ancient Order of Hibernians, The Working Men's Party who organized against the excesses of the 1877 depression, all the way to the present era when the Communist Party was banned (during this country's fascist takeover), and the Black Panther Party in the practical sense assaulted and banned.[2]

The hypocrisy of Amerikan fascism will not allow it to openly declare that it does hold political offenders—thus the hundreds of versions of conspiracy laws and the highly sophisticated frame-up. This is the first point of attack in the educational sense. Why do prisons exist in such numbers, what is the real underlying economic motive of crime, and the diacritical breakdown of types of offenders or victims? If offenders is the better term it must be clearly presented that the language of the law is definitely weighted and deceptive, it should be clear that when one "offends" the totalitarian state it is patently not an offense against the people of that state, offending the state translates into an assault upon the privilege of the privileged few.

Could anything be more ridiculous than the officious titles to indictments reading: "The People of the State . . . vs. Bobby Seale and Ericka Huggins" or "The People of the State . . . vs. Angela Davis and Ruchell Magee." What people are referred to?—clearly the hierarchy, the armed minority.

Then in the John Doe cases where an actual robbery or theft was committed, we must elucidate the real causes of economic crimes; or any crime, of passion against repression, the thrill crime, we must be all inclusive. All crime is motivated by simple economic oppression, or the psycho-social effects of an economic order that was decadent 100 years ago. Objective socio-economic conditions equals social productive or counter-productive activity, in all cases determined by the economic system, the method of economic organization, the maintenance of that organization against the forces of progress that would change it. Even the psychology of the sick individual, perpetrator of a "thrill crime" must ultimately be traced to a sick society.

Prisoners must be reached and made to understand that they are victims of social injustice. This is my task working from within (while I'm here—my persuasion is that the war goes on no matter where one may find himself on bourgeois dominated soil). The sheer numbers of the prisoner class and their terms of existence make them a mighty reservoir of revolutionary potential. Working alone and from within a steel enclosed society there is very little that people like myself can do to free the retrained potential revolutionary. That is part of the task of the "Prison Movement." "The People of the State . . . vs. John Doe" is as tenuous as the clearly political frame-ups. It's like stating "The People vs. The People." Man against himself.

The "Prison Movement" serves another important political end. It makes the ruling class conscious of our determination to never surrender our economic right to hold the implements of production in our own hands short of physical death. Detention will not check our movement. The August 7th[3] movement and all actual acts of, and attempts to, put the keeper to death serve this notice best. They also hint at the ultimate goal of revolutionary consciousness at every level of struggle, the major level at the point of production, and all the substructural levels. The goal is always the same: the creation of an infrastructure capable of fielding a people's army.

There should be no one among us who still doesn't understand that revolution is aggressive, and that the making of demands on the manipulators of the system, that they cannot or will not meet must eventually move us all into a violent encounter with that system one day. These are the terminal years of capitalism and as we move into significant areas of antiestablishment activities, history clearly forewarns us that when the prestige of power fails a violent episode precedes its transformation.

We can attempt to limit the scope and range of violence in revolution by mobilizing as many partisans as possible at every level of socio-economic life, but considering the hold that the ruling class of this country has on the apolitical in general and its history of violence, nothing could be more predictable than civil disorders, perhaps even civil war. I don't dread either, for there are no good aspects of monopoly capital, no good or beneficial guarantees, so no reservations need be recognized in its destruction. No interpretation of what revolution will be is required really, not in the U.S., not in the face of monopoly capital. As it stands above us monopoly capital is an obstruction that leaves us in the shade and has made us its servant. It must be completely destroyed, not rejected, not simply transformed, but destroyed utterly, totally, ruthlessly, relentlessly—as immediately as possible terminated!

With this as a common major goal it would seem that unitarian conduct of all parties concerned in active antiestablishment struggle on various levels should find little difficulty in developing initiatives and new methods consistent with the goals of mass society.

Regretfully this has not been the case, although as I stated there can be detected in the prison movement the beginnings of a unitary current cutting across the ideological, racial and cultural barricades that have in all times past blocked the natural coalition of left wing forces. This brings us to another vital aspect of the activity surrounding political prisoners. Perhaps on our substructural level with steadily attentive efforts at building the united front we can provide an example for the partisans engaged at other levels of struggle. The issues involved and the dialectic which flows from the clear objective existence of overt oppression could be the basis of, or a spring board for our genuine entrance into the tide of increasing worldwide socialist consciousness. In clearing away the obstacles that preclude a united left for the defense of political prisoners and prisoners in general there must first be a renunciation of the idea that all participants must be of one mind and should work at the problem from a single party line or methodical singularity. The reverse of this is actually desirable. "From all according to ability." Each partisan, outside the vanguard elements, should proceed in a popularization strategy in the area of their natural environment, the places where they pursue their normal lives when not attending the rallies and demonstrations. The vanguard elements (organized party workers of all ideological persuasion) go among the people concentrated at the rallying point with elevation strategy, promoting commitment and providing concrete, clearly defined activity for them to popularize. The vanguard elements are first searching out people who can and will contribute to the building of the commune, the infrastructure—(with pen and clipboard in hand)—for those who cannot yet take that step a "packet" of pamphlets is provided for use in their individual pursuits.

Unity of the left factions in this substructural aspect of the movement, which centers around political prisoners and prisons in general, is significant then in several ways. With our example we can begin to break the old behavioral patterns that have repeatedly won bourgeois capitalism, its imperialism and fascism, life after death over the last several decades. We free a massive potential reservoir of partisans for cadre work, and finally we begin to address one of the most complex psychosocial by-products that economic man with his private enterprise has manufactured—Racism.

I've saved this most critical barrier to our needs of unity for last. Racism is a question of ingrained traditional attitudes conditioned through institutions—for some, it is as natural a reflex as breathing. The psychosocial effects of the dichotomous habitudes set up by a particularly sensitized racism compounded with the bitterest of class repression has served in the past to render us all practically inactive, and where we attempt progressive action, particularly impotent.

If a united left is possible in this country the major obstacle must be considered racism, white racism to be blunt. The categories can be best simplified by reducing them to three, the overt self-satisfied racist who doesn't deign to hide his antipathy, the self-interdicting racist who harbors and nurtures racism in spite of their best efforts, and the unconscious racist, product of preconceived notions that must be blamed on history.

I deny the existence of Black racism outright, by fiat I deny it. Too much Black blood has flowed between the chasm that separates the races, it's fundamentally unfair to expect the Black man to differentiate at a glance the self-accepting racist, the self-interdicting racist and the unconscious racist. The apologist's term "Black racism" is either a healthy defense reflex on the part of the sincere Black partisan attempting to deal with the realistic problems of survival and elevation, or the racism of the government stooge organs.

As Black partisans we must recognize and allow for the existence of all three types of racists, as we accept ourselves in relation thereto, but all must still be viewed as the effect of the system. It is a system that must be crushed first, for it continues to manufacture new and deeper contradictions of both class and race. Once it is gone we may be able to address in depth the effects of its presence but to a great extent, we must combat racism while we are in the process of destroying it. The psycho-social effects of hundreds of years of mutually exclusive attitudinal positions on race and class and symbols, hierarchy in general must be isolated.

The self-interdicting racist, no matter what his acquired conviction or ideology, will seldom be able to contribute with his actions in any really concrete way. Their role in revolution, barring a change of basic character, will be minimal throughout. Whether the basic character of a man can be changed at all is still a question. But . . . we have in the immediacy of the "issues in question" the perfect opportunity to test the validity of materialist philosophy again.

The need for unitarian conduct goes much deeper than the liberation of Angela [Davis], Bobby [Seale], Ericka [Huggins], [Ruchell] Magee, Los Siete [de la Raza], [Reies Lopez] Tijerina, white draft resisters and now the indomitable and faithful James Carr.[4] We have fundamental strategy to be proved—tested and proved. The activity surrounding the protection and liberation of people who fight for us is an important aspect of the struggle, but it is important only if it provides new initiatives that redirect and advance the revolution under new progressive methods. There must be a collective redirection of the old guard, the factory and union agitator, with pamphlet and silenced pistol, the campus activist who can counter the ill-effects of fascism at its training site, the *lumpen-proletarian* intellectuals with revolutionary scientific socialist attitudes to deal with the masses of street people living outside the system already. Black, Brown, White are victims, fight! At the end of this massive collective struggle we will uncover our new man; he is a creation of the process, the future, he will be better equipped to wage the real struggle, the permanent struggle after the revolution—the one for new relationships between man.

NOTES

Originally published in *If They Come in the Morning: Voices of Resistance*, ed. Angela Y. Davis and Bettina Aptheker (New York: The Third Press, 1971), 141–47.

1. *Editor's note:* Currently, there are some 2.5 million people held in detention or prisons in the United States.

2. *Editor's note:* The Working Men's Benevolent Association and Ancient Order of Hibernians were Pennsylvania labor organizations related to the "Molly Maguires." According to Eileen O'Gara, the

> "Molly Maguires" were miners in the anthracite coal region of Pennsylvania who organized into a union during the 1860s and 1870s. These miners were chiefly, although not exclusively, Irish and the union was called the Working Men's Benevolent Association. In general, the members of this union were also members of the Ancient Order of Hibernians, a semi-secret fraternal society, which had its origin in Ireland as a completely secret and anonymous association (Eileen O'Gara, "The Molly Maguires," *Student Web Projects*, 1998 www.providence.edu/polisci/projects/molly_maguires/ [24 April 2002]).

See Kevin Kenny, *Making Sense of the Molly Maguires* (New York: Oxford, 1998); S. B. Liljegren, *The Irish Element in the Valley of Fear* (Copenhagen: Uppsala, 1964). When he claims that the "Communist Party was banned," Jackson likely refers to the 1954 Communist Control Act, which, in effect, made membership in the Communist Party illegal in the United

States (Howard Zinn, *A People's History of the United States* [New York: Harper & Row, 1980], 422–23).

3. *Editor's note:* By "August 7th Movement," Jackson refers to his younger brother Jonathan's "revolutionary attempt to free several Black prisoners from the Marin County courthouse in August 1970." The attempt "ended in carnage. . . . Jackson, the judge he kidnapped, and all but one of the escaping prisoners died in the shooting outside the courthouse." Kathleen Neal Cleaver, "Back to Africa: The Evolution of the International Section of the Black Panther Party (1969–1972)," in *The Black Panther Party [Reconsidered]*, ed. Charles E. Jones (Baltimore: Black Classic Press, 1998), 235; Joy James, ed., *The Angela Y. Davis Reader* (Malden, Mass.: Blackwell, 1998), 10–11.

4. *Editor's note:* For further reading, see: Bettina Aptheker, *The Morning Breaks: The Trial of Angela Davis* (New York: International Publishers, 1975); *The Angela Y. Davis Reader*; Donald Freed, *Agony in New Haven: The Trial of Bobby Seale, Ericka Huggins, and the Black Panther Party* (New York: Simon and Schuster, 1973); Marjorie Heins, *Strictly Ghetto Property* (Berkeley, Calif.: Ramparts, 1972); David DeLeon, ed., *Leaders from the 1960s: A Biographical Sourcebook of American Activism* (Westport, Conn.: Greenwood, 1994), 156; James Carr, *BAD—The Autobiography of James Carr* (Dublin: Pelagian Press; reissued, AK Press, 2002).

Chapter Six

Dhoruba Bin Wahad

Dhoruba Bin Wahad (Richard Moore) was born in the South Bronx in 1944. Like most members of the Black Panther Party (BPP), he was young, only twenty-three, when he left a Bronx gang, the Disciple Sportsmen, and joined the newly formed New York Panther chapter in 1968. The New York chapter quickly became one of the four major chapters of the Oakland-based group, managing other chapters and branches along the Eastern Seaboard. Bin Wahad, a skilled orator and one of the party's early leaders, worked on tenants' rights, police brutality, and drug rehabilitation programs in Harlem, the South Bronx, and Brooklyn. He helped to develop the Lincoln Detox center, a hospital-based rehabilitation center that used acupuncture rather than methadone maintenance for drug addiction. It was possibly one of the earliest examples of the Rainbow Coalition, with the Young Lords Party and the Young Patriots Party joining with the BPP in a community effort to curtail drug abuse.

The New York Police Department (NYPD), in complicity with COINTELPRO operatives, indicted Bin Wahad and twenty other leaders of the New York BPP, the "New York 21," on April 2, 1969, for more than one hundred conspiracy charges that included plots to assassinate New York City police officers and dynamite city department stores, a botanical garden, a police station, and a railroad right-of-way. This case was a timely blow to one of the key arms of the national Black Panther organizing body. The charges were without foundation and would be dismissed later. However, in the aftermath of the arrests and warrants, the New York 21 were incarcerated, and the New York Panther leadership decimated by the spurious charges. Bin Wahad and Michael Cetewayo Tabor were released on bail and later fled the country during the trial because of a Federal Bureau of Investigation (FBI)-initiated plot to incite the national BPP leadership, under Huey Newton, to assassinate them. After two years in prison and an eight-month-long trial, all the Black Panther Party defendants, including Bin Wahad and Tabor in absentia, were acquitted by a jury. Jury deliberations lasted less than an hour, and the verdict was returned on May 13, 1971. Bin Wahad returned to the United States, yet remained underground.

The NYPD apprehended Bin Wahad outside an "after hours" bar in the Bronx in June of 1971 and charged him with the attempted murder of two police officers, Thomas Curry and Nicholas Binetti, in Manhattan two months earlier. The case that ensued set the precedent for what became known as the Joint Terrorist Task Force, a joint investigative effort among New York City Police, New York State Police, and the FBI. After three trials in the case of *The People v Dhoruba Bin Wahad*, he was convicted in July of 1973 and sentenced to twenty-five years to life. Two years later, the Church Committee Senate hearings brought COINTELPRO under (semi-) public scrutiny and Bin Wahad's lawyers subsequently filed a civil rights action to procure all documents pertaining to him and the Black Panther Party in New York. Five years later, they received over 300,000 highly excised and unreadable documents that disclosed forged letters, phone calls, and anonymous articles aimed at defaming the reputation, alliances, and unity of the BPP. Significantly, the documents also contained over two hundred previously undisclosed pages of three FBI reports pertaining to Bin Wahad's case, including a record of an anonymous call to the police in which the prosecution's key witness, Pauline Joseph, exonerated Bin Wahad.[1] The defense received the final set of "Newkill" (an acronym referring to killings in New York that the agency wanted to connect to the BPP) documents in 1987, twelve years after the initial civil rights action to procure the evidence. Citing the inconsistency and possible perjury of Pauline Joseph in the 1973 trial and conviction, Dhoruba Bin Wahad and his lawyers filed for a retrial. A New York Supreme Court granted a retrial on March 22, 1990, and released Bin Wahad from prison. The District Attorney's office dismissed his case on January 19, 1995, formally ending the twenty-six-year struggle that began with the New York 21 case in 1969.

Following two lawsuits in 1995 and 2000, Dhoruba Bin Wahad received settlements for personal damages from the FBI and the City of New York, respectively.[2] With these funds, Bin Wahad founded the Campaign to Free Black and New Afrikan Political Prisoners (formerly the Campaign to Free Black Political Prisoners and Prisoners-of-War) and established the Institute for the Development of Pan-African policy in Accra, Ghana.

REFERENCES

Bin Wahad, Dhoruba. "Beggars on Horseback." Unpublished essay, editor's papers.
———. "Cointelpro and the Destruction of Black Leaders and Organizations." *Bulletin in Defense of Marxism* (May 1993): 22–26.
———. Interview with Bill Weinberg. "Dhoruba Bin Wahad: Veteran Black Panther and 19-year Political Prisoner." *Shadow* 36 (6 March 2002). shadow.mediafilter.org/mff/s36/s36.dbw.html.
———. "Speaking Truth to Power: Political Prisoners in the United States." In *Criminal Injustice: Confronting the Prison Crisis*, ed. Elihu Rosenblatt. Boston: South End Press, 1996.

Boyd, Herb. "Ex-Panther's Lawsuit Settled." *Black World Today,* 9 December 2000. www. twbt.com (6 March 2002).

Churchill, Ward, and Jim Vander Wall. *Agents of Repression: The FBI's Secret Wars against the Black Panther Party and the American Indian Movement.* Boston: South End Press, 1998.

Fletcher, Jim, et al., eds. *Still Black, Still Strong: Survivors of the War against Black Revolutionaries.* New York: Semiotext(e), 1993.

Fraser, Gerald C. "F.B.I. Files Reveal Moves against Black Panthers." *New York Times,* 19 October 1980, late ed., A1

Heath, G. Louis, ed. *Off the Pigs!: The History and Literature of the Black Panther Party.* Metuchen, N.J.: Scarecrow Press, 1976.

Newton, Huey. *War against the Panthers: A Study of Repression in America.* New York: Harlem River Press, 1996.

People of the State of New York v Dhoruba Bin Wahad, Formerly Richard Moore. Lexis 1232. NY Sup. Ct., 8 February 1990.

People of the State of New York v Joan Bird and Afeni Shakur. Lexis 1791. NY Sup. Ct., 4 March 1971.

Richard Moore v New York State Board of Parole. Lexis 11746. NY Sup. Ct., 14 November 1990.

NOTES

Research and draft for this biography were provided by Yvette Koch.

1. See Gerald C. Fraser, "F.B.I. Files Reveal Moves against Black Panthers," *New York Times,* 19 October 1980, late ed., A1; *The People of the State of New York v Dhoruba Bin Wahad, Formerly Richard Moore,* Lexis 1232, NY Supreme Ct., 8 February 1990; and Ward Churchill and Jim Vander Wall, *Agents of Repression: The FBI's Secret Wars against the Black Panther Party and the American Indian Movement* (Boston: South End Press, 1998).

2. Herb Boyd, "Ex-Panther's Lawsuit Settled," *Black World Today,* 9 December 2000, www.tbwt.com/views/specialrpt/special%20report-2_12-09-00.asp (6 March 2002).

COINTELPRO and the Destruction of Black Leaders and Organizations

December 1992

The concept of a counterintelligence program is a strategy or a series of operations carried out, supposedly against a foreign government, designed to counter their intelligence work within the United States or within a particular society. It's a war strategy. But here it has mainly been employed against people of color. It was first employed against the CP USA [Communist Party USA]. Many of us who look back historically realize that it was also employed against the [Marcus] Garvey movement. In fact, that was the first time it was employed against an organized, modern national liberation movement. We also know, however, that the techniques of the counterintelligence program began on the plantation.

The most basic strategy of any counterintelligence program is to confuse the enemy and have them believing what you want them to believe. But also it has another aspect to it, the aspect that we know as terrorism—intimidation and violence, making examples of leaders, making examples of people who resist. The United States government perfected these techniques in Southeast Asia against the people's movement in Vietnam. Many of the police professionals who would later lead the war of suppression against the FALN[1] and the Black Liberation Army went on year-long sabbaticals to Vietnam to be trained in the Phoenix program. For those of you who may not be aware of it, the Phoenix program was a program carried out by the CIA, and its objective was to root out the infrastructure and the cadres and troops of the National Liberation Front, the so-called Viet Cong.[2] They killed over 50,000 people in this effort, many of whom were tortured and most of whom were murdered in their sleep, much like Fred Hampton [the Chicago Black Panther leader].

The techniques of "low intensity warfare," of counterinsurgency, of terrorism, these techniques were perfected over a period of time and were used in very effective ways against the Black liberation movement. Especially during periods of upsurge in our consciousness and our activities. Earlier in the century, when Marcus Garvey began to build the United Negro Improvement Association [UNIA], and built it into a national organization of over a million Black men and women, and became a significant threat in the eyes of the racist status quo in this society, the then fledgling FBI took on the task of destroying Marcus Garvey. They did destroy him in the sense that they managed to imprison him on false income tax evasion charges, deport him from the country, and use infiltrators and undercover agents to sow dissension within his organization.

The fragmentation of the UNIA led directly to the establishment of a number of organizations that we now know about. The primary one, of course, was the Nation of Islam, but other movements came out of the fragmented Garvey movement as well. It is important to understand that out of the fragmentation of that movement in the 1920s and early 1930s, the types of individuals that came forward to fill the vacuum that was left as a consequence of the most principled and militant nationalist leadership being eliminated, those who came forward were everything from charlatans to con artists, from buffoons to idiots. They came forward with various messages of liberation that, in and of themselves, may sound absurd to us today, but because of the desperation of oppressed people, because of the psychological preparation that slavery had made among Black people and people of color in this society, many fell victim to that. We know about Sweet Daddy Grace, we know about Father Divine, we know about the pie-in-the-sky, pork chop preachers who organized in the wake of the dissolution of that strong nationalist mass movement.[3]

The same thing happened in the 1970s once the militant, revolutionary wing of the Black movement was destroyed. We need to understand our movement very clearly. We need to analyze it very clearly. At the height of the Black liberation movement in 1969, the basis of its unity had already eroded. There were no longer mass mobilizations of Black people carried out by coalitions of forces that may have differed ideologically. What had happened? What had happened is that the Counterintelligence Program, in order to be effective, had to capitalize on the weaknesses of the Black community in general, and on the weaknesses of the Black movement in particular.

REPRESSION AND "LEADERSHIP SELECTION"

The Counterintelligence Program was very effective, but it would not have been as effective as it was had it not been for our weaknesses. Many of us talk about the Counterintelligence Program and the demise of the Black movement and we do not analyze our role in how things failed. Many of us do not realize, for instance, that the Counterintelligence Program did not just target organizations that were revolutionary. Many of us think that it's a badge of distinction when the government puts surveillance on us and goes after us. We feel that if the enemy is watching us, we must be doing something right. We feel that if the government is concerned about what we're saying, we must be saying something right. That's not the case.

The Counterintelligence Program went after buffoons and geniuses alike. It went after people whose ideology was clearly reactionary, whose ideology was clearly designed to co-opt a legitimate revolutionary consciousness on the part of Black folks, and it went after revolutionaries as well. It went after Dr. Martin Luther King, who everyone in this room knows was no revolutionary by any stretch of the imagination, who represented a particular class within the Black community, and represented them very effectively. That's not to say that Dr. Martin Luther King did not have the interests of Black people at heart, or that he was not a sincere individual or a sincere combatant in the struggle for civil rights, but it is to say that Dr. Martin

Luther King represented a tendency in the Black movement that was conciliatory. A tendency that was, at best, challenging the system in order to become part of it. But the Counterintelligence Program made Dr. Martin Luther King a number one target. At the same time it made Stokely Carmichael, Rap Brown, and SNCC [the Student Nonviolent Coordinating Committee] number one targets. At the same time it began to focus over eighty-five percent of its operations in the Black community on the Black Panther Party.

What we are saying here is that organizations from the Nation of Islam to the SCLC [the Southern Christian Leadership Conference, headed by Martin Luther King, Jr.] and organizations from cultural nationalist groups on the right to cultural nationalist groups on the left were all targets of the United States counterinsurgency and counterintelligence program. This being the case, we cannot but conclude that the basis for COINTELPRO, the reason that it existed and the reason that it went after Black activists, Black preachers, etc., was to weaken and destroy any kind of independent organizations of Black people that were not under the direct control of the racist forces in this country.[4]

It's very important to understand this, because today, we are confronted with the consequences of what happened. Today, many of the individuals who collaborated with the system, who benefited from the murders of Black Panthers, who benefited from the destruction of organizations that militantly espoused self-determination for Black people, are in positions of power and influence. These individuals have gotten to these positions because they identify on a very fundamental level with the system that oppresses us. This is important to us because the greatest task before us as a community, before we can even talk about challenging the power structure, is to "challenge, neutralize, and destroy," to use their terms, the Black middle class that identifies with the system. We have to completely strip them of their power. Their power, like the power of the preacher on the plantation, is derived from their direct relationship to the racists who control this society. This is why preachers in this city can endorse someone like [Senator Alphonse] D'Amato [R-NY], a known and vociferous enemy of people of color. Black so-called clergymen can endorse D'Amato. They can endorse him because they can pick up the phone and get a favor from him when we go to them crying about some injustice in our community and D'Amato responds to them.

Power and leadership in our community has always been a question of the relationship of the power base to the dominant power structure. This means that leadership behind closed doors is a way of life. This means that undercover deals are a way of life. This means that unprincipled opportunism is a quality that Black leaders must have in order to survive in this racist society. The fact that we have the leaders that we have, the fact that we have the Jesse Jacksons and the Wyatt T. Walkers and the David Dinkinses,[5] the fact that we have these individuals leading us today is a testimony to the effectiveness of the Counterintelligence Program. That's my major point.

Our failure to understand the limitations of cultural nationalism led to the situation in the 1960s in which cultural nationalists such as Ron Karenga could carry out the brutal assassination of Black Panthers at the behest of the Los Angeles Police Department and be invited today to the college campuses to pontificate. Would you invite Jonas Savimbi [the head of UNITA, the pro–South African government, CIA-supported Angolan counterrevolutionary organization] here to talk about his position in Angola? Would you sit here and listen to [the Zulu/South African reactionary chief and apartheid collaborator Gatsha] Buthelezi discuss why Inkatha is doing what it is doing? These are butchers of Black people. We do not understand why people who have participated in the murder of Black revolutionaries today are lauded as scholars and leaders in our community. Ron Karenga is but one of them. He is the most classic example of the Savimbis and the Buthelezis among us. I want you to understand that he was effective because he was a narrow cultural nationalist.[6]

CULTURAL NATIONALISM VS. REVOLUTIONARY NATIONALISM

Revolutionary nationalism represented the type of nationalism that understood that there was a common solidarity between all people under the same economic and social political system. This oppression has its historical roots in the development of European hegemony and power in the world. A revolutionary nationalist, therefore, understands that internationalism is based upon an ideology and understanding of who the enemy is, and what the limitations are of the enemy's program and ideology. Cultural nationalists, on the other hand, said that to be Black is sufficient, that our African-ness was so unique in and of itself that we need not aspire to struggle in any arena other than the arena of African culture; that we first of all had to become aware of how beautiful we were, and we first of all had to become aware of our ancient African traditions and ways.

Of course, I am not one to disparage our traditions and our ways and our ancestors. Our ancestors have gotten us here; our ancestors' spirits have provided for us in a society that was bent on our destruction. However, preceding every revolutionary struggle, cultural awareness arises and becomes a mass awareness. Preceding the upsurges of the 1960s Black people began to rediscover who they were. They began to take the conk out of their hair, started wearing their hair naturally. Black women started taking the makeup off their face and became proud of their big African lips. Black men stopped curling and frying and dyeing their hair; they started wearing Afros and dashikis. We started renaming ourselves in the tradition of our ancestors. We embraced religions that reflected who we were. This cultural awareness preceded revolutionary consciousness.

The enemy is a student of history. They know our history better than we do. They analyzed the history and religions and trends in society around the world and they came to certain conclusions. One of the conclusions they came to is that cultural nationalism in and of itself is reactionary. It will never lead to the empowerment of people until it is politicized. Once it is politicized, it can possibly become revolutionary. So the key was to stop the politicization of our cultural awareness. Therefore, individuals who preached narrow cultural nationalism had to be supported covertly, and they had to be promoted.

When the Black Panther Party came upon the scene in the 1960s, it was the first Black organization in contemporary times that, number one, was a cadre organization and, number two, had a revolutionary ideology that embraced the idea and notion that there were Black enemies of Black people based on their class consciousness. This was difficult for the cultural nationalists to deal with in the 1960s. I know. They were into having Black women walking three steps behind them. They were into speaking Swahili and refusing to talk to any white folks under any circumstances. They said that because the Black Panther Party had this position and this analysis, white folks were controlling it. They said that we were fraternizing with white people and there were white people in the Black Panther Party.

When you look at the counterintelligence documents, you see the FBI played on this. They sent false information and letters to the Black student unions around the country in order to keep the Panthers off the campus. And the way they would couch their letters was in the phrases and terminology of the cultural nationalists. The letters said that the Panthers were hanging out with white folks—with honkies—you know the terminology they used. They would bring in the local janitor of the FBI building and say, "Look, Brother Coon, why don't you write a letter for us? You know, use that ol' coon talk that you talk." Yeah, they did that. When they used to place their phone calls they used to get the janitors and the people who used to clean the offices in the FBI building to place the phone calls because they couldn't imitate the speech patterns of Black people, and they had no Black agents. This is all in the documents. This is all in the Church Committee investigation.

So we need to understand that cultural nationalism, historically, has been a brake on our revolutionary consciousness when the mass movement has no leadership. They understood this so well that they went after the most radical wing of the Black movement. They went after them with guns, indictments, and criminalization, and they boosted the reformist wing of the movement by giving them little carrots and tokens and antipoverty programs. They pushed forward the cultural nationalists to say that the most radical nationalists were people who subscribed to some white, leftist ideology.

REVOLUTION AND CULTURE

We have to be very clear that the Counterintelligence Program was not only a war strategy. It was a strategy designed to manipulate the political landscape of the Black community, manipulate it in a way that we would find ourselves twenty-three years later in the exact same position we were then. It's like *déjà vu*. If you ever look at some of the old speeches of Malcolm and look at some of the videos we're watching now, it's like we're talking about the same thing! [Heavy-weight boxing champion] George Foreman was on yesterday talking about decent housing and police brutality and how we're not going to stop until the police stop. All you had to do was to change the date from 1963 to 1992 and he would have been talking about the exact same thing we're talking about now.

So how is it that we've managed for twenty-five years to talk about the same thing? I'll tell you how it happens. Those individuals who embraced revolutionary ideas and principles first of all realized that without a radical transformation of society there will be no possibility of a new type of human being, a non-exploited human being. A human being that can give the best of himself or herself to society and thereby enrich themselves and enrich society in the process. Revolution means, for us, the destruction of oppressive and exploitative systems. This, of course, implies that if there is to be a revolution there have to be revolutionaries and a revolutionary movement, and this movement has to have a culture. It has to have a way to inspire and to communicate to its people. The culture that this society loves to appropriate, but seldom gives its due to, is the culture of Africans in diaspora. We all know that we are the lifeblood of an otherwise bloodless culture. We know that it is our speech, our style, our very existence that peoples of the world emulate when they emulate so-called American culture. It's our music that has become renowned worldwide. It is our poetry, our speech, our clothes; it is our very being.

Therefore, the arena that the Counterintelligence Program focused on the most was the arena of the mass culture. The mass culture is an area that is controlled by what? The mass media. There could be no mass culture in this multitribal society were it not for the electronic media. The mass culture is promoted and promulgated by the mass media. It was in the arena of the mass media that the revolutionary nationalists had to first be discredited. It was in the arena of the mass media or in the arena of the mass culture that our movement had to first be derailed. . . .

We have to take it to the streets. When we look at the films of the 1960s, when we look at the struggle that unfolded in the 1960s, there was always that fundamental beat in the street. It was always going on in the streets. Without that happening today, we are going to be subjected to definition by media. You can't win because they manufacture not only consent, they manufacture ideas. They are the masters at putting a spin on something. Madison Avenue pays individuals six-digit figures to figure out how to subliminally seduce people.

We are not up against a simple system that can be defeated only through debate of ideas. We have to begin to exert some serious force in this issue. Now I'm not an advocate of violence. I'm not an advocate of the mindless use of force. But I do think the judicious application of physical force can bring about a negotiated settlement of issues that are otherwise unresolvable. I think that once we have established that our children will no longer listen to us, then I think we will begin to listen to our children.

NOTES

This selection is an edited version of a talk given by Dhoruba Bin Wahad in Harlem on December 4, 1992, at an African International Forum entitled "Cointelpro, CovertAction, and the Destruction of Black Leaders and Organizations." The talk was transcribed by Lee DeNoyer. Originally published in *Bulletin in Defense of Marxism* 11, no. 106 (May 1993): 22–26.

1. *Editor's note:* Fuerzas Armadas de Liberación Nacional (Armed Forces of National Liberation) was an underground organization that acted as resistance toward the U.S. colonization of Puerto Rico. Between 1974 and 1980, the FALN was accountable for numerous actions against U.S. military, government, and economic sites that they held responsible for U.S. domination in Puerto Rico. By 1980, the U.S. government cracked down on the group through a series of arrests. Jan Susler, "Unreconstructed Revolutionaries: Today's Puerto Rican Political Prisoners of War," in *The Puerto Rican Movement*, ed. Andres Torres and Jose E. Velazquez (Philadelphia: Temple University Press, 1998), 145.

2. *Editor's note:* "Operation Phoenix" was an assassination program undertaken by the CIA in southern Vietnam. "Special Operations Groups (SOGs)," acting to suppress dissident voices, and other military and nonmilitary formations, operated in a widespread counterinsurgency program. At this time, a Special Operations Service (SOS) was developed in the United States under the FBI and CIA to create similar programs domestically. Ward Churchill and Jim Vander Wall, *Agents of Repression: The FBI's Secret Wars against the Black Panther Party and the American Indian Movement* (Boston: South End Press, 1988), 194–95; Stanton Shelby, *U.S. Army and Allied Ground Forces in Vietnam: Order of Battle* (Washington, D.C.: U.S. News Books, 1981), 251–53.

3. *Editor's note:* Sweet Daddy Grace and Father Divine were leaders of different religious "cult" groups in Harlem during the Depression. Sweet Daddy Grace formed the House of Prayer shortly after Father Divine created the Peace Mission. Healing sessions, spiritual gatherings, and Messianic hope served as a way of organizing members of the black community. Many of their adherents were former followers of Marcus Garvey, who prophesied a black messiah and redemption. Both groups organized against racial and economic oppression and attempted to formulate alternatives with their congregants. Robert Weisbort, *Father Divine and the Struggle for Racial Equality* (Urbana: University of Illinois Press, 1983), 60–63, 176–78.

4. *Editor's note:* COINTELPRO was not designed specifically for African Americans or black progressives. It was created and utilized against formations and individuals that challenged elite dominance and structural oppression; however, those disproportionately and violently victimized by COINTELPRO were African, Native, or Latino Americans.

5. *Editor's note:* Civil rights activist Jesse Jackson, Sr.; former Southern Christian Leadership Conference leader, New York Reverend Wyatt T. Walker; first elected black New York City mayor, David Dinkins.

6. *Editor's note:* The FBI's Counterintelligence Program employed operations in order to create dissension between the Black Panther Party (BPP) and Ron Karenga's US. Among the tactics used were planting cartoons of each organization characterizing the other in a negative way. US members killed BPP leaders John Higgins and Bunchy Carter. See *Agents of Repression*, 41; Charles E. Jones, ed., *The Black Panther Party [Reconsidered]* (Baltimore: Black Classic Press, 1998).

Chapter Seven

Jalil Abdul Muntaqim

Jalil Abdul Muntaqim (Anthony Bottom) was born on October 18, 1951, in Oakland, California, and grew up in San Francisco. Attracted to antiracist and civil rights activism in the 1960s, Bottom began organizing for the National Association for the Advancement of Colored People (NAACP) as an adolescent. In high school, he was often recruited to engage in "speak outs" on behalf of the Black Student Union (BSU). He also participated in street protests against police brutality.[1] After the assassination of Martin Luther King, Jr., in 1968, though, he became convinced of the need to use armed strategies to combat racist repression.[2]

At the age of eighteen, Muntaqim joined the Black Panther Party (BPP). During this time, between late 1968 and 1969, the black underground organization, later known as the Black Liberation Army (BLA), began to militarize.[3] The *New York Times* in 1971 defined the BLA as a "loosely knit amalgam of terrorists that arose out of a Black Panther faction." Muntaqim described the formation as "a politico-military organization, whose primary objective is to fight for the independence and self-determination of Afrikan people in the United States."[4]

While those in the Black Panther Party's aboveground offices focused on organizing, communicating with nationwide party affiliates and other revolutionary groups, and forming positive political and social relations with local black communities across the country, Muntaqim and fellow members of the underground became experts in military strategy and served as the essential "armed wing of the aboveground political apparatus."[5] When the party split (into Newton vs. Cleaver or West vs. East Coast factions), however, this balance of skills was disrupted and the BPP lost political support. The BLA continued the movement in their area of expertise—armed struggle. Lacking the indispensable political support of the BPP, and with the alienation of large segments of American and African American communities who disagreed with its violent tactics, the BLA faltered and was eventually destroyed.

On August 28, 1971, one week after a San Quentin prison guard shot and killed imprisoned BPP Field Marshall George Jackson, Muntaqim and Albert "Nuh"

Washington were arrested in California for the alleged attempted killing of a San Francisco police sergeant. New York police charged Muntaqim, Washington, and another BPP and BLA member, Herman Bell, with the May 21, 1971, killings of two Harlem police officers, Waverly Jones and Joseph A. Piagentini.[6] The shootout that led to the deaths of the two officers came only two days after two other NYPD officers were wounded by gunfire, an incident for which an anonymous informer declared the BLA responsible.[7] Using George Jackson's murder as substantiation for a motive of BLA retaliation, police entered the gun that Muntaqim held at the San Francisco shooting as evidence in the New York City murder trial.[8]

The FBI's COINTELPRO project to suppress radicals was effectively used to capture and convict Muntaqim, Washington, and Bell (Bell was arrested two years later) for the killings. They became known as the "New York Three." According to Ward Churchill and Jim Vander Wall, the FBI secured their convictions by coercion of witnesses and perjured testimonies.[9] While Muntaqim, Bell, and Washington received an evidentiary hearing in 1992, in which they successfully proved the government's suppression of evidence and its illegal conduct in their previous trial, their appeals were denied by the state and federal courts on the grounds that these violations, when considered separately, did not warrant a new trial.[10] Muntaqim and Bell remain incarcerated in New York. Albert "Nuh" Washington died of liver cancer in April 2000, in New York's Coxsackie Correctional Facility.[11]

Muntaqim has remained active as an educator and writer in support of prisoners' rights and social justice. In 1976, while at San Quentin prison, he launched the National Prisoners Campaign to petition the United Nations to recognize the existence of political prisoners in the United States.[12] Through the National Prisoners Afrikan Studies Project, he participates in the education of other inmates, and has filed numerous lawsuits on behalf of prisoners.[13] Muntaqim also conceived of the Jericho '98 March on Washington, which drew thousands to support of the freedom of U.S. political prisoners. With Bell, he helps to coordinate "Victory Gardens—Food for Harlem," a project that seeks to join rural and urban communities—through the farming and distribution of fresh food and the distribution of educational materials on amnesty/clemency campaigns for U.S. political prisoners—in political unity that transcends race and class divisions.

REFERENCES

Bell, Herman. "New York Three Update." June 1997. prisonactivist.org/pps + pows/ny3_update.html.

Can't Jail the Spirit: Political Prisoners in the U.S. 4th ed. Chicago: Committee to End the Marion Lockdown, March 1998.

Churchill, Ward, and Jim Vander Wall. *The COINTELPRO Papers: Documents from the FBI's Secret Wars against Dissent in the United States.* Boston: South End Press, 1990.

Fried, Joseph. "2 Policemen Slain by Shots in Back, 2 Men Sought." *New York Times*, 21 May 1971, 1.

Kaufman, Michael T. "Slaying of One of the Last Black Liberation Army Leaders Still at Large Ended a 7-Month Manhunt." *New York Times,* 16 November 1973, 10.

Muntaqim, Jalil Abdul. "The Cold War of the 90's." Made available on www.prisonactivist. org/pubs/jalil-cold-war-90s.html. Reprinted from Prison News Service, Issue #52, September–October 1995.

———. "Criminalization of Poverty in Capitalist America." Made available on www. prisonactivist.org/pubs/jalil-crim-pov.html. Reprinted from Chinosole, ed., *Schooling the Generations in the Politics of Prison.* Berkeley, Calif.: New Earth Publications, 1996.

———. "On the Black Liberation Army." *Arm the Spirit,* 18 September 1979.

———. "Statement for the September 21, 1996 founding rally of the know INJUSTICE Coalition." Dolores Park, San Francisco, 1996. Made available on www.prisonactivist.org/ pps+pows/jbottom.html.

New York State Task Force on Political Prisoners. "Clemency Petition." Editor' papers.

NOTES

Research and draft for this biography were provided by Elizabeth Kaufman.

1. "Jalil Muntaqim" in *Can't Jail the Spirit: Political Prisoners in the U.S. A Collection of Biographies,* 4th ed. (Chicago: Committee to End the Marion Lockdown, 1998), 99.

2. *Can't Jail the Spirit,* 99.

3. Jalil Muntaqim, "On the Black Liberation Army," *Arm the Spirit* (18 September 1979): 65.

4. "On the Black Liberation Army," 66.

5. "On the Black Liberation Army," 66.

6. Michael Kaufman, "Slaying of One of the Last Black Liberation Army Leaders Still at Large Ended a 7-Month Manhunt," *New York Times,* 16 November 1973, 10.

7. Joseph Fried, "2 Policemen Slain by Shots in Back; 2 Men Are Sought," *New York Times,* 21 May 1971, 1.

8. New York State Task Force on Political Prisoners, "Clemency Petition," 18.

9. Ward Churchill and Jim Vander Wall, *The COINTELPRO Papers: Documents from the FBI's Secret Wars against Dissent in the United States* (Boston: South End Press, 1990), 157.

10. Herman Bell, "New York Three Update," June 1997, prisonactivist.org/pps+pows/ ny3_update.html.

11. New York State Task Force on Political Prisoners, 19.

12. *Can't Jail the Spirit,* 100.

13. New York State Task Force on Political Prisoners, 17.

On the Black Liberation Army *(Abridged)*

September 18, 1979

INTRODUCTION: 1966–1971

The history of our national liberation struggle is one of the most important sources from which the political [parties], the oppressed masses and the liberation armed forces can draw lessons elucidating the nature of their oppression and the task before them: moving towards independence and freedom. In this article, I would like to present to the masses the general history of the evolution of the Black Liberation Army (BLA). This will be a brief historical overview. In order to protect people who are or were at one time associated with the BLA, it will not provide specific historical data.

The Black Liberation Army is a politico-military organization whose primary objective is to fight for the independence and self-determination of Afrikan people in the United States. The political determination of the BLA evolved out of the now-defunct Black Panther Party (BPP).

With the advent of the Black Panther Party for Self-Defense in October 1966, the question of armed struggle and resistance to racist oppression emerged as a plausible strategy in the developing liberation movement. In late 1968 and early 1969, the forming of a Black underground began. From Los Angeles, California, to Texas, Louisiana, Mississippi, and Alabama, armed units were formed and trained in rural areas, and caches of resources were established.

In the same period, in Oakland, San Francisco, Detroit, Chicago, Philadelphia, Ohio, and New York, and other communities across the country, Black Panther Party offices were being established to formulate a political relationship with the oppressed Black masses. From 1969 to 1972, the BPP came under vicious attack by the State and Federal governments. The federal government employed COINTELPRO (the FBI program implemented with cooperation from the CIA and local police departments) as a means to destroy the aboveground political apparatus that fielded the Black underground.[1] But it wasn't until 1969 that the BPP began its purge of many of its most trusted and militant members, many of whom eventually joined the Black underground.

By 1971, contradictions perpetuated by COINTELPRO within the leadership of the BPP caused the split between [Huey] Newton and [Eldridge] Cleaver, which eventually split the entire Black Panther Party into two major factions. It was this BPP split and factionalism that propelled the Black underground to initiate a consistent practice of armed struggle for Black liberation. The State's armed offensive to liquidate the Party in order to destroy aboveground activity for liberation also played into this development.

This is not to say that armed action by the Black underground against the State did not occur prior to the split. On the contrary, by 1971 the Black underground was becoming rich in experience in the tactics of armed expropriations, sabotage, and ambush-assaults.

THE "DEFENSIVE–OFFENSIVE": 1970–1971

Prior to the split, the Black underground had been the official armed wing of the aboveground political apparatus, and for that reason had restrained its military activity. It was not an autonomous entity. The Black underground, though experienced in many areas of tactical military guerrilla warfare, was still politically infantile. Although it was becoming organizationally sophisticated as a fighting apparatus, it did not establish an infrastructure completely separate from the aboveground BPP cadres and chapters. This would become one of the major detriments to the Black underground after the Black Panther Party split.

Based upon the split and factionalism in the BPP, and in the context of heightened repression by the State, the Black underground was ordered to begin establishing the capacity to take the "defensive–offensive" in developing urban guerrilla warfare. Hence, in 1971, the title "Black Liberation Army" (or "Afro-American Liberation Army") surfaced as the name of the nucleus of Black guerrilla fighters across the United States. This is not to say that the name Black Liberation Army was first used in 1971, for in late 1968, during a student strike and demonstration in Mexico City, many students and demonstrators were killed by Mexican police.[2] One of those students was reported to have had a piece of paper in his pocket upon which was written the name Black Liberation Army. Whether or not there was a connection between the fielding of the Black underground and the uprising in Mexico in 1968 is unknown.

Both before and after the split in the BPP and the call for the "defensive–offensive," the Black underground had committed many armed attacks against the State as part of the BPP (and, starting in May 1971, as the Black Liberation Army). Many of these are unrecorded. Here I would like to present the Justice Department–LEAA Task Force report on BLA activity. (It should be noted that these reports were recorded by the date when police agencies captured, killed, or in some way received information concerning BLA activity. They are, therefore, one sided and by no means indicative of all BLA activity in the last ten years.) . . .[3]

1976

The defensive–offensive politico-military initiatives launched in 1970–71 were based upon the degree of repression suffered in the Black community due to COINTELPRO police attacks. The politico-military policy at that time was to establish a *defensive* (self-defense) front that would *offensively* protect the above-ground forces, whose purpose and task were to develop a mass movement towards national liberation.

At this time, a historical transition was taking place. The civil rights movement had given way to the riotous 1960s, the creation of BPP chapters bravely fighting against police attacks in Black communities, and massive mobilizations in support of the Vietnamese national liberation war. Hence, the commencement of armed struggle by our forces responded to this historical transition and development.

But there was a problem: In the early seventies, the Black underground was the armed wing of the aboveground BPP. Unfortunately, the subsequent split and factionalism within the BPP obstructed logistics and communications between cadre(s) in the Black underground in various parts of the country. This created the greatest impediment to the advent of the Black Liberation Army, so that the commencement of armed struggle could be said to have been premature. Subjectively, our capacity to wage a sustained protracted national liberation war was undermined by the split in the aboveground political apparatus, for the underground still depended on the aboveground for logistics and communications. The Black underground was comprised of militants who had not grown to political maturity. As a result, the underground was left without a politico-military structure and strategy to merge into a national formation employing stable and mobile urban and rural guerrilla warfare in conjunction with the rising militancy of the oppressed masses.

STRATEGIC RETREAT: 1971–1975

By late 1971, the Black underground was ordered to begin a strategic retreat, to reorganize itself and build a national structure. The call for the strategic retreat was too late, however, for many cadres. Many of the most mature militants were already deeply underground, separated from those aboveground BPP members who continued to support armed struggle after the split. The repression of the State continued to mount, especially now that the Black underground was hampered by internal strife and isolated by the loss of the aboveground political support apparatus (and with virtually no support coming from existing Black community groups and organizations). At the same time, it must be stated, a major contradiction was developing between the Black underground and Euro-American forces employing armed tactics in support of the Vietnamese liberation struggle.[4]

By 1973–75, this contradiction became full-blown: Specific Euro-American revolutionary armed forces refused to give meaningful material and political support to the Black Liberation Movement, more specifically, to the Black Liberation Army. Thus, in 1974 the Black Liberation Army was without an aboveground political support apparatus; logistically and structurally scattered across the country without the means to unite its combat units; abandoned by Euro-American revolutionary armed forces; and being relentlessly pursued by the State's reactionary law enforcement agencies and programs. It was only a matter of time before the Black Liberation Army would be virtually decimated as a fighting clandestine organization.

CONTINUING THE FIGHT IN THE
COURTS AND PRISONS

By 1974–75, the fighting capacity of the Black Liberation Army had been destroyed. But the BLA as a politico-military organization had not been destroyed, because the imprisoned comrades continued attempting to escape and persisted in fighting their political trials. These efforts forged ideological and political theory concerning the building of the Black Liberation Movement and revolutionary armed struggle. In the courts, Black Liberation Army members sought to place the State on trial, to condemn the oppressive conditions in which Black people had to eke out an existence in racist America. These trials went on for several years, with the courts and police trying to use them to embellish their position as guardians of society. The State media projected the Black Liberation Army trials as instances of justice being served: to protect Black people from terrorism; to prevent these terrorists from starting racial strife between Black and white people; to protect the police, who are responsible for the welfare of the oppressed communities, etc. The captured and confined BLA members were labeled terrorist, criminal, racist—but never revolutionaries, never humanitarians, never political activists.

But the undaunted revolutionary fervor of captured BLA members continued to serve the revolution—even from within the courtrooms and the prisons. By placing the State on trial, the BLA was able to expose the contradiction between the falsehood—that the State protects the rights of all people—and the actuality—that the State only protects the rights of the capitalist-class bourgeoisie. The comrades on trial sought to undermine the State's attempts to play off the BLA as an insignificant group of crazies. Thus the BLA trials became forums to politicize the masses about the nature of the struggle and revolution. The trials served to organize people to support those being persecuted and prosecuted by the State. They became a means for the oppressed masses to build the capacity to protect themselves from future persecution. In this manner, the trials of the Black Liberation Army voiced the discontent, dissatisfaction, and disenfranchisement of Black people in racist America.

STRATEGIC CAMPAIGNS: 1975–1979

By late 1975, the Black Liberation Army established a Coordinating Committee, essentially comprised of imprisoned members and outside supporters who had emerged during the years of political prosecution in the courts. The first task of the Coordinating Committee was to distribute an ideological document depicting the theoretical foundations of the Black Liberation Army's political determination. This document was entitled "A MESSAGE TO THE BLACK MOVEMENT—A Political Statement from the Black Underground." The Message to the Black Movement put forth several political premises underlying the BLA's status as a revolutionary political-military organization fighting for national liberation of Afrikan people in the United States.

In late 1975 and 1976, the Coordinating Committee distributed the first BLA newsletter, an organizational publication designed to forge ideological and political clarity and unity among BLA members captured and confined in various parts of the country. The BLA newsletter began to serve as a means for BLA members to voice their understanding of the national liberation struggle, and in this way, for the entire organized body to share in ideas and strengthen our collective political determination as a fighting force. Over the years, the newsletter has helped to develop cadres inside and outside of prison and to broaden the capacity of the BLA to continue to serve the national liberation struggle.

In 1976, members of the Black Liberation Army launched a national campaign to petition the United Nations concerning the plight of political prisoners of war and conditions of the U.S. penal system, on behalf of the prison movement. This BLA-initiated and led U.N. Prisoners Petition Campaign virtually revitalized the prison movement across the country and forged the impetus behind the present Human Rights campaign to the United Nations.[5] The U.N. Prisoners Petition Campaign was the first to call for an international investigation into the conditions of U.S. prisons. It also called for the release of political prisoners of war to a non-imperialist country that would accept them. (This year, another national campaign, entitled "National POW Amnesty Campaign" has been launched.) Lastly, in 1976–77, the Coordinating Committee distributed a Study Guide to captured members of the BLA as a means to consolidate the ideological perspectives from which the BLA would provide political leadership to the national liberation struggle.

From 1974 to the present, the BLA has continuously provided ideological and political perspectives within the Black Liberation Movement, and in this way has given leadership to the movement. However, the Black Liberation Army still lacks principled support from progressive forces throughout the country. The primary reason for this lack of support is the fact that the BLA still calls for armed struggle and the building of a revolutionary armed front. The Black Liberation Army is a politico-military organization. In the last five years it has served to develop the mass movement to merge with the political determination of the Black underground. The merger is based upon the development of a national politico-military strategy in unity with the aspirations and strategic initiatives of various political organizations throughout the country. The Black Liberation Army has consistently called for the development of a Black Liberation Front or Black United Front, a united front of Black revolutionary nationalists to establish the political determination of the class and national liberation struggle towards independence and for the freeing of the land. At this stage, there are several areas of progress that may serve to strengthen, consolidate, and mobilize the national liberation struggle for the aspirations of the oppressed Black masses.

The building of the Afrikan National Prisoners Organization is a positive step for various progressive Black forces to develop principled working relationships, alliances, and coalitions, and further build towards the Black Liberation Front. Similarly, the National Black Human Rights Coalition will allow a greater number of Black organizations and groups representing oppressed Black masses to educate, organize, and mobilize against racist, capitalist imperialism in conjunction with the heightened struggles in Namibia and Azania [South Africa] and escalating human rights violations here in North America. But it is imperative that these new formations develop a struggle line that supports the need for armed struggle in the United States, and, therefore, the oldest revolutionary armed force in North America—the Black Liberation Army.[6]

It is practically 1980 and the Black Liberation Army (the Black underground) has been in existence for over ten years. The last ten years have been hard years of struggle. We have lost many comrades, we have made many mistakes, but we have never lied nor compromised our principles in struggle. The growth and development of the BLA depends on the growth and development of the entire class and national liberation struggle. The BLA's ability to build revolutionary armed struggle lies in the willingness of the oppressed masses to support the BLA. This means calling for the BLA to act and building areas of support in the work place, in the home, in the social places of entertainment, but most of all amongst the political organizations and groups with whom the oppressed masses are affiliated. It is essential and necessary that the general mass and popular movement understand the need for revolutionary armed struggle/forces. They must recognize that the existence of the Black Liberation Army is the foundation for the preservation of the class and national liberation struggle as the socio-economic conditions of U.S. monopoly capitalism worsen and as racist repression intensifies.

As mentioned earlier, another national political campaign has been launched. This new campaign calls for the release and/or exchange of captured members of the Black underground and other revolutionary forces across the country. But it must be understood that the principle objective of this campaign is also to build support for revolutionary armed struggle, employing international law and politics (specifically, Protocols of the Geneva Accords) concerning the existence of political prisoners of war in the United States. Supporting the release of political prisoners of war brings understanding of how these revolutionaries came to be imprisoned, of the need for them to be released, and of the need for revolutionary armed struggle. This is the challenge in uniting the mass and popular movements under the auspices of building the Black Liberation Front. It can only be realized by supporting the re-emergence of the Black underground, the Black Liberation Army.

SUPPORT THE BLACK LIBERATION ARMY
BUILD THE NATIONAL POW AMNESTY CAMPAIGN
FREE ALL POLITICAL PRISONERS OF WAR

Jalil Abdul Muntaqim
on behalf of the Black Liberation Army

NOTES

Originally written on September 18, 1979, and printed in the revolutionary prisoners' news-paper, *Arm the Spirit,* this essay has been edited for this volume.

1. *Editor's note:* FBI COINTELPRO activity against the Black Panther Party is docu-mented in depth in Ward Churchill and Jim Vander Wall, *The COINTELPRO Papers: Docu-ments from the FBI's Secret Wars against Dissent in the United States* (Boston: South End Press, 1992), 91–164. The counterinsurgency program embodied in COINTELPRO targeted a broad range of black groups and organizations, seeking to squash any development suspected of furthering black nationalist and liberationist politics.

2. *Editor's note:* Students initiated a strike in July of 1968 to demand educational reforms. The 118-day strike affected close to 150,000 students and was marked by tension and vio-lence between federal officials and student protestors. Hundreds of students were wounded and many were killed and imprisoned for their actions. Associated Press, "Big Student Strike On in Mexico City," *New York Times,* 10 August 1968, 5; Associated Press, "Deaths Put at 49 in Mexican Clash," *New York Times,* 4 October 1968, 1.

3. *Editor's note:* The LEAA was the Law Enforcement Assistance Administration, an agency set up by the Department of Justice in 1968 to channel federal funds to state and local police agencies. Widely regarded by radicals as a conduit for counterintelligence programs, it was abolished in 1982. For Muntaqim's reference to the Justice Department–LEAA Task Force report on BLA activity, see original publication of this piece.

4. *Editor's note:* The National Black Human Rights Coalition was an alliance of revolu-tionary nationalist forces that led a mass mobilization in front of the United Nations in New York City in November of 1979.

5. *Editor's note:* The Euro-American forces referred to were radical student groups. Their antiwar efforts, support for the Black Panther Party, and subsequent decline are documented in *The COINTELPRO Papers: Documents from the FBI's Secret Wars against Dissent in the United States,* 165, 171–76, 208–30.

6. *Editor's note:* The Deacons for Defense and Justice, formed in 1960, provided a model for the Black Panther Party, originally created as the Black Panther Party for Self-Defense in 1966, and the Black Liberation Army as well. For more information on the Deacons for Defense and Justice and the organization's founder, Robert F. Williams, see Timothy B. Tyson, *Radio Free Dixie: Robert F. Williams and the Roots of Black Power* (Chapel Hill: Univer-sity of North Carolina Press, 1999); and Robert Franklin Williams, *Negroes with Guns* (Detroit: Wayne State University Press, 1998; reprint).

Chapter Eight

Assata Shakur

Assata Shakur (JoAnne Chesimard) was born in 1947 in New York City. She spent most of her childhood in the segregated South, living in Wilmington, North Carolina, until her family relocated to Queens, New York, when she was a teenager. Shakur began her political education in radicalism when she enrolled as a student at Borough of Manhattan Community College (BMCC) in the mid-1960s. In the context of growing black consciousness and nationalist movements, she became involved with BMCC's black and African student organizations. Her activism expanded to include the black liberation, student rights, and anti–Vietnam War movements. After graduating from college, Shakur began working with the Black Panther Party (BPP), but differences and dissatisfaction with the Oakland-based national leadership led her to the Black Liberation Army (BLA), an underground, military wing of the Panthers largely based on the East Coast. A main target of the Federal Bureau of Investigation's COINTELPRO, Shakur was accused of numerous crimes and forced underground. Eventually in each of these cases, charges would be dropped or Shakur acquitted. In a May 1973 confrontation with New Jersey state troopers, she was seriously wounded, and her companion and BLA comember Zayd Malik Shakur was killed, along with state trooper Werner Foerster. Companion Sundiata Acoli (Clark Squire) escaped but was later apprehended. Following a change of venue in 1973 and a mistrial in 1974, in March 1977 Shakur was convicted as an accomplice to the murder of state trooper Foerster and of atrocious assault on trooper James Harper with intent to kill. Despite the testimony of expert witnesses that argued medical evidence showed Shakur could not have shot either trooper, the all-white jury, of whom five had personal ties to state troopers, convicted her. Although the trial was held in a county where frequent pretrial press reports proclaimed her guilt, the judge refused to allow any evidence of COINTELPRO repression to be entered into the case and refused to investigate a burglary of the office of her defense counsel and the destruction or disappearance of important defense trial documents during that break-in.[1]

Shakur escaped from New Jersey's Clinton Correctional Facility in 1979. Since the 1980s she has been in exile in Cuba, where she received political asylum. Shakur's controversial case and police and prosecutorial malfeasance were reintroduced to mainstream black America in the mid-1980s through African American news host Gil Noble's *Like It Is* TV talk show, based in New York City. In the 1990s, she appeared in various documentaries, including Cuban filmmaker Gloria Rolando's *Eyes of the Rainbow*, which intersperses images of a serene Shakur with African Orisha, or Yoruba female warrior deities of love and community. Her case has received support from a broad national and international spectrum. In 1998 media reported that the U.S. State Department was negotiating with the Cuban government to lift crippling sanctions and a forty-year embargo in exchange for the extradition of Shakur and ninety other U.S. political exiles. Defiantly, Shakur described herself as a "fugitive slave" and the woman who authorized the hunt and increased the bounty on her head, then New Jersey governor Christine Todd Whitman (current Environmental Protection Agency [EPA] head), as a "slave mistress."

Shakur's life and experience in the black liberation struggle, and the state campaign to criminalize her, are detailed in *Assata: An Autobiography*. In the memoir she contests depictions of her as a violent black female revolutionary and offers a complex portrait of a woman committed to freedom. Refusing to make revolutionary war synonymous with violence, she writes of a "people's war" that precludes elite vanguards (quoted in the introduction, her words bear repeating here):

> Some of the groups thought they could just pick up arms and struggle and that, somehow, people would see what they were doing and begin to struggle themselves. They wanted to engage in a do-or-die battle with the power structure in amerika, even though they were weak and ill prepared for such a fight. But the most important factor is that armed struggle, by itself, can never bring about a revolution. Revolutionary war is a people's war.[2]

REFERENCES

"Assata Shakur: The Continuity of Struggle," *Souls* 1, no. 2 (Spring 1999).

Bin Wahad, Dhoruba, Mumia Abu-Jamal, Assata Shakur in Jim Fletcher, Tanaquil Jones, and Sylvère Lotringer, eds. *Still Black, Still Strong: Survivors of the U.S. War against Black Revolutionaries*. New York: Semiotext(e), 1993.

Hinds, Lennox S. Foreword. *Assata: An Autobiography*. Chicago: Lawrence Hill Books, 1987.

Mealy, Rosemari. "Assata Shakur: The Life of a Revolutionary." *CovertAction Quarterly* 65 (Fall 1998).

Parenti, Christian. "Assata Shakur Speaks from Exile: Post-modern Maroon in the Ultimate Palenque." *Z Magazine* 11, no. 3 (March 1998).

Perkins, Margo V. *Autobiography as Activism: Three Black Women of the Sixties*. Jackson: University Press of Mississippi, 2000.

Ratner, Michael. "Immoral Bounty for Assata." *CovertAction Quarterly* 65 (Fall 1998).

Shakur, Assata. *Assata: An Autobiography*. Chicago: Lawrence Hill Books, 1987.

———— (as told to Ida E. Lewis). "Assata Shakur: Profiled and on the Run." *The New Crisis* 107, no. 6 (November/December 2000).

Williams, Evelyn. *Inadmissible Evidence: The Story of the African-American Trial Lawyer Who Defended the Black Liberation Army.* Brooklyn: Lawrence Hill Books, 1993.

NOTES

Research and draft for this biography were provided by Elizabeth Walsh.

1. Lennox S. Hinds, Foreword, *Assata: An Autobiography* (Chicago: Lawrence Hill Books, 1987), xi–xii.

2. Assata Shakur, *Assata: An Autobiography* (Chicago: Lawrence Hill Books, 1987), 242.

July 4th Address

July 4, 1973

BLACK BROTHERS, BLACK SISTERS, I want you to know that I love you and I hope somewhere in your heart you have love for me. My name is Assata Shakur (slave name JoAnne Chesimard), and I am a field nigga who is determined to be free by any means necessary. By that I mean that I can never be free unless all my people are free along with me. By that I mean that I have declared war on all forces that have raped our women, castrated our men and kept our babies empty-bellied.

I have declared war on the rich who prosper on our poverty, the politicians who lie to us with smiling faces, and all the mindless, heartless robots who protected them and their property.

I am a black revolutionary, and as such I am the victim of all the wrath, hatred and slander that amerikkka is capable of. Like all other black revolutionaries, I have been hunted like a dog, and like all other black revolutionaries, amerikkka is trying to lynch me.

I am a black revolutionary woman and because of this I have been charged with and accused of every alleged crime in which a woman was believed to have participated. The alleged crimes in which only men were supposed involved, I have been accused of planning. They plastered pictures alleged to be me in post offices, airports, hotels, police cars, subways, banks, television, and newspapers. They offered over fifty thousand dollars ($50,000) in rewards for my capture and they issued orders to shoot on sight and to shoot to kill.

I am a black revolutionary and, by definition, that makes me part of the Black Liberation Army. The pigs have used their newspapers and TV's to paint the Black Liberation Army to be vicious, brutal mad dog criminals. They have called us gangsters and gun molls and have compared us to such characters as John Dillinger and Ma Barker. It should be clear, it must be clear to anyone who can think, see or hear, that we are the victims. The victims are not the criminals.

It should also be clear to us by now who the real criminals are. Nixon and his crime partners have murdered hundreds of thousands of Third World brothers and sisters in Vietnam, Cambodia, Laos, Mozambique, Angola and South Africa. As was proven by Watergate, the top law enforcement officials in this country are a lying bunch of criminals. The president, two attorney generals, the head of the FBI, the head of the CIA, and half the White House staff have been implicated in the Watergate crimes.

THEY CALL US MURDERERS, but we did not murder over 250 unarmed black men, women and children, and wound thousands of others in the riots they provoked during the Sixties. The rulers of this country have always considered their property more important than our lives. They call us murderers, but we were not responsible for the more than 6,000 black people lynched by white racists. They call us murderers, but we were not responsible for the twenty-eight brother inmates and the nine hostages murdered at Attica.[1] They call us murderers, but we did not murder and wound over thirty unarmed black students in the Orangeburg massacre.[2] We did not shoot down and murder unarmed black students at Jackson State or Southern State either.[3]

They call us murderers but we did not murder Martin Luther King, Emmett Till, Medger Evers, Malcolm X,[4] George Jackson, Nat Turner, James Chaney and countless other black Freedom Fighters. We did not bomb four black little girls in a Sunday school.[5] We did not murder, by shooting in the back, sixteen-year-old Rita Lloyd, eleven-year-old Rickie Bodden, or ten-year-old Clifford Glover.[6]

They call us murderers, but we did not control or enforce a system of racism and oppression that systematically murders black and Third World people. Although black people supposedly comprise about fifteen percent of the total amerikkkan population, at least sixty percent of murder victims are black. For every pig that is killed in the so-called line of duty there are at least fifty black people murdered by police.

Black life expectancy is much lower than white and they do their best to kill us before we are born. We are burned alive in fire-trap tenements. Our brothers and sisters O.D. daily from heroin and methadone. Our babies die from lead poisoning. Millions of black people have died as a result of indecent medical care. This is murder. But they have the gall to call us murders.

THEY CALL US KIDNAPPERS, yet Brother Clark Squire [Sundiata Acoli] (who is accused along with me, of murdering a New Jersey state trooper), was kidnapped on April 2, 1969, from our black community and held on $100,000 ransom in the New York Panther 21 conspiracy case. He was acquitted on May 13, 1971 along with all the others of all 156 counts of conspiracy by a jury that took less than two hours to deliberate. Brother Squire was innocent. Yet he was kidnapped from his community and family. Over two years of his life were stolen, but they call us kidnappers. They call us kidnappers, but we did not kidnap the thousands of Brothers and Sisters held captive in amerikkka's concentration camps. Most of the prison population in this country are black and Third World people who can afford neither bail nor lawyers.

They call us thieves and bandits. They say we steal. But it was not us who stole millions of black people from the continent of Africa. We were robbed of our language, of our gods, of our culture, of our human dignity, of our labor and of our lives. They call us thieves yet it is not us who rip off billions of dollars every year through tax evasions, illegal price fixing, embezzlement, consumer fraud, bribes, kickbacks and swindles. They call us bandits, yet every time most black people pick up our paychecks we are being robbed. Every time we walk into a store in our neighborhood we are being held up. And every time we pay our rent the landlord sticks a gun in our ribs.

They call us thieves, but we did not rob and murder millions of Indians by ripping off their homeland, then call ourselves pioneers. They call us bandits, but it is not us who are robbing Africa, Asia and Latin America of their natural resources and freedom while the people are sick and starving. The rulers of this country and their flunkies have committed some of the most brutal, vicious crimes in history. They are the bandits. They are the murderers. And they should be treated as such. These maniacs are not fit to judge me, Clark Squire, or any other black person on trial in amerikkka. Black people should, and, inevitably must, determine our destinies.

EVERY REVOLUTION IN HISTORY has been accomplished by actions, although words are necessary. We must create shields that protect us and spears that penetrate our enemies. Black people must learn how to struggle by struggling. We must learn much by our mistakes.

I want to apologize to you, my black brothers and sisters, for being on the New Jersey Turnpike. I should have known better. The Turnpike is a check point where black people are stopped, searched, harassed, and assaulted. Revolutionaries must never be in too much of a hurry or make careless decisions. He who runs when the sun is sleeping will stumble many times.

Every time a black freedom fighter is murdered or captured the pigs try to create the impression that they have squashed the movement, destroyed our forces and put down the Black Revolution. The pigs also try to give the impression that 5 or 10 guerillas are responsible for every revolutionary action carried out in amerikkka. That is nonsense. That is absurd. Black revolutionaries do not drop from the moon. We are created by our conditions, shaped by our oppression. We are being manufactured in droves in ghetto streets; places like Attica, San Quentin, Bedford Hills, Leavenworth and Sing Sing. They are turning out thousands of us. Many jobless black veterans and welfare mothers are joining our ranks. Brothers and sisters from all walks of life who are tired of suffering passively make up the Black Liberation Army.

There is and always will be, until every black man, woman and child is free, a Black Liberation Army. The main function of the Black Liberation Army at this time is to create good examples to struggle for black freedom and to prepare for the future. We must defend ourselves and let no one disrespect us. We must gain our liberation by any means necessary.

It is our duty to fight for our freedom.
It is our duty to win.
We must love each other and support each other. We have nothing to lose but our chains!

IN THE SPIRIT OF:
RONALD CARTER
WILLIAM CHRISTMAS
MARK CLARK
MARK ESSEX
FRANK HEAVY FIELDS
WOODY CHANGA

OLUGBALA GREEN
FRED HAMPTON
LIL' BOBBY HUTTON
GEORGE JACKSON
JONATHAN JACKSON
JAMES MCLAIN
HAROLD RUSSELL
ZAYD MALIK SHAKUR
ANTHONY KIMU
OLUGBALA WHITE

NOTES

Originally published as JoAnne Chesimard, "To My People," in *The Black Scholar* vol. 5, no. 2 (October 1973): 16–27. An alternative version of this July Fourth statement appears in Evelyn Williams, *Inadmissible Evidence: The Story of the African-American Trial Lawyer Who Defended the Black Liberation Army* (Brooklyn, N.Y.: Lawrence Hill Books, 1993), 86–88. The memoir's dedication reads in part: "to all political prisoners, wherever they are confined within the mirrored noon of the dead."

1. Before Governor Nelson Rockefeller ordered the retaking of Attica Prison on September 13, 1971, three prisoners and one guard had been killed in the initial uprising. In the retaking of the prison, the National Guard killed ten guards and twenty-nine prisoners. See *Eyes on the Prize*, Pt. II, *A NATION of Law?* (Boston: Blacksides Production).

2. *Editor's note:* A February 8, 1968, demonstration in Orangeburg, South Carolina, "aimed against the exclusion of Blacks from a local bowling alley" resulted in the police murders of three black students: Henry Smith (age twenty), Delano Middleton (age seventeen), and Samuel Hammond (age nineteen). Along with these deaths, twenty-seven other students were shot by "wildly firing" police. The patrolmen were eventually pardoned for their acts. Jack Nelson and Jack Bass, *The Orangeburg Massacre* (New York: World Publishing, 1970).

3. *Editor's note:* On May 14–15, 1970, Jackson State (Mississippi) students protested racial intimidation and harassment by white motorists traveling on Lynch Street, a thoroughfare running through the campus, as well as the May 4, 1970, Kent State tragedy (in which four protestors were shot and killed by National Guard soldiers). When several white motorists reported that students had thrown rocks at them as they passed, police arrived, armed with carbines, submachine guns, shotguns, service revolvers, and some personal weapons. Although witnesses later attributed the rock throwing to nonstudents, the police opened fire just after midnight on May 15. Police shot twelve Jackson State students and killed Phillip Lafayette Gibbs (age twenty-one) and seventeen-year-old high school student James Earl Green. See Tim Spofford, *Lynch Street: The May 1970 Slayings at Jackson State College* (Kent, Ohio: Kent State, 1988).

4. *Editor's note:* Members of the Nation of Islam were arrested and convicted for their roles in the shooting of Malcolm X El Malik Shabazz in the Audubon Ballroom in Harlem, New York, in 1965. Allegations remain that the federal government (through FBI COINTELPRO) or the New York Police Department was complicit in the assassination.

5. *Editor's note:* Carole Robertson (age fourteen), Cynthia Wesley (age fourteen), Addie Mae Collins (age fourteen), and Denise McNair (age eleven) died in the racially motivated bombing of the Sixteenth Street Baptist Church in Birmingham, Alabama, on September 15, 1963. See Joy James, ed., *The Angela Y. Davis Reader* (Malden, Mass.: Blackwell, 1998), 4. Bryon Beckwith was convicted of and incarcerated for the murders in 2000.

6. *Editor's note:* On January 27, 1973, sixteen-year-old Rita Lloyd was shot and killed by New York City plainclothes patrolman Robert Milano in Brooklyn, N.Y. Police alleged that, while patrolling the area, Milano saw two girls, one of whom (Denise Bethel) was carrying a sawed-off shotgun. Claiming that when he attempted to disarm her, Bethel pointed her gun at him, Milano fired in what police called a "quick defensive reaction," missing Bethel and hitting Lloyd in the chest. Running from the scene, Lloyd collapsed in her home a block away; police claimed the patrolmen were unaware that Lloyd had been shot. Charges were never brought against Milano. See " 'Defensive' Police Shots Kill a Girl, 16." *New York Times*, 28 January 1973, 13.

On August 15, 1972, unarmed eleven-year-old Ricky Bodden was killed by a bullet fired by Officer Francis Ortolando as he and another youngster were "allegedly running from a stolen car." See: "Officer Who Shot Boy Faces Charge," *New York Times*, 27 June 1973, 55. On April 28, 1973, New York Police Officer Thomas Shea shot and killed ten-year-old Clifford Glover and was later acquitted. See Murray Schumach, "Police-Call Tape Played at Trial," *New York Times*, 24 May 1974, 37; Laurie Johnston, "Jury Clears Shea in Killing of Boy," *New York Times*, 13 June 1974, 1.

Chapter Nine

Safiya Bukhari-Alston

Safiya Bukhari-Alston (Bernice Jones) became involved with the Black Panther Party (BPP) in 1969, when she began working at the Panthers' Free Breakfast Program in Harlem. From 1969 to 1971, she served as a section coordinator, selling party newspapers, organizing cell units, and conducting political education classes. In 1971, following the Eldridge Cleaver–Huey P. Newton split,[1] Bukhari-Alston became the head of Information and Communication for the East Coast Black Panther Party, a position she would hold until she went underground in 1973.[2]

On the morning of December 27, 1973, Bukhari-Alston was arrested with Michael Maurice Alston, Neil O. Thompson, and Harold Simmons as they allegedly attempted to free six Black Liberation Army members from "the Tombs," the Manhattan House of Detention for Men. (Among those held at the Tombs were Francisco and Gabriel Torres, Jalil Muntaqim [Anthony Bottom], Herman Bell, and Henry Brown.) The four were detained by police next to an open manhole two blocks from the Detention Center, which the police alleged they were using to gain access to the prison. According to the *New York Times*, "all were charged with burglary, possession of burglars' tools (a screwdriver, the iron bar and the rope ladder) and criminal tampering (lifting the manhole cover)."[3] Bukhari-Alston recalls: "The only thing they could charge us with was third degree burglary on a sewer, which was laughed out of court."[4] Although there was a paucity of evidence against the defendants, the media sensationalized the arrests; using phrases like "Great Tombs Escape Fails at the Sewer,"[5] it emphasized the connections of those arrested to the BPP and to other alleged criminal charges. Nevertheless, charges were dismissed on January 22, 1974, for lack of evidence. In spite of (or because of) the acquittal, the police department issued a $10,000 reward for Bukhari-Alston, based on her membership in the Black Liberation Army (BLA), and failure to appear for trial, warranting that she be shot on sight. Bukhari-Alston went underground as unit coordinator of the Amistad Collective of the BLA.[6]

Bukhari-Alston was captured on January 25, 1975, in Norfolk, Virginia, after a shooting that left her fellow BLA members Kombozi Amistad dead, and Masai

Ehehosi shot in the face. Charged with felony murder, attempted robbery, and illegal possession of a weapon, she was convicted in a one-day trial at which she was not present, sentenced to forty years in prison, and sent to the Virginia Correctional Center for Women in Goochland. There, Bukhari-Alston spent her first twenty-one days in maximum-security segregation. She was only released into the general prison community after she threatened to file a lawsuit. Upon release, however, her movement remained largely restricted given her designation as a "security risk."[7]

Refused desperately needed medical attention and surgery by prison doctors, Bukhari-Alston filed suit against the Virginia Correctional Center for Women. Both the initial suit and the appeal were denied, however, on the grounds that "her complaint amount[ed] to a difference of opinion with prison medical personnel" about treatment. Refused medical care, considering herself a citizen of the Republic of New Afrika (RNA) and therefore a prisoner of war, Bukhari-Alston decided to escape on December 31, 1976. Recaptured on February 27, 1977, she was returned to the Virginia Correctional Center, and was sentenced to an additional year. By using lack of medical attention as a defense, however, she was able to at least secure outside medical treatment, although by this point she was forced to have a hysterectomy. Upon returning to prison, she served the next three years and seven months in maximum-security segregation and, once again, only secured her release into the general population through a lawsuit. In 1983, she was granted parole.[8]

Currently a legal advocate, Bukhari-Alston is cochair of the Jericho Movement, which does educational support work for political prisoners, and cochair of the New York–based Free Mumia Abu-Jamal Coalition.

REFERENCES

Bukhari, Safiya. "Coming of Age." *Notes from a New Afrikan P.O.W. Journal, Book 7*. New York: Spear & Shield Publications, 1979.
———. "The Death Penalty Is a Politically Repressive Tool." *The Machinery of Death: A Shocking Indictment of Capital Punishment in the United States*. Amnesty International USA, 1995.
———. "Interview with Safiya Bukhari-Alston." New York City, 27 September 1992. *Arm the Spirit*, 8 March 1995. burn.ucsd.edu/archives/atsl/1995.Mar/0017.html
———. "On the Question of Sexism within the Black Panther Party." *The Black Panther* I(2), 4 (Fall/Winter 1993). www.hartford-hwp.com/archives/45a/014.html
Jones, Charles E., and Judson L. Jeffries. "'Don't Believe the Hype': Debunking the Panther Mythology." In *The Black Panther Party [Reconsidered]*, ed. Charles E. Jones. Baltimore: Black Classic Press, 1998.
Montgomery, Paul L. "4 Seized Near Manhole in Alleged Plot to Free Black Army Friends in Tombs." *New York Times*, 28 December 1973, 1.
"Police Break Gang Plot?" *Tri-State Defender*, 5 January 1974, V.22; N.52, 2.
Safiya Asya Bukhari, a/k/a Bernice Jones v Virginia Correctional Center for Women. No. 75-1809,

United States Court of Appeals for the Fourth Circuit, 530 F.2d 967; 1975 U.S. App. LEXIS 11791. Submitted October 28, 1975; Nov. 24, 1975.

"3 in an Alleged Plot to Free 6 at Tombs Released by Judge." *New York Times*, 24 January 1974, 41 col. 4.

Umoja, Akinyele Omowale. "Set Our Warriors Free: The Legacy of the Black Panther Party and Political Prisoners." In *The Black Panther Party [Reconsidered]*, edited by Charles E. Jones. Baltimore: Black Classic Press, 1998.

United States of America v Bernice Jones, a/k/a Safiya Asya Bukhari, a/k/a/ Beverly Dunlap. United States Court of Appeals for the Fourth Circuit, 529 F.2d 518; 1976 U.S. App. LEXIS 12725. Submitted December 30, 1975; February 23, 1976.

NOTES

Research and draft for this biography were provided by Nicole Kief.

1. In the early 1970s, tensions within the Black Panther Party grew as Huey P. Newton and Eldridge Cleaver took increasingly divergent stances on the role of the party, both tactically and ideologically. These tensions played out as a broader conflict between New York and Oakland chapters of the BPP, and escalated when Newton expelled several prominent party members in 1971. The conflict turned deadly when two members, Robert Webb and Samuel Napier, were murdered, and several others left the party as a result. See: Ollie A. Johnson, "Explaining the Demise of the Black Panther Party: The Role of Internal Factors," in *The Black Panther Party [Reconsidered]*, ed. Charles E. Jones (Baltimore: Black Classic Press, 1998), 400–2.

2. "Interview with Safiya Bukhari-Alston."

3. "4 Seized Near Manhole in Alleged Plot to Free Black Army Friends in Tombs," *New York Times*, 28 December 1973.

4. "Interview with Safiya Bukhari-Alston."

5. "Interview with Safiya Bukhari-Alston."

6. "Interview with Safiya Bukhari-Alston"; "4 Seized Near Manhole in Alleged Plot to Free Black Army Friends in Tombs"; "Police Break Gang Plot?" *Tri-State Defender*, 5 January 1974; "3 in an Alleged Plot to Free 6 at Tombs Released by Judge," *New York Times*, 24 January 1974.

7. "Interview with Safiya Bukhari-Alston"; Akinyele Omowale Umoja, "Set Our Warriors Free: The Legacy of the Black Panther Party and Political Prisoners," in *The Black Panther Party [Reconsidered]*, 428–29; Safiya Bukhari-Alston, "Coming of Age," *Notes from a New Afrikan P.O.W. Journal*, Book 7 (New York: Spear & Shield Publications, 1979); *United States of America v Bernice Jones*, December 30, 1975.

8. "Interview with Safiya Bukhari-Alston"; *Safiya Asya Bukhari v Virginia Correctional Center for Women*, October 28, 1975.

Coming of Age: A Black Revolutionary
1979

Greek mythology tells the story of Minos, ruler of the city of Knossus. Minos has a great labyrinth (maze) in which he keeps the Minotaur, a monster half man and half bull, whose victims were boys and girls who would make it to the center of the maze only to be killed when they came face to face with the Minotaur. If an intended victim chanced to survive the encounter with the Minotaur, they perished trying to find their way out of the many intricate passages. Finally, Theseus of Athens, with the help of Ariadne, Minos's daughter, enters the labyrinth, slays the beast and finds his way out by following the thread he had unwound as he entered.

The maturation process is full of obstacles and entanglements for anyone, but for a Black woman in America it has all the markings of the Minotaur's Maze. I had to say that, even though nothing as spectacular takes place in the maturation process of the average Black woman—it didn't happen to me—but the day-to-day struggle for survival and growth reaps the same reward in the end in ten thousand different ways. The trick is to learn from each defeat and become stronger and more determined . . . think and begin to develop the necessary strategies to insure the annihilation of the beast. . . .

I am one of a family of ten children. My parents were strict and religious, but proud and independent. One of the strongest influences of my childhood was my mother constantly telling us to hold our heads up and be proud because we were just as good or better than anyone else, and to stand up and fight for what you believe to be right.

There was a lot of competition in my family. Had to be with ten children (all two years apart) growing up, each trying to live up to the other or be better. We were determined not to be caught up in the rut of the ghetto. We were going to get out . . . so each of us worked on our separate goals—ten *individuals*—one family, in our separate world.

We believed that with the right education we could "make it"—so that's the route we took searching for the "American Dream." I was going to be a doctor.

In my second year of college I pledged a sorority—it was here that the rose colored glasses were cracked and rays of reality were allowed to filter in.

The sorority had decided to help "disadvantaged" children as one of our projects for the year and we were trying to decide what country to work with when one of the Sisters suggested that we work in the ghettos of New York. Personally, I'd never even thought of people in the United States being disadvantaged, but only too lazy to work and "make it." I was in for one of the biggest rude awakenings of my life.

A few of us were sent to Harlem to investigate the situation. We talked to people on the street, in the welfare centers, from door to door, and watched them work and play, loiter on the corners and in the bars. What we came away with was a story of humiliation, degradation, deprivation and waste that started in infancy and lasted until death . . . in too many cases, at an early age.

Even at this point, I didn't see this as affecting me personally, only as a sorority project . . . sort of a tourist who takes pity on the less fortunate.

The sorority decided to do what we could to help the children. The Black Panther Party had a Free Breakfast Program to feed the children going on. I had a daughter of my own at this point and decided that I would put my energies into this.

I couldn't get into the politics of the Black Panther Party, but I could volunteer to feed some hungry children; you see, children deserve a good start and you have to feed them for them to live to learn. It's hard to think of reading and arithmetic when your stomach's growling.

I'm not trying to explain the logic of the Free Breakfast Program for children, but to show how I had to be slowly awakened to the reality of life and shown the interconnection of things.

Every morning, at 5:00 my daughter and I would get ready and go to the Center where I was working on the Breakfast Program—cook and serve breakfast, sometimes talk to the children about problems they were encountering and sometimes help them with their homework. Everything was going along smoothly until the number of children coming began to fall off. Finally, I began to question the children and found out that the police had been telling the parents in the neighborhood not to send their children to the Program because we were "feeding them poisoned food."

It's one thing to hear about underhanded things the police do—you can ignore it then—but it's totally different to experience it for yourself—you either lie to yourself or face it. I chose to face it and find out why the police felt it was so important to keep Black children from being fed that they told lies. I went back to the Black Panther Party and started attending some of their Community Political Education Classes.

FIRST ENCOUNTER WITH THE POLICE

It wasn't long after that when I was forced to make a decision about what direction I was going in politically. I was on 42nd Street with a friend when we noticed a crowd gathered on the corner. In the center of the crowd was a Panther with some newspapers under his arm. Two police officers were also there. I listened to see what was going on. The police was telling the Panther he couldn't sell newspapers on the corner and he was insisting that he could. Without a thought, I told the police that the Brother had a *constitutional right* to disseminate political literature anywhere, at which point, the police asked for my identification and arrested the Sister and myself, along with the Brother who was selling the papers.

I had never been arrested before and I was naive enough to believe that all you had to do was be honest and everything would work out all right. I was wrong again. As soon as the police got us into the back seat of their car and pulled away from the crowd the bestiality began to show. My friend went to say something and one of the police officers threatened to ram his nightstick up her if she opened her mouth again, and ran on in a monologue about Black people. I listened and got angry. . . .

At the 14th Precinct they separated us to search us. They made us strip. After the policewoman had searched me, I remember one of the male officers telling her to make sure she washed her hand so she wouldn't catch anything.

That night, I went to see my mother, explained to her about the bust and about a decision I'd made. Momma and Daddy were in the kitchen when I got there—Daddy sitting at the table and Momma cooking. I remember telling them about the bust and them saying nothing. Then I told them about how the police had acted and them still saying nothing. Then I told them that I couldn't sit still and allow the police to get away with that. I had to stand up for my rights as a human being. I remember my mother saying, ". . . if you think it's right, then do it." I went back to Harlem and joined the Black Panther Party.

I spent the next year working with welfare mothers, Liberation Schools, talking to students, learning the reality of life in the ghettos of America and re-evaluating a lot of the things I had been taught about the "land of the free and the home of the brave."

It was about this time that I quit school and went to look for a full-time job. I had education and skills but there was always something wrong. It didn't dawn on me what it was until I went to ITT and applied for a job as a receptionist-clerk and they told me I was *over qualified.* I ended up working for my friend's mother in her beauty parlor and spent all of my spare time with the Party.

By the summer of 1970 I was a full time Party member and my daughter was staying with my mother. I was teaching some of the Political Education classes at the Party office and had established a Liberation School in my Section of the community. I had listened to the elderly while they told me how they couldn't survive off their miserly social security checks—not pay rent and eat, too—so they pay their rent and eat from the dog food section of the supermarket or the garbage cans. I had listened to the middle-aged mother as she told of being evicted from her home and sleeping on a subway with her children because the welfare refused to give her help unless she signed over all the property she had, and out of desperation, fraudulently received welfare. I had watched while a mother prostituted her body to put food in the mouth of her child and another mother, mentally broken under the pressure, prostituted her eight-year-old child. I had seen enough of the ravages of dope, alcohol and despair to know that a change had to be made so the world could be a better place for my child to live in.

My mother had successfully kept me ignorant of the reality of the plight of Black people in America—now I had learned it for myself—but I was still to learn a harsher lesson: The Plight of the Slave Who Dares to Rebel.

TURBULENT TIMES

The year 1971 saw many turbulent times in the Black Panther Party and changes in my life. I met and worked with many people who were to teach me and guide me: Michael (Cetewayo) Tabor of the Panther 21; Albert (Nuh) Washington, and "Lost One" who was responsible for my initial political education, Robert Webb. Cet taught me to deal principledly; Nuh taught me compassion, and Robert taught me to be firm in my convictions.

When the split went down in the Black Panther Party I was left in a position of Communications and Information Officer of the East Coast Black Panther Party. It wasn't until much later that I was to find out how vulnerable that position was.

Many of the members of the Party went underground to work with the Black Liberation Army (BLA). I was among those elected to remain aboveground and supply necessary support. The murders of youths such as Clifford Glover, Tyrone Guyton, etc., by police, and retaliation by the BLA with the assassinations of police officers Piagentini and Jones and Rocco and Laurie, made the powers that be frantic.[1] They pulled out the stops in their campaign to rid the streets of rebellious slaves.

By the spring of 1973, Comrades Assata Shakur and Sundiata Acoli were captured, along with Nuh and Jalil (Anthony Bottom) and Twyman Meyers[2] was on the FBI's Most Wanted List, and I was still traveling back and forth across the country trying to build necessary support mechanisms.

In 1972 I recognized the need for something other than myself to depend on. You see, in less than two years I'd aged to the point where I realized that nothing is permanent or secure in a world where it's who you know and what you have that counts. I'd seen friends and loved ones either killed or thrown in prison and associates that I'd once thought would never go back, turn states or go back into the woodwork. Nuh turned me on to Islam, which gave me a new security, sense of purpose and dignity.

By 1973 I'd begun to receive a lot of flak from the police because of what they "suspected" I might be doing. Actually it was because I didn't have a record, they couldn't catch me doing anything and I continued to actively and vocally support the BLA members . . . also my homework had been done so well in the community that the community's support was there also.

CAPTURE

On January 25, 1975 myself and some other members of the Amistad Collective of the BLA went into the country in Virginia to practice night firing. We were to leave

Virginia that night on our way to Jackson, Mississippi because I wanted to be there on Sunday to see someone. We decided to stop by a store before we went back to the crib we were staying at so we could pick up some cold cuts to make sandwiches with so we wouldn't have to stop at any roadside restaurants on the way down. We drove around looking for an open store. When we came to one I told the Brothers to wait in the car and I'd go in the store and be right back.

I entered the store, went past the registers, down an aisle to the meat counter and started checking them for all-beef products. I heard the door opening and looked up to see two of the brothers coming in—didn't give it a thought—went back to what I was doing when out of the corner of my left eye I saw a rifle pointed toward the door, in the manager's hand. I quickly got into an aisle just as the firing started. Up to this point I had heard no words spoken. With the first lull in shooting, Kombozi [Amistad] (one of my bodyguards and also a member of the Amistad Collective) came down the aisle towards me. He was wearing a full-length army coat. It was completely buttoned. As he came toward me he told me he was shot. I didn't believe him, at first, because I saw no blood and his weapon wasn't drawn. Then, he insisted again so I told him to lie down on the floor and I'd take care of it.

Masai [Ehehosi] (my co-defendant) had apparently made it back out the door when the firing started because just then he came back to the door and tried to draw the fire so we could get out. I saw him get shot in the face and stumble backwards out the door. I looked around for a way out and realized there was none. I elected to play it low-key in order to try and get help for Kombozi as soon as possible. I was to learn that the effort was wasted. The manager of the store and his son, Paul Green, Sr. and Jr. stomped Kombozi to death in front of my eyes. Later, when I attempted to press counter-charges of murder against them, the Commonwealth attorney called it "justifiable" homicide.

Five minutes after the shoot-out went down the FBI was on the scene. The next morning they held a press conference saying I was notorious, dangerous, etc., and known to law enforcement agencies nationwide—and my bail was set at one million dollars on each count. I had five counts.

TRIAL AND IMPRISONMENT

On April 16, 1975, after a trial that lasted one day, we were sentenced to forty years, and that night I arrived here at the Virginia Correctional Center for Women in Goochland.

Directly following my arrival I was placed in the Maximum Security building and there I stayed until, after being threatened with court action, they released me to general population. The day after my release to general population I was told that the first iota of trouble that I caused I would be placed back in the Maximum Security building and there I would stay.

At that point, and for the next two years, my emphasis was on getting some medical care for myself and the other women here and educational programs and activities, the priority being on medical care for myself. Inside the prison I was denied it (the general feeling was they couldn't chance hospitalization for fear I'd escape so rather than chancing my escape they preferred to take a chance on my life). In the courts they said they saw no evidence of inadequate medical care, but rather, a difference of opinion on treatment between me and the prison doctor.

The "medical treatment" for women prisoners here in Virginia has got to be an all-time low, when you got to put your life in the hands of a "doctor" who examines a woman who has her right ovary removed and tells her there's tenderness in her right ovary; or when this same "doctor" examines a woman who has been in prison for six months and tells her she's six weeks pregnant and there's nothing wrong with her and she later finds her baby has died and mortified inside of her; or when he tells you you're not pregnant and three months later you give birth to a seven pound baby boy; not to mention prescribing Maalox for a sore throat and diagnosing a sore throat that turns out to be cancer.

In December of 1976 I started hemorrhaging and went to the clinic for help. No help of any consequence was given, so I escaped. Two months later I was recaptured. While on escape a doctor told me that I could either endure the situation, take painkillers, or have surgery. I decided to use the lack of medical care as my defense for the escape and by doing so do two things: (1) expose the level of medical care at the prison, and (2) put pressure on them to give me the care I needed.

I finally got to the hospital in June of 1978. By that time it was too late, I was so messed up inside that everything but one ovary had to go. Because of the negligence of the "doctor" and the lack of feeling of the prison officials, they didn't give a damn, I was forced to have a hysterectomy.

When they brought me back to this prison in March of 1977, because of the escape, they placed me in Cell 5 on the segregation end of the Maximum Security building—the same room they placed me in on April 16, 1975. To date, I'm still in that cell, allegedly because of my escape, but in actuality because of my politics.

How do I know? Because since my being returned to this institution on March 24, 1977 other women have escaped and been brought back and have been released to general population—and yesterday (after twenty-two months) my co-defendant on the escape charge was okayed for release to general population. I was denied.

Despite all of the emotional and physical setbacks I've experienced, I've learned a lot. I've watched the oppressor play that same old game on Black people they've been playing for centuries—divide and conquer. Black women break under pressure and sell their men down the river and then the oppressor separates the women from their children. In two strokes the state does more damage than 30 years in prison could have done if the women had supported the men.

And now, more than ever before, Black women—New Afrikan women—have developed a mercenary outlook on life. They are not about family, community and us as a people anymore. They're about looking good, having fun and "making it." Women's liberation is what they're talking about, failing to grasp the realization that true women's liberation for Black women will only come about with the liberation of Black people as a whole, so that for the first time since our forefathers were snatched from the Afrikan continent and brought to America as slave labor, we can be a family, and from that family build a community and a Nation.

The powers that be were totally disconcerted when Black mothers, wives, daughters and Black women in general stood by and, in a lot of cases, fought beside their men when they were captured, shot or victimized by the police and other agents of the government. They were frightened of the potential to wreak havoc that Black women represented when Black women began to enter into the prisons and jails in efforts to liberate their men. They were spurred into action when they were confronted with the fact that Black women were educating their children from the cradle up about who the real enemies of Black people are and what must be done to eliminate this ever present threat to the lives of Black people.

During the last four years of my incarceration I've watched and didn't speak because I didn't want to chance alienating the "left" as Black men and Black women have fooled themselves into believing that we were "making progress" because (1) Patricia Harris, a Black woman, is part of the U.S. president's cabinet, and (2) Andrew Young is the Ambassador to the U.N.—failing to realize that it's all politics—American style. And, twenty women of all races are working together for Women's Liberation. There is no real progress being made. As a matter of fact, one of [former president Jimmy] Carter's best friends, Vernon Jordan, head of the Urban League, had to concede in his annual economic review *The State of Black America, 1979,* that the "income gap between Blacks and whites is actually widening."[3]

The sacrifices Black women have made in search of Black womanhood, like the sacrifices made by the people of Knossus in its efforts to slay the Minotaur, have been many, harsh and cruel—but We too can slay the beast (in our case American racism, capitalism and sexism) and out of the ashes build a free and independent Black Nation in which We can take our rightful place as Women, Wives and Mothers, knowing our children will live to be men and women, our men will be allowed to recognize their manhood—support and defend their families with dignity.

TOGETHER BUILDING A FUTURE FOR OURSELVES!
Build to Win!

COMING OF AGE: AN UPDATE [JANUARY 18, 1980]

It's two years since I wrote the original article . . . lots of things have happened . . . Assata Shakur was liberated; Imari Obadele[4] was released . . . the Klu Klux Klan regrouped and revamped;[5] sixteen Black children are missing and presumed to be dead in Atlanta;[6] eight Black men murdered in Buffalo;[7] pregnant Black women shot in Chattanooga;[8] Ronald Reagan will take office in two days.[9]

It's two months since I was released from the Maximum Security Building (after spending a total of three years and seven months) . . . had to go to court to do it . . . it too was an eye opening experience . . . they said the reason they were keeping me housed in that building was because I was a "threat to the security of the free world."

What can I say? It seems that the political scene in America has come full circle and Black people are once again the scapegoats for everything that goes wrong in white America. They no longer feel the need to pacify us with poverty programs and token jobs.

Sitting in a Maximum Security cell for three years and seven months afforded me an opportunity to reflect upon my life and the lessons I was forced to learn . . . but now the learning process is over . . . it is time to put what I've learned into practice . . . freedom will only be won by the sweat of our brows.

AFTERWORD 12 YEARS LATER

Yesterday, October 21, 1994, we buried a close comrade, friend and brother—Breeze Barrow. Less than two weeks ago, we buried another close comrade, friend, mentor and father figure—Nathaniel Shanks. Both of these brothers were strong Panthers and had been on the streets holding the line, maintaining the stand while we had been locked down in the dungeons of this country.

Reverberating through my mind for years has been the incantation of Che Guevara, "Wherever death may surprise us, it will be welcome as long as this our battle cry reach some receptive ear and new hands reach out to intone our funeral dirge with the staccato of machinegun fire and new cries of battle and victory." Now, today, this minute, this hour (as Malcolm would say) I've come to realize that picking up the gun was/is the easy part. The hard part is the day to day organizing, educating and showing the people by example what needs to be done to create a new society. The hard painstaking work of changing ourselves into new beings, of loving ourselves and our people and working with them daily to create a new reality . . . this is the first revolution, that internal revolution.

I'm coming to understand what they meant when they sang the words, "The race is not given to the swift, nor is it given to the strong, but to him that endures to the end," and what was meant by the fable of the "hare and the tortoise." Some people declare themselves to be revolutionaries, members of one organization or another i.e., I was one of the first Panthers, or I used to be a Panther . . . and only come out when there's some major celebration where Panthers are on display . . . and live off of their former glory, not understanding that it's not about what you used to be, but what are you doing now. They ran a quick race, utilizing all for the moment and grew tired and gave up. It may take a little longer to do it the hard way, slow and methodical, building a movement step-by-step and block-by-block, but doing it this way is designed to build a strong foundation that will withstand the test of time and the attack of the enemy.

If we truly are to create a new society, we must build a strong foundation. If we truly are to have a new society, we must develop a mechanism to struggle from one generation to the next. If we truly are to maintain our new society after we have won the battle and claimed the victory, we must instill into the hearts and minds of our children, our people, ourselves this ability to struggle on all fronts, internally and externally, laying a foundation built upon a love for ourselves and a knowledge of the sacrifices that went before and all we have endured.

There is much to be done to achieve this. There is a long road ahead of us. Let's do it.

NOTES

Originally published in *Notes from a New Afrikan P.O.W. Journal*, Book 7. Spear & Shield Publications.

1. *Editor's note:* On April 28, 1973, police officer Thomas Shea, searching for "two black males in their early 20's," shot and killed ten-year-old Clifford Glover in a South Jamaica, N.Y., lot after pursuing Glover and his fifty-year-old stepfather, Add Armstead. Shea was later acquitted. Murray Schumach, "Police-Call Tape Played at Trial," *New York Times*, 24 May 1974, 37; Laurie Johnston, "Jury Clears Shea in Killing of Boy," *New York Times*, 13 June 1974, 1.

Fourteen-year-old Tyrone Guyton was killed on November 1, 1973, by police from the Emeryville, Calif., Police Department in what many black activists and community members regarded as racist murder. In protest against his murder and the murder of several other black youths by police, including Clifford Glover, Claude Reese, Alberto Terrones, and Derrick Browne, the Jonathan Jackson/Sam Melville Unit of the New World Liberation Front (Symbionese Liberation Army) bombed the Emeryville Police Station on November 13. "Symbionese Liberation Army Communiqué #1," *Claycheck* www.claykeck.com/patty/docs/comm1.htm; "Communiqué Issued by the Symbionese Liberation Army (under the name 'New World Liberation Front') following the bombing of the Emeryville Police Station on August 13, 1975" *Claycheck*, www.claykeck.com/patty/docs/comm813.htm.

New York Police Officers Joseph A. Piagentini and Waverly M. Jones were murdered in Harlem on May 21, 1971. While the legitimacy of the evidence in the prosecution's case was questionable, Black Liberation Army members Jalil Abdul Muntaqim (Anthony Bottom), Herman Bell, and Albert "Nuh" Washington were convicted of the murders. Muntaqim was denied parole in 2002, and Bell is up for parole in 2004; Albert "Nuh" Washington died of liver cancer in April of 2000 while still incarcerated in New York. "New York State Task Force on Political Prisoners: Clemency Petition."

New York Police officers Rocco Laurie and Gregory Foster were murdered on January 27, 1972. While no witness could confidently identify the killer(s), members of the Black Liberation Army were accused of the murders. See: Gerald C. Fraser, "4 at Murder Site Testify at Trial," *New York Times*, 30 January 1974, 21; Associated Press, "Murder Witness Recants on Identity," *New York Times*, 31 January 1974, 37.

2. *Editor's note:* Twyman Ford Meyers, twenty-three-year-old Black Liberation Army member, was killed in a shootout with the FBI and New York Police Department officers on November 14, 1973. See: John T. McQuiston, "Fugitive Black Militant Is Killed in Bronx Shootout with Police," *New York Times,* 15 November 1973, 93.

3. *Editor's note:* Vernon Jordan, *The State of Black America* (New York: National Urban League, 1979).

4. *Editor's note:* Imari Obadele, former president of the Republic of New Afrika, was accused of "encouraging" the August 18, 1971, murder of a Mississippi police officer at the organization's headquarters and charged with the murder, despite the release, on grounds of self-defense, of others accused. See Associated Press, "Black Convicted in Police Slaying," *New York Times,* 7 May 1972; Associated Press, "4 Black Separatists Freed, Leader Is Held for Inquiry," *New York Times,* 12 October 1971, 18.

5. *Editor's note:* In the late 1970s and early 1980s, the Ku Klux Klan witnessed a resurgence in visibility and membership in the United States and Canada. The Anti-Defamation League of B'nai B'rith estimated that in 1980, the Klan boasted 10,000 members and 100,000 "sympathizers" in twenty-two states, representing the largest increase in membership in ten years. A Justice Department study during the same year warned that the "Invisible Empire, Knights of the Ku Klux Klan," a faction headed by Bill Wilkinson, posed a serious threat because of its use of violence. See "US Study Urges Agencies to Cooperate against Klan," *New York Times,* 24 November 1980, A19; "Ku Klux Klan Is Seeking New Members in Toronto," *New York Times,* 30 June 1980, A8.

6. *Editor's note:* Between August 1979 and January 1981, sixteen black children, two girls and fourteen boys, disappeared from their homes in and around Atlanta; several of the bodies were found suffocated, bludgeoned, shot, or strangled. Police reported that they were "baffled by the absence of an apparent motive for the slayings." See "Hundreds Search in Atlanta after the Discovery of Skeletons," *New York Times,* 11 January 1981, 20.

7. *Editor's note:* On September 22–24, 1980, four African American men were shot in the head in Buffalo. On October 8 and 9 of the same year, two black Buffalo taxi drivers were murdered and found with their hearts cut out. On December 29 and 30, two more black men were fatally stabbed in Buffalo and Rochester respectively. In addition, three African Americans and one Latino were stabbed to death in New York City, an incident police suspected to be linked to at least some of the Buffalo-area murders. Although Joseph Christopher, a white private in the U.S. Army, was convicted of three of the Buffalo shootings, the decision was overturned by the New York State Court of Appeals in 1985. See "Murder Convictions Against '22-Caliber Killer' Overturned," *Los Angeles Times,* 6 July 1985, 11; "Inquiry on Killings Shifted to Georgia," *New York Times,* 26 April 1981, 43.

8. *Editor's note:* Bukhari-Alston likely refers to the killing of thirty-year-old Dorothy Brown, a pregnant black woman, by a white police officer in Jackson, Mississippi, on August 29, 1980. Police contend that, upon receiving a call from neighbors claiming that Brown was drunk and threatening them with a gun, Officer Gary King arrived on the scene and, when himself threatened with Brown's weapon, shot her four times. Witnesses, however, claim that Brown had calmed down prior to King's arrival. On September 6, black and some white members of the community marched in front of City Hall protesting Brown's death and calling for the resignation of Police Chief Ray Pope, accused of covering up numerous incidents of police brutality against African Americans. See "Blacks in Jackson, Miss. Protest Killing of Woman," *New York Times,* 7 September 1980, Z30.

9. *Editor's note:* Ronald Reagan was inaugurated as the fortieth president of the United States on January 20, 1981.

Chapter Ten

Sundiata Acoli

Sundiata Acoli (Clark Squire) was born on January 14, 1937, in Decatur, Texas, and raised in Vernon, Texas. After graduating from Prairie View A&M College of Texas with a degree in mathematics, he worked for the National Aeronautics and Space Administration (NASA) for a period of time and then worked for thirteen years in computer technology in the New York area.

The murder of three civil rights workers, Andrew Goodman, Michael Schwerner, and James Chaney, in Mississippi by Klansmen in 1964 initiated Squire into political activism. This event was intended to intimidate many of the volunteers for the campaign against racial segregation in Mississippi. Squire, though, joined the summer project started by the Student Nonviolent Coordinating Committee (SNCC) and Council of Federated Organizations (COFO) in order to fight racial discrimination. During this "Freedom Summer of 1964" informal schools were created for the literacy and political education of the black community, and the Mississippi Freedom Democratic Party (MFDP), which propelled SNCC activist Fannie Lou Hamer to national prominence, was founded.

Acoli joined the Harlem branch of the newly formed Black Panther Party (BPP) and served as its finance minister. He was arrested on April 2, 1969, in the Panther 21 conspiracy case (see the biography of Dhoruba Bin Wahad). The Panther leaders were eventually acquitted of all charges but extended incarceration prior to and during their trials, and self-exile as fugitives, rendered many incapable of organizing in African American communities.

Due to the extensive targeting of Black Panthers by the FBI's COINTELPRO, Acoli considered the underground a necessity in order for Panthers to escape government and police assaults. The U.S. government considered the liberation movement a terrorist organization. In witness testimony for Sekou Odinga's[1] trial, Acoli argued that "'police pressure' had forced him . . . and others to go 'underground' with their activities . . . [because] a lot of Panthers were getting killed."[2]

On May 2, 1973, Sundiata Acoli, Assata Shakur, and Zayd Malik Shakur were stopped for an alleged traffic violation by state troopers on the New Jersey Turnpike searching for black militants. In the ensuing shootout, in which Panther Zayd Sha-kur and police officer Werner Foerster were killed, and Assata Shakur wounded, Acoli escaped only to be captured two days later. Inconclusive and contradictory ballistics evidence obscures how Trooper Foerster was killed. The two bullets that were found in Foerster's body were revolver bullets rather than those of a pistol, the type of weapon found in the pulled-over vehicle. Considerable controversy, includ-ing allegations of prosecutorial malfeasance, surrounded the trial.[3] Nonetheless, Assata Shakur and Sundiata Acoli were convicted of the murder of Trooper Foerster in separate trials, both with all-white juries. They were each sentenced to life plus thirty years in prison. (Shakur escaped from prison in 1979.)

Acoli was confined in Trenton State Prison, a Management Control Unit (MCU) created for him and other politically associated prisoners. For five years, he lived in an isolation cell smaller than the Society for the Prevention of Cruelty to Animals' standard space requirement for a German shepherd.[4] Suffering from tuberculosis, Acoli was transferred in September of 1979, even though he had no federal charges or sentences, to one of the highest-security prisons in the United States, Marion Control Unit prison, cited by Amnesty International for its human rights abuses.[5] He, as were other political prisoners, was locked down twenty-three hours a day in a stripped cell. Acoli was in Marion for eight years before he was transferred in July 1987 to Leavenworth, Kansas. In the fall of 1992, he was eligible for but denied parole, and the New Jersey Parole Board (his trial took place in New Jersey) ruled, in its twenty-minute hearing, that he would only be eligible again after another twenty years. Acoli was not allowed to attend the parole meeting. He is currently incarcerated in the USP Allenwood in White Deer, Pennsylvania, in the general population. Following September 11, 2001, Sundiata Acoli was placed in solitary confinement and held incommunicado until January 3, 2002.

REFERENCES

Acoli, Sundiata. "A Brief History of the Black Panther Party and Its Place in the Black Liber-ation Movement." Marion Penitentiary. April 2, 1985. Sundiata Acoli Freedom Cam-paign. afrikan.i-dentity.com/sundiata/.

———. "Hands Off Assata!" Statement of Sundiata Acoli for October 5, 1998, Demonstra-tion against H.C.R. 254. Sundiata Acoli Freedom Campaign. afrikan.i-dentity.com/sundiata/.

———. "Unique Problems Associated with the Legal Defense of Political Prisoners and Pris-oners of War." *Southern University Law Review*. Southern University Law Center, 1996.

Churchill, Ward, and Jim Vander Wall. *Agents of Repression: The FBI's Secret Wars against the Black Panther Party and the American Indian Movement*. Boston: South End Press, 1988.

Foner, Philip S., ed. *The Black Panthers Speak*. Philadelphia: Lippincott, 1970.

Hanley, Robert. "At 2 Brink's Trials, Accusations and New Motions." *New York Times*, 23 August 1983, Late City Final Edition.

Kaufman, Michael T. "Seized Woman Called Black Militants' 'Soul'." *New York Times*, 3 May 1973.

Lubasch, Arnold H. "Convicted Killer Defends 'Revolutionary' Acts at U.S. Brink's Trial." *New York Times*, 16 August 1983, Late City Final Edition.

Sullivan, Joseph F. "Gunfight Suspect Caught in New Jersey." *New York Times*, 4 May 1973.

———. "Panther, Trooper Slain in Shoot-Out." *New York Times*, 3 May 1973.

"Sundiata Acoli." *Can't Jail the Spirit: Political Prisoners in the U.S. A Collection of Biographies*. 4th ed. Chicago: Committee to End the Marion Lockdown, 1998.

"Sundiata Acoli: New Afrikan Liberation Fighter." *Revolutionary Worker* #941. January 25, 1998. rwor.org/a/v19/940-49/941/acoli.htm.

Umoja, Akinyele Omowale. "Repression Breeds Resistance: The Black Liberation Army and the Radical Legacy of the Black Panther Party." In *Liberation, Imagination, and the Black Panther Party: A New Look at the Panthers and Their Legacy*, edited by Kathleen Cleaver and George Katsiaficas. New York: Routledge, 2001.

NOTES

Research and draft for this biography were provided by Hana Tauber.

1. Sekou Mgobogi Abdullah Odinga is a New Afrikan Prisoner of War. In 1965, Odinga became a member of the Organization of African American Unity (OAAU, founded by Malcolm X in 1965). After Malcolm X's death, Odinga became involved with the New York chapter of the Black Panther Party. Due to increased police surveillance and repression, Odinga went underground in 1969. Captured in 1981, he was charged with six counts of attempted murder of police officers (during a police chase in which Mtayari Shabaka Sundiata was killed by police) and nine acts of a Racketeer Influenced and Corrupt Organization Act (RICO) indictment. Odinga was sentenced to twenty-five years to life for the attempted murders and twenty years and a $25,000 fine for two counts of the RICO indictment (which addressed the liberation/escape of Assata Shakur and the expropriation of money from an armored truck). He is incarcerated in Marion, Illinois. See *Can't Jail the Spirit: Political Prisoners in the U.S. A Collection of Biographies*, 5th ed. (Chicago: Committee to End the Marion Lockdown, 2002), 142–44.

2. Arnold H. Lubasch, "Convicted Killer Defends 'Revolutionary' Acts at U.S. Brink's Trial," *New York Times*, 16 August 1993.

3. See: Lennox Hinds, foreword to *Assata: An Autobiography* (Chicago: Lawrence Hill Books, 1987); and Evelyn Williams, *Inadmissible Evidence* (Brooklyn: Lawrence Hill Books, 1993).

4. *Can't Jail the Spirit*, 5th edition.

5. See the Amnesty International report on Marion, "Allegations of Ill-treatment in Marion Prison, Illinois, USA," AMR 51/26/87, May 1987.

An Updated History of the New Afrikan Prison Struggle *(Abridged)*

The New Afrikan liberation struggle behind the walls refers to the struggle of Black prisoners, "behind the walls" of U.S. penal institutions, to gain liberation for ourselves, our people, and all oppressed people. We of the New Afrikan Independence Movement spell "Afrikan" with a "k" as an indicator of our cultural identification with the Afrikan continent and because Afrikan linguists originally used "k" to indicate the "c" sound in the English language. We use the term "New Afrikan," instead of Black, to define ourselves as an Afrikan people who have been forcibly transplanted to a new land and formed into a "new Afrikan nation" in North America.

THE BLACK LIBERATION ERA

Black Panthers Usher in the Black Liberation Movement

Midstride the 1960s, on February 21, 1965, Malcolm [X] was assassinated, but his star continued to rise and his seeds fell on fertile soil. The following year, October 1966, in Oakland, California, Huey P. Newton and a handful of armed youths founded the Black Panther Party for Self Defense on principles that Malcolm had preached—and the Black Liberation Movement (BLM) was born.

Subsequently the name was shortened to the Black Panther Party (BPP) and a ten-point program was created which stated:

> We want freedom. We want power to determine the destiny of our Black community.
> We want full employment for our people.
> We want an end to the robbery by the CAPITALIST of our Black community.
> We want decent housing, fit for the shelter of human beings.
> We want education for our people that exposes the true nature of this decadent American society. We want education that teaches us our true history and our role in the present day society.
> We want all Black men to be exempt from military service.
> We want an immediate end to POLICE BRUTALITY and MURDER of Black people.
> We want freedom for all Black men held in federal, state, county and city prisons and jails.
> We want all Black people when brought to trial to be tried in court by a jury of their peer group or people from their black communities, as defined by the Constitution of the United States.

We want land, bread, housing, education, clothing, justice and peace. And as our major political objective, a United Nations-supervised plebiscite to be held throughout the Black colony in which only Black colonial subjects will be allowed to participate, for the purpose of determining the will of Black people as to their national destiny.

The Panthers established numerous programs to serve the Oakland ghetto—free breakfasts for children, free health care, free day-care, and free political education classes. The program that riveted the ghetto's attention was their campaign to "stop police murder and brutality of Blacks." Huey, a community college pre-law student, discovered that it was legal for citizens to openly carry arms in California. With that assurance the Black Panther Party began armed car patrols of the police cruisers that patrolled Oakland's Black colony. When a cruiser stopped to make an arrest, the Panther car stopped. They fanned out around the scene, arms at the ready, and observed, tape recorded, and recommended a lawyer to the arrested victim. It didn't take long for the police to retaliate. They confronted Huey late one night near his home. Gunfire erupted, leaving Huey critically wounded, a policeman dead and another wounded. The Panthers and the Oakland/Bay community responded with a massive campaign to save Huey from the gas chamber. The California Senate began a hearing to rescind the law permitting citizens to openly carry arms within city limits. The Panthers staged an armed demonstration during the hearing at the Sacramento Capitol to protest the Senate's action, which gained national publicity.[1] That publicity, together with the Panthers' philosophy of revolutionary nationalism, self-defense, and the "Free Huey" campaign, catapulted the BPP to nationwide prominence.

But not without cost. On August 25, 1967, J. Edgar Hoover issued his infamous Counter Intelligence Program (COINTELPRO) memorandum which directed the FBI (and local police officials) to disrupt specified Black organizations and neutralize their leaders so as to prevent "the rise of a Black messiah."[2]

Attacks Increase on Revolutionaries

The Panthers rolled eastward, establishing offices in each major northern ghetto. As they went, they set up revolutionary programs in each community that were geared to provide community control of schools, tenant control of slum housing, free breakfast for school children, free health, day-care, and legal clinics, and free political education classes for the community. They also initiated campaigns to drive dope-pushers and drugs from the community, and campaigns to stop police murder and brutality of Blacks. As they went about the community organizing these various programs they were frequently confronted, attacked, or arrested by the police, and some were even killed during these encounters.

Other revolutionary organizers suffered similar entrapments. The Revolutionary Action Movement's (RAM) Herman Ferguson and Max Stamford were arrested in

1967 on spurious charges of conspiring to kill civil rights leaders. In the same year Amiri Baraka a.k.a. LeRoi Jones (the poet and playwright) was arrested for transporting weapons in a van during the Newark riots and did a brief stint in Trenton State Prison until a successful appeal overturned his conviction. SNCC's Rap Brown, Stokely Carmichael, and other orators were constantly threatened or charged with "inciting to riot" as they crisscrossed the country speaking to mass audiences. Congress passed so-called "Rap Brown" laws to deter speakers from crossing state lines to address mass audiences lest a disturbance break out leaving them vulnerable to federal charges and imprisonment.[3] And numerous revolutionary organizers and orators were imprisoned.

This initial flow of revolutionaries into the jails and prisons began to spread a revolutionary nationalist hue through New Afrikans behind the walls. New Afrikan prisoners were also influenced by the domestic revolutionary atmosphere and the liberation struggles in Afrika, Asia, and South America. Small groups began studying on their own, or in collectives, the works of Malcolm X, Huey P. Newton, *The Black Panther Newspaper* [Intercommunal News Service], *The Militant Newspaper*, contemporary national liberation struggle leaders Kwame Nkrumah, Jomo Kenyatta, Frantz Fanon, Che Guevara, Fidel Castro, Ho Chi Minh, and Mao Tse-tung, plus Marx, Lenin, and Bakunin too. Increasing numbers of New Afrikan and Third World prisoners became more conscious of national liberation politics. The percentages of New Afrikan and Third World prisoners increased while the number of White prisoners decreased throughout U.S. prisons. Under this onslaught of rising national liberation consciousness, increased percentages of New Afrikan and Third World prisoners, and decreased numbers of White prisoners, the last of the prisons' overt segregation policies fell by the wayside.

THE NEW AFRIKAN INDEPENDENCE MOVEMENT

The seeds of Malcolm took further root on March 29, 1968. On that date the Provisional Government of the Republic of New Afrika (RNA) was founded at a convention held at the Black-owned Twenty Grand Motel in Detroit. Over 500 grassroots activists came together to issue a Declaration of Independence on behalf of the oppressed Black Nation inside North America, and the New Afrikan Independence Movement (NAIM) was born.[4] Since then, Blacks desiring an independent Black Nation have referred to themselves and other Blacks in the U.S. as New Afrikans.

That same month, March 1968, during Martin Luther King's march in Memphis, angry youths on the fringes of the march broke away and began breaking store windows, looting, and firebombing. A sixteen-year-old boy was killed and fifty people were injured in the ensuing violence.[5] This left Martin profoundly shaken and questioning whether his philosophy was still able to hold the youth to a nonviolent commitment. On April 4th he returned to Memphis, seeking the answer through one more march, and found an assassin's bullet. Ghettos exploded in flames one after another across the face of America. The philosophy of Black Liberation surged to the forefront among the youth.

But not the youth alone. Following a series of police provocations in Cleveland, on July 23, 1968, New Libya Movement activists there set an ambush that killed several policemen. A "fortyish" Ahmed Evans was convicted of the killings and died in prison ten years later of "cancer."[6]

More CIA dope surged into the ghettos from the Golden Triangle of Southeast Asia.[7] Revolutionaries stepped up their organizing activities on both sides of the walls. Behind the walls the New Afrikan percentage steadily increased.

THE STREET GANGS

There were numerous Black, White, Puerto Rican and Asian street organizations, i.e., "gangs," in New York City during the 1950s. Among the more notorious Black street gangs of the era were the Chaplains, Bishops, Sinners, and Corsair Lords; also there was the equally violent Puerto Rican Dragons. All warred against each other and other gangs that crossed their paths.

By the 1960s, the post–World War II heroin influx had taken its toll. Most of the New York street gangs faded away. Their youthful members had succumbed to drugs, either through death by overdose, or had ceased gang activities in order to pursue full time criminal activities to feed their drug habit or were in prison because of drug-crime activities or youth gang assaults and killings.

Lumumba Shakur, warlord of the Bishops, and Sekou Odinga, leader of the Sinners, were two such youths who had been sent to the reformatory for youth gang assaults. They graduated up through the "Gladiator Prisons"—Woodburn and Comstock—to mainline Attica, became politicized by the stark brutal racism in each prison and at age twenty-one were spit back upon the streets. When the Panthers reached the east coast in 1968, Lumumba and Sekou were among the first youths to sign up. Lumumba opened the Harlem Chapter of the Black Panther Party as its Defense Captain. Sekou opened the Queens Chapter as a Lieutenant and later transferred to Harlem to co-head it with his boyhood pal, Lumumba.

ORIGIN OF THE GANGSTER
DISCIPLES STREET GANG

The Gangster Disciples were founded in the 1960s in Chicago under the name "Black Disciples" by the late David Barksdale, known historically in gang circles as King David.[8] The group's name was later changed to "Black Gangster Disciples" and later still the name was shortened to "Gangster Disciples," or simply as "GD." Its gang colors are blue and black.[9]

COINTELPRO ATTACKS

In 1969 COINTELPRO launched its main attack on the Black Liberation Movement. It began with the mass arrests of Lumumba Shakur and the New York Panther 21. It followed with a series of military raids on Black Panther Party offices in Philadelphia, Baltimore, New Haven, Jersey City, Detroit, Chicago, Denver, Omaha, Sacramento, and San Diego, and was capped off with an early morning four hour siege that poured thousands of rounds into the Los Angeles BPP office. By mid morning, hundreds of angry Black residents gathered at the scene and demanded that the police cease-fire. Fortunately Geronimo ji-Jaga, decorated Vietnam vet, had earlier fortified the office to withstand an assault, and no Panthers were seriously injured. However, repercussions from the event eventually drove him underground. The widespread attacks left Panthers dead all across the country—Fred Hampton, Mark Clark, Bunchy Carter, John Huggins, Walter Toure Pope, Bobby Hutton, Sylvester Bell, Frank "Capt. Franco" Diggs, Fred Bennett, James Carr, Larry Robeson, John Savage, Spurgeon "Jake" Winters, Alex Rackley, Arthur Morris, Steve Bartholemew, Robert Lawrence, Tommy Lewis, Nathaniel Clark, Welton Armstead, Sidney Miller, Sterling Jones, Babatunde Omawali, Samuel Napier, Harold Russle, and Robert Webb among others.[10] In the three years after J. Edgar Hoover's infamous COINTELPRO memorandum, thirty-one members of the BPP were killed,[11] nearly a thousand were arrested, and key leaders were sent to jail. Others were driven underground. Still others, like BPP field marshal Donald "D.C." Cox, were driven into exile overseas.

The RNA was similarly attacked that year. During their second annual convention in March 1969, held at Reverend C. L. Franklin's New Bethel Church in Detroit, a police provocation sparked a siege that poured 800 rounds into the church. Several convention members were wounded; one policeman was killed, another wounded, and the entire convention, 140 people, was arrested en masse. When Reverend Franklin (father of "The Queen of Soul," singer Aretha Franklin) and Black State Representative James Del Rio were informed of the incident they called Black judge George Crockett, who proceeded to the police station where he found total legal chaos. Almost 150 people were being held incommunicado. They were being questioned, finger printed, and given nitrate tests to determine if they had fired guns, in total disregard of fundamental constitutional procedures. Hours after the roundup, there wasn't so much as a list of persons being held and no one had been formally arrested. An indignant Judge Crockett set up court right in the station house and demanded that the police either press charges or release their captives. He had handled about fifty cases when the Wayne County prosecutor, called in by the police, intervened. The prosecutor promised that the use of all irregular methods would be halted. Crockett adjourned the impromptu court, and by noon the following day the police had released all but a few individuals who were held on specific charges.[12] Chaka Fuller, Rafael Vierra, and Alfred 2X Hibbits were charged with the killing. All three were subsequently tried and acquitted. Chaka Fuller was mysteriously assassinated a few months afterwards.[13]

On Friday June 13, 1969, Clarence 13X, founder of The Five Percenters, was mysteriously assassinated in the elevator of a Harlem project building by three male Negroes.[14] His killers were never discovered but his adherents suspect government complicity in his death.[15] News reports at the time hinted that BOSS instigated the assassination to try to ferment a war between the NOI and The Five Percenters.[16]

Revolutionaries nationwide were attacked and/or arrested—Tyari Uhuru, Maka, Askufo, and the Smyrna Brothers in Delaware, JoJo Muhammad Bowens and Fred Burton in Philadelphia, and Panthers Mondo we Langa, Ed Poindexter, and Veronza Daoud Bowers, Jr., in Omaha.

Police mounted an assault on the Panther office in the Desiree Projects of New Orleans which resulted in several arrests. A similar attack was made on the Peoples Party office in Houston. One of their leaders, Carl Hampton, was killed by police and another, Lee Otis Johnson, was arrested later on an unrelated charge and sentenced to forty-one years in prison for alleged possession of one marijuana cigarette.

THE RISE OF PRISON STRUGGLES

Like the Panthers, most of those arrested brought their philosophies with them into the prisons. Likewise, most had outside support committees to one degree or another so that this influx of political prisoners linked the struggle behind the walls with the struggles in the outside local communities. The combination set off a beehive of political activity behind the walls, and prisoners stepped up their struggle for political, Afrikan, Islamic, and academic studies, access to political literature, community access to prisons, an end to arbitrary punishments, access to attorneys, adequate law libraries, relevant vocational training, contact visits, better food, health care, housing, and myriad other struggles. The forms of prison struggle ranged from face-to-face negotiations to mass petitioning, letter writing and call-in campaigns, outside demonstrations, class action law suits, hunger strikes, work strikes, rebellions, and more drastic actions. Overall, all forms of struggle served to roll back draconian prison policies that had stood for centuries and to further the development of the New Afrikan liberation struggle behind the walls.

These struggles would not have been as successful, or would have been much more costly in terms of lives lost or brutality endured, had it not been for the links to the community and the community support and legal support that political prisoners brought with them into the prisons. Although that support was not always sufficient in quantity or quality, or was sometimes nonexistent or came with hidden agendas, or was marked by frequent conflicts, on the whole it was this combination of resolute prisoners, community support, and legal support which was most often successful in prison struggles.

THE CHANGING COMPLEXION OF PRISONS

As the 1960s drew to a close New Afrikan and Third World nationalities made up nearly fifty percent of the prison population. National liberation consciousness became the dominant influence behind the walls as the overall complexion neared the changeover from White to Black, Brown, and Red. The decade long general decrease in prisoners, particularly Whites, brought a drop of between 16,000[17] and 28,000[18] in total prison population. The total number of White prisoners decreased between 16,000 and 23,000 while the total number of New Afrikan prisoners increased slightly or changed insignificantly over the same period.[19] Yet the next decade would begin the period of unprecedented new prison construction, as the primary role of U.S. prisons changed from "suppression of the working classes" to "suppression of domestic Black and Third World liberation struggles inside the U.S."

ORIGIN OF CRIP[20]

There existed street organizations in South Central, Los Angeles, before the rise of the Black Panther Party. These groups, criminal in essence, were indeed the wells from which the Panthers would recruit their most stalwart members. Alprentice "Bunchy" Carter, who chartered the first L.A. Chapter of the Party was the leader of perhaps the most violent street organizations of that time—the Slausons. James Carr, former cell mate of Comrade George Jackson, and author of *BAD*, was a member of the Farmers. There were the Gladiators, the Businessmen, the Avenues, Blood Alley, and the Rebel Rousers to name but a few.

After the 1965 rebellion in Watts, there came an unsteady truce of sorts that caused the street organizations to focus on a larger, more deadly enemy—the L.A.P.D. [Los Angeles Police Department]. So, by the time the Black Panther Party came to L.A., in 1968, a shaky peace existed among the larger groups. The Party offered the street combatants a new direction in which to vent their anger, respond to injustice and represent their neighborhoods.

By and large, the Party usurped the youthful rage and brought the street organizations of that time to an end. Of course, the U.S. government also did its share by drafting young brothers into the Vietnam War.

These, however, were the storm years of COINTELPRO and the Party was the focal point. Thus, by late '69, the aboveground infrastructure of the BPP was in shambles due to its own internal contradictions and subsequently the weight of the state. Confusion set in among the people creating, if you will, a window of opportunity of which both the criminals and the counter revolutionists in the government took advantage.

Community Relations for an Independent People (CRIP) was a city funded team post (meeting place) on the east side of South Central L.A. that played host to some of the area's most rowdy youth. One such brother was Raymond Washington, who at that time belonged to a young upstart clique called the Baby Avenues. The team post became center ground to an ever widening group of youth who eventually took its title, CRIP, as a name and moved westward with it. With the vanguard in shambles and the local pigs turning a deliberate deaf ear, the CRIPs flourished rapidly. In its formative years, the Party's influence was evident. For the same uniform/dress code of the Party's influence was that of the CRIPs. Yet, a sinister twist developed whereas New Afrikan people were targets of the young hoodlums. And with no vanguard forces readily available to teach and train these youth, they spiraled out of control, taking as their nemesis the Brims who later developed into the city wide Bloods. The founding of the CRIPs is established as 1969. Their gang color is blue, and sometimes also the color white.

ENTER THE 1970s

A California guard, rated as an expert marksman, opened the decade of the 1970s with the January 13th shooting at close range of W. L. Nolen, Cleveland Edwards, and Alvin "Jug" Miller in the Soledad prison yard. They were left lying where they fell until it was too late for them to be saved by medical treatment. Nolen, in particular, had been instrumental in organizing protest against guard killings of two other Black prisoners—Clarence Causey and William Powell—at Soledad in the recent past, and was consequently both a thorn in the side of prison officials and a hero to the Black prison population.[21] When the guard was exonerated of the triple killings two weeks later by a Board of Inquiry, the prisoners retaliated by throwing a guard off the tier.

George Jackson, Fleeta Drumgo, and John Cluchette were charged with the guard's death and came to be known as the Soledad Brothers. California Black prisoners solidified around the Soledad Brothers case and the chain of events led to the formation of the Black Guerrilla Family (BGF). The Panthers spearheaded a massive campaign to save the Soledad Brothers from the gas chamber. The nationwide coalescence of prisoners and support groups around the case converted the scattered, disparate prison struggles into a national prison movement.

On the night of March 9, 1970, a bomb exploded, killing Ralph Featherstone and Che Payne in their car outside a Maryland courthouse where Rap Brown was to appear next day on "Inciting to Riot" charges. Instead of appearing, Rap went underground, was captured a year later during the robbery of a Harlem so-called "dope bar," and was sent behind the walls. He completed his sentence and was released from prison.[22]

On August 7, 1970, Jonathan Jackson, younger brother of George, attempted to liberate Ruchell "Cinque" Magee, William Christmas, and James McClain from the Marin County courthouse in California. Jonathan, McClain, Christmas, and the trial judge were killed by SWAT teams who also wounded the prosecutor and paralyzed him for life. Miraculously, Ruchell and three wounded jurors survived the fusillade. Jonathan frequently served as Angela Davis's bodyguard. She had purchased weapons for that purpose, but Jonathan used those same weapons in the breakout attempt. Immediately afterward she became the object of an international "woman hunt." On October 13, Angela was captured in New York City and was subsequently returned to California to undergo a very acrimonious trial with Magee. She was acquitted on all charges. Magee was tried separately and convicted on lesser charges. He remains imprisoned to date, over three decades all total, and is our longest held political prisoner.[23]

ORIGIN OF THE BLOODS[24]

Most South Central street organizations, commonly called "gangs," "sets," or "orgs.," take their names from prominent streets: Slauson, Denver Lane, Piru, Hoover, etc., that run through their neighborhood. The CRIPs had already formed, were massed up and rolling together. Their strength attracted other sets to become CRIPs. As they moved into territories occupied by other South Central organizations, they clashed with and met stiff resistance from those neighborhood sets who did not want to align with or be taken over by them.

Among those gang leaders resisting the CRIP invasion were Peabody of the Denver Lanes, Puddin of the Westside Pirus, Rooster of the thirty Pirus, and the Westside Brims, perhaps the most well known and respected of the lot, although their leader is unknown today. Using their prestige and influence, the Brims began going into other neighborhoods to start other Brim families and to recruit other sets to join their side in opposition to the CRIPs. As the various sets began hooking up with each other and the Brims, they formed a loose coalition whose main point in common was their opposition to the CRIPs. In the early 1970s, the federation solidified and formally united into the citywide Bloods. They adopted the color red as their banner; they also use the colors green or brown.

Prison is a normal next stop for many gang members. The first Bloods sent to Chino, a mainline California prison, are commonly referred to in Blood circles as the "First Bloods to walk the line at Chino." To increase their prison membership and recruitment, they created a Bloodline (BL) Constitution patterned after the constitution of the BGF, a Panther-influenced group already established in the California prison system at the time. The BL Constitution contained the Blood's code of conduct, history, and by-laws and was required reading for each new recruit. To speed up recruitment, the older "First Bloods" made reading the constitution an automatic induction into their ranks and thereafter began tricking young prisoners into reading it. Once read, the new recruit could only reject membership at the risk of serious bodily harm.

The press-ganging of young recruits at Chino set off ripples of dissatisfaction and breakaways among Bloods in other California prisons. Those disaffected centered around Peabody at Old Folsom prison who took parts from the BL and the BGF constitutions and created a new United Blood Nation (UBN) Constitution designed to unify all Bloods in prison. Since then, Bloods have chosen which constitution they would come under.

Blood members under either the BL or UBN Constitution are held to a higher standard than other members; they hold positions and are similar to the Officer's Corps of a military organization. Those Bloods not under a constitution are the foot soldiers. The BL and UBN organization spread throughout the California prison system, and are strictly prison organizations. Once a Blood leaves prison he returns to his old neighborhood set. From South Central, the Bloods spread to Pasadena, Gardenia, San Diego, Sacramento, Bakersfield, and throughout the state and its prison system.

CALIFORNIA BAY AREA GANGS[25]

San Francisco's Bay Area gangs or "clicks" can be traced back to the early 1960s and are usually identified by, or named after, their neighborhoods or communities. Most of those functioning today came from splinter groups of the BPP after it broke up.

In Oakland, the 69th Street Mob, founded by Felix Mitchell in the early 1970s, still exists despite the government's best efforts to derail it. In East Oakland the Rolling Twenties and the 700 Club, along with the Acorn Gang in West Oakland, are the powerhouse clicks on the streets.

In San Francisco, there is Sunnydale and Hunters Point, the city's largest street gang, which is divided into several clicks—Oakdale, Harbor Road, West Point, etc. East Palo Alto is the home of the Professional Low Riders (PLR) who are a major influence in the South Bay Area—and in Vallejo there is the North Bay Gangsters and Crestview.

Most Bay Area gangs don't have colors but align primarily on the basis of money and hustling endeavors. Many are associated with the Rap music industry and with various prison groups—the 415s, BGF, or ANSARs.

GROWTH OF THE GANGSTER DISCIPLES

In 1970, Gangster Disciple (GD) Larry Hoover was convicted for a gang related murder and sentenced to a 150 to 200 year state sentence. He's the current leader of the GDs and runs the syndicate from an Illinois prison cell.

As drugs flooded into the Chicago ghettoes, young Black men flooded into the Illinois prisons where they were given GD application forms to fill out. If their references proved solid, they were indoctrinated into the gang. Everyone who joined had to memorize the GD's sixteen-rule code. The GDs spread throughout the Illinois and Midwest prison systems. The flow of GDs back into the streets enabled them to expand their street network which is an intricate command and control structure, similar to a military organization.[26]

COMRADE GEORGE ASSASSINATED

On August 21, 1971, a guard shot and killed George Jackson as he bolted from a control unit and ran for the San Quentin wall. Inside the unit lay three guards and two trustees dead. The circumstances surrounding George Jackson's legendary life and death, and the astuteness of his published writings,[27] left a legacy that inspires and instructs the New Afrikan liberation struggle on both sides of the wall even today, and will for years to come.

September 13, 1971, became the bloodiest day in U.S. prison history when New York's Governor Nelson Rockefeller ordered the retaking of Attica prison. The previous several years had seen a number of prison rebellions flare up across the country as prisoners protested widespread maltreatment and inhumane conditions. Most had been settled peaceably with little or no loss of human life after face to face negotiation between prisoners and state and prison officials. At Attica Black, Brown, White, Red, and Yellow prisoners took over one block of the prison and stood together for five days seeking to negotiate an end to their inhumane conditions. Their now famous dictum declared, "We are men, not beasts, and will not be driven as such." But Rockefeller had presidential ambitions. The rebelling prisoners' demands included a political request for asylum in a non-imperialistic country. Rockefeller's refusal to negotiate foreshadowed a macabre replay of his father John D's slaughter of striking Colorado miners and their families decades earlier. Altogether forty-three people died at Attica. New York State trooper bullets killed forty people—thirty-one prisoners and nine guards—in retaking Attica and shocked the world by the naked barbarity of the U.S. prison system. Yet the Attica rebellion too remains a milestone in the development of the New Afrikan liberation struggle behind the walls, and a symbol of the highest development of prisoner multinational solidarity to date.

NEW WORLD CLASHES WITH THE NATION OF ISLAM

In 1973 the simmering struggle for control of Newark's NOI [Nation of Islam] Temple No. 25 erupted into the open. Warren Marcello a New World [of Islam] member assassinated NOI Temple No. 25 Minister Shabazz. In retaliation several NWI members were attacked and killed within the confines of the New Jersey prison system, and before the year was out the bodies of Marcello and a companion were found beheaded in Newark's Weequahic Park. Ali Hassan, still in prison, was tried as one of the co-conspirators in the death of Shabazz and was found innocent.

THE BLACK LIBERATION ARMY

COINTELPRO's destruction of the BPP forced many members underground and gave rise to the Black Liberation Army (BLA)—a New Afrikan guerrilla organization. The BLA continued the struggle by waging urban guerrilla war across the U.S. through highly mobile strike teams.[28] The government's intensified search for the BLA during the early 1970s resulted in the capture of Geronimo ji-Jaga in Dallas, Dhoruba Bin-Wahad and Jamal Joseph in New York, Sha Sha Brown and Blood McCreary in St. Louis, Nuh Washington and Jalil Muntaqim in Los Angeles, Herman Bell in New Orleans, Francisco and Gabriel Torres in New York, Russell Maroon Shoats in Philadelphia, Chango Monges, Mark Holder, and Kamau Hilton in New York, Assata Shakur and Sundiata Acoli in New Jersey, Ashanti Alston, Tarik, and Walid in New Haven, Safiya Bukhari and Masai Gibson in Virginia, and others. Left dead during the government's search and destroy missions were Sandra Pratt (wife of Geronimo ji-Jaga, assassinated while visibly pregnant), Mark Essex, Woodie Changa Green, Twyman Kakuyan Olugbala Meyers, Frank "Heavy" Fields, Anthony Kimu White, Zayd Shakur, Melvin Rema Kerney, Alfred Kambui Butler, Ron Carter, Rory Hithe, and John Thomas, among others.[29] Red Adams, left paralyzed from the neck down by police bullets, would die from the effects a few years later.

Other New Afrikan freedom fighters attacked, hounded, and captured during the same general era were Imari Obadele and the RNA-11 in Jackson, Mississippi,[30] Don Taylor[31] and De Mau Mau of Chicago, Hanif Shabazz, Abdul Aziz, and the VI-5 in the Virgin Islands, Mark Cook of the George Jackson Brigade (GJB) in Seattle, Ahmed Obafemi of the RNA in Florida, Atiba Shanna in Chicago, Mafundi Lake and Sekou Kambui in Alabama, Robert Aswad Duren in California, Kojo Bomani Sababu and Dharuba Cinque in Trenton, John Partee and Tommie Lee Hodges of Alkebulan in Memphis, Gary Tyler in Louisiana, Kareem Saif Allah and the Five Percenter-BLA-Islamic Brothers in New York, Ben Chavis and the Wilmington 10 in North Carolina, Delbert Africa and MOVE members in Philadelphia, and others doubtless too numerous to name.[32]

POLITICAL CONVERTS IN PRISON

Not everyone was political before incarceration. John Andaliwa Clark became so, and a freedom fighter par excellence, only after being sent behind the walls. He paid the supreme sacrifice during a hail of gunfire by Trenton State Prison guards. Hugo Dahariki Pinell also became political after being sent behind the California walls in 1964. He has been in prison ever since. Joan Little[33] took an ice pick from a White North Carolina guard who had used it to force her to perform oral sex on him. She killed him, escaped to New York, was captured, and forced to return to the same North Carolina camp where she feared for her life. Massive public vigilance and support enabled her to complete the sentence in relative safety and obtain her release. Dessie Woods[34] and Cheryl Todd, hitching through Georgia, were given a ride by a White man who tried to rape them. Woods took his gun, killed him, and was sent to prison where officials drugged and brutalized her. Todd was also imprisoned and subsequently released upon completion of the sentence. Woods was denied parole several times, then finally released.

Political or not, each arrest was met with highly sensationalized prejudicial publicity that continued unabated to and throughout the trial. The negative publicity blitz was designed to guarantee a conviction, smokescreen the real issues involved, and justify immediate placement in the harshest prison conditions possible. For men this usually meant the federal penitentiary at Marion, Illinois. For women it has meant the control unit in the federal penitentiary at Alderson, West Virginia, or Lexington, Kentucky. In 1988 political prisoners Silvia Baraldini, Alejandrina Torres, and Susan Rosenberg won a D.C. District Court lawsuit brought by attorneys Adjoa Aiyetoro, Jan Susler, and others. The legal victory temporarily halted the practice of sending prisoners to control units strictly because of their political status. The ruling was reversed by the D.C. Appellate Court a year later.[35] Those political prisoners not sent to Marion, Alderson, or Lexington control units are sent to other control units modeled after Marion/Lexington but located within maximum security state prisons. Normally this means twenty-three hour a day lockdown in long term units located in remote hinterlands far from family, friends, and attorneys, with heavy censorship and restrictions on communications, visits, and outside contacts, combined with constant harassment, provocation, and brutality by prison guards.

EFFECT OF CAPTURED FREEDOM FIGHTERS ON PRISONS

The influx of so many captured freedom fighters (i.e., prisoners of war—POWs) with varying degrees of guerrilla experience added a valuable dimension to the New Afrikan liberation struggle behind the walls. In the first place, it accelerated the prison struggles already in process, particularly the attack on control units. One attack was spearheaded by Michael Deutsch and Jeffrey Haas of the People's Law Office, Chicago, which challenged Marion's H-Unit boxcar cells. Another was spearheaded by Assata Shakur and the Center for Constitutional Rights which challenged her out of state placement in the Alderson, West Virginia, control unit.

Second, it stimulated a thoroughgoing investigation and exposure of COINTELPRO's hand in the low-intensity warfare waged on New Afrikan and Third World nationalities in the U.S. This was spearheaded by Geronimo ji-Jaga with Stuart Hanlon's law office in the West and by Dhoruba Bin-Wahad with attorneys Liz Fink, Robert Boyle, and Jonathan Lubell in the East.[36] These COINTELPRO investigations resulted in the overturn of Bin-Wahad's conviction and his release from prison in March 1990 after he had been imprisoned nineteen years for a crime he did not commit.

Third, it broadened the scope of the prison movement to the international arena by producing the initial presentation of the U.S. political prisoner and prisoner of war (PP/POW) issue before the UN's Human Rights Commission. This approach originated with Jalil Muntaqim, and was spearheaded by him and attorney Kathryn Burke on the West Coast and by Sundiata Acoli and attorney Lennox Hinds of the National Conference of Black Lawyers on the East Coast.[37] This petition sought relief from human rights violations in U.S. prisons and subsequently asserted a colonized people's right to fight against alien domination and racist regimes as codified in the Geneva Convention.

Fourth, it intensified, clarified, and broke new ground on political issues and debates of particular concern to the New Afrikan community, i.e., the "National Question," spearheaded by Atiba Shanna in the Midwest.[38]

All these struggles, plus those already in process, were carried out with the combination in one form or another of resolute prisoners, and community and legal support. Community support when present came from various sources—family, comrades, friends; political, student, religious, and prisoner rights groups; workers, professionals, and progressive newspapers and radio stations. Some of those involved over the years were or are: the National Committee for Defense of Political Prisoners, the Black Community News Service, the African Peoples Party, the Republic of New Afrika, the African Peoples Socialist Party, The East, the BlissChord Communication Network, Liberation Book Store, WDAS Radio Philadelphia, WBLS Radio New York, WBAI Radio New York, Third World Newsreel, *Libertad* (political journal of the Puerto Rican Movimiento de Liberación Nacionál [MLN]), the Prairie Fire Organizing Committee, the May 19th Communist Organization, the Madame Binh Graphics Collective, The Midnight Express, the Northwest Iowa Socialist Party, the National Black United Front, the Nation of Islam, *Arm The Spirit*, Black News, International Class Labor Defense, the Real Dragon Project, the John Brown Anti-Klan Committee, the National Prison Project, the House of the Lord Church, the American Friends Service Committee, attorneys Chuck Jones and Harold Ferguson of Rutgers Legal Clinic, the *Jackson Advocate* newspaper, Rutgers law students, the Committee to End the Marion Lockdown, the American Indian Movement, and others.

THE END OF THE 1970s

As the decade wound down, the late 1970s saw the demise of the NOI following the death of Elijah Muhammad and the rise of orthodox Islam among significant segments of New Afrikans on both sides of the wall. By 1979 the prison population stood at 300,000, a whopping 100,000 increase within a single decade.[39] The previous 100,000 increase, from 100,000 to 200,000, had taken thirty-one years, from

1927 to 1958. The initial increase to 100,000 had taken hundreds of years, since America's original colonial times. The 1960s were the transition decade of White flight that saw a significant decrease in both prison population and White prisoners. And since the total Black prison population increased only slightly or changed insignificantly over the decade of the insurgent 1960s through 1973, it indicates that New Afrikans are imprisoned least when they fight hardest.

The decade ended on a master stroke by the BLA's Multinational Task Force, with the November 2, 1979, prison liberation of Assata Shakur—"Soul of the BLA" and preeminent political prisoner of the era. The Task Force then whisked her away to the safety of political asylum in Cuba where she remains to date.[40]

THE DECADE OF THE 1980s

In June 1980, Ali Hassan was released after sixteen years in the New Jersey state prisons. Two months later, five New World of Islam (NWI) members were arrested after a North Brunswick, New Jersey, bank robbery in a car with stolen plates. The car belonged to the recently released Ali Hassan, who had loaned it to a friend. Ali Hassan and fifteen other NWI members refused to participate in the resulting mass trial which charged them in a Racketeering Influenced Corrupt Organization (RICO) indictment with conspiracy to rob banks for the purpose of financing various NWI enterprises in the furtherance of creating an independent Black Nation. All defendants were convicted and sent behind the walls.

The 1980s brought another round of BLA freedom fighters behind walls— Basheer Hameed and Abdul Majid in the 1980s; Sekou Odinga, Kuwasi Balagoon, Chui Ferguson-El, Jamal Joseph again, Mutulu Shakur, and numerous BLA Multinational Task Force supporters in '81; and Terry Khalid Long, Ojore Lutalo, and others in 1982. The government's sweep left Mtayari Shabaka Sundiata dead, Kuwasi Balagoon subsequently dead in prison from AIDS, and Sekou Odinga brutally tortured upon capture, torture that included pulling out his toenails and rupturing his pancreas during long sadistic beatings that left him hospitalized for six months.

But this second round of captured BLA freedom fighters brought forth, perhaps for the first time, a battery of young, politically acute New Afrikan lawyers— Chokwe Lumumba, Jill Soffiyah Elijah, Nkechi Taifa, Adjoa Aiyetoro, Ashanti Chimurenga, Michael Tarif Warren, Evelyn Williams, Joan Gibbs, Florence Morgan, and others. They are not only skilled in representing New Afrikan POWs but the New Afrikan Independence Movement too, all of which added to the further development of the New Afrikan liberation struggle behind the walls.

The decade also brought behind the walls Mumia Abu-Jamal, the widely respected Philadelphia radio announcer, popularly known as the "Voice of the Voiceless." He maintained a steady drumbeat of radio support for MOVE prisoners.

He was driving his cab on the night of December 9, 1981, when he happened to spot a policeman beating his younger brother.

Mumia stopped, got out of his cab and was shot and seriously wounded; the policeman was killed. Mumia now sits on death row in greatest need of mass support from every sector, if he's to be saved from the state's electric chair.[41]

Kazi Toure of the United Freedom Front (UFF) was sent behind the walls in 1982. He was released in 1991. In 1983, the United States Penitentiary (USP) at Marion, Illinois, was permanently locked down, and the entire prison was converted into one huge control unit making it the nation's first control prison. The concept would spread across country in the next decade.

The New York 8—Coltrane Chimurenga, Viola Plummer and her son Robert "R.T." Taylor, Roger Wareham, Omowale Clay, Lateefah Carter, Colette Pean, and Yvette Kelly—were arrested on October 17, 1984, and charged with conspiring to commit prison breakouts and armed robberies, and to possess weapons and explosives. However, the New York 8 were actually the New York 8 + because another eight or nine people were jailed as grand jury resisters in connection with the case. The New York 8 were acquitted on August 5, 1985.

That same year, Ramona Africa joined other MOVE comrades already behind the walls. Her only crime was that she survived Philadelphia Mayor Goode's May 13, 1985, bombing which killed eleven MOVE members, including their babies, families, home, and neighborhood.

The following year, on November 19, 1986, a twenty-year old Bronx, New York, youth, Larry Davis—now Adam Abdul Hakeem—made a dramatic escape during a shootout with police who had come to assassinate him for absconding with their drug sales money. Several policemen were wounded in the shootout. Adam escaped unscathed but surrendered weeks later in the presence of the media, his family, and a mass of neighborhood supporters. After numerous charges, trials, and acquittals in which he exposed the existence of a New York police controlled drug ring that coerced Black and Puerto Rican youths to push police supplied drugs, he was sent behind the walls on weapon possession convictions. During incarceration, numerous beatings by guards confined him to a wheelchair for several years.

On July 16, 1987, Abdul Haqq Muhammad, Arthur Majeed Barnes, and Robert "R.T." Taylor, all members of the Black Men's Movement Against Crack, were pulled over by state troopers in upstate New York, arrested, and subsequently sent to prison on a variety of weapon possession convictions. Each completed his sentence and returned to the streets and the struggle.

Herman Ferguson, at sixty-eight years of age, voluntarily returned to the U.S. on April 6, 1989, after twenty years of exile in Ghana, Afrika, and Guyana, South America. He had fled the U.S. during the late 1960s after the appeal was denied on his sentence of three and a half to seven years following a conviction for conspiring to murder Civil Rights leaders. Upon return he was arrested at the airport and was moved constantly from prison to prison for several years as a form of harassment.

Only after serving his full sentence was he released back into the streets where he continues the struggle for Afrikan liberation.

The 1980s brought the Reagan era's rollback of progressive trends on a wide front and a steep rise in racist incidents, White vigilantism and police murder of New Afrikan and Third World people. The CIA flooded South Central, Los Angeles, with cheap "crack" cocaine and guns. It set off a tidal wave of internecine violence that eventually engulfed communities of color all across the country.

Like the CRIPs, the Bloods were initially influenced by the Black Panther Party, but with the deluge of CIA-Contra crack and guns into South Central, and with no revolutionary vanguard to direct them, the Bloods took the path of least resistance. Using their statewide network, rocks, firepower, and Blood rap videos and tapes, they spread their enterprise eastward through cities big and small.

The Reagan 1980s also brought about the rebirth and reestablishment of the NOI under the leadership of Minister Louis Farrakhan, the rapprochement with the Soviet Union, a number of New Afrikan POWs adopting orthodox Islam in lieu of revolutionary nationalism, the New Afrikan People's Organization (NAPO) and its chairman, Chokwe Lumumba's emergence from RNA as a banner carrier for the New Afrikan Independence Movement (NAIM), the Malcolm X Grassroots Movement (MXGM), the New Orleans assassination of Lumumba Shakur of the Panther 21, and an upsurge in mass political demonstrations known as the "Days of Outrage" in New York City spearheaded by the December 12th Movement and others.

The end of the decade brought the death of Huey P. Newton, founder of the Black Panther Party, allegedly killed by a young Black Guerrilla Family adherent on August 22, 1989, during a dispute over "crack." Huey taught the Black masses socialism and popularized it through the slogan "Power to the People!" He armed the Black struggle and popularized it through the slogan "Political Power grows out of the barrel of a gun."[42] For that, and despite his human shortcomings, he was a true giant of the Black struggle, because his particular contributions are comparable to that of other modern-day giants, Marcus Garvey, Elijah Muhammad, Malcolm X, and Martin Luther King, Jr.

AIDS, crack, street crime, gang violence, homelessness, and arrest rates all exploded throughout the Black colonies. The prison population on June 30, 1989, topped 673,000, an incredible 372,000 increase in less than a decade, causing the tripling and doubling of prison populations in thirty-four states, and sizable increases in most others.[43] New York City prisons became so overcrowded that they began using ships as jails. William Bennett, former U.S. Secretary of Education and then so-called Drug Czar, announced plans to convert closed military bases into concentration camps.

The prison-building spree and escalated imprisonment rates continued unabated. The new prisoners were younger, more volatile, with long prison sentences, and were overwhelmingly of New Afrikan and Third World nationalities, including women who were being incarcerated at increasing rates. Their percentage of the prison population rose to five percent in 1980 from a low of three percent in 1970.[44]

Whites continued to be arrested at about the same rate as in Western Europe while the New Afrikan arrest rate surpassed that of Blacks in South Africa. In fact, the U.S. Black imprisonment rate was now the highest in the world,[45] with ten times as many Blacks as Whites incarcerated per 100,000 population.[46]

THE 1990s AND BEYOND

As we began to move through the 1990s, the New Afrikan liberation struggle behind the walls found itself coalescing around campaigns to free political prisoners and prisoners of war, helping to build a national PP/POW organization, strengthening its links on the domestic front, and building solidarity in the international arena. 1991 brought the collapse of the Soviet Union and the end of the Cold War. It freed many of the CIA's Eastern Europe personnel for redeployment back to America to focus on the domestic war against people of color. In the same manner that COINTELPRO perfected techniques developed in the infamous Palmer raids at the end of WWI and used them against the Communist Party-USA, SCLC, SNCC, BPP, NOI, RNA, and other domestic movements, repatriated CIA operatives used destabilization techniques developed in Eastern Europe, South Africa, Southeast Asia, etc., to wreak havoc in New Afrikan and other domestic communities of color today.

Although the established media concentrated on the sensationalism of ghetto crack epidemics, street crime, drive-by shootings, and gang violence, there was a parallel long, quiet period of consciousness raising in the New Afrikan colonies by the committed independence forces. The heightened consciousness of the colonies began to manifest itself through apparent random sparks of rebellion and the rise of innovative cultural trends, i.e., Rap/Hip Hop "message" music, culturally designed hair styles, dissemination of political/cultural video cassettes, resprouting of insurgent periodicals, and the resurrection of forgotten heroes; all of which presaged an oppressed people getting ready to push forward again. Meanwhile the U.S. began building the ADX Control Prison at Florence, Colorado, which would both supersede and augment USP Marion, Illinois. ADX at Florence combined, in a single hi-tech control prison complex, all the repressive features and techniques that had been perfected at USP Marion.

In 1992, Fred Hampton, Jr., son of the martyred Panther hero, Fred Sr., was sent behind the walls. He was convicted of the firebombing of a Korean "deli" in Chicago in the aftermath of the Simi Valley, California, verdict that acquitted four policemen of the Rodney King beating which set off the Los Angeles riots.

In 1994, Shiriki Uganisha responded to the call of POWs Jalil Muntaqim, Sekou Odinga, Geronimo ji-Jaga, and Mutulu Shakur, by hosting a national conference in Kansas City, Missouri, where various NAIM organizations discussed forming themselves into a National Front. After a year of holding periodic negotiations in various cities, the discussion bore fruit in Atlanta, Georgia. On August 18, 1995, NAPO

[New Afrikan People's Organization], the December 12th Movement, MXGM [Malcolm X Grassroots Movement], The Malcolm X Commemoration Committee (MXCC), the Black Cat Collective (BCC), International Campaign to Free Geronimo, the Sundiata Acoli Freedom Campaign (SAFC), and various other POW and grassroots organizations formally unified under the banner of the New Afrikan Liberation Front (NALF), headed by Herman Ferguson. . . .

The mid decade also brought forth a growing right wing White militia movement that had obviously studied the tactics and language of the 1960s left wing movements—and which culminated in the bombing of the Oklahoma City Federal Building causing 168 deaths and a claim of POW status by the subsequently captured and convicted suspect, Timothy McVeigh. He had been an All-American boy, a blond haired, blue-eyed patriot who enlisted in the army to defend the American way of life that he so fervently believed in. He rose rapidly through the military ranks (private to sergeant) in two years, and was accepted into the Special Forces: the elite, top four percent of the military's forces. There he learned something that average thinking persons of color have known most of their lives.

In an October 1991, letter to his sister and confidant, Jennifer, McVeigh disclosed his revulsion at being told that he and nine other Special Forces commanders might be ordered to help the CIA "fly drugs into the U.S. to fund covert operations" and "work hand in hand with civilian police agencies" as "government paid assassins."[47]

Disillusioned and embittered with the U.S. government, McVeigh soon afterwards left military service, gravitated deeper into the right wing militia circles and surfaced four years later upon his arrest in the Oklahoma City bombing case.

The mid 1990s found White anarchists Neil Batelli and Mathias Bolton collaborating with Black POWs Ojore Lutalo, Sekou Odinga, and Sundiata Acoli which resulted in the transformation of their local New Jersey Anarchist Black Cross into an ABC Federation (ABCF) which now serves as a role model of the proper way for organizations to provide principled political and financial support to PP/POWs of all nationalities. The period also witnessed the resprouting of Black revolutionary organizations patterned after the BPP—the Black Panther Collective, the Black Panther Social Committee, the New Black Panthers, and the Black Panther Militia—along with the NOI's Minister Louis Farrakhan's emergence at the October 16, 1995 Million Man March (MMM) in Washington, D.C., as an undeniable force on the New Afrikan, Islamic and world stage. In the meantime, the U.S. moved further to the right with the passage of a series of racist, anti-worker legislation. The government passed the NAFTA bill to legitimize the private corporations' policy of sending U.S. jobs overseas. California passed Proposition 209 which killed Affirmative Action programs throughout the state. Then, it passed Proposition 187, which implemented statewide racist anti-immigration legislation. The Federal government killed Black voting districts and passed Clinton's Omnibus Crime Bill which greatly increased the number of crime statutes, death penalty statutes, policemen and armaments; arrest of people of color; youths tried as adults; 3-strike convictions, and prison expansion projects.

The so-called "War on Drugs" sent Blacks and other people of color, more commonly associated with crack cocaine, to prison in droves while allowing White offenders to go free. Five grams of crack worth a few hundred dollars is punishable by a mandatory five-year prison sentence, but it takes 500 grams, or $50,000 worth of powdered cocaine, more commonly associated with wealthier Whites, before facing the same five years.[48] In the mid '90s, 1600 people were sent to prison each week, every three out of four were either Black or Latino,[49] with the rate of Afrikan women imprisonment growing faster than that of Afrikan men.[50]

Blacks were ninety percent of the federal crack convictions in 1994.[51] The normal assumption follows that Blacks are the majority of crack users. Wrong! Whites are the majority of crack users[52] but were less than four percent of the crack convictions[53] and no White person had been convicted of a federal crack offense in the Los Angeles area since 1986[54] nor ever in Chicago, Miami, Denver, or sixteen states according to a 1992 survey.[55] As a result, there are now more Afrikan men in prison than in college[56] and one out of every three Afrikan men aged nineteen to twenty-nine are in prison, jail, or on probation or parole.[57] Most of the convictions were obtained by an informant's tainted testimony only, no hard evidence, in exchange for the informant's freedom from prosecution or prison.

After lobbying Congress for a few years, Families Against Mandatory Minimums (FAMM), a predominately White lobby group, succeeded in getting the harsh mandatory sentences lowered for marijuana and LSD convictions. Both drugs are more commonly associated with White offenders and FAMM's success resulted in the release of numerous White offenders from long prison sentences.

Blacks and other prisoners of color patiently waited for similar corrections to be made to the gross disparity between crack and powdered cocaine sentences. Several years passed before the answer came during a 1995 C-SPAN TV live broadcast of the Congressional session debating the disparity in sentencing. The Congress voted to continue the same 100 to 1 disparity between crack and powder cocaine sentences. Instantly, prisons exploded in riots, thirty-eight in all, although most were whited-out of the news media while across the country, prison officials instituted a nationwide federal prisons lock down. The disparity in crack/powder cocaine sentencing laws remains to date; the only change made was the removal of the C-SPAN TV channel from all federal prisons' TVs.

Only two prison elements grew faster than the Afrikan prison population. One was the number of jobs for prison guards[58] and the other was prison slave labor industries.[59] A California guard with a high school diploma makes $44,000 after seven years, which is more than the state pays its PhD public university associate professors and is $10,000 more than its average public school teacher's salary.[60] The national ratio for prisons is one guard for each 4.38 prisoners,[61] meaning that each time the state locks up five new prisoners, usually Black or others of color, they hire another prison guard, usually White, since most prisons are built in depressed, rural White areas to provide jobs to poor, unemployed White populations.

After decades of the U.S. loudly accusing China of using prison labor in their export products, the U.S. quietly removed its ban against the sale of U.S. prison products to the public. It set off a stampede by Wall Street and private corporations—Smith Barney, IBM, AT&T, TWA, Texas Instruments, Dell Computers, Honda, Lexus, Spalding, Eddie Bauer, Brill Manufacturing Co.,[62] and many others—to shamelessly invest in prisons, set up slave labor factories in prisons and to exploit every facet of the prison slave labor industry for super profits while callously discarding civilian workers for prison slave laborers.[63]

From 1980 to 1994, prisoners increased 221 percent, prison industries jumped an astonishing 358 percent, and prison sales skyrocketed from $392 million to $1.31 billion. By the year 2000, it is predicted that 30 percent of prisoners (or 500,000) will be industry workers producing $8.9 billion in goods and services.[64]

Although crime has been decreasing for five straight years, as we approach the new millennium, we find that prison expansion has continued at record pace and that the prison population has mushroomed over the last decade to an astonishing 1.75 million souls[65]—the majority of whom are Black, period—not counting the half million persons in county and city jails for a grand sum of 2.25 million prisoners total. The prisons/jails have been majority Black since 1993 when Blacks ascended to fifty-five percent. Other prisoners of color made up eighteen percent and Whites shrunk to twenty-seven percent of the prison population. There are now over two Blacks for every White prisoner,[66] and the ratio increases daily.

The incarceration of women continues to accelerate. There are over 90,000 women in prison today, fifty-four percent are women of color and the vast majority of women in prison are single mothers. Upon imprisonment they lose contact with their children, sometimes forever. There are 167,000 children in the U.S. whose mothers are incarcerated.[67]

The term "crime" has become a code word for "Black and other people of color." The cry for "law and order," "lock 'em up and throw away the key," and for "harsher prisons" is heard everywhere. Nothing is too cruel to be done to prisoners. Control units and control prisons abound across the landscape and prison brutality and torture is the order of the day. The "War on Drugs" continues apace, by now transparent to all as a "war, actually a pre-emptive strike, on people of color" to knock out our youth—our warrior class—and to decrease our birth rate, destabilize our families, re-enslave us through mass imprisonment, and ultimately to eliminate us. The threat is serious and real. To ignore it would be at our own peril.

Despite government mass imprisonment of our youth and covertly fomenting deadly internecine wars among Black street gangs, the abhorrence of the Afrikan community and persistent "Peace Summits" sponsored by Afrikan spiritual, community, and prison leaders have produced somewhat positive, although checkered results. The Gangster Disciples, at Larry Hoover's direction, have struggled to transform their image from a criminal organization to a formidable organization for grassroots empowerment called "Growth and Development." Throughout Chicago's ghettoes they have organized neighborhood cleanups and food drives in which hundreds of bags of Cornish hens and soul food dinners were given away to the poor.

Their political action committee, 21st Century, financed Chicago voter registration drives, conducted gang "peace summits," and held rallies in support of health care reform that eventually won support from the ghetto schools, churches, and community leaders which gave them a measure of mainstream political power. Former GD "war counselor," Wallace "Gator" Bradley ran for Alderman and lost both times, but in January 1994, he was admitted to the White House with Jesse Jackson to speak with Clinton about "combating crime." The GD's power continues to grow although in May 1997, still imprisoned Larry Hoover and six associates were found guilty of narcotic conspiracy.[68]

A shaky peace maintains between the Bloods and CRIPs despite intermittent flare-ups and constant provocations by police to reignite the conflict. Gradually, some Blood and CRIP sets in the West are changing their focus and becoming more involved in endeavors that uplift and protect the New Afrikan community. The Bloods and CRIPs joined the armed contingent led by Dr. Khalid Muhammad and Aaron Michaels of the New Black Panthers of Dallas, Texas, which confronted the Klan demonstration in Jasper, Texas following the brutal pick-up murder there by White racists of a Black hitchhiker, James Byrd, Jr. Some Latin King[69] sets in New York City are doing similar positive work for the Puerto Rican community which is likely the main reason for the recent mass roundup and arrest of ninety-four Latin Kings in New York. Latin Kings were in the streets on Racial Justice Day and took part in the takeover of the Brooklyn's D.A. Office to demand justice for the police murders of Yong Xin Huang and Anibal Carasquillo. When Francis Livoti, cop murderer of Anthony Baez was acquitted in 1996, the Latin Kings joined other protesters in the Bronx. They were among the first on the train to Brooklyn as news of the police rape/torture of Abner Louima hit the streets. Their leader, King Tone, a.k.a. Anthony Fernandez, and a Latin King contingent marched in the October 22, 1997, National Day of Protest Against Police Brutality. The Latin Kings also took part in the protest to demand a new trial for death-row Political Prisoner Mumia Abu-Jamal.[70] Similar positive results have been obtained on occasions by The Code in their work with the Black street organizations of Brooklyn and Queens, New York.

Over the last two decades, the GDs have grown to roughly 30,000 members with GD Chapters in about thirty-five states, primarily in the midwest.[71] The Bloods have reached New York City, and have sets in almost every state. They became the first Black street gang to spread coast to coast in both streets and prisons.[72] Today there are approximately 235 sets of CRIPs in L.A. and the surrounding area. Reportedly, there are CRIP sets in seventeen states and thirty-six cities, including New York. Government sources put their collective number at 90,000. Sanyika Shakur asks rhetorically, "Had we not begun as predators of New Afrikans would we have been allowed to last this long?"[73]

The latter part of the decade witnessed the June 17, 1997, release of BPP/BLA POW Geronimo ji-Jaga after twenty-seven years of unjust imprisonment. He was met with a tumultuous welcome home from the masses wherever he traveled and he confirmed their faith in him by immediately re-immersing himself in the struggle for New Afrikan independence and liberation of all oppressed peoples. In solidarity with the unprecedented gathering two years earlier of more than a million Black men at the Million Man March, three heroic grassroots sisters: Phile Chionesu, Asia Coney, and Nadirah Williams saw their works and faith materialize on October 25, 1997, when over a million Black women gathered at Philadelphia, Pennsylvania, for the Million Woman March. South Africa's Mother of the Struggle, Winnie Mandela, was the key note speaker, along with the Honorable Congresswoman Maxine Waters, and the just released POW Geronimo.[74]

Under POW Jalil Muntaqim's overall leadership, the NALF in conjunction with Jericho 98 Organizing Committee's Herman Ferguson and Safiya Bukhari brought the Jericho March to fruition on March 27, 1998. It was the first national demonstration of its kind on behalf of all PP/POWs in the U.S. Thousands of people of all nationalities from all over the country converged in Washington, D.C., to march from Malcolm X Park to the White House and around it several times, calling for U.S. recognition of, and amnesty for, all PP/POWs incarcerated in the U.S. Geronimo delivered the key note address at the main demonstration across the street in Lafayette Park. Other notable representatives of the people's struggle speaking at the event were Ramona Africa, Kathleen Cleaver, Angela Davis, Benjamin Muhammad (formerly Ben Chavis), Dennis Banks, Alejandro Molina, Julia Wright, Josefina Rodriguez, Alan Berkman, Ali Bey Hassan, Chief Billy Tyak, La Tanya White and many more—each calling for the release of all PP/POWs from prison and an end to the U.S.'s oppressive domination of the poor and people of color.

On September 5, 1998, thousands of Black and other youths of color throughout the country gathered at the Million Youth March/Movement in Harlem, New York, and Atlanta, Georgia. The Million Youth Movement in Atlanta was sponsored by Minister Louis Farrakhan of the NOI, Kweisi Mfume of the NAACP and Jesse Jackson of the Rainbow-Push Coalition. The major theme was that Black youth should be "God-centered" in their preparations to take the reins of leadership in the next century. The Million Youth March in Harlem was spearheaded by Dr. Khalid Muhammad of the New Black Panthers, Attorney Roger Wareham of the December 12th Movement, Attorney Malik Shabazz, and Erica Ford of The Code. The major theme centered around a Black youth "Struggle Agenda" for the coming century, namely:

> Freedom,
> Reparations for the Black Nation,
> Freeing all PP/POWs,
> Control of the Politics and Economics of our Communities,
> Building Independent Institutions in our Communities,
> Control of our Cultural and Intellectual Properties,
> End Police Brutality, Harassment, and Murder of Black People,
> End Racism,
> Self Determination for the Black Nation

Speeches were made by Damien of Harlem's Boys Choir, Farrakhan Muhammed—son of Dr. Khalid, Phile Chionesu, Dr. Josef Ben-Jochannan, Dr. Leonard Jeffries, Attorneys Malik Shabazz and Roger Wareham, Ernie Longwalker and Warrior Woman, Minister Conrad Muhammed, Al Sharpton, and others. Messages were read from various PP/POWs. Valentine, a spectator and twenty-three-year-old member of the United Blood Nation, said one reason he came was "to show his organization had positives" and "to bring understanding." He wore a red and white bandanna around his head to represent his group, and a Million Youth March dog collar around his neck.[75] Dr. Khalid Muhammad's speech concluded the March at which time, a police helicopter buzzed low over the dispersing crowd, and a police contingent rushed the stage to cut off the sound system. A melee ensued leaving one spectator and fifteen police injured. The Harlem community was incensed at Mayor "Adolph" Giuliani and the police department for their racist/fascist posture leading up to and throughout the March, and for their brazen provocations at its end, all of which fell short of their intended effect.

The New Afrikan struggle behind the walls now follows the laws of its own development, paid for in its own blood, intrinsically linked to the struggle of its own people, and rooted deep in the ebb and flow of its own history. To know that history is to already know its future development and direction. The times are serious. Our youth, our women, and therefore our very survival as a people are at stake. We need only, both inside and out, to unite around a struggle agenda, organize, and fight for it, and we shall win without a doubt.

Sundiata Acoli
USP Allenwood
White Deer, PA
December 7, 1998

NOTES

Orignally published by the New Afrikan Peoples Organization; adapted from Acoli's 1992 essay, "The Rise and Development of the New Afrikan Liberation Struggle behind the Walls."

1. Bobby G. Seale, *Seize The Time* (New York: Vintage Books, 1968).

2. *Editor's note:* See Ward Churchill and Jim Vander Wall, *The COINTELPRO Papers: Documents from the FBI's Secret Wars against Dissent in the United States* (Boston: South End Press, 1990), 396.

3. *Editor's note:* The Civil Rights Act was passed in 1968. Its "conspiracy" provision—popularly known as "The Rap Brown Law"—made it a federal crime to cross state lines "with intent to incite riot," or theoretically advocate social change.

4. Chokwe Lumumba, "20th Anniversary Commemoration of the Historic New Bethel Incident," *By Any Means Necessary!* 55, no. 2 (1989): 11.

5. Phil Serafino, "Fight For Economic Rights: Memphis Sanit Workers Urged on Anniversary of King Assassination," *Daily Challenge* (7 April 1989).

6. *Editor's note:* See "Fred Ahmed Evans Dies of Cancer at 46; Jailed for Role in '68 Ohio Riot," *New York Times*, 27 February 1978, D7.

7. *Editor's note:* For state complicity in the drug trade, see: Alfred W. McCoy, *The Politics of Heroin: CIA Complicity in the Global Drug Trade* (Chicago: Lawrence Hill, 1991, revised edition); Dan Baum, *Smoke and Mirrors: The War on Drugs and the Politics of Failure* (New York: Little, Brown, 1996); and Alexander Cockburn and Jeffrey St. Clare, *Whiteout: The CIA, Drugs, and the Press* (New York: Verso, 1999).

8. The "Latin Kings" street organization, officially named the Almighty Latin King and Queen Nation, is thought to be traceable back to the same "King David" who founded the Gangster Disciples but time constraints did not permit the author to pursue verification. Robert D. McFadden, "94 in Latin Kings Are Arrested Citywide," *New York Times*, 15 May 1998, states that the Latin Kings were founded in 1945 by Hispanic inmates in a Chicago jail and later established chapters in the Midwest and Northeast.

Editor's note: For recent documentation on the Latin Kings, see Dave Brotherton and Luis Barrios, *Between Black and Gold: The Street Politics of the Almighty Latin King and Queen Nation* (New York: Columbia University Press, 2003).

9. From author's conversation with, and paper provided by, Derek "D" Williams of the Gangster Disciples.

10. "Fallen Comrades," *The Black Panther* (Spring 1991): 6–7.

11. Lowell Bergman and David Weir, "Revolution on Ice," *Rolling Stone* (6 September 1975): 41–49.

12. Dan Georgakas and Marvin Surkin, *Detroit: I Do Mind Dying* (New York: St. Martin's Press, 1975), 66–68.

13. See Lumumba, "New Bethel Incident," 16.

14. See Prince A. Cuba, "Black Gods," 61.

Editor's note: "Prince A. Cuba" is formally listed as author of *Before Adam* (n.d.) and *Musa and the All-Seeing Eye* (1991), both published by United Brothers and Sisters.

15. Frank Faso, "Kenyatta's Pal is Killed, Cops See Muslim War," *New York Daily News*, 14 June 1969.

16. *Editor's note:* BOSS (Bureau of Special Services) was a division of the New York Police Department that spied on and attempted to disrupt black and Puerto Rican radical groups in the 1970s (see: *Court Action Quarterly* no. 67, Spring–Summer 1999). The Five Percent Nation was a religious organization that split from the Nation of Islam in 1964.

17. *Sourcebook of Criminal Justice Statistics—1986* (Washington, D.C.: U.S. Government Printing Office, 1987), 400.

18. See Calahan, *Correction Statistics*.

19. Author's conclusions based on results of his calculations using data from both Calahan's *Correction Statistics* and *Sourcebook of Criminal Justice Statistics—1986*.

20. From a paper "Origin of the CRIP," submitted to the author by Sanyika Shakur, author of *Monster* and an early CRIP member, and through author's conversations with CRIP member, "Popa" Scott and his close affiliate Marcus Dean.

21. Ward Churchill and Jim Vander Wall, *Agents of Repression* (Boston, Mass.: South End Press, 1988), 410.

22. *Editor's note:* In 2002, H. Rap Brown, now known as Jamil Abdullah Al-Amin, was sentenced to life in prison for the killing of Deputy Sheriff Rickey Kinchen. See: Alan Judd, "Al-Amin Sentenced: Strong Emotions For and Against," *Atlanta Journal-Constitution*, 14 March 2002.

23. *Editor's note:* See Jonathan Jackson, Jr., Foreword, in George Jackson, *Soledad Brother* (Chicago: Lawrence Hill Books, 1994).

24. From the author's conversations with Murdock Vinegar and "Steve-O" Geeot, members of the Bloods, and Marcus Dean of the Bay Area Gangs.

25. From author's conversation with, and paper submitted by, Marcus Dean of the Bay Area Gangs.

26. See "Gangster Disciples" [unpublished paper? N.d.], author's papers.

27. George Jackson, *Blood In My Eye* (New York: Bantam Books, 1972).

28. Sundiata Acoli, *Sunviews* (Harlem, N.Y.: Sundiata Acoli Freedom Campaign, 1981).

29. Assata Shakur, *Assata: An Autobiography* (Westport, Conn.: Lawrence Hill & Co., 1987).

30. Imari Obadele, *Free the Land!* (Wash., D.C.: The Malcolm X Society, 1984).

31. On May 17, 1991, Don Taylor died of cancer at the Stateville, Illinois, prison.

32. *Editor's note:* See Mumia Abu-Jamal, *All Things Censored* (New York: Seven Stories Press, 2000).

33. *Editor's note:* See "Joan Little Pleads Guilty of Escaping," *New York Times*, 13 July 1978, A16.

34. *Editor's note:* See "Around the Nation: 100 March in Plains, Ga. to Protest Woman's Jailing," *New York Times*, 5 July 1978, A11.

35. On Sept. 8, 1989, the D.C. Court of Appeals reversed the decision of the D.C. District Court in *Baraldini v Thornburgh.*

36. Dhoruba Bin-Wahad, *People of the State of New York v Dhoruba Bin-Wahad*, Index #3885-71, New York, April 1988, Motion to Vacate Conviction Pursuant to CPL 440.10. See Appendix containing 243 pages of COINTELPRO files pertaining to Dhoruba alone.

37. See Acoli, *Sunviews*, 26.

38. Atiba Shanna, *Notes From An Afrikan P.O.W. Journal*, Books 1–7 (Chicago, IL: Spear and Shield Publications, 1968).

39. See Note 17 in *Sourcebook of Criminal Justice Statistics—1986.*

40. See Shakur, *Autobiography.*

41. Marpessa D. Kupendua, "Mumia Jamal: Popular Reporter Fighting For Life," *The Last Trumpet*, Vol. 1, No. 1 (1989): 10.

42. *Editor's note:* See Mao Zedong, *Quotations from Chairman Mao Tse-tung* (Peking: Foreign Languages Press, 1966).

43. "Prison Population Sets a Year's Record, Early," *New York Times*, 11 September 1989.

44. See Calahan, *Correction Statistics.*

45. Steve Whitman, "The Crime of Black Imprisonment," *The Chicago Tribune*, 28 May 1987.

46. Unitarian Universalist Service Committee, "Crime and the News Media," 1988.

47. Jo Thomas, "McVeigh Letters Before Blast Show the Depth of His Anger," *New York Times*, 1 July 1998.

48. "Cocaine and Federal Sentencing Policy," *U.S. Sentencing Commission* (February 1995): 124–34.

49. "Slave Labor Behind Bars," *The Revolutionary Worker* (29 October 1995): 8–9.

50. Marc Mauer and Tracy Huling, "Young Black Americans and the Criminal Justice System: Five Years Later" (Washington, D.C.: The Sentencing Project, 1995), 18–20.

51. *New York Times*, 28 October 1995.

52. Dan Wiekel, "War on Crack Targets Minorities Over Whites," *Los Angeles Times*, 21 May 1994.

53. Op cit., *New York Times*, 28 October 1995.

54. Op cit., *Los Angeles Times*, 21 May 1994.

55. *Chicago Tribune*, 30 October 1995.

56. Nancy Kurshan and Steve Whitman, "The Continuing Crime of Black Imprisonment" (Chicago, IL: The Committee to End the Marion Lockdown, 1994).

57. Op cit., The Sentencing Project, 1.

58. Fox Butterfield, "Political Gains by Prison Guards," *New York Times*, 7 November 1995.

59. Butterfield, "Political Gains by Prison Guards."

60. Butterfield, "Political Gains by Prison Guards."

61. Butterfield, "Political Gains by Prison Guards."

62. Op cit., *The Revolutionary Worker*, 29 October 1995.

63. *Editor's note:* See *The Celling of America: An Inside Look at the U.S. Prison Industry*, ed. Daniel Burton-Rose with Dan Pens and Paul Wright (Monroe, Maine: Common Courage Press), 1998.

64. *The Revolutionary Worker*, 29 October 1995.

65. Fox Butterfield, "Prison Population Growing Although Crime Rates Drop," *New York Times*, 9 August 1998.

66. "Black Youths and the Criminalization of a Generation," *The Revolutionary Worker*, 30 August 1998.

67. Meg Henson Scales, "Women in Prison—Hidden Victims of the State," 23 January 1998, email, dharlem@pipeline.com.

68. See "Gangster Disciples."

69. Unauthored, "Operation Crown: The Political Persecution of the Latin Kings," *The Revolutionary Worker*, 31 May 1998.

70. Ibid.

71. See "Gangster Disciples."

72. See "Origin of the Bloods," unpublished paper, author's possession.

73. See "Origin of the CRIP," unpublished paper.

74. *Editor's note:* See Jack Olson, *Last Man Standing: The Tragedy and Triumph of Geronimo Pratt* (New York: Doubleday, 2000).

75. "Million Youth Marching," *The Final Call*, 15 September 1998.

Chapter Eleven

Lorenzo Komboa Ervin

Lorenzo Komboa Ervin was born March 30, 1947, in Chattanooga, Tennessee. A street gang member in his preteen years, at twelve he joined a local National Association for the Advancement of Colored People (NAACP) youth group and participated in the 1960 sit-in protests against racial discrimination in public accommodations. In 1965, Ervin was drafted for the Vietnam War and served two years in the U.S. Army before being court-martialed for his radicalism and antiwar organizing.[1]

In 1967, Ervin joined the Student Nonviolent Coordinating Committee (SNCC). "I learned a lot about internal democracy by being a part of SNCC," Ervin writes in *Anarchism and the Black Revolution*, "[about] how it could make or break an organization, and how it had so much to do with the morale of the members." SNCC, he explains, "developed a working style that was very anti-authoritarian and unique to the civil rights movement."[2] Ervin joined the Black Panther Party (BPP) between 1967 and 1968. He credited his brief period with the Panthers as another valuable learning experience: "It taught me," he recalled, "about the limits of—and even the bankruptcy of—leadership in a revolutionary moment . . . a realization that many times leaders have one agenda, followers have another."[3]

After nationwide riots followed Martin Luther King, Jr.'s 1968 assassination, a grand jury in Hamilton County, Tennessee, began to investigate "SNCC and the Black Power movement's role in planning disturbances in the city of Chattanooga."[4] Fearing "gun-running" charges against him and other SNCC activists and threats of violence from the police and Klansmen, Ervin left the city and went into hiding. The Federal Bureau of Investigation (FBI) utilized the 1968 Civil Rights Act to pursue him on charges of allegedly "bombing Klan offices and smuggling guns to be used during a civil disturbance."[5] That act, which became known as the "Rap Brown Law," made it a federal crime to cross state lines to "incite a riot," that is, engage in political agitation.

On February 25, 1969, armed with a revolver, Lorenzo Ervin hijacked a St. Louis-to-San Juan, Puerto Rico, jetliner, rerouting it to Cuba.[6] There, Ervin surrendered to Cuban authorities. In Atlanta on March 10, 1969, he was indicted by a federal grand jury and a warrant was issued. The following month, with a Cuban passport, he flew to Czechoslovakia, where he was given political asylum.[7] In Prague, Ervin traveled to the American embassy to renounce his American citizenship and was subsequently detained to face charges in the United States. Ervin alleges that he was coerced to sign "voluntary" repatriation papers. While being escorted by embassy personnel to the airport, he escaped.[8] Found on September 22, 1969, in a youth hostel in East Berlin, he was arrested by U.S. agents and forcibly repatriated to stand trial on charges of air piracy and kidnapping.[9] After the FBI arrested him at John F. Kennedy International Airport on September 24,[10] the *New York Times* reported that he had "voluntarily returned."[11]

On July 6, 1970, he was sentenced by an all-white jury in a Georgia court to concurrent life imprisonment on two counts of aircraft hijacking. This was the first life sentence ever imposed on a hijacker.[12] During his fifteen-year incarceration, he was moved approximately every two years between prisons in the South and Midwest, yet continued to organize against racism and for prisoners' human rights.

For his political activity, he was frequently held in solitary confinement. Yet Ervin remained politically engaged: while held in prison in Marion, Illinois, he joined the "Marion Brothers," a group of prisoners who fought in federal courts for general prisoners' rights. The Marion Brothers focused their work specifically on the abhorrent treatment received in the infamous Marion Control Unit. Their work gained the attention of Amnesty International, which castigated prison authorities for violating the United Nations Standard Minimum Rules for the Treatment of Prisoners.[13] Ervin's work with the Marion Brothers helped build international interest in his case. During the late 1970s, he was "adopted" by European anarchist organizations that popularized his case and that of other political prisoners, protesting European visits by then president Jimmy Carter.[14] Due to protest and support campaigns, Ervin was released from a Memphis, Tennessee, prison in December of 1983.

After his release, Ervin returned to Chattanooga, where he remained active with Concerned Citizens for Justice, a local civil rights group organizing against police brutality and the Ku Klux Klan.[15] Ervin's continued activity led to his arrests on a number of political resistance cases, most notably those of the "Chattanooga 8" and "Chattanooga 3."[16]

REFERENCES

Abron, JoNina M. *Protest.* www.protest.net/view.cgi?view = 1933 (14 March 2002).

———. "State's High Court Nixes Chattanooga 8 Case over Arrest." *Tri-State Defender,* 21 March 2001, A1.

Committee to Defend the Chattanooga 3. "Lorenzo Returned to Court and Has Been Assigned a New Prosecutor and Judge." *Infoshop,* 1999. www.infoshop.org/komboa_ervin.html (14 March 2002).

Ervin, Lorenzo Komboa. "Anarchism and the Black Revolution." *Anarchist People of Color*. www.illegalvoices.org/apoc/books/abr/index.html (14 March 2002).

———. *Anarchism and the Black Revolution*. Philadelphia: Mid-Atlantic Anarchist Publishing Collective, 1993.

———. "Behind the Walls of Prison." In *Race Traitor*, edited by Noel Ignatiev and John Garvey, 59–66. New York: Routledge, 1996.

———. "A Call for Amnesty for Black Political Prisoners and POWs." *Black Autonomy*. www.afrikan.net/black.autonomy/farc43.html (14 March 2002).

———. "The Racist Frame-Up of the Chattanooga Three Continues." *Indymedia*, 2001. www.indymedia.org/news/2001/01/1315.php (14 March 2002).

———. "Update on Komboa Ervin and Chattanooga 3 Case." *Infoshop*, 1999. www.infoshop.org/news4/komboa2.html (14 March 2002).

"Hijacker Diverts Plane to Denmark." *New York Times*, 6 June 1970, 62.

"Hijacker of Plane to Cuba Gets First Life Sentence for Offense." *New York Times*, 7 July 1970, 58.

"Hijacking Suspect Seized at Kennedy." *New York Times*, 25 September 1969, 21.

"Jet with 68 Hijacked to Cuba; 'Big Bore,' One Passenger Says." *New York Times*, 26 February 1969, 94.

Lorenzo Edward Ervin, Jr. v Billy Ray Lanier. No. 74 C 1681, United States District Court for the Eastern District of New York, 404 F. Supp. 15; 1975 U.S. Dist. LEXIS 15135 (November 24, 1975).

United States of America v Lorenzo Edward Ervin, Jr. No. 30442 Summary Calendar, United States Court of Appeals for the Fifth Circuit, 436 F.2d 1331; 1971 U.S. App. LEXIS 12329 (January 18, 1971).

NOTES

Research and draft for this biography were provided by Christopher Muller.

1. Lorenzo Komboa Ervin, *Anarchism and the Black Revolution* (Philadelphia: Mid-Atlantic Anarchist Publishing Collective, 1993), 95.

2. *Anarchism and the Black Revolution*, 95.

3. *Anarchism and the Black Revolution*, 92–93.

4. *Anarchism and the Black Revolution*, 92–93.

5. See: Ward Churchill and Jim Vander Wall, *Agents of Repression* (Boston: South End Press, 1988), 354.

6. "Jet with 68 Hijacked to Cuba; 'Big Bore,' One Passenger Says," *New York Times*, 26 February 1969, 94. The flight was later identified as "Eastern Airlines Flight 955." "Hijacker of Plane to Cuba Gets First Life Sentence for Offense," *New York Times*, 7 July 1970, 58.

7. *Lorenzo Edward Ervin, Jr. v Billy Ray Lanier*, No. 74 C 1681, United States District Court for the Eastern District of New York, 404 F. Supp. 15; 1975 U.S. Dist. LEXIS 15135 (November 24, 1975).

8. *Lorenzo Edward Ervin, Jr. v Billy Ray Lanier*, No. 74 C 1681.

9. *Lorenzo Edward Ervin, Jr. v Billy Ray Lanier*, No. 74 C 1681.

10. "Hijacking Suspect Seized at Kennedy," *New York Times*, 25 September 1969, 21.

11. "Hijacker Diverts Plane to Denmark," *New York Times*, 6 June 1970, 62.

12. "Hijacker of Plane to Cuba Gets First Life Sentence for Offense." According to court transcripts, Ervin "was convicted by a jury of aircraft piracy in violation of 49 U.S.C.A. §1472(i) [*1332] (1963), and of kidnapping in violation of 18 U.S.C.A. §1201 (1966). In closing argument, Ervin's council argued that "the issue, instead of being whether or not this man committed the acts charged in the indictment, whether he is guilty of air piracy and whether he is guilty of kidnapping, are, instead, whether because of his mental condition, the lay term being 'insanity,' he is legally responsible for those acts." *United States of America v Lorenzo Edward Ervin, Jr.*, No. 30442 Summary Calendar, United States Courts of Appeals for the Fifth Circuit, 436 F.2d 1331; 1971 U.S. App. LEXIS 12329 (January 18, 1971). In e-mail correspondence in September 2002, Ervin argued that "the legal use of the 'insanity' defense was designed" to discredit his political motives. (L. Ervin e-mail, September 2002, editor's papers.)

13. Amnesty International USA, *Allegations of Mistreatment in Marion Prison, Illinois, U.S.A.* May 1987 (Doc. #AMR 51/26/87).

14. *Anarchism and the Black Revolution*, 96.

15. Concerned Citizens for Justice was succeeded by the "Ad Hoc Coalition against Racism and Police Brutality," *Anarchism and the Black Revolution*.

16. See JoNina M. Abron, "State's High Court Nixes Chattanooga 8 Case over Arrest," *Tri-State Defender*, 21 March 2001, A1; Committee to Defend the Chattanooga 3, "Lorenzo Returned to Court and Has Been Assigned a New Prosecutor and Judge," *Infoshop* 1999, www.infoshop.org/komboa_ervin.html (14 March 2002); JoNina M. Abron, "Stop the Legal Railroading of the Chattanooga 3," *Protest*, 2000, www.protest.net/view.cgi?view=1933 (14 March 2002); and Lorenzo Komboa Ervin, "The Racist Frame-Up of the Chattanooga Three Continues," *Indymedia*, 2001, www.indymedia.org/news/2001/01/1315.php (14 March 2002).

Anarchism and the
Black Revolution (*Abridged*)

1979

ANARCHIST VS. MARXIST-LENINIST THOUGHT
ON THE ORGANIZATION OF SOCIETY

Historically, there have been three major forms of socialism—Libertarian Socialism (Anarchism), Authoritarian Socialism (Marxist Communism), and Democratic Socialism (electoral social democracy). The non-Anarchist Left has echoed the bourgeoisie's portrayal of Anarchism as an ideology of chaos and lunacy. But Anarchism, and especially Anarchist-Communism, has nothing in common with this image. It is false and made up by its ideological opponents, the Marxist-Leninists.

It is very difficult for the Marxist-Leninists to make an objective criticism of Anarchism as such, because by its very nature it undermines all suppositions basic to Marxism. If Marxism and Leninism ([and] its variant which emerged during the Russian Revolution) is held out to be the working class philosophy, and the proletariat cannot owe its emancipation to anyone but the Communist Party, it is hard to go back on it and say that the working class is not yet ready to dispense with authority over it. [V. I.] Lenin came up with the idea of the transitional State, which would "wither away" over time, to go along with Marx's "dictatorship of the proletariat." The Anarchists expose this line as counter-revolutionary and sheer power-grabbing, and over seventy-five years of Marxist-Leninist practice have proven us right. These so-called Socialist States produced by Marxist-Leninist doctrine have only produced Stalinist police states, where workers have no rights, and a new ruling class of technocrats and party politicians have emerged, and the class differential between those the State favored over those it didn't created widespread deprivation among the masses and another class struggle. But instead of meeting such criticisms head on, they have concentrated their attacks not on the doctrine of Anarchism, but on particular Anarchist historical figures, especially [Mikhail] Bakunin ([Karl] Marx's main opponent in the First International).[1]

Anarchists are social revolutionaries who seek a stateless, classless, voluntary, cooperative federation of decentralized communities based upon social ownership, individual liberty, and autonomous self-management of social and economic life.

The Anarchists differ with the Marxist-Leninists in many areas but especially in organization building. They differ from the authoritarian socialists in primarily three ways: they reject the Marxist-Leninist notions of the vanguard party, democratic centralism and the dictatorship of the proletariat, and Anarchists have alternatives for each of them. The problem is that almost the entire Left (including some Anarchists) is completely unaware of Anarchism's tangible structural alternatives of the catalyst group, Anarchist consensus, and the mass commune.

The Anarchist alternative to the vanguard party is the catalyst group. The catalyst group is merely an Anarchist-Communist federation of affinity groups in action. The catalyst group, or revolutionary anarchist federation, would meet on a regular basis or only when necessary, depending on the wishes of the membership and the urgency of social conditions. It would be made up of representatives from the affinity group (or the affinity group itself), with full voting rights, privileges, and responsibilities. It would both set policies and future actions to be performed. It would produce both Anarchist-Communist theory and social practice. It believes in the class struggle and the necessity to overthrow Capitalist rule. It organizes in the communities and workplaces. It is democratic and has no authority figures like a party boss or central committee.

In order to make a revolution, large-scale, coordinated movements are necessary, and their formation is in no way counter to Anarchism. What Anarchists are opposed to is hierarchical, power-tripping leadership which suppresses the creative urge of the bulk of those involved, and forces an agenda down their throats. Members of such groups are mere servants and worshippers of the party leadership. But although Anarchists reject this type of domineering leadership, they do recognize that some people are more experienced, articulate, or skilled than others, and these people will play leadership action roles. These persons are not authority figures, and can be removed at the will of the body. There is also a conscious attempt to routinely rotate responsibility and to pass on these skills to each other, especially to women and people of color, who would ordinarily not get the chance. The experience of these persons, who are usually veteran activists or better qualified than most at the moment, can help form and drive forward movements, and even help to crystallize the potential for revolutionary change in the popular movement. What they cannot do is take over the initiative of the movement itself. The members of these groups reject hierarchical positions (anyone having more official authority than others), and unlike the Marxist-Leninist vanguard parties, the Anarchist groups won't be allowed to perpetuate their leadership through a dictatorship after the revolution. Instead, the catalyst group itself will be dissolved and its members, when they are ready, will be absorbed into the new society's collective decision-making process. Therefore, these Anarchists are not leaders, but merely advisors and organizers for a mass movement. . . .

Anarchism is not confined to the ideas of a single theoretician, and it allows individual creativity to develop in collective groupings, instead of the characteristic dogmatism of the Marxist-Leninists. Therefore, not being cultist, it encourages a great deal of innovation and experimentation, prompting its adherents to respond realistically to contemporary conditions. It is the concept of making ideology fit the demands of life, rather than trying to make life fit the demands of ideology.

Therefore, Anarchists build organizations in order to build a new world, not perpetuate domination over the masses of people. We must build an organized, coordinated international movement aimed at transforming the globe into a mass commune. . . .

WHERE IS THE BLACK STRUGGLE
AND WHERE SHOULD IT BE GOING?

Some, usually comfortable Black middle class professionals, politicians or business-men who rode the 1960s Civil Rights movement into power or prominence, will say that there is no longer any necessity to struggle in the streets during the 1990s for Black freedom. They say that we have "arrived" and are now "almost free." They say our only struggle now is to "integrate the money," or win wealth for themselves and members of their social class, even though they give lip service to "empowering the poor." Look, they say: we can vote, our Black faces are all over TV in commercials and situation comedies, there are hundreds of Black millionaires, and we have political representatives in the halls of Congress and State houses all over the land. In fact, they say, there are currently over 7,000 Black elected officials, several of whom preside over the large cities in the nation, and there is even a governor of a Southern state who is an African-American. That's what they say. But does this tell the whole story?

The fact is that we are in as bad or even worse a shape economically and politically as when the Civil Rights movement began in the 1950s. One in every four Black males are in prison, on probation, on parole, or under arrest;[2] at least one-third or more of Black family units are now single parent families mired in poverty; unemployment hovers at 18–25 percent for Black communities; the drug economy is the number one employer of Black youth; most substandard housing units are still concentrated in Black neighborhoods; Blacks and other non-Whites suffer from the worst health care; and Black communities are still underdeveloped because of racial discrimination by municipal governments, mortgage companies and banks, who "redline" Black neighborhoods from receiving community development, housing and small business loans which keep our communities poor. We also suffer from murderous acts of police brutality by racist cops which have resulted in thousands of deaths and wounding, and internecine gang warfare resulting in numerous youth homicides (and a great deal of grief). But what we suffer from most and what encompasses all of these ills is the fact that we are an oppressed people, in fact a *colonized people*, who are subject to the rule of an oppressive government. We really have no rights under this system, except that which we have fought for and even that is now in peril. Clearly we need a new mass Black protest movement to challenge the government and corporations and expropriate the funds needed for our communities to survive.

Yet for the past twenty-five years the revolutionary Black movement has been on the defensive. Due to co-optation, repression, and betrayals of the Black Liberation movement of the 1960s, today's movement has suffered a series of setbacks and has now become static in comparison. This may be because it is just now getting its stuff together after being pummeled by the State's police agencies, and also because of the internal political contradictions which arose in the major Black revolutionary groups like the Black Panther Party, Student Nonviolent Coordinating Committee (SNCC or "snick" as it was called in those days), and the League of Revolutionary Black Workers, which I believe were factors which led to the destruction of the 1960s Black Left in this country. Of course, many blame this period of relative inactivity in the Black movement on the lack of forceful leaders in the mold of Malcolm X, Martin Luther King [Jr.], Marcus Garvey, etc., while other people blame the "fact" that the Black masses have allegedly become "corrupt and apathetic," or just need the "correct revolutionary line."

Whatever the true facts of the matter, it can clearly be seen that the government, the capitalist corporations, and the racist ruling class are exploiting the current weakness and confusion of the Black movement to make an attack on the Black working class, and are attempting to totally strip the gains won during the Civil Rights era. In addition there is a resurgence of racism and conservatism among broad layers of the White population, which is a direct result of this right-wing campaign. Clearly this is a time when we must entertain new ideas and new tactics in the freedom struggle.

The ideals of Anarchism are something new to the Black movement and have never really been examined by Black and other non-White activists, but put simply, it means that the people themselves should rule, not governments, political parties, or self-appointed leaders in their name. Anarchism also stands for the self-determination of all oppressed peoples, and their right to struggle for freedom . . . by any means necessary.

So what road is in order for the Black movement? Continuing to depend on opportunistic Democratic hack politicians like Bill Clinton or Ted Kennedy, the same old group of middle class sell-out leaders of the Civil Rights lobby, one or another of the authoritarian Leninist sects, who insist that they and *they alone* have the correct path to "revolutionary enlightenment"; or finally building a grassroots revolutionary protest movement to fight the racist government and rulers? Only the Black masses can finally decide the matter, whether they will be content to bear the brunt of the current economic depression and the escalating racist brutality, or will lead a fightback. Anarchists trust the best instincts of the people, and human nature dictates that where there is repression, there will be resistance, where there is slavery, there will be a struggle against it. The Black masses have shown they will fight, and when they organize they will win!

A CALL FOR A NEW BLACK PROTEST MOVEMENT

Those Anarchists who are Black like myself recognize that there has to be a whole new social movement which is democratic on the grassroots level and is self-activated. It will be a movement which is independent of the major political parties, the State and the government. It must be a movement which, although it seeks to expropriate government money for projects which benefit the people, does not recognize any progressive role for the government in the lives of the people. The government will not free us, and is part of the problem, rather than part of the solution. In fact, only the Black masses themselves can wage the Black freedom struggle, not a government bureaucracy (like the U.S. Justice Department), reformist civil rights leaders like Jesse Jackson, or a revolutionary vanguard party on their behalf.

Of course, at a certain historical moment a protest leader can play a tremendous revolutionary role as a *spokesperson* for the people's feelings, or even produce correct strategy and theory for a *certain period* (Malcolm X, Marcus Garvey, and Martin Luther King, Jr. come to mind), and a "vanguard party" may win mass support and acceptance among the people for a time (e.g., the Black Panther Party of the 1960s); but it is the Black masses themselves who will make the revolution, and once set spontaneously in motion, know exactly what they want. Though leaders may be motivated by good or bad, eventually they will act as a brake on the struggle, especially if they lose touch with the freedom aspirations of the Black masses. Leaders can only really serve a legitimate purpose as an advisor and catalyst to the movement, and should be subject to *immediate recall* if they act contrary to the people's wishes, and of course in that kind of limited role they are not leaders at all, they are *community organizers*.

The dependence of the Black movement on leaders and leadership (especially the Black bourgeoisie) has led us into a political dead end. We are expected to wait and suffer quietly until the next messianic leader asserts himself, as if he or she were "divinely missioned" (as some have claimed to be). What is even more harmful is that many Black people have adopted a slavish psychology of "obeying and serving our leaders," without considering what they themselves are capable of doing. Thus they prefer to bemoan the brutal facts, for year after year, of how Brother Malcolm X was taken away from us rather than trying to analyze the current situation and then carrying on his work in the community. Some mistakenly refer to this as a "leadership vacuum." The fact is that there has not been much *movement* in the Black revolutionary movement since his assassination and the virtual destruction of groups like the Black Panther Party. We have been stagnated by middle class reformism and misunderstanding. We need to come up with new ideas and revolutionary formations in how to fight our enemies. We need a new mass protest movement. It is up to the Black masses to build it, not leaders or political parties. They cannot save us. We can only save ourselves.

WHAT FORM WILL THIS MOVEMENT TAKE?

If there was one thing which was learned by Anarchist revolutionary organizers in the 1960s, you don't organize a mass movement or a social revolution just by creating one central organization, such as a vanguard political party or a labor union. Even though Anarchists believe in revolutionary organization, *it is a means to an end*, instead of the ends itself. In other words, the Anarchist groups are not formed with the intention of being permanent organizations to seize power after a revolutionary struggle. But rather to be groups which act as a catalyst to revolutionary struggles, and which try to take the people's rebellions, like the 1992 Los Angeles revolt, to a higher level of resistance.

Two features of a new mass movement must be the intention of creating dual power institutions to challenge the state, [and] the ability to have a grassroots autonomist movement which can take advantage of a pre-revolutionary situation to go all the way. *Dual power* means that you organize a number of collectives and communes in cities and towns all over North America, which are in fact liberated zones, outside of the control of the government. *Autonomy* means that the movement must be truly independent and a free association of all those united around common goals, rather than membership as the result of some oath or other pressure. So how would Anarchists intervene in the revolutionary process in Black neighborhoods? Well, obviously North American or "White" Anarchists cannot go into Black communities and just proselytize, but they certainly should work with non-White Anarchists and help them work in communities of color. (I do think that the example of the New Jersey Anarchist Federation and its loose alliance with the Black Panther movement in that state is an example of how we must start.) And we are definitely not talking about a situation where Black organizers go into the neighborhood and win people to Anarchism so that they can then be controlled by Whites and some party. This is how the Communist Party and other Marxist groups operate, but it cannot be how Anarchists work. We spread Anarchist beliefs not to "take over" people, but to let them know how they can better organize themselves to fight tyranny and obtain freedom. We want to work with them as fellow human beings and allies, who have their own experiences, agendas, and needs. The idea is to get as many movements of people fighting the state as possible, since that is what brings the day of freedom for us all a little closer.

There needs to be some sort of revolutionary organization for Anarchists to work on the local level, so we will call these local groups *Black Resistance Committees*. Each one of these Committees will be Black working class social revolutionary collectives in the community to fight for Black rights and freedom as part of the Social Revolution. The Committees would have no leader or "party boss," and would be without any type of hierarchy structure; they would also be anti-authority. They exist to do revolutionary work, and thus are not debating societies or a club to elect Black politicians to office. They are revolutionary political formations, which will be linked with other such groups all over North America and other parts of the world in a larger movement called a *federation*. A federation is needed to coordinate the actions of such groups, let others know what is happening in each area, and to set down widespread strategy and tactics. (We will call this one, for want of a better name, the "African Revolutionary Federation," or it can be part of a multi-cultural federation.) A federation of the sort I am talking about is a mass membership organization, which will be democratic and made up of all kinds of smaller groups and individuals. But this is not a government or representative system I am talking about; there would be no permanent positions of power, and even the facilitators of internal programs would be subject to immediate recall or have a regular rotation of duties. When a federation is no longer needed, it can be disbanded. Try that with a Communist party or one of the major Capitalist parties in North America!

NOTES

Originally released in its entirety as a pamphlet in 1979, this version is excerpted from a 1993 reprint by the Mid-Atlantic Anarchist Publishing Collective in Philadelphia.

1. *Editor's note:* Mikhail Aleksandrovich Bakunin (1814–1876) was one of the earliest theorists of anarchism. See: Mikhail Aleksandrovich Bakunin, *God and the State* (Freeport, N.Y.: Books for Libraries Press, 1971) and *Marxism, Freedom and the State* (London: Freedom Press, 1950).

2. *Editor's note:* According to the Sentencing Project's mid-year 2001 statistics, one in every eight African American males in the twenty-five to thirty-four age range is incarcerated in prison or jail on any given day. See *New Inmate Population Figures Show Continued Growth, Prospects for Change in Policy Unclear*, www.sentencingproject.org/news/inmatepop-apr02.pdf.

Chapter Twelve

Mumia Abu-Jamal

Mumia Abu-Jamal (Wesley Cook) and his twin brother, Wayne, were born in Philadelphia on April 24, 1954. While in junior high Abu-Jamal joined a march of schoolchildren protesting for black studies classes. While a high school student, he and three friends protested a rally for Southern segregationist George Wallace's presidential campaign. When they were subsequently attacked by whites on the subway, Abu-Jamal appealed to a passing police officer for help. Instead of assistance, he was kicked and punched by the officer, injured past recognition, arrested, and charged with assault. In his book *All Things Censored*, Abu-Jamal writes that he has been "thankful to that faceless cop ever since, for he kicked me straight into the Black Panther Party."[1]

A founding member of the Philadelphia chapter of the Black Panther Party, Abu-Jamal soon found his passion in writing for their paper. He became the lieutenant of information for the Philadelphia Panthers when only fifteen. Like all Panthers working in Philadelphia, he was targeted and monitored by the Federal Bureau of Investigation's (FBI) domestic counterinsurgency program, COINTELPRO. Abu-Jamal remained a Panther until 1970, when factionalism and FBI deception crippled the party.

Attending Goddard College in Plainfield, Vermont, for several semesters between 1978 and 1980, he expanded his journalistic skills by working at the campus radio station. When he returned to Philadelphia, he did reporting on three stations. His career path, however, was continually blocked because of his political views.

One particularly contentious issue in his broadcasts was his coverage of MOVE, a revolutionary community based in Philadelphia. On August 8, 1978, officials flooded, tear-gassed, and shot into the MOVE compound. A police officer was killed, and a MOVE baby also died, allegedly murdered, although mainstream press denied the latter.[2] Nine MOVE members were convicted for the officer's death and were sentenced to thirty to one hundred years of imprisonment.[3] Abu-Jamal's anger about the siege, deaths, and incarceration of MOVE members highlighted his commentaries. Because of his support for the MOVE organization and his criticisms of the Philadelphia police and city administration, he was fired by a local radio station and Mayor Frank Rizzo,[4] a former police officer, threatened him at a press conference.[5]

Although he was still an influential journalist, the loss of his position made supporting his family, which included three children, difficult; consequently, he began driving a cab to supplement his income. After being robbed twice at gunpoint, Abu-Jamal legally bought a gun. While working as a cabbie on December 9, 1981, Abu-Jamal saw his brother, William Cook, being assaulted by a police officer. Abu-Jamal was shot while intervening, and a police officer, Daniel Faulkner, was killed. Abu-Jamal was charged with and convicted of Faulkner's death and sentenced to death following a trial presided over by pro-prosecutorial judge Albert F. Sabo.[6]

Abu-Jamal's past political activity with the Black Panther Party figured prominently in the prosecution's case for the death penalty and its strategy to portray him as a violent "cop-killer." In addition, his forcibly assigned attorney was unprepared and neglected to refute basic inconsistencies in the prosecution's case.[7] Consequently, Abu-Jamal chose to represent himself. Consistently maintaining his innocence, he has spent his sentence appealing his imprisonment and continuing his journalistic advocacy for social justice.

While incarcerated, Abu-Jamal obtained a B.A. from Goddard College, an honorary doctorate of law from the New College of California, a Blackstone School of Law paralegal degree, and completed a thesis for an M.A. in humanities history at California State University. He has published three books: *Live from Death Row*, *Death Blossoms*, and *All Things Censored*.[8] His death sentence was overturned in December of 2001 after a judge found that the instructions to the jury during his trial were unconstitutional.[9] Mumia Abu-Jamal remains on death row awaiting the outcome of appeals.

REFERENCES

Abu-Jamal, Mumia. *All Things Censored*. New York: Seven Stories Press, 2000.
———. *Death Blossoms: Reflections from a Prisoner of Conscience*. Farmington, Pa.: Plough Publishing House, 1997.
———. *Live from Death Row*. New York: Avon, 1996.
Amnesty International. *United States of America; A Life in the Balance: The Case of Mumia Abu-Jamal*. New York: Amnesty International Publications, 2000.
Bisson, Terry. *On a Move: The Story of Mumia Abu-Jamal*. Farmington, Pa.: Litmus Books, 2000.
Edginton, John. *Mumia: A Case for Reasonable Doubt?* Produced and directed by John Edginton. 72 min. Fox Lorber, 1997, 1996. Videocassette.
Ledbetter, James. "Silence of the Damned: Why America Won't Listen to Mumia Abu-Jamal." *The Village Voice*, 6 September 1994, 26–28.
Miller, Arthur. *Fair or Foul: The Case of Mumia Abu-Jamal*. Produced by Andy Halper and directed by Jeffery Nachbar. 45 min. Courtroom Television Network, 1996. Videocassette.

Rimer, Sara. "Death Sentence Overturned in 1981 Killing of Officer." *New York Times*, 19 December 2001.

Schooling the Generations in the Politics of Prison. Edited by Chinosole. Berkeley, Calif.: New Earth Publications, 1996.

"The Story of the MOVE Organization, from *20 Years on the MOVE.*" *Prison Activist Resource Center* (website). Available: www.prisonactivist.org/pps + pows/move-story.html.

Williams, Daniel R. "The Ordeal of Mumia Abu-Jamal." In *States of Confinement*, edited by Joy James. New York: St. Martin's, 2000.

NOTES

Research and draft for this biography were provided by Tiffany Bradley.

1. Mumia Abu-Jamal, *All Things Censored* (New York: Seven Stories Press, 2000), 104.

2. Gregory Jaynes, "Officer Killed as Philadelphia Radicals Are Evicted," *New York Times*, 9 August 1978, NJ21–NJ22.

3. Charles Sims Africa, Debbie Sims Africa, Delbert Orr Africa, Edward Goodman Africa, Janet Hollaway Africa, Janine Phillips Africa, Michael Davis Africa, and William Phillips Africa are all still incarcerated. Merle Austin Africa died in prison in 1998. For more information on the MOVE prisoners, see *Can't Jail the Spirit: Political Prisoners in the U.S.*, 5th ed. (Chicago: Committee to End the Marion Lockdown, 2002).

4. See: Joseph R. Daughen and Peter Binzen, *The Cop Who Would Be King: Mayor Frank Rizzo* (Boston: Little, Brown, 1977).

5. Terry Bisson, *On a Move: The Story of Mumia Abu-Jamal* (Farmington, Pa.: Litmus Books, 2000), 166.

6. *All Things Censored*, 272.

7. See his former attorney's article: Daniel R. Williams, "The Ordeal of Mumia Abu-Jamal," in *States of Confinement*, ed. Joy James. New York: St. Martin's, 2000.

8. Mumia Abu-Jamal, *Live from Death Row* (New York: Avon, 1996); *Death Blossoms: Reflections from a Prisoner of Conscience* (Farmington, Pa.: Plough Publishing House, 1997); *All Things Censored*.

9. Sara Rimer, "Death Sentence Overturned in 1981 Killing of Officer," *New York Times*, 19 December 2001.

Intellectuals and the Gallows

> Yond Cassius has a lean and hungry look; He thinks too much: such men are dangerous.
>
> —Caesar, to Antony; Shakespeare, *Julius Caesar*, Act 1, Scene ii

For academicians and intellectuals, the issue of capital punishment, as practiced in the United States, is a troubling challenge. This is especially so in the case of radical intellectuals, who by necessity form a lesser percentage of academicians, and as such may possess a lesser degree of institutional influence in the academy. The struggle such as one wages for respectability for his views, in a milieu that is, by its very nature, conservative and bound by tradition, may sap the needed energy to battle for larger extra-institutional causes, especially one as popularly projected as capital punishment.

The radical intellectual, struggling for her own place in an academy already under siege by market forces and political interference, may lack the stomach for engaging in external conflicts that are deemed "controversial" by the media projectors of the status quo, for even radical intellectuals must eat; and to eat means to affiliate with aggregates of intellectual organization and power (universities), if one wants to teach.

Nothing written in this essay will relieve the tension between one's fear and one's conscience, for nothing is more controversial in the American context than the state's role in determining whether its purported citizens should live or die. Such an inquiry involves an examination of American history, law, state power and race. It also implicitly involves one's stance vis-à-vis the state, and perhaps more unnervingly, public opinion. This very possibility causes some to shudder, and breeds silence in others.

The question then becomes, how can the truly radical intellectual work in such a milieu? How can s/he do both intellectual work and meaningful political work?

THE THREE PUBLICS

The answer is simply that they *must* do so, in spite of so-called public opinion, and indeed, because of it; for public opinion is, in truth, rarely the opinion of the public; it is more often the projection of powerful elites and monied interests. In his "Three Publics Theory," W. Russell Neumann argues that rather than see the public as a largely undifferentiated mass, it is more accurate to see three publics, each of varying sophistications, knowledge and involvement in the issues of the day.

The first public, representing about 20% of the whole, rises from an absolute low level of sophistication to about a third of the total population's and is deemed "unabashedly apolitical." The second public, about 75% of the populace, is marginally attentive to the political world, and does little more than vote. Their level of sophistication and involvement is middling, rising from the third to perhaps 55% at the periphery of this sector. The third public is the activist core, which comprises about 5% of the total.

This sophistication distribution provides some insight into results of opinion polls, and teaches caution in interpreting them. Neumann likens this sophistication breakdown to a kind of "political literacy":

> The apoliticals can be thought of as fundamentally illiterate, so they are naturally immune to repeated attempts to politicize and mobilize them. They lie below a critical threshold which puts them outside the flow of meaningful political communications. The middle mass can then be characterized as having modest literacy. They keep track of the most important issues with modest effort, but they lack the background information and rich vocabulary necessary for the quick and convenient processing of large amounts of political information. They can communicate political ideas, but they are hunt-and-peck typists. In contrast, the activists are avid readers and lucid speakers. Since virtually all of the professional politicians, journalists and political analysts fall into the highest stratum, they may well share an ingrained incapacity to understand that the vocabulary of politics is interpreted in somewhat different ways by the middle mass, and in stumbling across this phenomenon from time to time, they may mistake the middle mass for the apolitical stratum at the bottom of the continuum.[1]

Included in that "highest stratum," of course, are intellectuals, but rarely are these radicals (for, more often than not, they are stigmatized).

THE CASE OF ANGELA DAVIS

This is illustrated when one considers the notion of left-leaning public intellectuals. The names Angela Davis, Noam Chomsky, Maulana Karenga, and Cornel West leap to mind. Although these scholars represent a wide disparity of perspectives, all may lay some claim to a somewhat radical orientation. Davis is somewhat of an anomaly in this regard as her renown arises not from her remarkable academic or intellectual attributes, but from her historical intersection, interaction, support and proximity with the Black Panther Party, a black revolutionary organization that was involved in several violent conflicts with the state. As a Marxist scholar who stood in support of such a black liberation group, she was herself hounded, imprisoned, and vigorously prosecuted as a black political prisoner on murder, kidnapping and conspiracy charges, stemming from an unsuccessful breakout attempt of several black revolutionaries from the Marin County, California courthouse on 7 August 1970.[2] It is for this episode, then, that Professor Davis is known, and her large and impressive body of writings is relatively little known. She is rarely quoted in mainstream media, and her deeply informed point of view is rarely heard in the predominately white-bread, bourgeois realm of punditry. Indeed, one scholar notes her "iconographic status,"[3] as if frozen in the black power era of the early 1970s, while almost three decades of scholarly and popular writings remain virtually ignored. Even given the remoteness of her arrest and acquittal, school administrators have tried to demonize and challenge Davis' work and scholarship. In 1994, conservative state officials opposed her appointment to a University of California Presidential Chair, and in 1996, one Negro regent[4] castigated the University of California Professor of History of Consciousness for several of her speeches in support of affirmative action, writing: "Your record as a revolutionary is not merely disturbing but it may impair your effectiveness as a member of the faculty of one of this nation's most highly respected academic institutions."[5]

That such a craven political appointee would write such a thing to a distinguished scholar such as Davis, after over a quarter of a century of demonstrating her "effectiveness," is illustrative of the perils facing radical intellectuals.

It illustrates the institutional distaste with which radical intellectuals are held and the lingering threat posed by state actors who oppose radical pedagogy. In a profession where scholars are expected to "publish or perish," Professor Davis has published five books and over twenty-five scholarly articles. The threat arises, then, not because of her lack of scholarship, but because of her political stance.

THE CASE OF NOAM CHOMSKY

The case of linguist Noam Chomsky presents a far more common reflection of the way a radical intellectual is regarded in the United States. Although known in radical, academic and anti-war circles, he is virtually unknown by mainstream media consumers. Although regarded as a brilliant intellectual in the fields of linguistics, cognitive psychology, politics, and philosophy, his anti-imperialistic stance on issues of war and U.S. military aggression has led to his virtual silencing by the media. As early as 1972, Chomsky was named on the Nixon White House "Enemy List" (along with Daniel Ellsberg) for his anti-war intellectual work.[6] Although he is a prodigious writer (of some 70 books or so) who has been published by activist presses (like South End), Chomsky's work has been suppressed by publishers, and some notable media outlets have refused to print his letters or to do interviews with the scholar.[7]

Frequent coauthor Edward Herman notes:

Chomsky has never had an Op Ed column in *The Washington Post*, and his lone opinion piece in *The New York Times* was not an original contribution but rather excerpts from testimony before the Senate Foreign Relations Committee. *The New York Review of Books* exception closed down in 1973, not as a result of any change in Chomsky but following a sharp move to the right by the editors of the journal, who thereafter excluded a number of left critics.[8]

Herman collaborated with Chomsky on a number of works, among them
Counter-Revolutionary Violence: Bloodbaths in Fact and Propaganda (1973) which was
published by a subsidiary of Warner Communications.[9] Robert Barsky's work on
Chomsky's intellectual life and development details the treatment of a text that
sought to describe the horrendous violence perpetrated against the Vietnamese
people by the United States:

> *Counter-Revolutionary Violence* was suppressed by Warner Communications, the giant
> parent company of the publisher Warner Modular. This, in itself, sounds implausible:
> an American megacorporation decides to destroy a book it has already published. Fur-
> thermore, because Warner Modular refused to stop distributing the book after Warner
> Communications issued the order to kill it, the parent company actually put the pub-
> lisher out of business. It gets worse. The book appeared in French translation (*Bains de
> sang*) the following year (1974), but, Chomsky insists, it was "mistranslated to satisfy
> the ideological needs of the French left at that time. . . ."[10]

We need not discuss Messrs. Karenga and West at this juncture, for as we have
seen, the state and the corporate media utilize various strategies to threaten or minimize the status of scholars who dare question the status quo. Radical scholars who
opt to oppose the elite should be mindful of our cited examples, as one contem-
plates assuming such a stance.

RESPONDING TO REPRESSION
WITH ORGANIZATION

It is necessary for us to recognize similar coping strategies employed by Davis and
Chomsky to somewhat mitigate their silencing by the corporate media. Both scholars either developed or affiliated with external social-political structures with which
they organized challenges to the status quo. For Davis, the Communist Party-USA
fulfilled that role, as later did the Committees of Correspondence. Before joining a
wing of the CPUSA, Davis swam in the ambiguity between being a full member
and a "fellow traveler" of the earliest formation of the Black Panther Political Party
of Los Angeles, California, an affiliate of the Oakland office.[11]

Similarly (if not to the same degree) Chomsky has either been on the periphery
or in collectives with other activists. Although not a member, Chomsky was "fairly
close to" the Zionist-Socialist youth group Hashomer Hatzair, although he found
their Marxist-Leninist ideology a bit hard to take.[12] He has chosen to participate in
the South End Press and Z *Magazine* collectives, both of which have published the
bulk of his books and articles. Both had their birth in the Rosa Luxemburg student
group at MIT, where Chomsky served as a student advisor.[13]

Messrs. Karenga and West are active in external groups. Karenga formed the US
organization, and advanced an African-oriented philosophy termed Kawaida. West
is active in the W. E. B. Du Bois Institute at Harvard, and holds a leading position

in the Democratic Socialists of America [West resigned from Harvard in 2002 to take a position at Princeton]. Speaking of W. E. B. Du Bois, we are reminded of one of the most brilliant radical intellectuals of the nineteenth and twentieth centuries, and a man who remained so highly regarded precisely because he committed class betrayal, and used his scholarship to demystify and expose the evils of American white supremacy.

But, it is equally important for us to recognize the achievements of organic intellectuals, uneducated radical activists, who used their inherent wisdom to touch people, to organize them, and to move them; folks like Marcus Garvey, Noble Drew Ali, Hon. Elijah Muhammad, Malcolm (X) Shabazz, Huey P. Newton, Eldridge Cleaver, John Africa, and the list goes on. These radicals and revolutionaries knew that to move an inherently conservative, post-agricultural, oppressed people took enormous effort, untold heartbreak, and a genius unlearned in the master's house; yet they did it. There is a lesson in these examples, for radical intellectuals; that they can, indeed *must*, to quote a Maoism, "learn from the people."

THE RADICAL ANTI-DEATH PROPOSAL

What we have learned is that radical scholars must organize externally to practice their politics and beliefs, for the academic milieu will not suffice. This principle holds true for those radical intellectuals who feel compelled to intervene in the troubling challenge posed by the American practice of death. There are a number of organizations that have either prison or death row as their focus, and would be enriched by the insights and energies of radical thinkers. Radical historians may present linkages between the peculiar American practice of lynchings and the contemporary practice of capital punishment. Radical sociologists might attempt longitudinal studies of those held on death row, or an examination of their families. Radical psychologists might examine how people handle such extended periods of pronounced isolation. Radical philosophers might examine the political usages and advantages of the death penalty to politicians seeking higher office. Radical lawyers and legal scholars might examine the treatment of legal principles by jurists who are called to try, resolve, and develop precedents in capital case jurisprudence.

As Chomsky and Herman noted in *Manufacturing Consent: The Political Economy of the Mass Media*,[14] the mainstream media serves the ruling class interests by derogation, illusion, obfuscation and lies. In the case of radical intellectual antagonists the weapon of choice is to "disappear" them. By so doing they hope to minimize, frustrate and destroy any meaningful critique of the established order.

But there is a method to their madness. The muffling of such critiques has a larger objective: the stifling of the growth and development of popular movements that challenge the status quo, and the rulers. Intellectuals, as a rule, serve the interests of power and capital. Yet it needn't be this way.

With work, with heart, and with daring, they can begin to serve popular interests, and indeed, radical ones. America's fatal addiction to death can be broken, and the role of radical intellectuals can be pivotal to that success. As we have seen, however, no critique is free from reprisal.

You may be targeted. You may be vilified. You may be threatened. You may even be "disappeared."

Yet this world, and life itself, is broader than the ivory towers of academia. Make external connections. Build bridges to the larger, nonacademic community. Establish social, political and communal networks. The word radical means "from the roots"—so, build roots! Touch base with real folks, and work for the only real source of liberty—life!

Ona Move!
Long Live John Africa!

NOTES

Originally published in *Radical Philosophy Newsletter* 49 (September 1999): 1, 3–5.

1. W. Russell Neumann, "The Paradox of Mass Politics: Knowledge and Opinion in the American Electorate," in *Political Psychology: Classic and Contemporary Readings*, ed. Neil J. Kressel (New York: Paragon House, 1993), 258.

2. Davis was acquitted of all charges on June 4, 1972.

3. Joy James, ed. *The Angela Y. Davis Reader* (Walden, Mass.: Blackwell, 1998), 19.

4. *Editor's note:* Abu-Jamal refers here to anti-affirmative action activist Ward Connerly.

5. *The Angela Y. Davis Reader*, 22 n.19.

6. *New York Times*, June 27, 1972.

7. Robert F. Barsky, *Noam Chomsky: A Life of Dissent* (Cambridge: MIT, 1997), 31.

8. Robert F. Barsky, *Noam Chomsky*, 162; Edward S. Herman, "Pol Pot, Faurrison and the Process of Derogation," in *Noam Chomsky: Critical Assessments*, ed. Carlos P. Otero (New York: Routledge, 1994), 3:599.

9. *Editor's note:* Noam Chomsky and Edward S. Herman, *Counter-Revolutionary Violence: Bloodbaths in Fact and Propaganda* (Andover, Mass.: Warner Modular, 1973).

10. Robert F. Barsky, *Noam Chomsky*, 160

11. Joy James, *The Angela Y. Davis Reader*, 8–10.

12. Robert F. Barsky, *Noam Chomsky*, 76.

13. Rosa Luxemburg (1870–1919) was a socialist theorist and agitator in Germany.

14. *Editor's note:* Noam Chomsky and Edward S. Herman, *Manufacturing Consent: The Political Economy of the Mass Media* (New York: Pantheon, 1988; reissued 2002).

Part Two

INTERNATIONALISTS AND
ANTI-IMPERIALISTS

Chapter Thirteen

Mutulu Shakur

Mutulu Shakur (Jeral Wayne Williams) was born on August 8, 1950, in Baltimore, Maryland, and grew up in Queens, New York. Shakur's first involvement with political struggle began with New York's Ocean Hill-Brownsville for decentralization and parental-community control of the public school. The movement's relative success led to further civil rights activism.

In 1970, Shakur began his career as an acupuncturist and health care worker. Joining the Lincoln Hospital Detoxification Program in the Bronx, he used acupuncture in the detoxification programs of thousands of drug-addicted patients. In 1978, he earned a Doctor of Acupuncture degree from the Quebec Institute of Acupuncture, and also that year he cofounded the Black Acupuncture Advisory Association of North America (BAAANA) and the Harlem Institute of Acupuncture. Between 1978 and 1982, extending his medical work, he treated not only drug addicts but elderly and poor patients unable to receive affordable, quality health care.[1]

Ten years earlier, at the age of eighteen, he had been a "founding citizen" of the Provisional Government of the Republic of New Afrika (RNA), which called for reparations as well as an independent black nation within the South. While serving as a leader and providing security in the RNA, Shakur also worked with the New York chapter of the Black Panther Party (BPP). Following the split in the party, he became a member of the Black Liberation Army (BLA);[2] yet throughout the 1970s, Shakur largely focused on his work as an RNA leader. Because of his political activities, the Federal Bureau of Investigation (FBI) began filing regular surveillance reports on Shakur when he was nineteen.[3] In the 1970s, he founded and directed the National Task Force for COINTELPRO Litigation and Research to increase public awareness of the FBI counterintelligence program at a time when few were informed of its existence.

On November 2, 1979, armed BLA members conducted what was described by prison authorities as a "well planned and arranged" action at the Clinton Correctional Institution for Women in New Jersey that resulted in the escape of Assata

Shakur, the prominent BLA leader imprisoned for her alleged role in a 1973 shoot-out on the New Jersey Turnpike. Mutulu Shakur was implicated in the escape by police and subsequently increasingly targeted by them.

On October 20, 1981, an attempted holdup of a Brink's armored truck resulted in the deaths of Brink's guard Peter Paige, police officer Waverly Brown, and Sergeant Ed O'Grady. Although Shakur was not immediately charged and arrested, the Brinks robbery led to a series of legal battles that resulted in his trial and conviction in federal court under the Racketeer Influenced and Corrupt Organizations Act (RICO) for conspiracy and participation in "racketeering enterprise, bank robbery, armed bank robbery, and bank robbery murder."[4] Shakur's defense team argued for an international tribunal to judge him, arguing that Shakur's actions were political and not criminal: the 1977 United Nations amendments to the 1949 Geneva Convention on Human Rights include the clandestine resistance of national liberation movements.

Since his incarceration in 1986, Mutulu Shakur has helped found a youth prisoner organization, the Islamic Young Men's Movement, and played a central role in negotiating a truce between the Bloods and the Crips at Lompoc Penitentiary. A member of the National Committee to Free Political Prisoners prior to his own incarceration, he has supported movements to free political prisoners such as Herman Ferguson, Mumia Abu-Jamal, Sundiata Acoli, and other incarcerated RNA, BLA, and New Afrikan activists.

REFERENCES

"In US-Brink's Trial, New Afrika Wins." *New Afrikan: Organ of the Provisional Government of the Republic of New Afrika* 9, no. 3 (December 1983).

"Memorandum Opinion." *Shakur v Federal Bureau of Prisons, et al.*, U.S. District Court for the District of Columbia. Civil Action No. 96-646. February 3, 1998.

"Memorandum Opinion and Order." *Mutulu Shakur and Marilyn Buck v United States of America.* U.S. District Court for the Southern District of New York. 97-CV-2908. January 13, 1999.

Odinga, Sekou, Hanif Shabazz Bey, Mutulu Shakur, Kojo, Jalil Muntaqim, Jihad Mumit, Sundiata Acoli, and Geronimo ji Jaga. "Statement in Support of Consolidation from New Afrikan POWs and Political Prisoners in Lewisburg, Pennsylvania, New York, and California Prisons: Toward the Objective of Building a National Liberation Front." *Jericho Movement* (commemorative newspaper for March 27, 1998, march in Washington, D.C.).

Shakur, Mutulu. "Another Crime Bill?" www.efn.org/~ironplow/mutulush.

———. "Mutulu Shakur: New African Political Prisoner." In *Can't Jail the Spirit: Political Prisoners in the U.S.* 1st ed. Chicago: Editorial El Coqui, 1988.

Shoats, Russell. "Black Fighting Formations: Their Strengths, Weaknesses, and Potentialities." In *Liberation, Imagination, and the Black Panther Party*, edited by Kathleen Cleaver and George Katsiaficas. New York: Routledge, 2001.

NOTES

Research and draft for this biography were provided by Will Tucker and Tiffany Bradley. Although we were unable to provide biographies of Mutulu Shakur's coauthors, we were able to obtain the following information. Mark Cook, the only African American man arrested for the actions of the George Jackson Brigade (of which Bo Brown was a member), served the longest prison term of convicted Brigade members. *Independentista* Adolfos Matos received clemency from President Bill Clinton; he currently lives in Puerto Rico.

1. Mutulu Shakur, "New Afrikan Political Prisoner," in *Can't Jail the Spirit: Political Prisoners in the U.S.*, 4th ed. (Chicago: Committee to End Marion Lockdown, 1998), 148.

2. For details on the Newton/Cleaver–East/West split of the BPP, see Donald Cox, "The Split in the Party," in *Liberation, Imagination, and the Black Panther Party*, ed. George Katsiaficas and Kathleen Neal Cleaver, 119–22 (New York: Routledge, 2001). The BLA is examined in Russell Shoats, "Black Fighting Formations: Their Strengths, Weaknesses, and Potentialities," in *Liberation, Imagination, and the Black Panther Party*, 128–38.

3. "Dr. Mutulu Shakur," *Jericho*; Shakur, "New Afrikan Political Prisoner," 149–50.

4. "Memorandum Opinion and Order," *Mutulu Shakur and Marilyn Buck v United States of America*. U.S. District Court for the Southern District of New York, 97-CV-2908, January 13, 1999.

Genocide against the Black Nation in the U.S. Penal System *(Abridged)*

Mutulu Shakur, Anthony X. Bradshaw, Malik Dinguswa,
Terry Long, Mark Cook, Adolfo Matos,
and James Haskins
1988

We specifically charge that the government of the United States is practicing genocide through behavior modification and counterinsurgency and low intensity warfare techniques in its state and federal prisons.

We submit that behavior modification as practiced in United States prisons incorporates techniques from both counterinsurgency–low intensity warfare, and psychology for political and military objectives. The implementation of this strategy in the United States penal system is the result of research conducted by government scientists and counterinsurgency agents who studied the theories and works of experts in the distinct fields of behavior therapy (synonymous with behavior modification), insurgency, and low intensity warfare.

Every aspect of this behavior modification program violates the human rights of those persons subjected to it, and it is this treatment that is vehemently complained about by political prisoners and POWs [prisoners of war]. This program involves a scientific approach in targeting special prisoners with the aim of achieving political objectives. Each targeted prisoner is observed to determine his or her leadership potential, religious beliefs, aspirations, and, most importantly, to record his or her reaction to the experiments being implemented. The sole purpose of the program is for government agents to learn lessons from how political prisoners suffered and reacted during experiments; then use those findings to formulate a broad plan to be implemented against the people in society at large who are the ultimate targets.

The oppressive conditions and the experiments conducted in the U.S. penal system, as implemented by prison officials, are evidence of a psychological war being waged against political prisoners[1] who come from a people involved in a struggle of resistance. When the behavior modification program conducted by the government is viewed in the light of the "Geneva Accord" mandates, one can only conclude that the United States Government's actions are criminal and violate international human rights laws. Accordingly, the United States Government's acts should be regarded as war crimes.

Specifically, the U.S. Government is in violation of Article I of the Geneva Convention on the prevention and punishment of the crime of genocide, which was approved by the United Nations General Assembly on December 9, 1948, and the U.S. Government is in violation of resolution 260, III, which entered into force on

January 12, 1951.[2] In this resolution "the contracting parties confirmed that genocide, whether committed in time of peace or in time of war, is a crime under international law which they undertake to prevent and punish." According to Article
II, genocide is defined as any of the following acts committed with the intent to
destroy, in whole or in part, a national, ethnic, racial, or religious group such as:
(a) killing members of the group; (b) causing serious bodily harm or mental harm
to members of the group; (c) deliberately inflicting on the group conditions of life
calculated to bring about its destruction in whole or in part; (d) imposing measures
intended to prevent births within the group; or (e) forcibly transferring children of
the group to another group.

Having reviewed the list of acts that constitute the crime of genocide, as set forth
by the Geneva Convention, we submit that the behavior modification program
being carried out in the United States penal system is a scientific form of genocide
waged against the Black Nation, and it is a continuance of the nefarious tactics
employed by the government over the years to subjugate the Black Nation. On
learning of the use of behavior modification techniques to further counterinsurgency–low intensity warfare objectives, especially in light of the government's
intended broad application, all caring people should be shocked.

Behavior modification is a complex science composed of information from psychology, sociology, philosophy, anthropology, and even some aspects of biology. By
definition "behavior modification" broadly refers to the systematic manipulation of
an environment for the purpose of creating a change in individual behavior.

We submit that Black people were in fact the first experimental targets of group
behavior modification. Furthermore, current data and statistics on the prison situation support our contention that Black people inside state and federal prisons today
remain the prime targets of the government's program. Moreover, we discovered
during our research that the psychological warfare being waged in the U.S. penal
system was planned as far back as the early 1960s because the government foresaw
that Black people, like those in prison, would revolt against oppression. Black people's conduct, like that of many people throughout history, validates the axiom that
"oppression breeds resistance."

In 1961, a social scientist, Dr. Edward Schein, presented his ideas on brainwashing at a Washington, D.C., meeting convened by James V. Bennett, then director
of the Federal Bureau of Prison Systems; the meeting was attended by numerous
social scientists and prison wardens.[3] Dr. Schein suggested to the wardens that
brainwashing techniques were natural for use in their institutions. In his address on
the topic "Man Against Man," he explained that in order to produce marked
changes of behavior and/or attitude it is necessary to weaken, undermine or remove
the supports of old patterns of behavior and old attitudes: "Because most of these
supports are the face-to-face confirmation of present behavior and attitudes, which
are provided by those with whom close emotional ties exist." This can be done by
either "removing the individual physically and preventing any communication with
those whom he cares about, or by proving to him that those whom he respects are

not worthy of it, and indeed should be actively mistrusted." Dr. Schein then provided the group with a list of specific examples such as:

1. Physical removal of prisoners to areas sufficiently isolated to effectively break or seriously weaken close emotional ties.
2. Segregation of all natural leaders.
3. Use of cooperative prisoners as leaders.
4. Prohibition of group activities not in line with brainwashing objectives.
5. Spying on the prisoners and reporting back private material.
6. Tricking men into written statements which are then shown to others.
7. Exploitation of opportunists and informers.
8. Convincing the prisoners that they can trust no one.
9. Treating those who are willing to collaborate in far more lenient ways than those who are not.
10. Punishing those who show uncooperative attitudes.
11. Systematic withholding of mail.
12. Preventing contact with anyone non-sympathetic to the method of treatment and regimen of the captive populace.
13. Building a group among the prisoners convincing them that they have been abandoned by and totally isolated from the social order.
14. Disorganization of all group standards among the prisoners.
15. Undermining of all emotional supports.
16. Preventing prisoners from writing home or to friends in the community regarding the conditions of their confinement.
17. Making available and permitting access to only those publications and books that contain materials which are neutral to or supportive of the desired new attitudes.
18. Placing individuals into new and ambiguous situations for which the standards are kept deliberately unclear and then putting pressure on them to conform to what is desired in order to win favor and a reprieve from the pressure.
19. Placing individuals whose willpower has been severely weakened or eroded into a living situation with several others who are more advanced in their thought reform and whose job it is to further the undermining of the individuals' emotional supports which were begun by isolating them from family and friends.
20. Using techniques of character invalidation, e.g., humiliations, revilement, shouting to induce feelings of guilt, fear and suggestibility, coupled with sleeplessness, and exacting prison regimen and periodic interrogational interviews.
21. Meeting all insincere attempts to comply with cellmates' pressures with renewed hostility.
22. Repeated pointing out to prisoner by cellmates of where he was in the past, or is in the present, not even living up to his own standards or values.

23. Rewarding of submission and subservience to the attitudes encompassing the brainwashing objective with a lifting of pressure and acceptance as a human being.
24. Providing social emotional supports which reinforce the new attitudes.

Following Schein's address, Bennett commented, "We can perhaps undertake some of the techniques Dr. Schein discussed and do things on your own. Undertake a little experiment with what you can do with the Muslims. There is a lot of research to do. Do it as groups and let us know the results."

Approximately eleven years after that significant meeting, it was confirmed that Schein's ideas and objectives were in fact being implemented inside the prisons. In July 1972, the Federal Prisoner's Coalition, in a petition to the United Nations Economic and Social Council, asserted that the Asklepieion program conducted at the Marion, Illinois, federal penitentiary was directly modeled on methods of thought control/reform. The petition contains a point-by-point comparison between Schein's address, and the goals and structure of the Asklepieion program.[4]

We should not overlook the fact that prison officials will also use drugs as a method of control. In fact, we have discovered that most of the drugs used by prison officials today are far more detrimental in their relative potency than those used in earlier years.[5] It is not unusual inside the prisons today to see prisoners exhibiting "zombie-like-behavior" as a result of the type of drugs administered to them against or with their consent. In many prisons it is a prerequisite for some prisoners to take certain prescribed drugs in order to be released from solitary confinement. There are several courts that support the forcible use of drugs by prison officials, thus leaving the way open for the use of drugs as a hands-on tactic.

Whether or not one responds with a shocked conscience on learning of the behavior modification experiments, one should bear in mind that the behavior modification experiments are conducted to achieve warfare objectives. Nevertheless, the judicial branch of government, by not intervening to order the executive branch [Reagan/Bush administrations] to cease their deleterious program and practices, supports the daily abuses arising out of the behavior modification program. . . .

We submit that the captured Black Nation was and remains a prime target of the government's strategy of behavior modification counterinsurgency and low intensity warfare. Evidence of the government's strategy is revealed by the exceptionally harsh treatment inflicted on Black prisoners—especially those prisoners who are committed to the Black Liberation Movement's struggle for self-determination.

It is important to understand that the prisons in the United States have always been operated primarily by white administrators predominantly working with white prison guards. This combination of factors renders the Black prisoner excessively vulnerable to and a prime target of unbridled racism and brutality.

Also, we must not overlook the fact that there are prisoners from other oppressed Nations inside the United States and from the Caribbean Islands who, as they fight for their national liberation, are also targeted by this government. . . . The Puerto

Rican National Liberation Movement in Puerto Rico and in the United States has been a prime target of the U.S. government, and the government has used the most severe tactics of counterinsurgency and low intensity warfare against them for over a half century. Since United States troops invaded the island in 1898, the people have used every method within their reach to terminate the colonial structure designed and imposed on them by their U.S. colonizers. . . . UN General Assembly Resolution 3030 states that "The General Assembly . . . reaffirms the legitimacy of the people's struggle for liberation from colonial and foreign domination and alien subjugation by all available means, including armed struggle." The American Government has assassinated members of the Puerto Rican movement; it has tortured and maimed its political prisoners; it has used frame-ups for imprisonment; it has transferred the Puerto Rican leadership from the Island of Puerto Rico to prisons deep inside the United States, thus, denying the leadership the opportunity to maintain a community with other activists.[6]

Another example of U.S. imperialism appears in the government's handling of incarcerated Black and Latin freedom fighters from the Caribbean. Many of these prisoners are politically opposed to the "puppet regimes in their Caribbean Islands that America controls."[7] Consequently, these dissident prisoners also become targets of the government's counterinsurgency and low intensity warfare. (It should also be understood that because of the geo-political and economic objectives the United States is carrying out in these underdeveloped and developing nations many social crimes are committed on these islands and these crimes are a direct result of America's intervention.) After arriving on U.S. soil, though, the prisoners from the Caribbean Islands become socially, politically and culturally active in the prison system, and their experiences incline them to create unbreakable bonds between themselves and the other Black freedom fighters inside the United States.

To fully appreciate the overall effect of behavior modification and low intensity warfare on those prisoners subjected to it, more research will have to be done. But we feel that it is safe to say, in view of the incarceration of freedom fighters from the Caribbean in this prison system, and their resulting political and cultural isolation, that they are very, very much enmeshed in the U.S. government's counterinsurgency–low intensity warfare and behavior modification programs.

The citing of Blacks from the United States and the Caribbean and Puerto Ricans from the United States and Puerto Rico[8]—all freedom fighters of color—gives rise to the question: Are white anti-imperialists prisoners also targeted by the government's programs? When white anti-imperialists are charged and brought before judicial tribunals, often U.S. judges maintain that because the white anti-imperialists are not victims of oppression, they have no justification for participating in resistance. This position rejects a political stance based on the "necessity defense" of the "Nuremberg Principle" [see Marilyn Buck's essay that follows]. Furthermore, it is natural for caring people to sympathize with and support those who resist being oppressed. However, when the white anti-imperialists do get involved in the resistance and are placed in prison, a racist government can discourage other whites from aligning themselves with Blacks in struggle by the severe, at times cruel, treatment it inflicts on anti-imperialists.

We charge that there is and has been a very clear and systematic program of low intensity warfare in motion in America's prisons based on "mentacide"—the ruthless manipulation of people's minds that reduces them to broken subjects.

Isolation and sensory deprivation as it is practiced in prisons across America is a definite aspect of the oppressor's controlled environment. Through isolation, and through the systematic removal, inclusion, or manipulation of key sensory stimuli, the government can attack a prisoner's mind and reduce him or her to a warped, subservient state characterized by feelings of lethargy, listlessness and hopelessness . . . in short, a prisoner develops the feeling of being "more dead than alive."

They combine sensory stimuli with a nutritiously deficient diet, that leaves one feeling hungry, lethargic, and depressed (ultimately with self-destructive thoughts). Government officials know exactly what they are doing; they know precisely what their "scientific" experiments will entail. In this they are again in violation of international standards.[9]

The penal system is designed to break minds, to create warped and aberrant personalities, and isolation and sensory deprivation play a singular and unique role in this.[10]

In general, all prisoners are targeted. (Even the staff themselves become victimized by the same system they blindly seek to uphold: you cannot dehumanize people without yourself becoming dehumanized in the process.) Yes, all prisoners are targeted, and the harshness of their treatment varies only in degree, with the most severe treatment being meted out to those with some political consciousness. They concentrate punishment on the political prisoner because the political prisoner has the clearest understanding of the prevailing exploitative relationships, and so has the greatest potential for awakening and organizing the rest of the prisoners.

In prison, isolation and sensory deprivation, deficient diets, confinement within a limited space, denial of privacy, lack of natural light and fresh air, lack of comradeship, lack of undisturbed sleep, lack of proper health care, lack of educational and recreational outlets—all reduce one to an existence of lifelessness.

This is war. This is a war of attrition, and it is designed to reduce prisoners to a state of submission essential for their ideological conversion. That failing, the next option in deadly sequence is to reduce the prisoners to a state of psychological incompetence sufficient to neutralize them as efficient, self-directing antagonists. That failing, the only option left is to destroy the prisoners, preferably by making them desperate enough to destroy themselves. The purpose of this isolation and sensory deprivation is to disrupt one's balance, one's inner equilibrium, to dehumanize the prisoner, to depersonalize him, to strip him of his unique individuality, rendering him pliant in the hands of his vicious captors.

We note that amongst the many effects of the process is the disruption of the biological time clock, neuropathic disorders, bio-chemical degeneration, depression, apathy, chronic rage reaction, defensive psychological withdrawal, loss of appetite (or the opposite extreme), weight loss, and the exacerbation of pre-existing medical problems.

There are important and relevant international bodies that exist to uncover and redress human rights violations.[11] But what we ask—those of us who have been victimized—is "Where are the stringent voices of those international bodies as, day in and day out, our rights and dignity, are offended and trampled on over and over again?" Is everyone so inexorably chained to partisan politics that they refrain from applying their conscience until given the nod by party bigwigs? The world can see what goes on in the tombs of America as Black people are being slowly strangled and suffocated to death. . . .

Yes, the world can see what goes on. Yet there remains a deadly chorus of silence, a conspiracy of silence.

We charge the American Government with genocide. In clear, unequivocal terms, we charge the American government with genocide against the captive Black people in America who are perpetually under siege.

NOTES

Originally published in unedited form in *Schooling the Generations in the Politics of Prison*, ed. Chinosole (Berkeley, Calif.: New Earth Publications, 1996).

1. When the term "political prisoner" is used in this paper, it is not limited to those who are incarcerated as a result of their political beliefs, actions, or affiliations. The term includes persons in prison for social crimes who became politicized inside prison walls, and who oriented their lives around the struggle for social justice and national liberation. Such persons as MALCOLM X, GEORGE JACKSON, THE ATTICA WARRIORS, and the many other men and women of yesterday and today's struggle would be and are encompassed in the term.

2. Essentially, the Nuremberg principle makes war crimes indefensible despite military orders. See Marilyn Buck, "The Struggle for Status Under International Law" [found in this anthology].

Editor's note: The U.S. Congress ratified the UN Convention against Genocide in 1988, adding crippling amendments; then-president Ronald Reagan signed it into law that same year.

3. Information concerning that historical meeting is found in Alan W. Scheflin, *The Mind Manipulators* (Grosset and Dunlap, 1978); and the pamphlet *Breaking Men's Minds* on behavior control in Marion, Illinois.

4. See Scheflin, *Mind Manipulators*.

Editor's note: Asklepieion (from Asklepios, a Greek deified for his healing powers) was the name given to a behavior modification program based on Transactional Analysis (TA) and applied in several maximum-security prisons in the United States beginning in the 1970s.

5. The drug thorazine (chlorpromazine) was one of the first anti-schizophrenia drugs used in the United States and was generally given to prisoners in earlier years. This drug, which produces "zombie-like-behavior" in the individual, has been used as the standard against which the newer drugs are compared. (See Arnold A. Lazarus, *The Practice of Multi-*

modal Therapy [Baltimore: Johns Hopkins University Press, 1989, paperback reprint edition].) Although thorazine is still being used by prison officials today, new drugs called prolixin (fluphenazine) and haldol (haloperidol) are increasingly prescribed. Prolixin has a relative milligram potency of 70:1 to thorazine, and haldol has a potency of 100:1 to thorazine; both can cause drastic mental and physical side effects.

6. A Senate committee chaired by Senator Frank Church [D-Idaho] in 1975 evaluated the riots and rebellion that swept the United States during the development of the Liberation Movement in the 1960s era, and the government's use of illegal and deadly means to counter protest movements.

7. Again, the U.S. Government is clearly violating international standards by transferring Puerto Rican and Caribbean political prisoners into U.S. prisons. On March 3, 1989, the U.N. General Assembly passed Resolution 43/173, also called "Body of principles for the protection of all persons under any form of detention or imprisonment." Principle 20 states, "If a detained or imprisoned person so requests, he shall if possible be kept in a place of detention or imprisonment reasonably near his usual place of residence."

8. The exploitative and brutal control the United States wields over the Caribbean Islands is evinced by its cowardly attack on Grenada, its intervention in Michael Manley's government during the Jamaican election, and the continual colonization of the Virgin Islands. One salient consequence of the U.S. exploitation of the Caribbean is the influx of Rastafarian and progressive prisoners from the Islands into U.S. prisons.

9. See *Covert Action Information Bulletin*, issue number 31, wherein Susan Rosenberg speaks about the horrendous conditions under which she, Silvia Baraldini and Alejandrina Torres were confined in the Lexington High Security Unit. UN Resolution 43/173, Principle 22, passed into effect on March 19, 1989, states the following: "No detained or imprisoned person shall, even with his consent, be subjected to any medical or scientific experimentation which may be detrimental to his health."

10. See Scheflin, *The Mind Manipulators*. It contains information on some of the techniques used on prisoners; its list of the chapters includes "Assaulting the Mind"; "Tampering with the Mind"; "Ruling the Mind"; "Amputating the Mind"; "Pruning the Mind"; "Rewiring the Mind"; "Blowing the Mind"; "Castrating the Mind"; "Robotizing the Mind."

11. We do not mean to imply that these international bodies have not done some outstanding work. We acknowledge that these bodies have monitored certain regions and countries, and they have called attention to human rights abuses occurring in those areas. What we do charge, however, and feel most strongly about, is that these same international bodies have been virtually silent with regard to the brutal treatment of Blacks in America, a people who have never had any real rights in America. We are calling attention to this neglect. (See Marilyn Buck "The Struggle for Status Under International Law.")

Chapter Fourteen

Marilyn Buck

Marilyn Buck was born in 1947, in Temple, Texas, the daughter of a nurse and an Episcopal minister active in the civil rights movement. She herself first became politically active while a student at the University of Texas, and later at the University of California-Berkeley, where she protested against sexism and the Vietnam War and supported the Black Power movement. In 1967, Buck attended a teacher-organizer school led by Students for a Democratic Society (SDS) in Chicago and briefly edited the SDS's national newsletter, *New Left Notes*. Committed to educational organizing, in 1968, she returned to California and began with San Francisco Newsreel, a radical filmmaking collective. Buck also worked in solidarity with indigenous groups and the black liberation movement, the Black Liberation Army (BLA), and international organizations struggling in Vietnam, Palestine, and Iran.

In 1973, Marilyn Buck became a target of the Federal Bureau of Investigation's (FBI) COINTELPRO campaign against the Black Liberation Army and the Weathermen. Captured in her apartment in San Francisco, she was held on a $100,000 cash bail for purchasing ammunition under a false ID and for an application for a social security card using an alias.[1] Convicted, Buck was sentenced to ten years, an unusually long term for a minor offense. The FBI accused her of being a member of the BLA and increased surveillance of Buck during her incarceration, monitoring her contacts with friends and political associates who corresponded with and visited her.

Sent to an experimental behavior modification program at the Federal Women's Prison in Alderson, West Virginia, Buck endured psychological torture used in U.S. prisons to "neutralize" prisoners who pose the threat of political dissidence or escape. In 1977, she did not return from a work furlough; she escaped and went underground, where she continued anti-imperialist and antiracist activism.

In 1979, when Black Panther–BLA leader Assata Shakur successfully escaped from a New Jersey prison, Buck was suspected as an accomplice. In October 1981, along with codefendants Mutulu Shakur, Sekou Odinga, Silvia Baraldini, and others, she was indicted in a conspiracy that included Assata Shakur's escape and the

"Brink's robbery" in Rockland County, New York, which resulted in the killing of two policemen and a guard.[2] Buck was captured in Dobbs Ferry, New York, in 1985.[3]

For the next five years, Buck faced four separate trials.[4] In 1987, she went on trial for conspiracy under the Racketeer Influenced and Corrupt Organizations Act (RICO), used in counterinsurgency because it turned politically subversive movements into "criminal" organizations. Baraldini and Odinga were convicted in the first RICO trial.[5] Buck and Mutulu Shakur were convicted in 1987 in the second RICO conspiracy trial, charged with conspiracy to commit armed bank robbery in support of the New Afrikan Independence struggle.[6] She was sentenced to fifty years in addition to twenty years of previous convictions and ten years for the resistance conspiracy case (see Evans et al. biography in this volume) for a total of eighty years.[7]

Trained as a literacy teacher, Marilyn Buck has worked in prison with immigrant women and women pursuing their graduate equivalent degrees (GEDs). Laura Whitehorn recalls witnessing Buck—then her prison cellmate—quietly getting up at five o'clock in the morning to tutor women who wanted to learn confidentially and teaching yoga classes and conducting HIV/AIDS education and support work with other prisoners.[8] Studying for a master's in poetics, she continues to write and publish poetry, and until recently wrote a column, "Notes from the Unrepenitentiary," in *Prison Legal News*. In the 1990s, she translated articles for the Chicago monthly journal *Latin America Update*.

Marilyn Buck received a Pen Prison Writing Prize (April 2001) for her volume of poetry, *Rescue the Word*. Her poems also appear in *Concrete Garden*, *Sojourner*, *BLU Magazine*, *Prosodia X*, *2001*, and the anthologies *Hauling Up the Morning, Voices of Resistance; Doing Time: 25 Years of Prison Writing*; and *Wall Tappings: An International Anthology of Women's Prison Writings, 200 A.D. to the Present*. Following the September 11, 2001, tragedy, under the orders of Attorney General John Ashcroft, she was taken out of general population in her Dublin, California, prison and placed in isolation for several weeks, denied contact with family, friends, and attorneys.

REFERENCES

Baraldini, Sylvia, Marilyn Buck, Susan Rosenberg, and Laura Whitehorn. "Women's Control Unit." In *Criminal Injustice: Confronting the Prison Crisis*, edited by Elihu Rosenblatt. Boston: South End, 1996.

Buck, Marilyn. "On Self-Censorship." Berkeley, Calif.: Parentheses Writing Series, Small Press Distribution, 1995.

———. "On the Burning of African American Churches." *Prison News Service* 55 (Summer/Fall 1996).

———. "Prisons, Social Control, and Political Prisoners." *Social Justice* 27, no. 3: 200.

———. *Rescue the Word: Poems*. San Francisco: Friends of Marilyn Buck, 2001.

———. "Thoughts on the Surrender of Kathy Power." *Downtown*, New York, 1993. www.

etext.org/Politics/Arm.The.Sp...oners/marilyn-buck.interview.december-93 (17 March 2002).

———, and Laura Whitehorn. "Legal Issues for Women in Federal Prisons: FCI Dublin California." *The Legal Journal* 10, no. 11 (Winter 1996).

———. "Interview with Resistance in Brooklyn." In *Enemies of the State: A Frank Discussion of Past Political Movements, Victories and Errors, and the Current Political Climate for Revolutionary Struggle Within the U.S.A.* Toronto: Resistance in Brooklyn and Arm the Spirit, 2001.

Can't Jail the Spirit: Political Prisoners in the U.S. 5th ed. Chicago: Committee to End the Marion Lockdown, 2002.

Heidhues, Lee Ross. "Law 'N' Order Judge Presides at Trial of Accused BLA Member." *Sun Reporter*, 11 August 1973, N33.

Lubasch, Arnold H. "2 Ex-Fugitives Convicted of Roles in Fatal Armored-Truck Robbery." *New York Times*, 12 May 1988, B4.

"Marilyn Buck Page." *Prison Activist Resource Center.* www.prisonactivist.org/pps + pows/marilynbuck/ (27 February 2002).

Resistance Conspiracy. San Francisco: Bay Area Committee to Support the Resistance Conspiracy Defendants [distributor]; Oakland: Peralta Colleges Television (PCTV) Production Company, 1990. Videocassette.

Treatster, Joseph B. "Marilyn Buck: A Fugitive and Long a Radical." *New York Times*, 23 October 1981, B5.

NOTES

Research and draft for this biography were provided by Martha Oatis.

1. Lee Ross Heidhues, "Law 'N' Order Judge Presides at Trial of Accused BLA Member," *Sun Reporter*, 11 August 1973, N33.

2. Joseph B. Treatster, "Marilyn Buck: A Fugitive and Long a Radical," *New York Times*, 23 October 1981, B5.

3. Arnold H. Lubasch, "2 Ex-Fugitives Convicted of Roles in Fatal Armored-Truck Robbery," *New York Times*, 12 May 1988, B4.

4. "Marilyn Buck," in *Can't Jail the Spirit: Political Prisoners in the U.S.*, 5th ed. (Chicago: Committee to End the Marion Lockdown, 2002), 193.

5. Silvia Baraldini was repatriated to Italy where she is under house arrest; Mutulu Shakur and Sekou Odinga are incarcerated in the United States. See Shakur's biography in this volume.

6. "Marilyn Buck Page," Prison Activist Resource Center, www.prisonactivist.org/pps + pows/marilynbuck/ (19 Apr. 2002).

7. See "Marilyn Buck," *Can't Jail the Spirit*, 5th edition (Chicago: Committee to End Marion Lockdown, 2002), 193. In 1973, Marilyn Buck received a fifteen-year sentence; in 1985, a five-year sentence for a felony, transporting firearms; a five-year sentence for failure to return from furlough; fifty years for Assata Shakur's escape and Brink's robbery; in 1990, ten years for the Capitol bombing. The total of eighty-five years—minus five years served concurrently—resulted in an eighty-year prison term.

8. Conversation with Laura Whitehorn, 25 March 2002.

The Struggle for Status under International Law: U.S. Political Prisoners and the Political Offense Exception to Extradition

INTRODUCTION

In the following paper I discuss how I came to study international law and the political status of prisoners. I begin with my relationship to the history of the legal development of the status question inside the U.S., and from my own experience. Though not academically trained in international law, all of my previous political education—both experiential and formal—prepared me for this learning process.

I conclude with the collective work of my codefendants, Dr. Mutulu Shakur, my own, and others as we labor to produce a legal brief in response to Judge Charles S. Haight's questions regarding "The Political Offense Exception to Extradition (POEE)," and legal and political status, i.e. standing as political prisoners and/or prisoners of war.[1] I did not do the majority of the writing. I had to appear for trial every day, rising at 4:00 AM to change into my court clothes in order to be transported from the jail to the courthouse. I did not attend legal meetings until after 6:00 or 7:00 PM, after I had returned from court and changed back into prison uniform. Other political prisoners held with us at the Metropolitan Correction Center in New York City (MCC-NY) contributed to this collective product.

NEW LEFT ACTIVISM

In the 1960s the U.S. was ablaze with social and political conflict and strife. The Civil Rights movement exploded into the Black Power and Black Liberation movement. Demonstrations for civil rights and political rights escalated into demands for self-determination. The Universal Declaration of Human Rights, signed by the U.S. in 1948, reflected on the official level of social, political and economic struggles worldwide, including in the United States. In 1966, the UN International Covenant on Civil Rights and Political Rights was elaborated. It too responded to post–World War II anti-colonial struggles, articulating some of the demands and aspirations of oppressed and exploited peoples worldwide. Here in the U.S. activists had been demanding civil rights since before the return of Black troops from WWII to Jim Crow America; now activists were demonstrating against apartheid, sitting in at lunch counters and traveling South as Freedom Riders to challenge *whites only*, and protesting against the U.S. war in Vietnam. The Black Panther Party (BPP) demanded the right to self-determination and to self-defense for Black people; in one electrifying demonstration in 1967, they stood with firearms before the California State House in Sacramento. Civil disobedience as well as active resistance burgeoned. Activists were arrested, went to jail, got bail and continued social protests.

By the end of the 1960s, political activists were being imprisoned for their radical challenge to the status quo. The questions about prisons and prisoners, and the role of incarceration in the suppression of political dissent and opposition, rose to the forefront. More and more political militants and activists spent years in jail awaiting trial or as convicted persons—Huey P. Newton and countless other Black Panthers, Ahmed Evans of the Revolutionary Action Movement (RAM), draft resisters, Puerto Rican Nationalists, and North American anti-imperialists, anti-war activists and pacifists. Thousands of political activists were inducted into Federal Bureau of Investigation (FBI) files and logged on to jail and prison rolls. They were incarcerated with other women and men who had originally been imprisoned for social and economic offenses—social prisoners. Prisoners were being treated as beasts, not men (or women). Some of those prisoners became politically conscious and struggled for human rights within the prisons.

Those of us in the political and social movements who were not in jail or prison poured a lot of energy into supporting all those women and men who had fallen into the hands of the State's repressive apparatus—the "criminal justice" system. In that period, we made little distinction about "political status": if one was in the State's clutches and/or was resisting dehumanization, support was given. By the early 1970s a debate began on who was or was not a political prisoner.

AN EXISTENTIAL QUESTION:
THE EXPERIENCE OF POLITICAL DETENTION

In 1973, the question of who and what is a political prisoner became an existential question for me. As an anti-imperialist and an internationalist, I supported and worked in solidarity with Black Liberation forces including the Black Liberation Army (BLA). Suddenly, in the dawn hours of March 22, 1973, with the kicking-in of a door, I became a political prisoner. I was convicted for buying firearms and sentenced to ten years in prison, unheard of at the time for such a minor offense (but in retrospect a short sentence for the betrayal of white supremacist culture). I went from trial to trial and was moved from jail to jail, isolation cell to isolation cell. I finally in the fall of 1974, for no other reason than "political association," was dumped into the then-experimental behavior modification program at the Federal Women's Prison at Alderson, West Virginia. After more than thirteen months of "behavior modification" (which consisted primarily of isolation and segregation with no discernible goals to be met to tend the process), I was released into the general population. There I met Lolita Lebron, the Puerto Rican Nationalist political prisoner who had been in prison since March 1, 1954. For several years we spent a lot of time together. From her I learned about other women political prisoners who had been there at different times—other Puerto Rican Nationalists such as

Blanca Canales, Isabel Rosado, and American Elizabeth Gurley Flynn, a Communist. I met another political prisoner there as well, a pacifist Roman Catholic nun, Sister Jane. Most importantly, I learned from Lolita resistance, commitment and about *being* a political prisoner. She was a shining example of commitment to her people and of human dignity under adverse conditions.

I had experience as a political prisoner, including the particular repression we were subject to at times. (Those imprisoned for political actions and offenses are considered to be the "worst of the worst." We are subject to preventive detention or astronomically high bails; courtroom security is used to prejudice the jury; we receive disproportionate sentences; and we are subjected to isolation and efforts to break or destroy those who do not repent our political ideologies.) Nevertheless I had little knowledge of the history of political prisoners in the U.S. I began to read about the history and traditions of U.S. political prisoners: the *Amistad* rebellion and trial, Joe Hill, Emma Goldman, Sacco and Vanzetti, the Rosenbergs, Francisco Flores Magon, Don Pedro Albizu Campos and Don Juan Corretjer, the Communists imprisoned because of the HUAC (House Un-American Activities Committee) "red scare" hearings in the 1950s, as well as countless others.

In 1978, I was granted a work furlough. I did not return. I continued my political activism underground until 1985 when I was captured.

NATIONAL LIBERATION, INTERNATIONAL LAW AND POLITICAL PRISONERS

The concept of political prisoner is as old as the history of political conflicts between and within nations and states. That prisoners of such conflicts were recognized as political prisoners has not always been a certainty. Most nation-states unequivocally condemn the political opposition and militancy as "criminal." Nonetheless, at the end of the Second World War, European and American statesmen sat down to define war, conflicts and the rules of war for the modern world, as well as to outlaw genocide and civilian murder and displacement. The Nuremberg Charter, as well as the Geneva Conventions of 1949, were elaborated.

The rule of and interpretation of international law have become broader in reach since the Second World War. For those who have been imprisoned because of their involvement in struggles against colonial oppression and for human rights— including inside the U.S. itself, it has been necessary to demand and advocate for recognition and inclusion of those struggles under international law. Forces of national liberation and anti-imperialism—excluded from the community of nations because of their colonial status—had staged wars of national liberation. Anti-colonial warfare—unconventional warfare—challenged the narrowness of the conventions, given that the conventions were elaborated relative to conventional warfare in the imperialist, developed nations. Many of the progressive changes in international law have been primarily impelled by those nations most excluded—the former and current colonies. (The Soviet Union had argued that all wars that were "just" might not adhere to prevailing legal standards; thus while wars of national liberation were considered just they did not necessarily gain UN support until such time as it was clear about the outcome of many of those wars.) On June 8, 1977, the Additional Protocols (I and II) to the Geneva Conventions of August 12, 1949, were adopted by the Diplomatic Conference on Reaffirmation and Development of International Humanitarian Law applicable to Armed Conflict. These Protocols expanded the Geneva Convention to protect those fighting against colonialism and foreign domination. The spirit of Article 45, as well as the entire Additional Protocol I, was to confer as liberally as possible prisoner of war protections on legitimate national liberation combatants. The U.S. refused to sign Protocol I. As was stated in our *Memorandum in Support of Defense Motion to Dismiss the Indictment*, November 2, 1987:

> A major reason why the United States refused to ratify this Protocol was because the spirit and intent of the Protocol conflicts with the government's repressive approach that uses law to criminalize participants in liberation struggles.[2]

POLITICAL PRISONERS IN THE 1960s

In the 1960s, political movements had declared that those who had acted in concert with those movements and were imprisoned for their actions were political prisoners. Many Black Liberation Movement "cases" were supported worldwide, especially those of Angela Davis, Huey P. Newton, and the Panther 21. Weathermen, pacifists, draft resisters and anti-imperialists also became political prisoners. Some social prisoners, like George Jackson and the Soledad Brothers, and later the San Quentin Six and Ruchell Magee, had actively opposed the racism and inhumane conditions inside prisons. They had become politicized and had paid heavy prices. They too were recognized and supported as political prisoners. The U.S. judiciary and the repressive apparatus officially denied the political nature of all those cases, relying on the FBI's Counterintelligence Program, COINTELPRO, to quell political dissent and to maintain or restore the status quo in society.

After the defeat of the U.S. by the Vietnamese in 1975, and its other losses in Southeast Asia, the State's repressive apparatus intensified its program to restore "order" in U.S. society. It sought to reassure or deceive the international community, as well as its own citizens, that the U.S. was indeed the leading stable force of democracy and human rights worldwide.

In the early 1970s, in the course of the domestic battles against the war in Vietnam, when the Weather Underground bombed the Capitol, it was treated as a political attack. Thereafter, during the Reagan regime, in response to ongoing domestic left political struggles, the State reconfigured its definition of "terrorism" to include political actions of dissent, opposition and resistance. Thus, in 1983 when the Capitol was bombed, it was decried and propagandized as a "terrorist" attack although the action did not fall under the Geneva Convention's definition of terrorism; i.e. military acts of violence against the civilian population to inspire fear and subjugation. Those who were arrested or captured for political actions and protests were demonized as terrorists, not recognized as political activists. They were subjected to extreme security measures: isolation, overwhelming use of armed force to regulate their movements as political prisoners, and a steady stream of media propaganda.

The process of delegitimization of political resistance was under way.

DIFFERENT DEFINITIONS (1): U.S. V. LEFT POLITICAL MOVEMENTS: COINTELPRO

The U.S. government asserts that there are no political prisoners in the United States. It maintains this assertion in relation to countries with (military) dictatorships that are friendly to the U.S. While it may have signed, in part, the 1977 Additional Protocols, its practice has been to assert that political prisoners and prisoners of war (POWs) exist only in those countries that are considered inimical to or that impede U.S. interests, such as Cuba and Libya. The U.S. response to international covenants, the Geneva Conventions in particular, is to say that there are no conditions or situations of conflict within the U.S. that would result in political prisoners. It refuses to acknowledge its colonial relationships or conflicts with Puerto Rico, Native Americans, or African descendants of slaves. In 1988, in the course of the RICO (Racketeer Influenced and Corrupt Organization) conspiracy case against Dr. Mutulu Shakur and me, the Executive branch of the government submitted a brief in response to an order by Judge Charles S. Haight, which states:

it is well accepted in customary international law, the Geneva Convention, and the Protocols that the use of force by the regular military forces of a State in resisting rebels or insurgents by force is need[ed] before any situation can be properly described as an armed conflict (whether international or internal).[3]

It is the view of the Government that the actual application of the Geneva Conventions requires a political judgment on whether an international or internal armed conflict is present. Whether such a conflict of hostilities exists in a particular case presents a question that is appropriately reserved to the political branches of governments.[4]

Thus, those persons arrested for their political activities are seen and treated as outlaws and criminals. To admit that there are political prisoners would open the U.S. to scrutiny over its own anti-democratic and repressive practices toward its own populations (and other nations). This would be tantamount to officially acknowledging that serious national conflicts exist within its borders.

. . . [A]ny decision that an armed conflict exists would have serious foreign policy and legal ramifications. Under traditional international law, for example, it would give rise to neutral rights, and thus confer the right on the belligerents (e.g. the United States and the "Republic of New Afrika") to search and seize certain neutral vessels engaged in commerce to ensure that contraband (e.g. weapons) is not being shipped to the other belligerent. It is extremely unlikely that other countries would tolerate action by the so-called "Republic of New Afrika."[5]

Despite its denials of the existence of political conflicts, the government's repressive measures and programs to monitor, control and destroy rising political movements and struggles is well-documented. COINTELPRO was the government's most developed political police program to fend off and undermine those political movements that have demanded the same liberation and justice advocated by the U.S. in those areas of the world where it has sought to gain both economic and political footholds. It arose out of the U.S.'s post–World War II "cold war" program of political control and repression. Its antecedents lie in FBI programs such as COMINFIL (for communist infiltrators operating) in the 1950s in the wake of the HUAC hearings and imprisonment of "communists" who refused to bow before its ideological inquisition, coupled with the trial and execution of the Rosenbergs for espionage. Among its earliest targets was the Puerto Rican Independence movement, the Civil Rights movement, and Communists and Socialists who had not capitulated before HUAC. By the late 1960s, COINTELPRO had issued its infamous dicta about preventing the rise of a Black Messiah and the necessity to "neutralize" any potential Black leadership or movement.

Under the umbrella of COINTELPRO, the FBI, Central Intelligence Agency (CIA) and local police agencies employed nefarious, illegal activities against political activists across the Left spectrum, including white Leftists that supported the Black struggles and opposed the war in Vietnam. If the local police agencies were not before that time invested as a political, military force in what the U.S. government characterized as "actions to protect U.S. democracy against Communism," they quickly took on that mantle, particularly in communities of oppressed national "minorities."

After some of its most blatant activities were exposed and protested by the targets of its attacks, a Congressional investigation—the Church committee—was initiated. "COINTELPRO essentially federalized the local police for its politically repressive purposes, and military intelligence played a major role in the successful implementation of the program."[6]

Throughout the 1970s, the National Black Task Force for COINTELPRO Litigation and Research, led by Dr. Shakur and Muntu Matsimela, played an important role in uncovering some of the government's illegal actions against political activists and political prisoners. Through the Freedom of Information Act (FOIA) a number of abuses were uncovered and a civil suit, *Clark v Gray*, was filed through the efforts of the Black Task Force. It was subsequently settled by the government before trial. (The Task Force also played an instrumental role in building political prisoner support work.) In the late 1970s, COINTELPRO was ostensibly dismantled after such scrutiny, but the Joint Terrorist Task Force (JTTF) was created to take over the functions of COINTELPRO and continue its program of intensified repression.

DIFFERENT DEFINITIONS (2):
LEFT POLITICAL MOVEMENTS V. U.S.

Where one stands in the world shapes and defines what one sees as reality. Those of us who believe in human rights, including the right to self-determination for peoples and nations, have a different worldview, experience and definition of political prisoners and prisoners of war. This worldview is diametrically opposed to the U.S. view of both international and domestic law.

We recognize that there has been an ongoing, historical conflict within the body politic of the U.S.A. Founded on genocide and slavery under the guise of "Manifest Destiny," the United States developed as the dominant modern capitalist nation-state, and as a profoundly anti-democratic, white supremacist society with internal and external colonies. This fundamental anti-democracy shaped late U.S. twentieth-century strategies to maintain power and a modicum of social stability.

The United States has never redressed the injustices of slavery, neither through reparations nor cessation of hostilities against Black communities nationwide. It has not withdrawn from Puerto Rico despite repeated UN votes for decolonization. Both situations are unresolved political conflicts. Therefore, the U.S. is fundamentally in violation of common international law as it has developed since the Second World War, despite the fact that it ostensibly subscribes to the rule of international law while claiming paradoxically that it is not bound by international law.

> International law is part of our law, and must be ascertained and administered by the courts of justice of appropriate jurisdiction.[7]

> It is now established that customary law in the United States is a kind of federal law, and like treaties and other international agreements, it is accorded supremacy over State law by Article VI of the Constitution.[8]

The government argues that the judicial branch only enforces that which the legislative and executive branches devise as current law. On the one hand the State represents the body of law as the immutable neutral foundation of society. On the other hand, it denies the political and selective nature of the law. Laws had to be forcibly changed to outlaw slavery (reinstated in the Thirteen Amendment, for prisoners), to protect workers' and immigrants' rights. Political movements and their political prisoners have had not only to struggle for human rights and against exploitation and oppression in the social-political realm, but have had to do battle in the legal realm as well.

Over a period of twenty years the concept of "political prisoner" developed from the practice and experience of people detained and imprisoned for their beliefs and actions. By the late 1970s, there were prisoners from the Black Liberation movement—the Panthers in particular—along with several U.S. anti-imperialists and anarchists, who had been imprisoned since the late 1960s for their political activities. Once the 1977 Additional Protocols were signed, political prisoners began to demand that they be treated as political prisoners and prisoners of war according to international law. The concept of the political offenses and political "crimes" began to be integrated into legal defenses in order to challenge criminal charges, criminalization, and the attempts of the U.S. to hide its endemic social-political contradictions and conflicts.

These legal claims—as challenges to the criminalization of political opposition—eventually became sharper and more clearly defined. The definition of U.S. political prisoners was agreed to by a number of movements (and their political prisoners) concerned with national self-determination, justice and human dignity. The Introduction to the fourth edition of *Can't Jail the Spirit* discusses the concept of political prisoner status:

> Political prisoners exist as a result of real political and social conflicts in the society. There is no society free of contradictions and therefore no society that does not have political prisoners. The absurd position of the U.S. government that it alone has no political prisoners is consistent with its position that there are no legitimate social or political movements struggling for fundamental change. The strategy of criminalization and isolation of political prisoners, i.e. the denial of their existence in part allows the U.S. to propagate the lie that U.S. society has achieved social peace, and that whatever dissent there is functions solely within the existent bourgeois democratic framework.[9]

Our movements here in the U.S., as well as liberation-directed movements in other nations and even some foreign states, are clear that there are political prisoners and POWs in the U.S. After every major attack by the State in which political activists have been arrested, we have mounted a defense struggle in the realm of the domestic, criminal court both to challenge the criminal charges and to argue for treatment as such under international law.

In 1977, William Morales, a Puerto Rican *independentista* was arrested in New York after a pipe bomb exploded prematurely in his hands. He refused to participate in a "criminal" trial based on his declared status as a prisoner of war under the Geneva Conventions. This case was one of the first to challenge the right of the U.S. to try him under criminal because as a colonial fighter he was eligible for POW status under international law. Morales [who escaped to Cuba] relied on the eighty-year history of struggle against Puerto Rico's colonial status, led by Don Pedro Albizu Campos and the Puerto Rican Nationalist Party, five militants who were at that time still imprisoned after at least twenty-four years of incarceration.

Within a few years thereafter, a large number of other political militants were captured, arrested and charged as "criminals" or "terrorists"—two terms increasingly conflated in order to heighten fears of terrorist attacks on civilians and civil society and thereby to justify brutal, inhumane treatment of prisoners.

BUT FOR THE EXPERIENCE

Had I not been captured, I would not have studied international law relating to political conflict and political prisoners/POWs. The experience of being a political prisoner motivated my studies. Prior to my arrest, I did not see such study to be my responsibility. My attentions and efforts were focused elsewhere in other arenas: I was immersed in other strategies both to support and to free political prisoners, many of whom had been subjected to harsh, extreme treatment inside prison.

Once again captive, Dr. Mutulu Shakur mobilized me to study international law in order to advance the struggle in international terms and to better attack politically the indictment against us. During my first trial, for escape, in West Virginia, I acted as my own attorney. I argued a "necessity defense" that had been developed at the end of the 1970s, principally by the prisoners of the anti-nuclear movement. The "necessity defense" was based on the Nuremberg Principles embodied in the Treaty of London, to which the U.S. is a signatory. It provides that

individuals have international duties which transcend the national obligations of obedience imposed by the individual state.[10]

The principles recognized in the Judgment of the Nuremberg Tribunal impose on individuals the affirmative duty to prevent the commission of crimes as enumerated therein at Article 6.[11]

Investigating the "necessity defense," I began my engaged analysis of international law and political prisoner status. Although I had prepared a necessity defense with the help and advice of attorneys, I was not allowed to present it except to the extent that I could elaborate the concept in my opening and closing statements. I was convicted, sentenced and returned to New York.

A STUDY OF INTERNATIONAL LAW: THE NATURE OF CONFLICT AND POLITICAL STATUS

In New York, I was to stand trial for a RICO conspiracy. I began to prepare my defense case with my attorneys, and was fully engaged in all aspects. I focused on challenging the evidence, which we did successfully, initially, at lower court levels. My knowledge or understanding of the international legal tradition that defined the concept of political prisoner was still limited. However, I was in the company of a number of other political prisoners and POWs—Grand Jury resisters, comrades from the New Afrikan Independence Movement, other North American anti-imperialists, Puerto Rican political prisoners, as well as an Irish Republican Army member, Joe Doherty. For years Joe had been fighting in the U.S. courts for political asylum against the demand by the British government that he be returned to political detention there. He had based his legal battle in international law and the Political Offense Exception to Extradition (POEE).

In interactions limited by security attempts to keep us separate, political prisoners discussed both the international and domestic laws concerning the definition and status of U.S. political prisoners. Recognizing the import of the POEE, Dr. Shakur began to explore its possibilities and educated the political prisoners, attorneys, and law student paralegals. We analyzed the history of political prisoners' challenges to U.S. criminal law, read previous briefs, and translated that history into a legal argument. Under Dr. Shakur's direction, an argument was developed that the POEE must not be limited to extradition only since it is the method used in most Western alliance countries as a guide to evaluate the political character of an offense and its common criminal elements.

The conspiracy charge against us was defined by the U.S. Justice Department as an enterprise for political purposes; that is, to free political prisoners and provide economic support for the New Afrikan Independence Movement. Nevertheless, the conspiracy and the substantive acts and counts were indicted criminal offenses. We participated in the trial to challenge the evidence against us. We also consistently showed the political nature of the acts, particularly in cross-examination of the government's central witness, a former political associate of Dr. Shakur who had succumbed to FBI/JTTF coercion and had been well-paid to elaborate upon the prosecution's conspiracy case.

We argued for political prisoner status under international law based on the Geneva Conventions (1949), incorporated the International Covenant on Civil and Political Rights,[12] and developed arguments using the Political Offense Exception to Extradition (POEE). Led by Dr. Shakur and Joe Doherty, we studied these particular aspects of international law. We referred to other political challenges to criminalization by other political prisoners and POWs including William Morales and Sekou Odinga, a New Afrikan POW comrade and codefendant in our RICO indictment.

At the beginning of our trial in November 1987, Dr. Shakur filed a "Motion to Dismiss the Indictment" based on his status as a POW. I did not seek POW status because for a Euro-American citizen of the U.S., not a colonial subject, the same arguments could not be made relative to a "civil" war. In an earlier trial it had been decided, for political reasons, that the (white) North American anti-imperialists, though acting in solidarity and in concert with the New Afrikan Independence forces, would declare themselves as political prisoners and allies.

Dr. Shakur argued that African peoples inside the United States constituted a

New Afrikan nation by virtue of their historical relation to the land in the South, and that as a citizen and militant of the Republic of New Afrika, he had a legitimate right to defend his nation against the white supremacist, genocidal war that the U.S. had been waging against New Afrikan people as colonial subjects. In his petition, *Memorandum in Support of Defense Motion to Dismiss the Indictment,* he argued that the Political Offense Exception to Extradition could be extended to political conflict inside the United States.

According to the Quinn Court, there are two distinct categories of political offenses: "pure political offenses" and "relative political offenses."

> Pure political offenses are acts aimed or directed at the government and have none of the elements of ordinary crimes . . . The definitional problems focus around the second category of political offenses—the relative political offenses. These include "otherwise common crimes committed in connection with a political act," or common crimes . . . committed for political motives or in a political context.[13]

> It is the fact that the insurgents are seeking to change their governments that makes the political offense exception applicable, not the reasons for wishing to do so or the nature of the acts by which they hope to accomplish that goal.[14]

He argued that within the POEE, treaties and international norms, there are various tests known as the Anglo-American test, which are the primary tests used by the judiciary to evaluate the character of the acts charged by the country demanding extradition of the defendants.

In January 1988, after the Government had filed its response to Dr. Shakur's motion, the Judge directed the Government to answer five questions "regarding the possibly political character of the acts charged in the indictment." (See SSS 82 CR. 312-CSH, *Memorandum Opinion and Order* by Charles S. Haight, Judge, Southern District of New York, January 19, 1988.) Those questions were:

1. What role, if any, did the United States play in the development of the 1977 protocols proposed as amendments to the 1949 Geneva Prisoner of War Convention?
2. What is the history and present status of the United States' position with respect to the 1977 protocols?
3. Do the 1977 protocols reflect the current state of international law on the issue of when prisoner-of-war treatment must be accorded to accused persons?
4. Assuming that the United States has not adopted the 1977 protocols, but that the protocols do reflect current international law, is this Court required or permitted to decline to analyze the present motion under the principles enunciated therein? Cf. *Filartiga v Pena-Irala,* 630 F.2d 876 (2d. Cir. 1980)
5. Analyzed under the principles enunciated in the 1977 protocols, should the criminal enterprise charged in the indictment be regarded as an insurgency?

The AUSAs—Attorneys for the United States of America or federal prosecutors—forwarded the Court's order to the Department of State to make the responding brief. Abraham D. Sofaer, Legal Advisor to the Department of State, together with others, including the Chief of the Office of the Judge Advocate General of the Department of the Army and Office of the General Counsel of the Department of Defense responded.

The government's political brief argued essentially that any decision on POW (or political) status or declaration that a conflict exists is reserved to the political branches:

> . . . even were the court otherwise inclined to address the defendant's contention, it should take into account that there is an "absence of judicially discoverable and manageable standards" for determining whether hostilities or armed conflict exist for purposes of such laws and treaties.[15]

The government dismissed outright any condition of the Political Offense Exception to Extradition as not applicable.

> The political offense exception referred to by the defendants is relevant as a matter of law solely in cases involving extradition. Under no circumstances is it a defense to prosecution in the United States. (Cites omitted) (*Government Brief*, 2)

We responded to that brief. In March 1988, we had requested that a number of potential political prisoner witnesses for the defense case be brought to New York. The Judge ordered Sekou Odinga and Cecil Ferguson, both comrades already convicted in our own case; David Gilbert, an anti-imperialist comrade who had been convicted in New York state courts for participation in an action that included both New Afrikans and North American anti-imperialists and was one of the substantive acts charged in our own case; Susan Rosenberg, an anti-imperialist comrade indicted in the instant RICO conspiracy but who had been *nolled* [i.e., the government chose not to prosecute but declined to drop charges] in order to focus the prosecution on Dr. Shakur and me; Nuh Washington, a Black Liberation Army combatant imprisoned since 1971 in NY state prisons; and Geronimo ji Jaga Pratt, a Black Panther Minister of Defense who was falsely imprisoned for twenty-seven years as a target of COINTELPRO.

We held joint legal meetings nightly after Dr. Shakur and I returned from court. Each evening was a legal education session on points of international law regarding political prisoners, definitions of combatants and non-combatants and on the POEE and its possible application to our situation inside the U.S. We approached the subject from the point of view that the court had the discretion to address this issue:

> The "political offense exception" to extradition arose in Europe and America because democratic governments supported the right of individuals "to resort to political asylum to foster political change." The underlying tenets of domestic extradition law arise from

(1) the desire to insulate the executive involvement in the extradition determination, which is made by the Court; and, (2) the political decision that the executive should not help another country suppress its own internal political dissent. These concerns have governed American extradition policies for 150 years.[16]

In order to respond to Judge Haight's questions and challenge the government's response to those same questions we immersed ourselves deeper into the case law and the theories behind international conventions and laws, in particular the Political Offense Exception to Extradition, given that the major point of contention was whether the crimes charged were political or not.

By the time we had read and discussed a significant amount of case law and international covenants related to political conflict, political offenses and judicial authority, we felt confident to write a response brief to answer the government's misrepresentations of international law. We were advised by our attorneys, Chokwe Lumumba, Jill Soffiyah Elijah and Judith Holmes, each of whom brought her or his own area of expertise and experience. Our response brief began by arguing that the U.S. political stance relative to Protocol I was based on its own history and policies. It had historically denied that political conflicts have existed internally. We argued that

The real issue, assuming that the Protocols do reflect current international law, is whether there are controlling executive or legislative acts that preclude the Court from recognizing international law applicable to this case.[17]

We also challenged the government's assertion that if Congress doesn't ratify a law of nations then that law is not controlling.

The Senate's failure to ratify the Protocols means that these amendments do not have the status of a United States treaty. But, if the Protocols do indeed express contemporary international law, the Senate's non-ratification merely means that no codification on how such international law may or may not apply in the United States has been established.[18]

In response to Judge Haight's final question, we argued that the Black Liberation struggle was indeed an ongoing internal conflict.

Given the body of factual data in defendant's [Dr. Shakur] affidavit about the war against New Afrikans and the Black Liberation Movement, and the massive documentation the Church Committee revealed that chronicled the government's "secret war" involving the Army, the CIA, the FBI, the IRS and the state and local police against the Black Liberation Movement, such actions taken against any foreign nation would clearly constitute overt "acts of war" in international law. Any person captured would be considered a prisoner of war.[19]

The government's reply to the Court's fifth question, asking whether the criminal enterprise charged in the indictment should be regarded as an insurgency as analyzed under the 1977 Protocols, evaded the central issue: whether the conspiracy charged is a part of the ongoing conflict between Black people in America and the United States government. . . . The RICO statute has become a tool for criminalizing political movements that has enabled the government to define the New Afrikan Independence Movement as a criminal enterprise.[20]

Dr. Shakur posited that the Court could grant relief under the provisions for international armed conflict because the requirements for such an evaluation existed despite the U.S. government's denials; i.e., the Political Offense Exception to Extradition could be applied by the Court to grant us political status.

In re *Doherty*, 599 F. Supp. 270, 27 (S.D.N.Y. 1984) elaborated a more flexible standard for applying the political offense exception. It stated:

The court rejects the notion that the political offense exception is limited to actual armed insurrections or more traditional and overt military hostilities . . .[21]

Finally we made an "interest of justice argument and application" in which we argued that the case presented by the State pointed out the relative political nature of the acts and of the defendants. We asked that the Court hold fact-finding hearings on our political status.

In the Documentation/Appendix, *The Defendants' Memorandum* in *Reply to the Government's Response to the January 19, 1988 Order of Judge Charles S. Haight* (as printed in *Wazo Weusi*) lays out all of our arguments based on the substance of the learning experience that occurred not only for myself but for all of us involved, both defendants and attorneys.

AFTERWORD

Both Dr. Shakur and I were found guilty of the RICO conspiracy and all the substantive acts therein. Post trial, as part of the defense's sentencing briefings, Judge Haight ruled against Dr. Shakur's POW petition and our joint request to be treated as political prisoners and to be allowed to go into exile to a country that would grant us political asylum. However, he accepted the government's argument that he had no jurisdiction to rule on our political status given there was no precedent in U.S. law not related to extradition. He carried forward the criminalization process by sentencing us under criminal law guidelines.

In 1989, a campaign to demand amnesty for all political prisoners and POWs (of the progressive and Left movements)—Freedom Now—was launched. In 1990, the campaign culminated in an international tribunal on U.S. political prisoners and prisoners of war. The work we had done was useful in that tribunal. Nevertheless, the work we did remains to be evaluated under changed political conditions. Perhaps our work will contribute to changes in the political conditions and, ultimately, in the law itself. Radical change generally precedes any change in the law. The law is the foundation stone of the political and social order as it has been and is not what it is to become.

NOTES

Unedited version originally published in *Prior Learning Component #2* (Fall/Winter 1999).

1. *Editor's note:* The Political Offense Exception to Extradition (POEE) was established as international law in the Geneva Convention. Article 44 combined with Additional Protocol I (1977) of the Geneva Convention expands the categories of individuals who can be defined as prisoners of war. The United States has refused to obey the POEE; such action would acknowledge that there are political crimes in the United States. Mutulu Shakur, Marilyn Buck, Geronimo Pratt, Albert "Nuh" Washington, Sekou Odinga, Cecilio Chui Ferguson El, Susan Rosenberg, and David Gilbert, "Prisoners of War: The Legal Standing of Members of National Liberation Movements," in *Cages of Steel: The Politics of Imprisonment in the United States*, ed. Ward Churchill and Jim Vander Wall (Washington, D.C.: Maisonneuve, 1992).

2. *Defendants' Memorandum*, 128.

3. (Cites omitted.) See: *Government Brief in Response to Memorandum Order of January 19, 1988*, 16.

4. (Cites omitted.) *Government Brief*, 19.

5. *Government Brief*, 22–23.

6. See *The Select Committee Report*. Supra at 785–835. (*Defendants' Memorandum*, 134).

7. *The Paquete Habana*, 175 U.S. 677, [1900].

8. Restatement [Third] of the Foreign Relations Law of the U.S., Part I, Ch. 2, [1987] [Introductory Note].

9. *Can't Jail the Spirit*, 4th ed. (Chicago: Committee to End the Marion Lockdown), 19.

10. *Treaty of London*, August 8, 1945, 59 Stat. 1544, 1548 Article 8.

11. Brief Supporting Charges that the United States Federal Government has Acted as an International Criminal Conspiracy and a Criminal Organizations with Regard to the Political Incarceration and Commission of Human Rights Violations Against White, North American Revolutionaries and Activists, Marilyn Kalman, Attorney at Law, San Francisco, CA, October 2–4, 1992, 2.

12. G. A. Resolution 2200A[XXI], 21 U.N. GAOR Supp. [No. 16] at 52, U.N. Doc. A/6316 [1966], 999 U.N.T.S. 171, *entered into force* Mar. 23, 1976.

13. *Quinn v Robinson*, supra at 793–794, cited in SSS 82-CR.312 CSH, Memorandum in Support of Defense Motion to Dismiss the Indictment, November 2, 1987, 44–45.

14. *Quinn v Robinson*, 783 F. 2d at 805, Memorandum in Support of Defense Motion to Dismiss the Indictment, November 2, 1987, 47.

15. (Case law cites omitted.) *Government Brief*, 24.

16. *Defendants' Memorandum*, 138.

17. *Defendants' Memorandum*, 131.

18. *Defendants' Memorandum*, 132.

19. *Defendants' Memorandum*, 133.

20. *Defendants' Memorandum*, 135.

21. *Defendants' Memorandum*, 139.

Chapter Fifteen

Rita Bo Brown

Born in 1947, Bo (Rita Darlene) Brown grew up in a white working-class neighborhood in Klanmath, Oregon. Her first experience with the U.S. prison system came when she was sentenced to seven months at Terminal Island Penitentiary for stealing forty dollars from the post office in Seattle where she worked. Upon release, she returned to Seattle and became involved in prison and lesbian rights work, helping to found Leftist Lezzies, an organization to combat the invisibility of lesbians in the antiwar movement. Eventually, Brown became a member of the George Jackson Brigade; her involvement with the Brigade and its armed robberies led to eight additional years of incarceration.[1]

Based in Seattle, the Brigade emerged as a multiracial, nonhomophobic, anticapitalist, anti-imperialist underground organization. It was largely composed of individuals who were former prisoners, or had used or advocated armed struggle in opposition to U.S. policies and in solidarity with Native struggles for sovereignty, Seattle Auto Workers' strikes, and Washington State prisoners' human rights. In solidarity with the United Farm Workers, the Brigade allegedly bombed a Safeway supermarket; in support of the American Indian Movement, the organization allegedly bombed the Bureau of Indian Affairs in Everett, Washington, and the Federal Bureau of Investigation (FBI) office in Tacoma, Washington.

The Brigade publicized the political nature of its actions through communiqués distributed to news media across the country, announcing the bombings and explaining their political motivations. Attempting to make a distinction between terrorism and the Brigade's actions, Brown asserted in an article in the feminist publication *Off Our Backs*:

> Terrorism is armed action which deliberately and callously ignores the welfare of the people. It is the institutionalized sick violence of the ruling class and its police forces— i.e., the senseless bombings of Viet Nam; the Attica massacre; the Kent State massacre; the Jackson State massacre; the individual murders of Clifford Grover, Karen Silkwood, and George Jackson; the continuing murders and sterilizations of Native Americans and Puerto Ricans. . . . "Armed Struggle" is the use of controlled violence such as

216

armed occupations, kidnappings, prisoner escapes, armed robberies, bombings, etc. A primary factor is that concern for the welfare of innocent people is *always* a vital part of the planning and execution of these actions."[2]

Bo Brown was finally captured on November 4, 1977, in Seattle, Washington, and extradited to Oregon that month to stand trial. Although charged with five counts of robbery and two weapons charges, all remaining charges were dropped when, on January 11, 1978, Brown pleaded guilty to a 1977 armed robbery of a Wilsonville Branch of the National Bank of Oregon. The press often covered news of the Brigade's activities, yet the FBI allegedly withheld information from the media after Brown's arrest in order to limit publicity for the George Jackson Brigade. Limited media coverage made the organization of a political defense all the more difficult for Brown and her allies. Sentenced on February 21, 1978, to twenty years for robbery and an additional five years on the firearms charge, Brown appealed, arguing that she could not be sentenced to two consecutive terms for the same crime; the initial ruling was upheld.[3]

Once sentenced, Brown was held in solitary confinement in the Federal Correctional Institution in Pleasanton, California, until March 21, at which point she was transferred to the Federal Correctional Institution at Alderson, West Virginia. At Alderson, she was placed in the prison's Maximum Security Unit (MSU) in Davis Hall, which also housed Assata Shakur. Women in Davis Hall were locked in their cells the majority of the day, with exceptions for meals, two hours of personal visits, and, sometimes, for work.[4] While housed in Davis Hall, arguably the first special control unit for political women in the federal system, Brown and other inmates attempted to publicize the unfair conditions of the unit. After pressure from progressive segments of the legal community, community activists, and inmate activists, the MSU was terminated as a program; however, it continued to be used as a general punitive segregation unit and, occasionally, as a control unit. (Held there in the 1980s were Lucy Rodriguez, Haydée Torress, Dylcia Pagán, and Laura Whitehorn.)[5]

After Brown was released from prison in 1987, she cofounded Out of Control Lesbian Committee to Support Women Political Prisoners, and began support work for people with AIDS in prison, and for battered women convicted of killing their abusers.[6] Organized initially around the campaign to close the Lexington Control Unit for Women, Out of Control now works to support women political prisoners. Brown also participated in the Jericho '98 Campaign to Free Political Prisoners and Prisoners of War and the Norma Jean Croy Support Committee for the release of Norma Jean Croy, a Native lesbian wrongfully imprisoned for nineteen years. Brown has directed and produced *Shasta Woman*, a documentary on Croy's case.[7]

REFERENCES

Brown, Bo. "White North American Political Prisoners." In *Criminal Injustice: Confronting the Prison Crisis*, edited by Elihu Rosenblatt. Boston: South End Press, 1996.

————, et al. "Reflections on Critical Resistance." *Social Justice: A Journal of Crime, Conflict and World Order* 27, no. 3 (Fall 2000).

Burton-Rose, Daniel. "Guerrillas in Our Midst: Where Do Armed Revolutionaries in the US Go after They Lay Down Their Arms?" *Lip Magazine*, 15 February 1999.

"Member of Revolutionary Group Arrested by the F.B.I. in Seattle." *New York Times*, 6 November 1977, 34 col. 6.

Moira, Fran. "25 Years for Rita Brown." *Off Our Backs* 8, no. 5 (31 May 1978), Washington, D.C.: 8.

Rita Darlene Brown v Kenneth R. Neagle. United States District Court for the Southern District of West Virginia, Beckley Division, 486 F. Supp. 364; December 10, 1979.

United States of America v Rita Darlene Brown. United States Court of Appeals, Ninth Circuit, 602 F.2d 909, August 22, 1979.

Winn, Scott. "Seattle Welcomes Back Radical Queer Activists from the 1970s: An Interview with Lesbian activist Bo (Rita D. Brown)." *Seattle Gay News Online.* www.sgn.org/Archives/sgn.8.13.99/bo-sgn.htm.

————. "Talkin' About a Revolution: An Interview with Prison Rights Activist Bo Brown." *Real Change.* www.realchangenews.org/pastarticles/interviews/fea.bo.html.

"Woman Admits Bank Robbery." *New York Times*, 12 January 1978.

NOTES

Research and draft for this biography were provided by Nicole Kief.

1. Scott Winn, "Talkin' About a Revolution: An Interview with Prison Rights Activist Bo Brown," *Real Change*, n.d. www.realchangenews.org/pastarticles/interviews/fea.bo.html; Bo Brown, "25 Years for Rita Brown," *Off Our Backs* 8, no. 5 (31 May 1978), Washington, D.C.; Scott Winn, "Seattle Welcomes Back Radical Queer Activists from the 1970s: An Interview with Lesbian Activist Bo (Rita D. Brown)," *Seattle Gay News Online*, n.d., www.sgn.org/Archives/sgn.8.13.99/bo-sgn.htm.

2. "25 Years for Rita Brown," 8.

3. "Member of Revolutionary Group Arrested by the F.B.I. in Seattle," *New York Times*, 6 November 1977, 34 column 6. *United States of America v Rita Darlene Brown.* United States Court of Appeals, Ninth Circuit, 602 F.2d 909, August 22, 1979.

4. See "25 Years for Rita Brown," *Off Our Backs.*

5. See "25 Years for Rita Brown"; "MSU Plays Hide and Seek," "Prisoner Subjected to Arbitrary Punishment"; *Rita Darlene Brown v Kenneth R. Neagle*, United States District Court for the Southern District of West Virginia, Beckley Division, 486 F. Supp. 364; December 10 1979; and "Rita D. Brown Harassed, Transferred"; Winn, "Talkin' About a Revolution."

6. See www.prisonactivist.org/ooc/.

7. Daniel Burton-Rose, "Guerrillas in Our Midst: Where Do Armed Revolutionaries in the US Go After They Lay Down Their Arms?," *Lip Magazine*, 15 February 1999, www.lipmagazine.org/articles/featrose_9.htm.

White North American Political Prisoners

October 1992

I am very honored to be here today, at this tribunal condemning 500 years of genocide and celebrating 500 years of resistance. I came to speak about some thirty-five
white political prisoners presently being held in U.S. prisons and jails—many of
whom are imprisoned because of their solidarity with oppressed nations and peoples
in the United States and around the world. I speak from experience and deep feeling, for I am a former political prisoner myself, having spent eight and a half years
in federal prisons around the country because of my actions as a member of the
George Jackson Brigade. In those years I was moved from prison to prison. During
that time I spent almost a year in isolation in Davis Hall at Alderson.[1] This was the
first special control unit for political women in the federal system. Sister Assata
Shakur and I were held there along with reactionary and Nazi prisoners—the government's threat to us was very clear. I was also kept for extra long periods in isolation and threatened and harassed specifically because I am a Lesbian. This was not
all that unusual treatment, however, for my experience mirrors that of all the political prisoners. Yet our very existence is still denied by the U.S. government and not
seen or understood by most people in this country.

The strategy of the U.S. government towards all political prisoners and POWs
held in prisons is to criminalize them—to disguise their political identities under
the rhetoric of criminal activity. But they are not criminals. All of these white
North American political prisoners have been convicted of and imprisoned for
activities that are strictly political in nature. These political prisoners and POWs
are not a new phenomenon but are part of the history of the resistance in the Americas. In fact, under international law as well as the Constitution of the United
States, people not only have the right, but the absolute responsibility to resist the
illegal policies and practices of the oppressor and colonizing nation. And that's
what they have done.

The North American political prisoners draw on a history of resistance that
includes the anti-slavery/abolitionist movement, those who helped in the Underground Railroad, women's rights activists, labor and working-class organizers, and
supporters of anti-colonialism and anti-militarism. Some of their names are familiar: John Brown, Emma Goldman, Eugene Debs, Ruth Reynolds, and Ethel and
Julius Rosenberg; but most of the names of our historical grandmothers and grand-
fathers remain unknown to us because the historians don't want us to know about
them. Some of these political prisoners come from working-class or poor communities, some were already ex-cons, and still others were college students, but a common thread runs through all their stories—the decision to take action. Action in
support of self-determination; action against racism; action against U.S. military
and nuclear policy; action against apartheid in South Africa and action in solidarity

with workers and poor people around the world. In order to understand them and their situation better we have to go back a little in history.

If you were living in this country in the 1960s and 1970s, you had to be affected by the struggles for freedom and social justice. Products of those times, many of the women and men in prison today were active in support of the civil rights movement and were influenced by the demand for self-determination by Malcolm X and the organizing of Martin Luther King, both of whom would be assassinated by 1968. Others worked with the Black Panther Party (BPP), often in defense of BPP members who were imprisoned for political activities. Many came to work also with Native-American, Mexicano/Chicano, and other Third World liberation struggles. Along with millions of others, they consistently opposed U.S. policy in Vietnam and were part of the antiwar movement. There were mass demonstrations throughout the country, marches on Washington, student strikes, sit-ins, and the burning of draft cards. There were also thousands of acts of sabotage against academic, corporate, military, and government targets that ranged from property damage to bombings. This was also the period when women began to be more conscious about their own oppression and began to demand liberation and when Lesbians and gay men came out of the closet and went into the streets demanding an end to gay oppression.

During these years a prisoner's rights movement developed, led mostly by Black prisoners and with close ties to the BPP and other community groups. Many of the white political prisoners worked with these organizations and thus came to better understand the integral part that prisons play in this society. They came to understand this country needs to control its people and criminalize, jail, or kill those whom it either can't control or doesn't need. The government's response to this legitimate protest and sense of empowerment was swift, repressive and violent. COINTELPRO, the FBI's counter-intelligence program, was responsible for the destruction of the BPP and the disruption of the American Indian Movement. Hundreds of BPP members and other Black activists, like Fred Hampton and Bunchy Carter, were killed or jailed. The same was true for Native people struggling for sovereignty.

This period also saw the killing of students at Kent and Jackson State universities and the widespread use of grand jury witch hunts that were designed to further disrupt legal organizations. Out of these experiences came the understanding that U.S. society is based on the rape and plunder of Native lands, the expropriation of the life and labor of African slaves, and the class exploitation of European, Asian, and Mexican workers. People were enraged at the racism so basic to this country and were determined not to be a part of it. Many began to see that there was a connection between the colonialism here at home and the war of imperialism in Vietnam.

It was during this time that activists in various parts of the country independently decided to begin armed resistance, expropriations, and sabotage. These were difficult steps to take but were all done in pursuit of their vision for change. This vision included changing centuries-old oppressive practices that promote hatred and that create psychological and physical damage and destruction. It meant creating a society based on self-determination for oppressed peoples both inside and outside the United States, based on an end to white supremacy, a society that was not based on class divisions. It meant creating a society where Lesbians and gay men could be proud of who they were. And it meant creating a non-sexist society where women could be equal, free, and unafraid. Finally all these people are driven by a vision of a future based not on greed and profit but one that truly answers people's needs.

This vision and spirit of resistance continued to move North Americans to action during the 1970s and 1980s. Thousands of people organized to resist the building of nuclear weapons, the intervention in Nicaragua and El Salvador, and in solidarity with Black forces against apartheid in South Africa. Many whites demonstrated and organized against racism and the growth of the Klan and other white supremacist groups. Thousands of people signed pledges of resistance to participate in civil disobedience if Nicaragua was invaded and participated in these acts as intervention in Central America increased. Women marched *en masse* against cutbacks in reproductive rights and protected abortion clinics against attacks. Lesbians and gay men demanded that the society deal with the AIDS pandemic and pushed for broader acceptance of Lesbian and gay rights. Again, during the Gulf War, thousands of white people joined in the streets protesting U.S. policy.

Not much has changed. We can understand the desire to resist very well. Genocidal conditions are increasing for Blacks and other communities of color. There is a rise of police brutality, drugs, and jailings and, as we all know, dramatic cuts to social services. Violence against women is increasing—a woman gets raped every two minutes. The right-wing scapegoats and whips up hysteria against gays and Lesbians with a propaganda campaign for their "family values." Abortion is all but gone; the courts are making one right-wing decision after another; and if we don't look out, soon we won't even have air we can breathe or earth we can stand on.

Before we get more specific about who the prisoners are, we'd like to take time to define what we mean by political prisoner. For some of us, this definition means those in prison as a direct result of their political actions, affiliations, and beliefs. Still others wish to extend that definition to those imprisoned for social crimes who have become politicized while inside prison and who therefore suffer extra repression for it. Some of us also think it important to extend the definition of political prisoner to those imprisoned for their sexual orientation (adopted by Amnesty International in 1992) and to those imprisoned for defending themselves against and/or fighting their abusers, such as women imprisoned for killing their batterers.

So let's get down to specifics. First, there are prisoners who consider themselves to be revolutionary anti-imperialists. The Jonathan Jackson–Sam Melville Brigade and United Freedom Front (UFF) were armed clandestine organizations that emerged from the experiences of working-class people in poor communities, in the military, and in prison.[2] The Jackson-Melville Brigade was held responsible for a number of bombings of government and corporate offices in the mid- to late-1970s. These actions raised the demands of independence for Puerto Rico and an end to

U.S. support for apartheid in South Africa, among other issues. The UFF operated from the early to mid-1980s and demanded the end of governmental and corporate support for South Africa, an end to U.S. intervention in Central America, and freedom for all political prisoners and POWs in U.S. prisons. Today the people charged with these acts are known as the "Ohio 7." They include Raymond Levasseur, Thomas Manning (both Vietnam Vets who had spent years in prison for social crimes), Jaan Laaman, Carol Manning, Richard Williams, Barbara Curzi, and Pat Gros Levasseur (these last two are both out on parole).

Other North American anti-imperialists were imprisoned for their direct aid to armed clandestine Black organizations in the early 1980s. Judy Clark [seventy-five to life], David Gilbert [seventy-five to life], and Kathy Boudin [twenty-five to life] are serving [virtual] life sentences in prison. They are charged with aiding an attempted expropriation (robbery for political reasons) of an armored truck in New York State in 1981. This action was claimed by the Revolutionary Armed Task Force. Marilyn Buck was also charged as a result of this action, as well as for assisting in the escape of Assata Shakur. Susan Rosenberg and Timothy Blunk were captured in 1984 on charges of conspiracy to possess explosives. Later they, along with Alan Berkman, Laura Whitehorn, Linda Evans, and Marilyn Buck, were charged with a number of bombings claimed by the Armed Resistance Unit and the Red Guerrilla Resistance. Included in these is the 1983 bombing of the Capitol in solidarity with the people of Grenada and in retaliation against the U.S. invasion that year. Other actions were taken against corporate and military targets in solidarity with the peoples of Central America and against intervention, against the Zionist occupation of Palestine, and to protest police killings of Black and Latino people in New York City.

Once again I come to my own background as a former member of the George Jackson Brigade. We were a multi-racial, armed organization that operated in the Northwest in the mid- to late-1970s. We took our name from George Jackson, the Black revolutionary who was assassinated in prison on August 21, 1971. We were composed mainly of working-class ex-convicts, and engaged in acts of armed resistance in solidarity with the struggle of Native people for sovereignty, in support of a strike by Seattle Auto Workers, and in support of struggles by Washington State prisoners for basic human rights. I've already told you that I was in prison for eight-and-a-half years. My comrades, Mark Cook, a Black prisoner [released in 2000], and Ed Mead, a white prisoner [released in 1994], remain in prison to this day for these actions.

There are also anti-authoritarian prisoners. Bill Dunne and Larry Giddings have been in prison since 1979 for participating in expropriations and the liberation of a comrade from jail. Richard Picariello [released in 1995, reimprisoned for alleged parole violations] has been in prison since 1977 for armed actions against U.S. oppression and imperialism. Due to be released after fifteen years, the state is scrambling to extend his sentence because he's dared to continue struggling from inside.

Next, I'd like to talk about those people who consider themselves part of the

Ploughshares. Taking their name from the famous biblical quote about turning swords into ploughshares, these anti-nuclear and anti-military activists come from a religious conviction and tradition that insists that they must not sit by while weapons of destruction are being made and used. Over the last ten years many have entered military bases and destroyed military property directly, while others have borne witness and engaged in symbolic acts. The most recent case is that of Peter Lumsdain and Keith Kjoller, who destroyed the Navstar computer—part of the United States' first strike capability—to the tune of two-and-a-half million dollars. They received eighteen months for this "crime."

Throughout the 1980s, the government also prosecuted members of the sanctuary movement. These include clergy, church workers, and lay activists who have "illegally" provided refuge to Central and South American refugees fleeing U.S.-sponsored repression in their homelands. Following an historic tradition, there are also military resisters. For example, Gilliam Kerley was sentenced to three years in prison plus a $10,000 fine not merely for refusing to register but because he persisted in organizing against registration and the draft. Military resisters continue to sit in jail as a result of their refusal to serve in the Gulf War. [After hard-fought campaigns, all of the military resisters—or at least those whose cases were publicized—were released by the end of 1994.—E.R.] The U.S. legal system is also used to serve the government's allies in effecting their own counter-insurgency programs. In so doing, it echoes and enforces U.S. foreign policy.

Along with Haitians, Central and South Americans, and other Third World people, there are several European nationals being held in U.S. prisons. Silvia Baraldini, a citizen of Italy, received a forty-year sentence for aiding in the escape of Assata Shakur. Although the Italian government has said that it wants her back in Italy to serve her time in an Italian prison—in accord with the Strasberg Convention—the U.S. Justice Department refused to let her go, claiming the Italians won't be harsh enough.[3] There are also nine alleged members or supporters of the IRA (Irish Republican Army) held in U.S. prisons by the U.S. government.

The same counter-insurgency tactics that have been detailed elsewhere have been used against white political prisoners. These include sophisticated spying and infiltration techniques, the jailing of many white activists for refusing to testify and/or cooperate with grand juries, the use of broad and vague conspiracy laws to criminalize people for association and belief and the use of preventative detention to deny bail. Laura Whitehorn was held without bail for four years before going to trial.

Finally, because they are political prisoners, they get some of the longest sentences in the world. Their political beliefs are used as a basis to impose sentences that are, in many instances, the equivalent of natural life in prison. The reason for this is that they are revolutionaries. For example, in 1986, a man convicted of planning and carrying out bombings—without making warning calls—of ten occupied health clinics where abortions were performed, was sentenced to ten years in prison and was paroled after forty-six months. In contrast, Raymond Levasseur was convicted of bombing four unoccupied military targets in protest against U.S. foreign policies, and sentenced to forty-five years in prison. A Ku Klux Klansman, charged with violations of the Neutrality Act and with possessing a boatload of explosives and weapons to be used in an invasion of the Caribbean island of Dominica received eight years.[4] Yet Linda Evans, convicted of purchasing four weapons with false ID, was sentenced to forty years—the longest sentence ever imposed for this offense.

Prisons are a horrible experience for everyone in this country. This was well documented in the Prison Discipline Study Report, issued in 1991.[5] This national survey revealed that both physical and psychological abuse, so severe that it approaches the internationally accepted definition for torture, are the norm in maximum-security prisons throughout the United States. That's the case for all prisoners. In this context the North American prisoners—like political prisoners everywhere—are systematically singled out for particularly severe sentences and constant harassment once incarcerated. This includes particular abuse directed at the women and Lesbians, including sexual assault and threats, often at the hands of male guards.

One of the most brutal weapons in the government's arsenal is the control unit prison. Its goal is to reduce prisoners to a state of submission, where it becomes possible to destroy their bodies, their spirit, their will, and ultimately their resistance and very self-definition. While officials claim that these units are only for the most violent disciplinary problems, more and more political prisoners are being placed there solely for their political beliefs. For instance, Alan Berkman, Raymond Levasseur, and Tom Manning were all sent directly to Marion Control Unit after sentencing. Silvia Baraldini and Susan Rosenberg, along with Puerto Rican POW Alejandrina Torres, were sent to the Lexington High Security Unit for two years in 1986. The justification: their political beliefs and associations. Once it was closed, as a result of a massive campaign inside and out, Susan and Silvia were sent to the new control unit for women at Marianna. Marilyn Buck was also sent there directly after sentencing.

In addition to isolation in control units, all political prisoners are more frequently subjected to cruel and inhumane punishment. This includes torture, sexual assault, strip and cavity searches (including those by male guards on women prisoners), punitive transfers, censorship, and denial of medical care, which has had grave consequences in several cases. Alan Berkman, suffering from Hodgkin's disease, nearly died several times while in prison because officials withheld necessary medical treatment. Silvia Baraldini's abdominal lumps, which anyone could feel, were ignored for months only to reveal that she had an aggressive form of uterine cancer. Silvia continues to have difficulty receiving medical attention.

Yet, imprisonment doesn't mean the end of these revolutionaries' organizing and political work. They continue once they're inside. For many of them, this has meant organizing resistance to oppressive prison policies, publishing prison newsletters, providing legal help and assistance, and facilitating courses, work stoppages and hunger strikes. For others it's also meant becoming AIDS activists. In fact, some of the women are responsible for developing the most comprehensive models (like AIDS Counseling and Education [ACE] at Bedford Hills and Pleasanton AIDS Counseling and Education [PLACE] at FCI-Dublin) for AIDS education and peer counseling in prisons in the country! But even in these cases, political prisoners are punished for being too successful in their work. For instance, Ed Mead, who organized Men Against Sexism at Walla Walla, was prevented from continuing his work on prisoner-on-prisoner rape. Bill Dunne was kept at Marion for years for publishing a newsletter there and David Gilbert was moved from place to place for developing work on AIDS in prison, and finally prevented from doing any work at all. Quite recently, Laura Whitehorn [released in 1999] was transferred from Lexington to Marianna after she participated in the first women's prison uprising in 20 years. Tim Blunk was moved back to Marion from Lewisburg after there was a strike there of Black and Puerto Rican prisoners.

Why does the government so determinedly continue to attack and repress these women and men once they are incarcerated? It needs to break their spirits and prevent them from continuing to educate and mobilize from within the prison walls. On the one hand, these prisoners are used as examples to intimidate whole movements and communities from continuing their resistance. The government wants it made very clear that the price one can pay for being a white person willing to take a stand against this racist and inhuman system is very high. On the other hand, they need these revolutionaries to be buried away and forgotten. We won't let that happen! Clearly now is a time for action. We too can follow the examples of these brave women and men who have given so much of their lives for freedom and justice. We must recognize who and what they are: political prisoners. We must demand their freedom so they can be back on the streets where they belong.

I know I speak for all the white political prisoners when I say that it's been a great honor to be able to speak to you today at this International Tribunal. All of us pledge to continue our resistance to the crimes outlined by today's speakers and commit ourselves to continue to work until there is a world where everyone can have true justice and freedom.

NOTES

Speech delivered at the International Tribunal of Indigenous Peoples and Oppressed Nations in the United States, October 3, 1992; published in E. Rosenblatt, ed. *Criminal Injustice* (Boston: South End, 1991).

1. *Editor's note:* "Davis Hall Alderson" refers to the Control Unit at FCI-Alderson, WV.

2. *Editor's note:* The group Brown calls the "Jonathan Jackson–Sam Melville Brigade" actually called itself the "Sam Melville/Jonathan Jackson Unit," and it operated in the Northeastern United States. This is not the same organization as the Jonathan Jackson–Sam Melville Unit of the New World Liberation Front, which took responsibility for bombings in California in the late 1970s and was affiliated with the Symbionese Liberation Army. Brown

herself was affiliated with the George Jackson Brigade, a group separate from those mentioned in this note.

3. *Editor's note:* The Strasberg Convention on human rights established that prisoners convicted outside their homeland should serve their time in their native country. Baraldini was returned to Italy in August 1999.

4. *Editor's note:* Don Black was no longer in the Klan when he and nine others were arrested preparing to sail to Dominica. He was released from prison after serving "more than two years" (Kent Faulk, "White Supremacist Spreads Views on Net," *Birmingham News,* 19 October 1997, 1). He violated the Neutrality Act, originally passed in 1935 to keep the United States out of a possible European war. The act prevents the exportation of arms, ammunition, and implements of war to any "belligerent" warring nations, defined at the discretion of the president. Amendments to the Neutrality Act in 1936 and 1937 expanded the provisions of the law to exclude loans to states at war and then to include civil wars under foreign wars as well.

5. *Editor's note:* See Prisoners' Rights Union, *Prison Discipline Study* (Sacramento, Calif.: Prisoners' Rights Union, 1991).

Chapter Sixteen

Raymond Luc Levasseur

Raymond Luc Levasseur was born October 10, 1946, into a family of poor French Canadian textile and shoe factory workers in Sanford, Maine. Reluctant to follow his grandparents and parents into the wage slavery of millwork, he went to work in a shoe factory at age seventeen. Resisting the debilitating effects of "speed ups" in production, he and coworkers stopped the machines, jamming them with a shoe—*le sabot*. "It was my first act of sabotage," writes Levasseur, "but a long way from my last."[1]

In 1965, he enlisted in the army. Two years later, he was radicalized by a tour of duty in Vietnam. There he witnessed racism against the Vietnamese and African American and Latino American soldiers and found that fighting against the Vietnamese right to self-determination contradicted his own beliefs in American ideals. Returning to the United States when his twelve-month tour ended, Levasseur moved to Tennessee and began college. He also began organizing with the Southern Student Organizing Committee (SSOC), which focused on ending the war and supporting black liberation and the efforts of workers fighting to unionize. Levasseur's activism with SSOC ended in 1969 after he was caught in an undercover police "sting" and was convicted of selling seven dollars' worth of marijuana. Although he had no prior convictions, Levasseur, known for his political activism, received the maximum sentence: five years. He was classified as an "agitator" upon entering prison.

As in most U.S. prisons, the population of Tennessee State Penitentiary was rife with racial tensions, tensions at times promoted and manipulated by guards. Levasseur, however, saw himself as a victim of Anglo-American supremacy and crossed the "color line" of segregated prison life. Consequently, he spent most of the next two years in solitary confinement.[2] Like many politicized prisoners of the era, Levasseur began studying the revolutionary theories of Mao Zedong, Che Guevara, Frantz Fanon, Rosa Luxemburg, Emma Goldman, and the Black Panther Party.

In 1971, Levasseur was paroled to Maine, where he organized for Vietnam Veterans against the War (VVAW). By 1973, influenced by the Black Panthers and Malcolm X, Levasseur viewed prisoners as key in social justice leadership. He became active in prisoners' rights organizations, including the Statewide Correctional Alliance for Reform (SCAR); there he organized community-based "survival programs" for prison families, including a community bail fund, a prisoners' union, an alternative paper, a martial arts program, and job, housing, and welfare initiatives. Echoing the Black Panthers, SCAR described survival as programs "pending significant social changes, survival pending revolutionary changes that would meet the needs of the people who suffer most from class and racist oppression."[3]

Organizing in Maine, Levasseur met his future common-law wife, Pat Gros, and Carol Ann and Tom Manning, with whom he would eventually go underground.

In March of 1975, he was arrested in Rhode Island with Students for a Democratic Society (SDS) activist Cameron Bishop, a fugitive on federal sabotage charges. After being released on bail, Levasseur went underground and learned that Pat was expecting the first of their three daughters.

The Levasseurs and their comrades spent the next ten years balancing the demands of family, clandestinity, and frequent moves from state to state, while continuing to organize. The Federal Bureau of Investigation (FBI)'s COINTELPRO and the BosLuc task force formed the largest FBI manhunt in history. The task force assembled to find Levasseur and his codefendants brought together elements of various task forces—including the Joint Terrorist Task Force. Federal agents apprehended Ray Luc Levasseur and Pat Gros-Levasseur along with Barbara J. Curzi, Jaan Laaman, and Richard Williams on November 4, 1984, in Ohio. The Mannings were captured five months later in Virginia. All defendants would eventually be known as the "Ohio Seven."

The government alleges that between 1974 and 1984 Levasseur and his comrades were members of the United Freedom Front (UFF) and the Sam Melville/Jonathan Jackson Unit (SM/JJU) (a group not connected with the one cited in Bo Brown's text), named after Sam Melville, a white prison activist killed by guards in the retaking of Attica prison in 1971, and Jonathan Jackson, the slain teenaged brother of George Jackson. These organizations claimed responsibility for a series of bombings of government and military buildings and corporate offices, including those of South African Airlines in New York City. No deaths occurred in any of these actions, but there were injuries in a Suffolk County courthouse bombing.[4] In 1986, a Federal Court in Brooklyn convicted members of the Ohio Seven of bombings against U.S. military facilities, military contractors, and businesses profiting from South African apartheid. Levasseur received forty-five years. (In a subsequent trial for sedition [in a RICO indictment], Levasseur represented himself and was acquitted, along with his codefendants.)

To serve his forty-five-year sentence, Levasseur was sent to the Control Unit at Marion Prison in Marion, Illinois, a prison that the United Nations has condemned for human rights abuses. Ostensibly, the "prison within a prison" is for the most violent prisoners, yet Levasseur had accumulated no prison violations. A prison administrator acknowledged that "the purpose of Marion is to control revolutionary attitudes in the prison system and society at large."[5] The only available work at Marion was in Federal Prison Industries, Inc., or UNICOR, producing military equipment for the Department of Defense. Levasseur's refusal to work for UNICOR likely led to his transfer in 1994 to the Federal Correctional Complex at Florence, Colorado, one of the most high-tech administrative segregation (ADX) units in the United States. In 1999, he was transferred to the Atlanta Federal Prison, and in December of that year, Ray Luc Levasseur was released from solitary confinement for the first time in thirteen years.[6] Raymond Luc Levasseur's writings appear on the website *Letters from Exile*.[7]

REFERENCES

Levasseur, Raymond Luc. "Dear Betty." *Letters from Exile*. March 1990. home.earthlink.net/~neoludd/betty.htm (18 March 2002).

———. "Death Chambers." *Letters from Exile*. home.earthlink.net/~neoludd/chambers.htm (18 March 2002).

———. "My Blood Is Quebecois." *Letters from Exile*. May 1992. home.earthlink.net/~neoludd/qbq.htm (18 March 2002).

———. "Raymond Luc Levasseur." In *Can't Jail the Spirit*, 182–83. Chicago: Committee to End the Marion Lockdown, 2002.

———. "The REEF." *Letters from Exile*. home.earthlink.net/~neoludd/reef.htm (18 March 2002).

———. "The Trial Statement of Ray Luc Levasseur." *Letters from Exile*. January 1989. (Opening Statement, 10 January 1989: Springfield, Mass.) home.earthlink.net/~neoludd/statement.htm (18 March 2002).

———. *Until All Are Free: The Trial Statement of Ray Luc Levasseur* (Pamphlet). London: Attack International, 1989.

NOTES

Research and draft for this biography were provided by Daniel Schleifer.

1. Ray Luc Levasseur, "My Blood Is Quebecois," *Letters from Exile*, May 1992, home.earthlink.net/~neoludd/qbq.htm (18 March 2002).

2. Ray Luc Levasseur, "Death Chambers," *Letters from Exile*, home.earthlink.net/~neoludd/chambers.htm (18 March 2002).

3. Ray Luc Levasseur, "Trial Statement," *Letters from Exile*, January 1989 (Opening Statement, 10 January 1989: Springfield, Mass.), home.earthlink.net/~neoludd/statement.htm (18 March 2002).

4. *Editor's note:* According to correspondence with Levasseur in 2002, the only injuries in any SMJJ/UFF bombing were at the Suffolk County courthouse in Boston where authorities

failed to heed a telephoned SMJJ warning to evacuate the facility. Suffolk was the first SMJJ bombing. No injuries resulted from subsequent bombings.

5. Ray Luc Levasseur, "Dear Betty," *Letters from Exile*, March 1990, home.earthlink.net/ ~neoludd/betty.htm (18 March 2002).

6. Ray Luc Levasseur, "The REEF," *Letters from Exile*, home.earthlink.net/~neoludd/ reef.htm (18 March 2002).

7. *Letters from Exile* is located at home.earthlink.net/~neoludd.

On Trial (Abridged)

January 10, 1989

I freely admit to being part of a revolutionary movement. The government cannot tolerate serious opposition to its own criminal policies, so they do what the prosecution are trying to do here. They want to criminalize my life, my values, and the organisations that they allege I've been part of.

They begin to do this in the indictment by talking about "manner and means." Use of fictitious identification, renting houses with names other than your own, using public telephones to communicate, private mailboxes. The possession of weapons. Practicing with weapons. Monitoring police activities. If you look at the context in which things are done, I think that in this case you are going to find out this is not criminal activity. You know, when I went to Vietnam I was twenty years old, I couldn't vote and I could not have a legal drink. So I did what a lot of other GI's did. I had a fake ID, so I could have a beer and celebrate the idea that I might get killed in another year to defend this system.

More to the point, if you want to stay alive and survive, you have to utilise these methods. In Nazi Germany if they hadn't had secret meetings (I'm talking about Jews, labor leaders, communists, gay people—everybody who the Nazis went after), if they hadn't used false passports, if they didn't carry a gun now and then, do you think more would have gotten killed? When the Nazis spread their fascism into France and you had a French government that collaborated with the Nazis, how far do you think the resistance would have got, if they had not utilised these types of methods? It had a hard enough time as it was.

And the same could be said for South Africa today that murders and tortures its opponents. They want you to carry a pass in South Africa today. So you are going to have to find something else if you don't want to end up in one of those South African prisons. Or the sanctuary movement today, which utilizes churches to move refugees through the country from Central America, refugees from wars that the United States is responsible for creating. Think for a minute about a woman named Harriet Tubman, who used to come through Springfield up to Amherst and into Canada. She carried a gun and she used a name other than her own and she used so-called safe houses. That is what the underground railroad was. How many of those slaves do you think would have made it if she hadn't done that? Part of what they were fleeing from was the Fugitive Slave Act. It was the law at the time.

I would like to digress for a minute and tell you why I'm choosing to defend myself. I was underground for ten years. It's not easy for me to stand here before you now and speak in what is essentially a public forum. What I'm simply trying to do is to add my voice to that of millions of others who cry freedom, from South Africa to Central America to the South Bronx in New York. They don't have much choice about it, and I don't have much choice. I'd rather not be here. But since I am, I want to defend myself and I want to defend the issues that I think are important. And the important issue here is the issue of human rights. I see that as a central part of this trial.

The prosecutor mentioned one of his snitch witnesses comes from Harvard University, and of course the prosecutor went to the same school. I can tell you that I never went to any prestigious law school. He has indicated that he is going to bring a computer in here to put on his table. You will not see any computer over there on my table. And I don't have a squad of FBI agents running my paperwork around for me. I do all my preparation from a prison cell. I'm one of over a hundred political prisoners in the United States, which the United States refuses to recognize.

The judge has said I don't have to ask questions, I don't have to testify, I don't have to cross-examine. But I do want to defend myself and I do want to participate in certain parts of this trial. What he didn't tell you is that he decides what it is I can do. I have a defense, but you are not necessarily going to hear it or see it. He makes that decision. That's the power he has. But if you don't hear it, it's not that I haven't tried.

You will see me angry in this trial. That anger will never be directed towards you. My anger is reserved for the government and some of the agents and witnesses who they're going to bring in here.

Now, over the years, after Vietnam, I felt I needed to engage in a self-education project. You will see a lot of material that was seized by the FBI. They seized everything in the house, including my kids' report cards, and a copy of the Bill of Rights. I monitored and collected a lot of data, research, fiscal data, articles documenting human rights violations in South Africa, Central America, human rights violations by this government. I collected information on military contractors—who they are selling their weapons to and how much they are getting for it. I tried to document every incident I could find where Black and Latino people were murdered by the police. And if I stood here now and started giving you each one of those names, I would still be standing here next week. I kept a file on the numbers of homeless and hungry and the numbers of unemployed. And there was a special notebook which I kept on prisons, documenting the guard murders of prisoners and, in particular, political prisoners. I documented civil rights violations and violations of international law.

The judge has said that you are triers of facts and I think you should look at the facts. But I'm going to ask you to look for something else. I'm going to ask you to look for the truth. Over the years, directly and indirectly, I have become aware that the United States government and some of the corporations headquartered in this country have been engaged in serious violations of international law, what are referred to as crimes against humanity and war crimes. The government has referred to communiqués that will come into evidence. The evidence is going to show that a lot of these bombings were done in support of freedom in South Africa. And that no other government in today's modern world is as close to being like Nazi Germany as the government of racist South Africa.

South Africa has a system called apartheid. Apartheid means hate Black people; segregate Black people. The United Nations has condemned apartheid as a crime against humanity. The closest ally to racist South Africa in this world is the United States government. The United Nations has condemned the collaboration of the US, including US corporations, with racist South Africa. There's a saying I once heard: "The blood of oppression in South Africa runs as deep as the mines." Because we know who works in the mines in South Africa—who mines the gold and diamonds—Black people. They do it for next to nothing. They do it for starvation wages. Because they've had their land stolen from them. Black people are 80% of the population and they don't even have the right to vote.

There was an action carried out by the Sam Melville/Jonathan Jackson Unit in 1976 against Union Carbide. It was right after the Soweto Uprising in South Africa in which 1,000 or more Black people, mainly women and children, were gunned down by South African troops. It started off as a student demonstration. People demanding to preserve their language and culture were shot in the back by the South African troops. The very first to be killed was Hector Pieterson, a young African boy. He was fourteen years old. Why were they gunned down? Because they were all in the streets of Soweto, a Black township, with their fists in the air shouting "*Amandla, Amandla*"—power that brings freedom. They want their country back. They want their land back. And they want their rights.

The Sam Melville/Jonathan Jackson Unit attacked the property of the Union Carbide Corporation while the US government was collaborating with the South African police and troops to kill 1,000 Black people. I'm here to support the liberation struggle in South Africa; these prosecutors are here to defend the interests of the United States government in South Africa. The United Freedom Front also paid a visit to the South African Airways office, a front for an office of the South African government in New York City. They did it there after there was a massacre in Lesotho, next to South Africa, where South African troops had gone in and gunned down Black activists. That's called a massacre. We're going to learn in this trial what the word "massacre" means.

American corporations are the legs upon which the racist system in South Africa walks. Troops in South Africa ride in General Motors trucks that are fuelled by Mobil Oil Corporation. So do the entire police and military system. In South Africa, those prisons, that pass system, all of that is computerized by corporations like IBM. The blood of innocent people must stir your conscience. I think that you ought to ask yourself a question throughout this trial, and that is: who are the real criminals? Those who support the racist system in South Africa or those who are opposed to it?

I believe that the evidence will show that there is a war in Central America and that it is a U.S.-sponsored war. This trial's going to have a lot to do with bombings. The United Freedom Front took responsibility for bombings of US military contractors and facilities. The evidence is going to show the UFF objected to the United States shipping bombs and armaments to the government of El Salvador which uses them to slaughter its own people. One of these particular bombs is a 750 pound fragmentation bomb. The prosecutor referred to 600 pounds of dynamite. This is one bomb that weighs 750 pounds. It's dropped by an A-37 Dragon Jet made by General Electric. That was also used in Vietnam. They're anti-personnel bombs. They explode before they hit the ground. That's not designed to destroy property as much as it's designed to kill people. And while we're standing here, there is a corporation up in Burlington, Vermont—General Electric—that is making machine guns that are going on this aircraft. The guns that the peasants in El Salvador refer to as flying death squads. The issue of state terrorism is going to be a central issue that comes up during this trial.

A lot of SM/JJ bombings were done in support of Puerto Rican independence and the release of Puerto Rican political prisoners. All national struggles in which people are trying to be free are close to my heart, but the struggle for Puerto Rico to be free is especially close to me. I have three young girls and I used to tell them bedtime stories about Puerto Rican patriots like Lolita Lebron and her compañeros who spent a quarter of a century in US prisons because they dared to take the struggle for a free Puerto Rico to the heart of the beast, right here in the United States. Half of the Puerto Rican population have been forced by economic conditions to migrate to this country. The American flag flies over Puerto Rico. While you think it may represent freedom here, it does not represent freedom to the vast majority of Puerto Rican people.

The United States invaded Puerto Rico ninety years ago and it has been militarily occupied since then. There are bases all over the nation of Puerto Rico. The United Nations has ruled that Puerto Rico is a colony of the United States and that colonialism is illegal under international law. I believe that it is inhumane by any standard to subject another country or another people to what you want to do. The United Nations has ruled that Puerto Rico is being held illegally, illegally occupied therefore it has the right to resist that occupation. And I support that. You are going to see evidence in this trial about the police murders of unarmed Puerto Rican men right here in Springfield. That is something the Sam Melville/Jonathan Jackson Unit felt was necessary to respond to. You will see evidence of the abusive treatment of Puerto Rican political prisoners held in the United States.

Like me, you probably hold high value and respect for the principles on which the American Revolution was founded, the Declaration of Independence and the Constitution. But as I look back at those documents and what they represent, I ask myself, I do not remember anybody conferring on this government or its military or police apparatus the right to engage in violations of human rights in the name of the American people. When I went to school as a kid I would do the pledge of allegiance all the time. But, based on my experience since then, I don't feel like I owe any blind allegiance to a system that is going to perpetuate this kind of suffering of people throughout the world—including here within the United States. I mentioned earlier that the question of killer cops is going to be an important issue in this trial. When officers of the New York City Police Department beat to death a young Black community artist named Michael Stewart, the United Freedom Front responded by supporting the Black communities in their struggle to stop killer cops.

There's little difference between a lynching by the KKK and a police officer who puts a bullet in the head of a young Black man, and it happens time and time again. And lest we think the Klan is not active, I expect that we're going to have a close look at the New York Police Department during this trial. I think what you are going to see is the largest Ku Klux Klan chapter in the Northeast.

The sedition law and the RICO law were addressed earlier and I now want to address them briefly.[1] Sedition laws in general have always been designed to break what has been a tradition of resistance and political activity in this country, whether it was Native American people resisting the theft of their land or slaves trying to be free, or union leaders or anti-war activists. And this specific sedition law, seditious conspiracy, has been almost exclusively used against Puerto Rican Independentistas, that is, advocates for a free and independent Puerto Rico. Now the government has expanded its use to try and target those who support Puerto Rican independence. You are going to see very clearly that I support Puerto Rican independence with all my heart. And I don't support it idly—I support it actively—I participate in the struggle.

The government wants you to believe that three people are going to conspire to overthrow the most powerful government on the face of the earth. Or eight people as the original indictment says. Or eighty or 800 for that matter. That is a fabrication. That goes against my political thinking. Because I don't think there's going to be significant social change in this country unless a lot of people participate and make it happen. That is what self-determination is all about.

They're spending over $10,000,000 on this trial to try to convince people that a 125-year sedition statute is going to keep the United States from sinking. What they are really looking for with their $10,000,000 is a government show trial. A propaganda trial. Sort of a version of what they used to have years ago where you take a dissident and you put him in a wooden stock and try to humiliate him, denigrate him, criminalize him. This is what they want to use the prosecution of myself and others for. As a warning to other political dissidents, to organizers, to revolutionaries. Against those who challenge a government conducting their bloody business as usual.

They want to see to it that I spend the rest of my life in prison. They want to make me bleed. One of the ways they do that is they go not just after me, but they go after everybody with whom I'm associated—friends, family, supporters. I've had friends subpoenaed before a grand jury that refused to testify; refused to give up information. They have been jailed. That's called political internment. Because you're jailed without a trial.

I was arrested in November 1984. Since I've been arrested, I've been beaten and I've been stun-gunned. A stun gun is like an electric cattle prod. I was arrested with my wife and our three children, who were four, six and eight at the time. Government agents attempted to bribe my eight-year-old daughter at the time. She wouldn't take a bribe. So they put her in a room with FBI agents and state police and they threatened her. There was a time when these agents sitting here and their colleagues were hanging from trees in the cemetery when my grandma died, because they thought that they could pick up on my whereabouts, because they think that my family is going to turn me in. I don't come from that kind of people. We don't turn each other in. We do not turn over for this government.

The treatment of the children at the time of our arrest [and that of] the children of Thomas and Carol Manning, who were grabbed and held for two months incommunicado, separate from their family members who pleaded to have them released—and ultimately they were released after [a hunger strike brought] widespread attention to the case—[reveals] the abuses that the government is prepared to carry out in an attempt to not only convict me and keep me in prison, but also to take that pound of flesh and hurt everybody that I'm associated with.

In June of 1984 it became public knowledge of the existence of a task force called BosLuc. You remember I said my middle name is Luc. Bos, B O S, Boston, Luc, L U C, my middle name. I was the target. This task force existed before June of 1984, but it became public knowledge in June of 1984. It had to because they put a bullet in the head of a kid named Ralph Richards. I read about it in the newspaper. How this kid had his hands up and he got shot in the head by the BosLuc agents. I felt that bullet had my name on it.

There's another reason for this prosecution and what the government is doing that sheds some light on their intent. Not only do they want to keep me in prison, but they want to put my wife in prison. If you listened to the prosecution earlier, you heard them characterise our marriage and our love for each other as if it were some kind of criminal enterprise. You know I'm separated from my three young daughters by prison walls and my wife brings them in to visit me, but the government isn't going to be satisfied until those three kids are orphans. That's the nature and extent of the punishment that they want to put out to anyone who even thinks of challenging this government's policies. . . .

It's hard to believe that those government prosecutors are going to build their careers on the backs of political prisoners and children who are left without their parents. But that's what they're doing. I want to just briefly address the issue of the RICO charges. Racketeering Influenced Corrupt Organizations. I can't tell you how insulted I am that these prosecutors charge me with being a racketeer. That law was passed in the 1970s and it was specifically passed to be used against real gangsters and real racketeers. "Racketeering Influenced and Corrupt Organizations"—I do not believe has the word revolutionary in it, or political dissident. They're trying to bend the law. . . . You cannot be a revolutionary and be a racketeer. It's a contradiction. It is either one or the other. You cannot support freedom struggles in South Africa or Central America or the Black nation within this country from the foundation of a criminal enterprise. It can't be done. History shows that.

I'm neither profit-oriented nor drug-oriented. In twenty-one years of political activity I've never done anything for personal gain or profit. Nothing. That has never been part of my motivation or intent. The government wants to charge that bombing the office of the South African government is an act of racketeering? A bombing that was done in response to a massacre in South Africa and to support the struggle for freedom there. This is an act of racketeering? No, it's an expression of support for freedom. It is that simple. If we could have Nelson Mandela here today, or Winnie Mandela, would they think attacking an office of the racist government of South Africa is an act of racketeering?

The government stood up for forty-five minutes essentially saying nothing more than that I'm a criminal and a racketeer and part of a criminal enterprise. That's not true. And I want to refute it and I want to put as much evidence in as I can to refute it. I want to participate in certain parts of this trial to refute it. If you want to see a corrupt and criminal enterprise let's take a good look at the highest levels of the United States government and what some of these military contractors are doing. Then we'll see what real corruption and criminality looks like.

These prosecutors do not represent the American people. They represent the government. And, since Vietnam, I have always made an important distinction between the two. I hope that you will. They're here to present certain interests and I'm here to defend certain issues. I began this by talking about children.[2] The children I began talking about were my own grandparents. They were merely children when they had to go to work in those mills and shoe factories. My grandfather was thirteen years old. That and my own experience I've outlined to you have left a deep imprint on me. And it does not leave me with any criminal intent or a criminal mind. It leaves me with the heart of a revolutionary, somebody who's committed to social justice.

My wife and I have a marriage. We don't have a criminal enterprise. I love her very much. We have three daughters. My oldest daughter is going to be thirteen day after tomorrow. We named each of our kids after their grandmothers, one of whom is sitting here now, and one after their great grandmother. Because we are proud of our working class roots and we're proud of our families.

I will remember the children of Vietnam, the suffering of those children who I saw there. But I also remember the beauty of their smiles. And I never have lost sight of what human potential there is in people. This is at the heart of what motivates me—my intent, my purpose, my goals, my values, this is where it's at. It's my commitment. This is what the government fears. That I didn't go back to that mill to make those shoe heels, that I took another course with my life. I have a commitment to a future that holds the human potential of poor and working class people as a great asset to be developed. A commitment to a future in which no child will ever have to suffer from racism, poverty or war. A future where justice brings peace for our children and generations to come.

Raymond Luc Levasseur
United States Courthouse
Springfield, MA

NOTES

Originally published in the pamphlet *Until All Are Free: The Trial Statement of Ray Luc Levasseur* (London: Attack International, 1989).

Editor's note: This excerpted opening statement was given at Raymond Luc Levasseur's RICO trial—a trial at which he was acquitted of seditious conspiracy and the government dismissed the RICO charges due to a "deadlocked" jury.

1. *Editor's note:* RICO (Racketeer Influenced and Corrupt Organizations Act; 18 U.S.C. §§ 1961–1968), officially designed as antiracketeering statutes to combat organized crime, has frequently been used against political dissidents.

2. *Editor's note:* Levasseur is referring to a section of his trial statement not included here.

Chapter Seventeen

Daniel J. Berrigan, S.J.

Born in 1921, Daniel Berrigan joined the Order of Jesus in 1939 and was ordained in 1952. In 1965, church officials exiled the young Jesuit priest indefinitely to South America for comments he made supporting a young Catholic man who immolated himself in protest of the U.S. war against Vietnam. Without a chance to say good-bye to family and friends, Berrigan departed, but after months of considerable petitioning pressure from students and laypeople, the Catholic hierarchy allowed him to return to the United States.

Daniel Berrigan and his younger brother, Philip Berrigan, were two of the most prominent and two of the first Roman Catholic priests to serve federal sentences for acts of political resistance in the United States during the antiwar and civil rights movements. (Philip Berrigan would later leave the priesthood and cofound Plowshares.) Their first sentence was for burning draft cards as members of the Catonsville Nine in 1969.[1] Their two most widely publicized actions were the 1968 Catonsville raid and participation in the Plowshares Eight witness, which entailed hammering nuclear warheads and pouring their blood on government documents in 1980.[2] Also that year, they traveled to Ireland to highlight the deplorable conditions and punishments endured by some four hundred Irish political prisoners and detainees held by the British.[3]

While incarcerated, the Berrigan brothers organized in prison, although they were often held incommunicado in solitary confinement and transferred from prison to prison without court orders. On several occasions they led strikes to protest parole boards' "arbitrariness and secrecy" and the Vietnam War.[4] They challenged abuse and corruption, initiating a strike after discovering that African Americans and ethnic minorities working in "the prison factory for slave wages . . . were making parts of fuses of bombs that were being dropped on Vietnam."[5]

Both Berrigans were heavily influenced by France's radical worker-priest movements, but they were radicalized by Martin Luther King, Jr.'s invitation to clergy to march in Selma, Alabama, in 1965. It was then, according to Berrigan, that the two "young working-class, Irish-American priests . . . stepped out of rhetoric, into the reality of action, and the realm of consequence."[6] Berrigan believed it necessary to develop strategies that were consistent with spiritual and political beliefs: "A revolution is interesting insofar as it avoids like the plague, the plague it promised to heal." This led to his criticisms of the Weathermen or the Weather Underground Organization (WUO). In 1969, the group of college-age European Americans emerged from the ranks of Students for a Democratic Society (SDS).[7] In 1970, the Weathermen allegedly planned to detonate a bomb filled with nails at a Reserved Officer Training Corps (ROTC) dance, but while constructing the bomb in New York City's West Village, they accidentally blew up a Manhattan townhouse in which they were working. Three members of the WUO—Teddy Gold, Diana Oughton, and Terry Robbins—were killed in the explosion. By 1976, the Weather Underground had disbanded.[8]

Berrigan was also underground at this time, eluding the FBI, which sought to arrest him for his role in the Catonsville Nine. On August 8, 1970, three days prior to his capture, Berrigan recorded a message to the Weather Underground, cautioning against the use of violence to engineer political revolution: "No principle is worth the sacrifice of a single human being." The WUO, which decided to cease actions with human targets, were receptive to this message.[9]

REFERENCES

Berrigan, Daniel. *America Is Hard to Find: Notes from the Underground and Letters from Danbury Prison*. New York: Doubleday, 1972.

———. "Daniel Berrigan: War in Heaven, Peace on Earth." *Spirituality Today* 40, no. 1 (Spring 1988). www.spiritualitytoday.org/spir2day/884013berrigan.html (18 March 2002).

———. *Lights on in the House of the Dead: A Prison Diary*. New York: Doubleday, 1974.

———. *Prison Poems*. Greensboro, N.C.: Unicorn, 1973.

———. *To Dwell in Peace: An Autobiography*. San Francisco: Harper & Row, 1987.

———. *The Trial of the Catonsville Nine*. Boston: Beacon, 1970.

———, and Robert Coles. *The Geography of Faith: Underground Conversations on Religious, Political and Social Change*. 30th Anniversary Edition. Woodstock, Vt.: Skylight Paths, 2001.

Berrigan, Daniel, and Lee Lockwood. *Daniel Berrigan: Absurd Convictions, Modest Hopes: Conversations after Prison with Lee Lockwood*. New York: Random House, 1972.

Berrigan, Philip, with Fred A. Wilcox. *Fighting the Lamb's War: Skirmishes with the American Empire: The Autobiography of Philip Berrigan*. Monroe, Maine: Common Courage, 1996.

Fox, Alan. "A Conversation between Daniel Berrigan and Alan Fox." *Rattle*. www.rattle.com/rattle11/poetry/interview.html (18 March 2002).

Jacobs, Harold, ed. *Weatherman*. Berkeley, Calif.: Ramparts Press, 1970.

NOTES

Research and draft for this biography were provided by Samuel Seidel.
1. The Berrigan brothers and seven others entered a draft board in Catonsville, Maryland,

removed 378 draft files, and burned them in the parking lot. See Daniel Berrigan, *The Trial of the Catonsville Nine* (Boston: Beacon, 1970).

2. The Berrigan brothers and six others entered a General Electric weapons manufacturing plant in King of Prussia, Pennsylvania, and damaged missiles. This was the beginning of the Plowshares Movement. The name of the movement came from the book of Isaiah's injunctions to "beat swords into plowshares." Since 1980, there have been over fifty Plowshares actions. See Philip Berrigan with Fred A. Wilcox, *Fighting the Lambs War: Skirmishes with the American Empire: The Autobiography of Philip Berrigan* (Monroe, Maine: Common Courage Press, 1996), 183–205.

3. Daniel Berrigan, "The Prisoners of Ulster," *New York Times*, 9 October 1980, A35.

4. Berrigan, *Fighting the Lamb's War*, 139.

5. Alan Fox, "A Conversation between Daniel Berrigan and Alan Fox," *Rattle*. www.rattle.com/rattle11/poetry/interview.html (18 March 2002).

6. Berrigan, *Fighting the Lamb's War*, 54 and 62.

7. Harold Jacobs, ed., *Weatherman* (Berkeley, Calif.: Ramparts Press, 1970).

8. Jonathan Lerner, "I Was a Terrorist," *Washington Post*, 24 February 2002.

9. Daniel Berrigan, *Daniel Berrigan: Absurd Convictions, Modest Hopes* (New York: Random House, 1972), 205.

Letter to the Weathermen

1972

Dear Brothers and Sisters,

Let me express a deep sense of gratitude that the chance has come to speak to you across the underground. It's a great moment; I rejoice in the fact that we can start a dialogue that I hope will continue through the smoke signals, all with a view to enlarging the circle. Indeed the times demand not that we narrow our method of communication but that we enlarge it, if anything new or better is to emerge. (I'm talking out of a set of rough notes; my idea is that I would discuss these ideas with you and possibly publish them later, by common agreement.)

The cold war alliance between politics, labor, and the military finds many Americans at the big end of the cornucopia. What has not yet risen in them is the question of whose blood is paying for all this, what families elsewhere are being blasted, what separation and agony and death are at the narrow end of our abundance. These connections are hard to make, and very few come on them. Many can hardly imagine that all being right with America means that much must go wrong elsewhere. How do we get such a message across to others? It seems to me that this is one way of putting the very substance of our task trying to keep connections, or to create new ones. It's a most difficult job, and in hours of depression it seems all but impossible to speak to Americans across the military, diplomatic, and economic idiocies. Yet I think we have to carry our reflection further, realizing that the difficulty of our task is the other side of the judgment Americans are constantly making about persons like ourselves. This determination to keep talking with all who seek a rightful place in the world, or all who have not yet awakened to any sense at all of the real world—this, I think, is the revolution. And the United States perversely and negatively knows it, and this is why we are in trouble. And this is why we accept trouble, ostracism, and fear of jail and of death as the normal condition under which decent men and women are called upon to function today.

Undoubtedly, the FBI comes with guns in pursuit of people like me because beyond their personal chagrin and corporate machismo (a kind of debased esprit de corps; they always get their man), there was the threat that the Panthers and the Vietnamese have so valiantly offered. The threat is a very simple one; we are making connections, religious and moral connections, connections with prisoners and Cubans and Vietnamese, and these connections are forbidden under policies which [FBI Director] J. Edgar Hoover is greatly skilled both in enacting and enforcing. They know by now what we are about; they know we are serious. And they are serious about us. Just as, with mortal fear, for the last five years they have known what the Vietnamese are about, and the Brazilians and Angolese and Guatemalans. We are guilty of making connections, we urge others to explore new ways of getting

242

connected, of getting married, of educating children, of sharing goods and skills, of being religious, of being human, of resisting. We speak for prisoners and exiles and that silent, silent majority which is that of the dead and the unavenged as well as the unborn. And I am guilty of making connections with you.

By and large the public is petrified of you Weather People.[1] There is a great mythology surrounding you—much more than around me. You come through in public as embodiment of the public nightmare, menacing, sinister, senseless, and violent: a spin-off of the public dread of Panthers and Vietcong, of Latins and Africans, of the poor of our country, of all those expendable and cluttering, and clamorous lives, those who have refused to lie down and die on command, to perish at peace with their fate, or to drag out their lives in the world as suppliants and slaves.

But in a sense, of course, your case is more complicated because your rebellion is not the passionate consequence of the stigma of slavery. Yours is a choice. It's one of the few momentous choices in American history. Your no could have been a yes; society realizes this—you had everything going for you. Your lives could have been posh and secure; but you said no. And you said it by attacking the very properties you were supposed to have inherited and expanded—an amazing kind of turnabout.

Society, I think, was traumatized by your existence, which was the consequence of your choice. What to do with Vietcong or Panthers had never been a very complicated matter, after all. They were jailed or shot down or disposed of by the National Guard. But what to do with you—this indeed was one hell of a question. There was no blueprint. And yet this question, too, was not long in finding its answer, as we learned at Kent State.[2] That is to say, when the choice between property and human life comes up close, the metaphor is once more invariably military. It is lives that go down. And we know now that even if those lives are white and middle-class, they are going to lie in the same gun sights.

The mythology of fear that surrounds you is exactly what the society demands, as it demands more and more mythology, more and more unreality to live by. But it also offers a very special opportunity to break this myth that flourishes on silence and ignorance and has you stereotyped as mindless, indifferent to human life and death, determined to raise hell at any hour or place. We have to deal with this as we go along; but from what values, what mentality, what views of one another and ourselves? Not from a mimicry of insanity or useless rage, but with a new kind of anger which is both useful in communicating and imaginative and slow-burning, to fuel the long haul of our lives.

I'm trying to say that when people look about them for lives to run with and when hopeless people look to others, the gift we can offer is so simple a thing as hope. As they said about Che [Guevara], as they say about Jesus, some people, even to this day; he gave us hope. So my hope is that you see your lives in somewhat this way, which is to say, I hope your lives are about something more than sabotage. I'm certain they are. I hope the sabotage question is tactical and peripheral. I hope indeed that you are uneasy about its meaning and usefulness and that you realize that the burning of properties, whether at Catonsville or Chase Manhattan or anywhere else, by no means guarantees a change of consciousness, the risk always being very great that sabotage will change people for the worse and harden them against enlightenment.[3]

I hope you see yourselves as Che saw himself, that is to say as teachers of the people, sensitive as we must be to the vast range of human life that awaits liberation, education, consciousness. If I'm learning anything it is that nearly everyone is in need of these gifts—and therefore in need of us, whether or not they realize it. I think of all those we so easily dismiss, whose rage against us is an index of the blank pages of their lives, those to whom no meaning or value have ever been attached by politicians or generals or churches or universities or indeed anyone, those whose sons fight the wars, those who are constantly mortgaged and indebted to the consumer system; and I think also of those closer to ourselves, students who are still enchanted by careerism and selfishness, unaware that the human future must be created out of suffering and loss.

How shall we speak to our people, to the people everywhere? We must never refuse, in spite of their refusal of us, to call them our brothers. I must say to you as simply as I know how; if the people are not the main issue, there simply is no main issue and you and I are fooling ourselves, and American fear and dread of change have only transferred themselves to a new setting.

Thus, I think a sensible, humane movement operates on several levels at once if it is to get anywhere. So it says communication, yes; organizing, yes; community, yes; sabotage, yes—as a tool. That is the conviction that took us where we went, to Catonsville. And it took us beyond, to this night. We reasoned that the purpose of our act could not be simply to impede the war, or much less to stop the war in its tracks. God help us; if that had been our intention, we were fools before the fact and doubly fools after it, for in fact the war went on. Still, we undertook sabotage long before any of you. It might be worthwhile reflecting on our reasons why. We were trying first of all to say something about the pernicious effect of certain properties on the lives of those who guarded them or died in consequence of them. And we were determined to talk to as many people as possible and as long as possible afterward, to interpret, to write, and through our conduct, through our appeal, through questioning ourselves again and again to discuss where we were, where we were going, where people might follow.

My hope is that affection and compassion and nonviolence are now common resources once more and that we can proceed on one assumption, the assumption that the quality of life within our communities is exactly what we have to offer. I think a mistake in [the Students for a Democratic Society] SDS's past was to kick out any evidence of this community sense as weakening, reactionary, counter-productive. Against this it must be said that the mark of inhumane treatment of humans is a mark that also hovers over us. And it is the mark of a beast, whether its insignia is the military or the movement.

No principle is worth the sacrifice of a single human being. That's a very hard statement. At various stages of the movement some have acted as if almost the opposite were true. As people got purer and purer, more and more people have been kicked out for less and less reason. At one remote period of the past, the results of such thinking were the religious wars, or wars of extinction. At another time it was Hitler; he wanted a ton of purity too. Another is still with us in the war against the Panthers and the Vietnamese. I think I'm in the underground because I want part in none of this inhumanity, whatever name it goes by, whatever rhetoric it justifies itself with.

When madness is the acceptable public state of mind, we're all in danger; for madness is an infection in the air. And I submit that we all breathe the infection and that the movement has at times been sickened by it too.

The madness has to do with the disposition of human conflict by forms of violence. In or out of the military, in or out of the movement, it seems to me that we had best call things by their name, and the name for this thing, it seems to me, is the death game, no matter where it appears. And as for myself, I would as soon be under the heel of former masters as under the heel of new ones.

Some of your actions are going to involve inciting conflict and trashing, and these actions are very difficult for thoughtful people. But I came upon a rule of thumb somewhere which might be of some help to us: Do only that which one cannot not do. Maybe it isn't very helpful, and of course it's going to be applied differently by the Joint Chiefs of Staff and an underground group of sane men and women. In the former, hypocritical expressions of sympathy will always be sown along the path of the latest rampage. Such grief is like that of a mortician in a year of plague. But our realization is that a movement has historic meaning only insofar as it puts itself on the side of human dignity and the protection of life, even of the lives most unworthy of such respect. A revolution is interesting insofar as it avoids like the plague the plague it promised to heal. Ultimately if we want to define the plague as death (a good definition), a prohuman movement will neither put people to death nor fill the prisons nor inhibit freedoms nor brainwash nor torture enemies nor be mendacious nor exploit women, children, Blacks, or the poor. It will have a certain respect for the power of the truth, a power which created the revolution in the first place.

We may take it, I think, as a simple rule of thumb that the revolution will be no better and no more truthful and no more populist and no more attractive than those who brought it into being. Which is to say, we are not killers, as America would stigmatize us, and indeed *as America perversely longs for us to be.* We are something far different. We are teachers of the people who have come on a new vision of things. We struggle to embody that vision day after day, to make it a reality among those we live with, so that people are literally disarmed by knowing us; so that their fear of change, their dread of life are exorcised, and their dread of human differences slowly expunged.

Instead of thinking of the underground as temporary, exotic, abnormal, perhaps we should start thinking of its implication as an entirely self-sufficient, mobile, internal revival community; the underground as a definition of our future. What does it mean, literally, to have nowhere to go in America, to be kicked out of America? It must mean—let us go somewhere in America, let us stay here and play here and love here and build here, and in this way join not only those who like us are kicked out also, but those who have never been inside at all, the Blacks and the Puerto Ricans and the Chicanos.

Next, we are to strive to become such men and women as may, in a new world, be nonviolent. If there's any definition of the new man and woman, the man or woman of the future, it seems to me that they are persons who do violence unwillingly, by exceptions. They know that destruction of property is only a means; they keep the end as vivid and urgent and as alive as the means, so that the means are judged in every instance by their relation to the ends. Violence as legitimate means: I have a great fear of American violence, not only in the military and diplomacy, in economics, in industry and advertising; but also in here, in me, up close, among us.

On the other hand, I must say, I have very little fear, from firsthand experience, of the violence of the Vietcong or Panthers (I hesitate to use the word violence), for their acts come from the proximate threat of extinction, from being invariably put on the line of self-defense. But the same cannot be said of us and our history. We stand outside the culture of these others, no matter what admiration or fraternity we feel with them; we are unlike them, we have other demons to battle.

But the history of the movement, in the last years, it seems to me, shows how constantly and easily we are seduced by violence, not only as method but as an end in itself. Very little new politics, very little ethics, very little direction, and only a minimum moral sense, if any at all. Indeed one might conclude in despair: the movement is debased beyond recognition, I can't be a part of it. Far from giving birth to the new man, it has only proliferated the armed, bellicose, and inflated spirit of the army, the plantation, the corporation, the diplomat.

Yet it seems to me good, in public as well as in our own house, to turn the question of violence back on its true creators and purveyors, working as we must from a very different ethos and for very different ends. I remember being on a television program recently and having the question of violence thrown at me, and responding—look, ask the question in the seats of power, don't ask me. Don't ask me why I broke the law; ask [Richard] Nixon why he breaks the law constantly; ask the Justice Department; ask the racists. Obviously, but for [Presidents Lyndon] Johnson and [Richard] Nixon and their fetching ways, Catonsville would never have taken place and you and I would not be where we are today; just as but for the same people SDS would never have grown into the Weather People or the Weather People have gone underground. In a decent society, functioning on behalf of its people, all of us would be doing the things that decent people do for one another. That we are forbidden to act, forced to meet so secretly and with so few, is a tragedy we must live with. We have been forbidden a future by the forms of power, which include death as the ordinary social method; we have rejected the future they drafted us into, having refused, on the other hand, to be kicked out of America, either by aping their methods or leaving the country.

The question now is what can we create. I feel at your side across the miles, and I hope that sometime, sometime in this mad world, in this mad time, it will be possible for us to sit down face to face, brother to brother, brother to sister, and find that our hopes and our sweat, and the hopes and sweat and death and tears and blood of our brothers and sisters throughout the world, have brought to birth that for which we began.

Shalom to you.

NOTES

On August 8, 1970, Daniel Berrigan recorded a message to the Weather Underground; the transcribed tape became the "Letter to the Weathermen"; it was published in 1971, in *The Village Voice*, and reprinted in 1972, in Berrigan's *America Is Hard to Find* (Garden City, N.Y.: Doubleday, 1972).

1. *Editor's note:* The "Weather People," also known as the Weatherman, the Weathermen, or the Weather Underground Organization, was an underground offshoot of Students for a Democratic Society (SDS).

2. *Editor's note:* Four whites, including students, were shot during a demonstration protesting the Vietnam War at Kent State University in Ohio on May 4, 1970.

3. *Editor's note:* The Berrigans burned draft records at Catonsville on May 17, 1968. "Chase Manhattan" refers to an action in the 1980s in which Daniel Berrigan and a group of theology students sat on the steps of Chase Manhattan Bank in protest of the bank's investments in apartheid South Africa.

Chapter Eighteen

Michele Naar-Obed

Michele Naar-Obed was born May 29, 1956, in Ossining, N.Y. She began her involvement in peace and social justice activism in 1991, in the context of a growing U.S. military presence in Saudi Arabia. At the time she was living in Baltimore, Maryland, and working as a pathologist's assistant in a community hospital. In reaction to the impending Gulf War, she became involved with Quaker peace activism in Baltimore, and committed her first act of civil disobedience the day after the bombing of Iraq began in January 1991. Naar-Obed and six others climbed on the roof of a National Guard armory and poured oil, sand, and their blood on the building's sign. All of the activists involved were charged with trespassing and destruction of government property. By the time they went to trial, the ground war had ended and sanctions were devastating Iraq (in a decade U.S. economic sanctions would lead to over a million civilian deaths). Rather than try to legally maneuver out of a prison sentence, Naar-Obed chose a stance based on political convictions. Nevertheless, she and her codefendants were acquitted on a legal technicality. She describes that first act of civil disobedience and the resulting trial as catalysts in her ideological and spiritual development: "I started to see that being a peace activist demanded more than reaction to an event. It's about saying *no* to, and resisting, what is morally wrong as well as saying *yes* to, and living, what is right. It has since become my full time and, hopefully, life-long commitment."[1]

Following her first trial, Naar-Obed continued in direct-action peace work, grounding her civil disobedience in spiritual and religious commitments: "[F]or me, this work needs to be grounded in faith and with the belief that God or some Divine Source exists. . . . Living a life of resistance to the violence of militarism in one of the most militarized nations in the world makes the most sense to me when I understand the significance of Christ's crucifixion and resurrection. That, too, is a life-long pursuit."[2]

The Plowshares movement, of which Naar-Obed is an active member, began in 1980 when then Catholic priests Daniel and Philip Berrigan and six others hammered and poured blood on two nose cones for nuclear warheads at a General Electric plant. Since this first act, there have been more than fifty Plowshares disarmament actions. Naar-Obed describes the Plowshares movement as an "effort to bring to life Isaiah's prophecy, 'They shall beat their swords into plowshares and spears into pruning hooks. Nation shall not wage war against nation nor shall they study war any more.'"[3] In May 1996, Naar-Obed was a defendant in the Jubilee Plowshares East trial, for her involvement in an August 7, 1995, act of civil disobedience in which she and three others symbolically disarmed a fast attack nuclear submarine at the Newport News, Virginia, shipyards, while on the same day two of their friends symbolically disarmed a Trident nuclear missile on the West Coast. For her role in this act of civil disobedience, Naar-Obed was imprisoned for eighteen months. As a condition of her parole, she was prohibited from visiting the Jonah House, a Christian Resistance community in Baltimore founded by Philip Berrigan and other peace activists in 1973, where she had lived with her husband and daughter for years.

In addition to her two trials for Plowshares actions, Naar-Obed has been tried in numerous smaller trials. For her nonviolent political activism, she has been sentenced to prison and jail terms on several occasions.

Author of a collection of essays, *Maternal Convictions*, on community, spirituality, and nonviolent resistance (abridged version of which appears below) and numerous articles for *Year One* and various Catholic Worker newsletters, Michele Naar-Obed currently lives with her husband, Greg Boertje-Obed, and their daughter, Rachel, at the Loaves and Fishes Catholic Worker Community in Duluth, Minnesota, and continues to write, speak, and act on behalf of peace and in opposition to U.S. militarism.

REFERENCES

Naar-Obed, Michele. *Maternal Convictions: A Mother Beats a Missile into a Plowshare*. Maple, Wisc.: Laurentian Shield Resources for Nonviolence, 1998. Available from the Catholic Worker Bookstore: www.catholicworker.com/bookstore/cwb-zmem.htm.

Obuszewski, Max, of the American Friends Service Committee in Baltimore. *Press Release—Protest Mistreatment of Plowshares by Baltimore Probation*. April 12, 1999, available online at csf.colorado.edu/forums/peace/apr99/0029.htm.

Rivera, John. "Jonah House Supporters Protest Probation Terms; 2 with Criminal Records Not Allowed to Live There." *Baltimore Sun*, 14 April 1999.

NOTES

Research and draft for this biography were provided by Elizabeth Walsh.

1. Michele Naar-Obed, *Maternal Convictions: A Mother Beats a Missile into a Plowshare* (Maple, Wisc.: Laurentian Shield Resources for Nonviolence, 1998), 7.

2. *Maternal Convictions*, 7–8.

3. *Maternal Convictions*, 5.

Maternal Convictions: A Mother Beats a Missile into a Plowshare (*Abridged*)

SPIRITUAL OPPRESSION

We are the only nation in the world that has ever dropped a nuclear weapon on human beings. We have spent more than $12 trillion for war and war preparations since 1945. Approximately $6 trillion of that has been spent on nuclear weapons. Our annual military budget is larger than the GNP of eight industrialized nations combined.

Why do so many people bury their heads in the sand with the help of mind-numbing television, drugs, alcohol and material consumption while our societal net unravels? Our cities are dying, the quality of public education is rapidly declining, health care is abysmal, the number of families living below the poverty line is ever-increasing, and this nation incarcerates more people per capita than any other industrialized nation in the world.

Life-sustaining and community-enhancing resources are decreasing exponentially. A country which is still viewed by most of the world as the richest and strongest is dependent on two death-dealing industries which dominate: weapons production and sales, and the prison industry.

Our air and water are polluted, our food is contaminated, and cancer has reached epidemic proportions. While most people point their finger at Joe Camel and the evil tobacco industry, there is a large body of evidence to condemn nuclear fallout from both weapons tests and accidents for much of the increase in lung cancer, according to the Worldwatch Institute and many other independent researchers and analysts. In September 1997 the National Cancer Institute released a study attributing 75,000 American citizen cancer cases to U.S. above ground nuclear testing in the 1950s and 1960s. According to the U.S. government itself—[Environmental Protection Agency] EPA and [Government Accounting Office] GAO reports in particular—the U.S. military is largely responsible for the pollution and devastation of our natural environment. They are virtually held unaccountable by the standard checks and balances and governmental regulations. Even when successfully sued by the states for violations of national environmental law, the Pentagon is able to overturn all challenges in the appellate courts. They are essentially lawless.

To underscore that phenomenon, Americans recently learned that during the 1950s our own military conducted secret medical experiments with radioactive material to understand the effects of nuclear weapons on human beings. Experiments were carried out on poor, pregnant mothers to study the effect of radioactivity on the fetus, on the mentally impaired, and on prisoners. Soldiers were sent to explosion sites as human guinea pigs—no more than test animals—to study the effects of nuclear fallout at varying distances from ground zero.

This was revealed by Energy Secretary Hazel O'Leary [in the Clinton Administration] somewhat after the time of the Iraq massacre, when Americans were notified that Saddam Hussein had gassed the Kurds. Neither behavior is excusable; *wake up, America! Something just as evil and criminal happened right here to us.*

Some of us from the Atlantic Life Community handed out informational leaflets about these nuclear experiments. Expecting the response to be outrage at the government and possibly a willingness to stand with us, we found instead that a common response was to tear the leaflet into pieces and throw it in our faces. Even that was actually a little more tolerable than watching people toss the leaflet aside as they might a candy bar wrapper. At least the first response showed emotion.

This made me realize how difficult it is to change hearts and minds about our military policies that victimize people on the other side of the world when most people don't seem to care about what's happening right here to their sons and daughters, sisters and brothers, and mothers and fathers.

I heard a Palestinian man speak about a group of people seeking to nonviolently resist Israeli occupation of their land. He challenged his fellow Palestinians to find 300 people who would literally be willing to give their lives to resist the oppressive occupation nonviolently. Within days 300 people came forward and they began a series of nonviolent actions to reclaim their land.

A young man from South Africa told of how university students would give up their education to join resistance groups during apartheid. Central Americans formed faith-based communities that are an envy to many of us North Americans.

These people were willing to give up their individual desires and even their lives for the communal good. They make sacrifices that most of us don't even dare to think about. Hearing these stories, I wonder why in our country it's often so difficult to get more than a handful of people to come to a vigil or even think about risking arrest.

One reason that comes to mind is that our oppression is much more subtle and insidious. It is more spiritual than physical in nature. Our oppressors work by taking over our hearts and minds rather than our "homelands." They work on stripping us of everything we know to be human and decent and loving. They fill us with images to make us afraid and to make us feel meaningless unless we have certain things. They work on making us believe that bombs are peacemakers and plowshares activists are violent. The idea of a know-nothing Generation X is marketed to become a self-fulfilling prophecy.

Even with the billion-dollar Wall Street goods-and-political-services propaganda ad machine, many Americans are beginning to realize that the American Dream is a lie. They are grasping that the void cannot be filled with materialism, consumerism or arrogant superiority.

Our souls yearn for community. It's natural to love and trust. It is not natural to kill, and it is not natural for a nation to be so obsessed with killing. We want community with each other and with our natural environment.

For most people, this spiritual discomfort has become a little more noticeable. For others, it has become unbearable. Jesus' warning now makes sense. Don't be afraid of those who can harm your body and do no more. Fear instead the one who can kill both body and soul and cast your soul into damnation (Luke 11: 4–5).

How do we resist this spiritual occupation? Where do we turn for guidance and example? How do we differentiate between truth and lies? Can we overcome our fears and misconceptions and come together as sisters and brothers? Can we go beyond our own self-interests and act as if we had the best interest of the next seven generations in mind? These are just some of the questions we must address if we have any hope of preserving our identity, our existence, and more importantly, our very souls.

THE PLOWSHARES WITNESS

There are numerous books written on the subject of the plowshare witness. The most complete, *Swords into Plowshares*, by Sr. Anne Montgomery and Art Laffin, gives an analysis and summary of every plowshare action up to 1996 and is an excellent resource, especially for anyone interested in direct disarmament.[1]

The plowshare witness is an attempt to bring Isaiah's vision (Isaiah 2:4) to life.[2] It envisions a time when all of God's people come together on the Holy Mountain to live as sisters and brothers. They come disarmed, personally and communally. It is a time when enemies put aside their differences and live together as described in the Peaceable Kingdom (Isaiah 11:6–9).

If we believe that the word of God applies to every generation throughout all of time, then we, this current generation of God's children, are called to bring the Word to life. This effort won't make sense to one who believes that the prophecies died with the prophets, or that our social responsibilities ended with Christ's crucifixion. It also won't make sense to one who believes in a final apocalyptic event resulting in the second coming of Christ to collect "the saved."

It will only make sense if one believes that we are required to live out God's commandments and God's vision, not only in our personal lives, but in our professional, communal, national, and international lives as well. It will make sense if we believe we have the responsibility to live out God's kingdom on earth: *"thy will be done, on earth as it is in heaven."* It will make more sense if we believe that it is the Christian responsibility to follow the nonviolent examples of Jesus as recorded in the Sermon on the Mount. It will only become palatable if one believes that the resurrection of the spirit through the Divine power of God is greater than persecution and that God has the final word even over death.

The plowshares witness is an act of direct disarmament, but the means are, in reality, symbolic. We who choose this witness beat the swords of our time, but we do this with small household hammers intending to convert, not destroy. We often spend months together in preparation and in prayer so that we can carry forth this action, not with malice or hate, but filled with hope and love for God's Creation. Thus our hammering is minimal and meant to be a symbolic attempt to begin the process of conversion.

Another symbol commonly used in plowshares witnesses is blood. The blood is often our own and is clinically drawn by a medical professional. It is poured out on the weapon to expose its destructive nature. During a time when weapons are becoming more high-tech, when soldiers can push buttons to destroy people thousands of miles away without having to see, hear, or smell death, and when the victims are referred to as "collateral damage," the pouring out of our blood is an attempt to make visible the bloody reality of war.

On a spiritual level, the blood also represents the blood of Christ. It is the blood of the new covenant, which requires love of enemy, forgiveness, and compassion.

Generally, plowshare witnesses are carried out on weapons that are nuclear-capable. These weapons not only violate God's law, but international law as well. The use, or threatened use, of weapons that cannot discriminate between soldier and civilian and are capable of mass destruction is illegal even under our own Constitution. Additionally, our Constitution states that international law supersedes local, state and federal law. So we have not only a moral right, but a legal right to use nonviolent direct action to stop the threat of criminal activity inherent in the manufacture of these weapons.

Another component of the plowshare witness is to stay with and take responsibility for the action after it's completed. This often means that we have to search out authorities to explain our act, and we attempt to indict them for participating in criminal activity under international law. We make no attempt to run or hide from our witness. To do so would reduce it to an act of vandalism.

Generally speaking, our indictments against the government and weapons manufacturers are ignored and we are the ones who are indicted, charged, and almost always convicted. The most common charges are trespass and destruction of government property, although some vindictive prosecutors have charged folks with sabotage.

The government has become very adept at silencing us in court. They have routinely invoked an *"in limine"*[3] motion preventing us from even using the words "international law" or "my religious beliefs" in our defense. In essence, the motion makes it impossible to speak about our moral, religious or political motivations without being further charged with contempt of court. Prosecution of the action is reduced to: Were you there? Did you intend to hit the weapon with the hammer? If so, you are guilty of trespass and destruction of property. If it wasn't such a flagrant display of injustice, it would be almost comical. Actually, in spite of it all, it *is* sometimes laughable.

Jail is almost inevitable, although there have been some judges who have shown their support in the sentencing phase, giving short or no jail terms at all. On the

average, prison sentences range from one to three years. None of us seek imprisonment, but we accept it as a consequence. Some accept it more joyfully than others.
The jail witness often becomes a focal point and a reminder. Most Americans have
notoriously short attention spans and the person in jail tends to nudge our consciences and challenge us with questions that would be easier left unanswered and
forgotten.

Is symbolic direct disarmament a violent action? That's a question that has
caused divisions even amongst the radical Catholics who agree with the practice of
civil disobedience.

The standard Webster dictionary gives the definition of violence as *"the exertion
of a physical force so as to injure or abuse."* Although this is a narrow definition, at
least part of the answer lies in the issue of intent. Individually and communally, the
intent of the plowshare witness is to symbolically convert. We don't use major
wrecking devices and we don't go with hopes of doing as much damage as possible
before being caught. We often are in a position to stop acting when we feel the
symbols have been brought to life and then to search out authorities to explain the
symbolism of our work.

Is it possible to do violence to property that has no right, morally or legally, to
exist? For property to be recognized as such means that it has a proper and life-
enhancing role for the good of society and creation. The weapons we choose to act
on are primarily first strike, nuclear-capable weapons which, if used, can destroy all
Creation as well as prohibit the normal reproduction of life for generations to come,
if not destroy it altogether. By their very existence, they endanger and intimidate
and hold the entire world hostage, creating an immoral ethic of might makes right.
Their illegality reduces them to dangerous contraband which would, under all other
circumstances, be disassembled or destroyed.

Governments appear to be unwilling or incapable of making any honest efforts
toward real disarmament. Politicians are stuck in the muck and mire of greed and
power. Assuming that decisions in a democracy are made by "we the people," then
"we the people" are trying to bring the issues of disarmament to debate through the
plowshare witness.

Contrary to government belief, there is no plowshare organization. Individuals
moved by their consciences come together to pray and discern. Out of that prayer
and reflection, an action plan may go forward. The first plowshares witness occurred
in 1980. Since then, there have been sixty worldwide.

GOOD NEWS PLOWSHARES

I have participated in two of them [Plowshares acts]. The first, which we called the
Good News Plowshares, took place on April 7, 1993, Good Friday. Kathy Boylan,
Greg Boertje-Obed and I had spent many months in preparation together. Greg
and I were married just three weeks before the action.

Our witness took place at the Newport News shipyard in Virginia. One of the largest shipyards on the East Coast, the majority of its contract work is for the military. Through public record, we were able to find out that it had contracts for aircraft carriers and fast attack nuclear submarines.

Our hope was to locate the fast attacks, which we learned would house twelve vertical launch cruise missiles that could be either nuclear or conventionally tipped. One cruise missile is capable of causing seventeen times the damage done to Hiroshima. Twelve missiles would cause 204 times more damage. We were able to verify that fast attack subs have a role in a first strike scenario and are considered to be a violation of international law.

At approximately 3 a.m., with blood, hammers, banners, and indictments in hand, we cut a hole in the chain link fence, slid down an embankment and made our way through the massive shipyard. We had no idea where we were going and were counting on the Spirit to guide us.

Time seemed distorted, like in a dream, but at some point before dawn, we literally ran into a submarine on dry dock. It was surrounded by scaffolding and the top, which is where we needed to go in order to hammer on the launching tubes for the cruise missiles, was about sixty-eighty feet up.

I'm not too fond of heights; once we reached a height of about twenty feet, I was ready to pour the blood, hit the massive hull with the hammer a few times, tie our banner to the scaffolding, and wait for a crane to get us down. Kathy and Greg kept climbing and, finally, so did I. When we reached the top, we saw a makeshift canvas tent. There, inside, were the launching tubes with their massive steel hatch covers open.

We poured our blood into the tubes, found a hunk of metal that appeared to line the inner part of the tube, removed it and hammered on the lip of the tube. We spray painted "*Christ Lives—disarm,*" "*Love,*" and "*Christ's cross.*" We hung up banners and sat together in prayer. We then introduced ourselves to some nearby workers, assured them we were acting nonviolently, and suggested they find a security officer.

During the actual witness, I felt as if I were in an altered state of mind. It was almost like watching another force use my body to carry out the act. I was in it but not in it. Once we broke that state of mind, the reality of being eighty feet up hit, and I could not imagine going down all that scaffolding. When we were finally escorted down, we learned that the other side of the sub had a sturdy and wide stairwell with hand railing set up against it. What a relief!

After many hours of interrogation by shipyard security and Navy investigators, we were brought before a magistrate and then to the city jail.

We had previously decided that we would not pay a bond to be released before trial and we would represent ourselves in court. Our testimony would be simple and spoken from the heart. It would be close to five months before we were finished with two trials; one for the misdemeanor trespass charge for which we were fined

$100, and the second for the felony destruction of property charge for which we received an eight-month sentence.

With the time already spent in jail and calculated good time, we had already completed our sentence. In essence, we were tried, convicted, sentenced and released all in one day. The witness was complete.

JUBILEE PLOWSHARES WITNESS

The second plowshare witness was a bit more complicated and as of this writing, I am still living through the consequences. This witness took place August 7, 1995, the fiftieth anniversary of the bombing of Hiroshima and Nagasaki. Our daughter Rachel was ten months old. The Jonah House community was ready and willing to support Greg and help raise her. But leaving her was a gut-wrenching decision for me.

Our group was divided into East and West Coast components, and we called ourselves the Jubilee Plowshares East and West. Our name was to symbolize the Year Jubilee, which, biblically, was the year when debts would be forgiven and the poor would be liberated. Our hope was to be liberated from the threat and debt of nuclear weapons.

The West Coast group was able to enter a Lockheed-Martin plant and make their way into a room where casings for the D5 Trident nuclear missiles were made. They hammered on the casings and poured blood on classified documents, were arrested, and remained in jail while awaiting trial. They were charged by the federal government with destruction of property, then convicted and sentenced to ten months in prison plus two years of supervised release (probation). They refused to cooperate with the conditions of supervised release, and both participated in another, the Prince of Peace, plowshares at a shipyard in Maine [and received] prison sentences for that action.

Our East Coast group made its way, once again, into the Newport News shipyard, walking by numerous security guards and checkpoints, as if we were invisible. This time we walked down a dock where three fast attack submarines were located. We got on board one that had the launching tubes installed and the hatches open. Again we hammered, poured blood, hung up banners and prayed. After a while, we were able to get the attention of a worker and to suggest that he inform security.

We were originally charged by the state but those charges were eventually dropped in lieu of federal government prosecution. The shipyard CEOs were highly embarrassed and livid that an ordinary group of people could get into a high security area undetected once again. They wanted to be certain that prosecution would be hard and heavy.

Two members of our group experienced personal crises while in jail. We all bonded out to regroup and support each other. Amy eventually plea-bargained with the state, while Rick, Erin, and I faced federal charges which included three counts of sabotage, destruction of property and conspiracy. We were facing a maximum of forty-five years in prison and $1.5 million in fines!

After much discussion, we decided to put on a serious legal defense and six lawyers (more of them than us) volunteered their services. They researched cases and worked up a string of motions in order to ensure that we would not be gagged by an *in limine* motion. We had expert witnesses prepared to testify about international law vis-à-vis the first strike capability of the fast attack submarine. We had Catholic bishops willing to testify that we were motivated by our faith and understanding of the Scriptures. We had people willing to fast and pray outside the courthouse for the duration of the trial and we had a sympathy reporter willing to do daily feature articles.

Following months of preparation, we went to our preliminary hearing where the motions to set the format of the trial would be heard. Twenty-one motions were presented by our lawyers and twenty-one motions were denied by Judge Rebecca Smith. There would be no expert witness testimony and we would not be allowed to talk about our religious, political or moral views, or mention the words international law. Grounds for a conviction of sabotage were reduced down to: did we intend to hit the metal with the hammer? If so, we had therefore intended to prevent the U.S. from defending itself in the event of war. It was an absurd judgment and even the prosecutor was shocked. He immediately offered to drop all charges if we pled guilty to one count of conspiracy to damage government property.

Rick, Erin and I spent four days together in prayer and discernment. We were physically, emotionally and spiritually tired. Our choices were to go ahead with a kangaroo court trial, face inevitable convictions on all five counts, and hope that we could win an appeal, or accept the plea bargain. We chose the latter. Erin, Rick and I were sentenced to eight, nine and eighteen months in prison, respectively. Four of Erin's eight months would be spent on home confinement. Additionally, we were given fines and restitution and three years of supervised release (some of the conditions of supervised release are detailed in the essay on community).

Accepting the plea bargain was an incredibly hard decision to make and one for which I still have not forgiven myself. I began the process of preparing for the witness while I was pregnant with Rachel. The witness was to be my gift to her and to all the children of the world. When we did the action, it was like giving birth all over again. It was an act that made the hope and promise of a better tomorrow alive.

The witness took on a life of its own and I believed it was my responsibility to nurture it, defend it, and keep it alive while the powers that be wanted to destroy it. When I accepted that plea bargain, I felt as if I were turning my back on it. I let it down. I no longer had the strength to defend it. With much remorse, I let it go with the hope that its life would be picked up and nourished by God and by others stronger than me. Maybe that's how the family of Moses felt when they floated him down the Nile in a basket.

The criticism of my decision to plea bargain is self-imposed. My community, and friends from the larger worldwide disarmament community, supported it. Nobody, to my knowledge, condemned us. The significance of the witness was not changed or diminished by accepting the plea. However, it still remains a decision that I will have to come to terms with. I continue to learn from it, and, in the process, grow deeper in faith.

ON COMMUNITY

People live in a growing state of fear of neighbor, both domestic and abroad. Fear and isolation seem to work in a sick symbiosis. The more one fears, the more one isolates, and the more one isolates, the more one fears. This twisted psychological development makes it very easy for the government to demonize and dehumanize people. Every young black male becomes suspect, foreigners become likely terrorists, poor people become lazy welfare trash, and on and on.

Thus, the significance and benefits of living communally grow more and more profound. It's an experience in which one constantly learns about human interaction and group dynamics.

We discern and pray together as a community and in the context of our faith. Our willingness to trust one another is essential to our existence.

I became especially aware of that during my last prison term. Rachel was essentially raised by Greg and other community members while I completed the Jubilee witness prison term. They were willing, and I had to let them, make the day-to-day decisions about her life. I had to trust that they would love her and discipline her when necessary. I had to trust in the values they would instill in her. She was twenty-three months old when I left for prison and had just turned three when I was released. I was away during one of the most formative years of her life.

Rachel thrived during my absence. She was given much love, and she in turn enriched the lives of those around her. Through this experience, she learned that her family goes beyond the bloodline. It will, we hope, help her to realize that she is part of a much larger family, the human family, and that all people are her brothers and sisters. Understanding this, being able to connect and identify with the human family, makes it harder to kill or allow a government to kill in our names.

Jonah House is part of an extended community which includes many of the Catholic Worker (CW) communities, though Jonah House itself is not a CW home. These communities differ from Jonah House in that a large part of the CW vision includes hospitality or direct service to the poor, and the majority of worker houses are funded by donation. The CW communities are much more experienced in breaking down the barriers of class and race through their efforts to live communally and equally with the poor.

Together, our communities make up, in the eastern states, a loose-knit larger group known as the Atlantic Life Community (ALC). The ALC meets twice each year to share and reflect together, strengthen our bonds, and deepen our commitments to peace and justice. We also try to meet at least once during the year to participate in a public witness denouncing violence.

Similarly, CWs and peace communities in the Southeast, Midwest, and West Coast gather periodically in work and support; there are also attempts to form community internationally.

We seem to be coming into a time for community awareness of our interdependence on each other. While each may always be autonomous in deciding how to live the vision of peace and justice, we cannot look at ourselves as separate entities. There is great strength in our unity; at a time when the government seems to be more oppressive and intolerant of dissent, that strength is imperative.

As I write this, I am forbidden by the federal courts to return to my home with the Jonah House community.[4] This is a condition of supervised release (probation) which will last for three years as a result of my participation in the Jubilee Plowshare witness. This is also a clear example of the government's attempt to break up community, knowing that resistance is virtually impossible without it.

Upon release from federal prison, I was forced to live in Norfolk, VA to meet probation requirements. In order for our family to be together, Greg and Rachel had to relocate from Jonah House to Norfolk. It was a painful separation for everyone, especially Rachel. In addition to keeping her from those she loved, she had to be taken out of her Headstart program that she enjoyed very much. While the officials in the government may think they are hurting me, it was my daughter who took the brunt of this spiteful tactic. Senator Barbara Mikulski [D-Maryland], Catholic bishops and hundreds of friends wrote the probation department requesting that I be able to return home, to no avail.

In addition to being banned from Jonah House, I was further forbidden from the Norfolk Catholic Worker. This community was very supportive of us after our plowshares action and remained so during our terms in prison.

By imposing such restrictions on plowshare activists, the government treats our work both as peacemakers and in service to the poor as criminal activity. For me to enter the Norfolk CW house to make sandwiches for the street breakfast, or to go to Mass, or to join in a bible study, are all considered criminal acts. In other words, to live out my faith is a crime. Never before has the government come down in this particular way on a peace activist, and there is great potential for this to become the new trend. (Indeed, the next plowshares prisoner to be released, Steve Baggarly, was forbidden to return to the CW home he and his wife founded in Norfolk, VA.)

Greg, Rachel and I were able to stay with a friend of the Norfolk CW and were able to find creative ways with the CW community to support each other. Eventually, we were all able to move to the Loaves & Fishes CW in Duluth, MN, where we plan to reside until my probation is terminated.

Children are remarkably resilient and Rachel has adapted well to all the changes. Her extended family and circle of friends has grown tremendously. Nevertheless, our family has been forced into exile. Trying to keep things in perspective, we are experiencing a small taste of what refugees from war-torn countries must feel. On a positive note however, the government has provided us with the opportunity to strengthen community ties between the East Coast and the Midwest.

Out of this experience I again raise the idea that we look at our communities as interdependent, recognizing autonomy yet realizing we exist for a bigger reason.

Can we become flexible enough to move within this wider understanding of community so that we can offer each other very real and practical support? Can we pool our resources and creativity so that we can continue to act faithfully yet deal with our limitations as human beings? Can we open ourselves up to one another, challenge and really walk with each other so that Isaiah's vision and Christ's example stay alive?

I believe that not only can we do this, but we have already begun to do it. The outpouring of support for Greg, Rachel and me has been incredible. I feel certain that the support we received was much more than personal and that there is a recognition that the act of resistance we did as family is necessary and needs to continue.

NOTES

Excerpted from Michele Naar-Obed, *Maternal Convictions: A Mother Beats a Missile into a Plowshare* (Maple, Wisc.: Laurentian Shield Resources for Nonviolence, 1998).

1. *Editor's note:* See Arthur J. Laffin and Anne Montgomery, eds., *Swords into Plowshares: Nonviolent Direct Action for Disarmament* (San Francisco: Harper & Row, 1987).

2. *Editor's note:* Isaiah 2:4: "They shall beat their swords into plowshares and their spears into pruning hooks. Nation shall not war against nation nor shall they study war any more."

3. *Editor's note:* Motions "*in limine*" seek to anticipate and control the trial's conduct.

4. *Editor's note:* Upon release from prison, Michele Naar-Obed, due to probation requirements, was prohibited from returning to Jonah House. She lived in exile of her home for sixteen months. She, her husband, and daughter spent six months with a friend from the Norfolk Catholic Workers, who had been supporters of the plowshare action and also housed other activists. For the next ten months, Naar-Obed's family lived with the Loaves and Fishes Catholic Worker community in Duluth, Minnesota. In defiance of probation, she and her family decided to return to Jonah House. Two months later, U.S. marshals arrested Michele and held her without bond pending a violation hearing. During her hearing one month later, U.S. Attorney General Ramsey Clark and Catholic Bishop Walter Sullivan testified as character witnesses. Sentenced to another year in federal prison without further probation requirements, she was released in June 2000 and remained with her family in Jonah House until June 2002. The family currently resides with Duluth's Loaves and Fishes Catholic Worker community.

Chapter Nineteen

Linda Evans, Susan Rosenberg, and Laura Whitehorn

Born in Fort Dodge, Iowa, in 1947, Linda Evans began her political activism in 1965, when she became involved with antiracist organizing as a student at Michigan State University. She worked with Students for a Democratic Society (SDS), organizing against the war in Vietnam and in support of Black liberation. In 1969 she traveled to Vietnam as part of a delegation from the antiwar movement. Evans was first arrested in 1970 on conspiracy charges of crossing state lines to incite a riot, and transportation of weapons. These charges were linked to Evans's work as an SDS regional organizer; charges were eventually dropped on the grounds of government misconduct: the prosecution's evidence was collected through illegal wiretaps.[1] By this time the Federal Bureau of Investigation (FBI)'s COINTELPRO had begun a systematic attack on SDS, including the use of extensive wiretaps and infiltrations.[2] In the early 1970s, Evans moved to Texas, where she was active in the women's liberation movement and the lesbian community, and involved in organizing support for grassroots African American and Chicano/Mexicano movements.[3] She was a member of a political guerrilla street theater group, an all-women's political band, and a political women's printing and graphics collective in Texas. She organized against the Ku Klux Klan, forced sterilization, and police brutality and fought racism, white supremacy, and Zionism as a member of the John Brown Anti-Klan Committee. She was also active in building solidarity for South African, Palestinian, and Central American liberation movements and organizing support for U.S. political prisoners. In 1985, fifteen years after her first arrest, Evans was arrested on charges of making false statements to acquire weapons. By this time she had developed an openly revolutionary stance in opposition to U.S. imperialism in Latin America, southern Africa, and other regions, and was working to develop clandestine armed struggle as a component of revolutionary strategy.[4] Although Evans's legal counsel informed her that she would likely receive a five-year sentence because of her political affiliations, the judge sentenced her to the maximum for each charge, and ordered that time be served consecutively: Linda Evans received a forty-year sentence.[5] She was also charged in the "Resistance Conspiracy" case while in prison and sentenced to federal prison in California. During her imprisonment, Evans worked as a "jailhouse lawyer," organized for prisoners' rights,[6] and worked as an HIV/AIDS peer counselor and educator. With Eve Goldberg, she coauthored the essay "The Prison Industrial Complex and the Global Economy."[7] Linda Evans was released on executive clemency by President Clinton in 2001, and has since continued to speak and organize for prisoners' rights and in opposition to the U.S. prison industrial complex and U.S. military and economic imperialism.

Susan Rosenberg was born in New York in 1955. A doctor of acupuncture, she worked with the Black Acupuncture Advisory of North America.[8] Rosenberg became involved with antiracist activism as a high school student in the early 1970s, organizing support for the Black Liberation and Puerto Rican independence struggles. She was involved with the student, antiwar, and women's movements. After going underground in the early 1980s, Rosenberg was arrested in New Jersey in 1984 on weapons possession charges. She was convicted and sentenced to fifty-eight years, sixteen times the national average for such an offense. The judge cited her political ideology as the reason for his decision.[9] Rosenberg had previously been charged in the 1981 "Brink's Robbery" case in New York, but these charges against her were dismissed for lack of evidence.[10] She had also been accused of being a participant in the escape of Assata Shakur from prison. As a result of her support for the Black Liberation Army, the FBI targeted Rosenberg.[11] In 1988, she was charged in the "Resistance Conspiracy" case, but these charges were also eventually dropped. In spite of over ten years in various forms of isolation and maximum-security conditions she continued to actively organize, teach, write, and overcome. She spent the last five years inside working as a writer and an HIV/AIDS peer educator and teacher. Her writing has appeared in journals and anthologies, including *Criminal Injustice* and *Doing Time: Twenty-Five Years of Prison Writing*.[12] She obtained her master's degree in writing in 2000. Along with Linda Evans, Susan Rosenberg was granted clemency by President Clinton in 2001. Since her release, Rosenberg has been working as a human rights and prisoner rights activist, writing a memoir, and teaching literature at the John Jay School of Criminal Justice in New York City.

Laura Whitehorn was born in 1945 in Brooklyn, New York. She began organizing in the 1960s, when as a college student she participated in the civil rights and antiwar movements. Since that time, she has been active in anti-imperialist and antiracist groups, and in the movements for women's and gay liberation. She graduated from Radcliffe College in 1966, and received her master's degree from Brandeis University, before deciding to leave graduate school because academia at that time seemed to her a poor place for the kind of activism she felt was needed. Before her imprisonment in 1985 she worked with Dr. Mutulu Shakur's National Task Force for COINTELPRO Litigation and Research to expose the FBI's COINTELPRO and organized in support of political prisoners and Puerto Rican prisoners of war and in support of prisoners' rights. She also worked actively in support of the Black Panther

Party and the Black Power movement. In the Boston area she collaborated with others to establish a women's school and helped lead a takeover of a Harvard building to protest Harvard's involvement in the war in Vietnam, an action that indirectly led to the establishment of a women's center in Cambridge that is still in existence. Several years later, during the infamous Boston busing controversy of 1974, she organized white leftists to defend the homes of black families who were the targets of white supremacist attack. In the late 1970s she moved to New York City and joined the John Brown Anti-Klan Committee to fight white supremacy and Zionism and the Madame Binh Graphics Collective, an anti-imperialist women's art group. In the early 1980s she went underground to engage in more militant forms of solidarity and resistance, hoping to build a clandestine revolutionary movement. In 1985, she was arrested by the FBI in Baltimore, and was eventually charged in the "Resistance Conspiracy" case. At the time of the "Resistance Conspiracy" indictment, Whitehorn had served three years in prison. She was placed under "preventive detention" and was denied bail on the grounds that she was an escape risk, partly based on a statement she made in court that she chose to live by "revolutionary and human principles."[13] Whitehorn was sentenced to twenty-three years for the "Resistance Conspiracy" case.

While imprisoned, Whitehorn worked on HIV/AIDS peer education. Throughout her years in prison she contributed her artwork to publications and exhibitions, and articles to journals and anthologies, including *Cages of Steel* and *States of Confinement* as well as a regular column in *Prison Legal News*. In August 1999, Whitehorn was released from prison upon completion of her sentence ("maxing out"—i.e., completing the sentence less federally mandated "good time"). She currently lives in New York City with her lover, Susie Day, and organizes in support of political prisoners. She has worked since her release as an associate editor at *POZ*, a national magazine for those affected by HIV, focusing on HIV and hepatitis C in the prisons.

All three women are known for their roles in the "Resistance Conspiracy" case. In 1988, Linda Evans, Susan Rosenberg, and Laura Whitehorn, along with Marilyn Buck, Tim Blunk, Alan Berkman, and Elizabeth Duke (who never went to trial and is still at large), were charged with conspiracy to carry out eight political bombings in Washington, D.C., and New York from 1983 to 1985. Targets of the bombings included the U.S. Capitol, to protest the invasion of Grenada, and the South African consulate, to oppose U.S. support for the apartheid regime. Other targets concerned Zionism and police brutality. No one was harmed in any of the bombings.

Government use of the criminal justice system as a domestic counterinsurgency program enabled the state to criminalize political dissidents as "terrorists."[14] Although some defendants had previously been convicted of the specific acts cited in the conspiracy charges, and the FBI admitted confusion about which individuals were actually involved in the bombings,[15] at trial, Evans, Whitehorn, and Buck pled guilty to the charges in exchange for charges being dropped against their codefendants, one of whom, Alan Berkman, was suffering from cancer and in need of competent medical treatment.[16] The plea agreement cut years off Berkman's projected sentence, allowing him to bypass a lengthy trial and arrive at a hospital in time to receive therapy for the effects of his cancer treatments.

REFERENCES

Baraldini, Silvia, Marilyn Buck, Susan Rosenberg, and Laura Whitehorn. "Women's Control Unit." In *Criminal Injustice: Confronting the Prison Crisis*, edited by Elihu Rosenblatt. Boston: South End Press, 1996.

Can't Jail the Spirit: Political Prisoners in the U.S. 4th ed. Chicago: Committee to End the Marion Lockdown, 1998.

Chevigny, Bell Gale, ed. *Doing Time: Twenty-Five Years of Prison Writing.* New York: Arcade Publishing; distributed by Time Warner Trade Publishing, 1999.

Churchill, Ward, and Jim Vander Wall, eds. *Cages of Steel: The Politics of Imprisonment in the United States.* Washington, D.C.: Maisonneuve Press, 1992.

———. *The COINTELPRO Papers: Documents from the FBI's Secret Wars against Dissent in the United States.* Cambridge, Mass.: South End Press, 1990.

De Vries, Sonja, and Rhonda Collins. *Out: The Making of a Revolutionary.* New York: Third World Newsreel, 2000. Videocassette.

Goldberg, Eve, and Linda Evans. "The Prison Industrial Complex and the Global Economy." San Francisco, Calif.: Agit Press, 1998. Prison Activist Resource Center. prisonactivist.org/crisis/evans-goldberg.html.

James, Joy, ed. *States of Confinement: Policing, Detention and Prisons.* Rev. ed. New York: St. Martin's, 2002.

O'Melveny, Mary. "Lexington Prison High Security Unit: U.S. Political Prison." In *Criminal Injustice: Confronting the Prison Crisis*, edited by Elihu Rosenblatt. Boston: South End Press, 1996.

Resistance Conspiracy. San Francisco: Bay Area Committee to Support the Resistance Conspiracy Defendants [distributor]. Oakland: Peralta Colleges Television Production Company, videocassette, 1990.

Whitehorn, Laura. "Resistance at Lexington." In *Criminal Injustice: Confronting the Prison Crisis*, edited by Elihu Rosenblatt. Boston: South End Press, 1996.

NOTES

Research and draft for this biography were provided by Elizabeth Walsh.

1. *Can't Jail the Spirit: Political Prisoners in the U.S.*, 4th ed. (Chicago: Committee to End the Marion Lockdown, 1998), 173. The charges were connected to Evans's organizing for "The Days of Rage," an antiwar action in Chicago in 1969 sponsored by the Weathermen section of SDS.

2. Ward Churchill and Jim Vander Wall, *The COINTELPRO Papers: Documents from the FBI's Secret Wars against Dissent in the United States* (Cambridge, Mass.: South End Press, 1990), 165–66.

3. "Linda Evans: Anti-Imperialist Political Prisoner," *Can't Jail the Spirit*, 173.

4. *Can't Jail the Spirit*, 173.

5. *Resistance Conspiracy* (San Francisco: Bay Area Committee to Support the Resistance Conspiracy Defendants [distributor]; Oakland: Peralta Colleges Television Production Company, videocassette, 1990).

6. *Can't Jail the Spirit*, 174.

7. Eve Goldberg and Linda Evans, "The Prison Industrial Complex and the Global Economy," prisonactivist.org/crisis/evans-goldberg.html.

8. Elihu Rosenblatt, ed., *Criminal Injustice: Confronting the Prison Crisis* (Boston: South End Press, 1996), 355.

9. Ann Nicholson, "Commutations Gained through Work of Law Faculty, Students," *Washington University Record*, Washington University in St. Louis, 6 April 2001.

10. "Communication Gained."

11. *Criminal Injustice*, 355.

12. See: Rosenblatt, *Criminal Injustice*, and Bell Gale Chevigny, ed., *Doing Time: Twenty-Five Years of Prison Writing* (New York: Arcade Publishing; distributed by Time Warner Trade Publishing, 1999).

13. Laura Whitehorn, "Preventive Detention: A Prevention of Human Rights?" in Ward Churchill et al., eds., *Cages of Steel*, (Washington, D.C.: Maisonneuve Press, 1992), 365–77.

14. *Resistance Conspiracy*.

15. *Cages of Steel*, 313.

16. "3 Plead Guilty to '83 Bombing," *New York Times*, 9 September 1990.

Dykes and Fags Want to Know

Interview with Lesbian Political Prisoners—
Linda Evans, Susan Rosenberg, and Laura Whitehorn
by the Members of QUISP

Early 1991

QUISP: I'm an activist; why haven't I heard of you before?

LAURA: I think it's because there's been a long time during which the "left" and progressive movements haven't really tried to know who's in prison—including but not limited to political prisoners and POWs. For instance, how many AIDS activists know about the many PWA's [Person/People with AIDS] in prison, and the horrible conditions they live in? Aside from Mike Riegle at *GCN* (*Gay Community News*), how many writers and media folks in our movements try to reach into the prisons to support lesbian and gay prisoners, whose lives are often made pretty rough by the pigs? [Riegel, a gay activist and writer who cofounded Boston's Prison Books program, died of AIDS in 1991.]

In general, this country tries to shut prisoners away and make people outside forget about us. In the case of political prisoners, multiply that times X for the simple fact that our existence is a danger to the smooth, quiet running of the system: our existence shows that this great demokkkracy is a lie. The government doesn't want you to know who we are—that's why they try so hard to label us "terrorists" and "criminals."

LINDA: Political prisoners have been purposely "disappeared" by the U.S. government, whose official position is that "there are no political prisoners inside the U.S." This is the way that the government denies both that the motivations for our actions were political and that the movements we come from are legitimate, popular movements for social change. The prison system isolates all prisoners from their communities, but especially harsh isolation is instituted against political prisoners: restricted visiting lists, frequent transfers to prisons far away from our home communities, mail censorship, "maximum security conditions," long periods of time in solitary confinement.

But our own political movement, too, has ignored the existence of political prisoners. I think this has largely been a product of racism—most U.S. political prisoners/POWs are Black and Puerto Rican comrades who have been locked up for over a decade. Unfortunately there has never been widespread support among progressive white people for the Black Liberation struggle, for Puerto Rican independence, or for Native American sovereignty struggles—and these are the movements that the Black/Puerto Rican/Native American political prisoners/POWs come from.

Also, many political activists have actually withheld support for political prisoners/POWs because of disagreements with tactics that were employed, or with actions of which the political prisoners have been accused or convicted. These disagreements are tactical in nature, and shouldn't be allowed to obscure the fact that we all have been fighting for justice and social change. This withdrawal of support leads to false divisions amongst us, and actually helps the state in its strategy to isolate political prisoners/POWs from our communities and political movements.

SUSAN: The activists/radicals of the late 1980s and 1990s have to reclaim the history of resistance that emerged and continued through the 1970s and 1980s. As long as the government and mass media get to define who and what is important then the real lessons contained in our and others' experiences will get lost. People haven't heard of us (except as a vague memory of a headline—if that) because there is a very serious government counter-insurgency strategy to bury the revolutionaries who have been captured in prison. I have been in prison six years and over half of that time was spent in solitary confinement or small-group isolation thousands of miles away from my community and family. My experience is similar to the 100–150 other political prisoners in the U.S. If the individuals from different movements (i.e., the Black, Puerto Rican, Native American and white movements who have seen the need for organized resistance to oppression) are destroyed it is a way to delegitimize the demands of the movements.

QUISP: Did you do it? Did the government misrepresent what you did? If so, how?

LAURA: Yes, I did it! I did (do) resist racism, sexism, imperialism with every fiber of my queer being, and I believe we need to fight for justice. The government's "version" of what I/we did is a complete lie, though, in that they call resistance a crime. It's sort of like the way [Senator] Jesse Helms [R-NC] calls us "sick"—he's as sick as you can get. On the morality meter he doesn't even make the needle move. Same way the U.S. government, a genocidal system, calls acts of revolutionary struggle "terrorist violence," and their system of law, "justice."

LINDA: Yes, I'm proud that I've been part of the struggle to build an armed clandestine resistance movement that can fight to support national liberation struggles, and that will fight for revolution in the U.S. Of course the government misrepresented what we did first of all by calling us "terrorists" to make people think we were a danger to the community, as if our purpose was to terrorize or kill people. Quite the contrary: all the armed actions of the last twenty years have been planned to minimize any risk of human life. This, of course, is in stark contrast to the actions of the terrorist government, which is responsible world-wide for supporting death squads and mercenary armies like the contras and [Jonas] Savimbi's UNITA[1] in

Angola, which supports the Israeli war of genocide against the Palestinians and the brutal system of apartheid, and which supports daily police brutality in Black and Third World communities here, even such acts as the aerial bombing of MOVE in Philadelphia in 1985, which killed eleven people and created a firestorm that left over 250 people homeless.

SUSAN: I have been a revolutionary for much of my life. A revolutionary in the sense that I believe in the need for profound social change that goes to the roots of the problem. Which I believe is systemic. Consequently I have along with others tried many methods of struggle to enact a strategy to win liberation and attack the state (government) as representative of the system. First as a peace activist in the late 1960s, then as a political activist in the 1970s, and then in joining the armed clandestine resistance movement that was developing in the 1980s. I am guilty of revolutionary anti-imperialist resistance. Of course the government has misrepresented me and all of us. The main form that has taken is to call us terrorists, which is something that couldn't be further from the truth. Just like all opposition to the cold war of the 1950s was labeled communist, the 1980s equivalent is terrorist. Now there are all kinds of terrorists according to the U.S.—all of it bullshit. I don't mean to beg the question in the specific. I believe that no revolutionary captured comrade says what they have or haven't done within their revolutionary work.

QUISP: Audre Lorde says the master's tools (violence) will never dismantle the master's house (the state).[2] How do you react to this?

LAURA: I don't think "violence" is just one thing, so I don't think it's necessarily "the master's tool." If revolutionaries were as vicious and careless of humanity and innocent human lives as the U.S. government is, then I think we'd be doing wrong. But when oppressed people fight for freedom, using "violent" means among others, I think we should support them. Would you have condemned African slaves in the U.S. for killing their slave masters, or for using violence in a struggle for freedom? To me, the issue is how do we fight effectively—and humanely—for liberation. As we build the struggle, we have to be very self-critical, very self-conscious about how we struggle as well as what we struggle for. But I think we also need to fight to win—and I think that means engaging in a fight for power. For the past five and more years, I've witnessed close up the violence—slow, brutal, heartless genocide against African American women. To refuse to fight to change that (and I don't believe we can fight for power completely "nonviolently") would, I think, be to accept the violence of the state in the name of rejecting the violence of revolutionary struggle.

LINDA: I disagree with posing the question in the way she does (or how the question does). I don't think the issue is violence, but rather politics and power. Around the world, imperialism maintains itself—keeps itself in power—by military power and the threat of violence wherever people struggle for change. Liberation movements have the right to use every means available to defeat the system that is oppressing and killing people. This means fighting back in self-defense, and it means an offensive struggle for people's power and self-determination. But reducing it to a tactical question of "violent means" doesn't recognize all the aspects of building a revolutionary movement that are crucial to actually mobilizing people, developing popular organizations, empowering oppressed groups within the people's movement like women and indigenous people, developing a revolutionary program that can really meet people's needs and that people will fight to make real. A slogan that embodies this for me comes from the Chinese Revolution: "Without mass struggle, there can be no revolution. Without armed struggle, there can be no victory."

SUSAN: I always took the quote from Audre Lorde to mean the opposite of what you say. Funny, no? I always interpreted her saying that to mean the master's tools being electoral/slow change. Well—there you go!

QUISP: Why is it important to support political as opposed to non-political prisoners? Shouldn't we be concerned about all prisoners?

LAURA: I think we should be concerned about all prisoners, and I don't think it's ever been we political prisoners who have promoted any irresolvable contradiction between us and the rest of the prisoners in the U.S. But within that, I think there is a particular need for progressive movements to defend political prisoners, because it's a part of fighting for the movements we come from. If you are fighting racism and homophobia, and there are people serving long sentences in prison for fighting those things, I think you advance the goals by supporting the prisoners. I also think that support for political prisoners helps expose how repressive and unjust the whole system is. That can also be an avenue to supporting all prisoners.

Support for political prisoners is a concrete act of resistance to the control the government keeps over all our minds: it fights the isolation and silencing of political prisoners and POWs. It asserts the legitimacy of resistance. And in my experience it is a major way that people outside become aware of the purpose and nature of the prison system as a whole.

LINDA: Yes—it's important for our movement to be concerned about all prisoners, and I think it's especially important for the lesbian and gay movement to concern ourselves with combating attacks on lesbian/gay prisoners, and supporting all prisoners with AIDS. Concerning ourselves with all prisoners, and with the repressive/warehousing role of prisons in our society is another way of fighting racism, since the majority of prisoners are from Third World communities. Prisoners get locked away—out of sight, out of mind—and the few prisoners' rights that were won in prison struggles are being undermined and cut back. Human rights are nearly nonexistent in prison, and without community support and awareness, the government can continue to escalate its repressive policies, and conditions will just steadily worsen. This is especially true for prisoners with AIDS, since the stigma attached to AIDS in society generally is heightened in prison. Prisoners with AIDS die at an even faster rate than PWAs on the outside because treatment is so sporadic, limited, and conditions are so bad. So I would never say for people to support political prisoners as opposed to nonpolitical prisoners. Our interests inside prison are definitely not in opposition to each other. All the political prisoners/POWs actively fight for prisoners' rights, and for changes in conditions that will benefit all prisoners. But it's important to build support specifically for political prisoners because we represent our movements, and it's a way for us to protect and defend the political movements we come from against government repression. For the movement on the outside to embrace and support political prisoners/POWs makes it possible for us to continue to participate in and contribute to the movement we come from and it makes it impossible for the government to isolate and repress us in their efforts to destroy our political identities.

SUSAN: All prisoners are in desperate need of support, and as the population gets greater (in prison) and the repression gets heavier the prisons will become a major confrontation within the society. If the prisons are to become a social front of struggle then there must be a consciousness developed to fight the dehumanization and criminalization that prison intends. Political prisoners are important to support because we are in prison for explicitly social/political/progressive goals. Our lack of freedom does affect how free you are. If we can be violated, so can you. There is no contradiction between political and social prisoners.

QUISP: How does being a lesbian fit in with your work?

LAURA: The same way it fits into my life—it is a basic, crucial part of my character, my outlook on things, my personality. Because I'm a lesbian, the fight against homophobia and sexism takes on particular importance. But really I think my lesbianism helps me care about the oppression of others by the imperialist system. So I think my lesbianism makes me a better anti-imperialist—it makes me fight all the harder. Being a lesbian in prison is often very hard, but being "out" gives me a lot of strength. I have to say that I am very proud when I hear or read about the struggles queers are waging out there.

LINDA: Being a lesbian has always been an important part of the reasons why I'm a revolutionary—even before I was self-conscious about how important this is to me! I don't separate "being a lesbian" from any other part of my life, or from my politics. Because I experience real oppression as a lesbian and as a woman, I am personally committed from the very core of my being to winning liberation for women, lesbians, and all oppressed people. This makes me more willing to take risks and to fight, because I have a vision of a society I want to live in, and to win for future generations, where these forms of oppression don't exist. I think being a lesbian has also helped me recognize the importance of mutual solidarity and support between the struggles of oppressed people, despite the sexism, heterosexism and racism that often interfere in the process of building these alliances. I really believe that we have a common enemy—the imperialist system—and that we have to support each other in all the forms our struggles against that enemy may take. These alliances need to be built in a way that respects the integrity of our various movements.

SUSAN: Well! Being a lesbian is part of the very fabric of my being—so the question is not really how it fits into my work, rather how conscious do I make my lesbianism in living in prison or in the life of resistance I lead. It alternates depending on what the conditions are. Recently I have "come out" because at this point I have chosen to be more consciously lesbian-identified. I have done this because I believe that as gay people we need more revolutionary visions and strategies if our movement is to become significant in linking the overturning of sexual oppression with other forms of oppression. The other reason I have felt compelled to be out is that the tightest, most important women in the community we live in are the butches. It is the butches who suffer most for their choices/existence in prison. In recognition of Pete, Cowboy, JuJu, Slimmie, and all the other sisters it seems only right. Finally—Laura and Linda have been out since the RCC6 [Resistance Conspiracy Case 6] began and it has been a very important political and personal experience for them and for us all.[3] They have through their struggles created an environment of love and solidarity that enabled me to subsequently "come out" as well.

QUISP: How have you struggled with sexism and heterosexism in the groups with which you have worked?

LAURA: Mostly by confronting people when I think they are being sexist or heterosexist, and by fighting for women's liberation and lesbian and gay liberation to be included not just as words but as real goals. The saddest times for me have been those times when I was in groups where we didn't do this. I think it's very important for people to be able to struggle for a variety of goals without setting up a hierarchy or exclusive list. I will continue to join groups whose main program is, for example, anti-racism or support for Palestine or Puerto Rico, because those things are just as necessary for my liberation as women's and lesbian liberation are. And I won't demand that my liberation be made a part of every agenda. But I won't ever deny my identity, my right to be respected, and the urgency and legitimacy of lesbian, gay and women's liberation, either.

SUSAN: I have become much more of a feminist over the last number of years— and by that I mean ideologically and politically I believe we have to examine the position of women, the structures of the society and how male dominance defines women's position in all things. I don't think in the past I fought against the subjugation of women and gay people enough. I substituted my own independence as a woman with actively struggling against political and social forms of oppression. For example: in Nicaragua now, the women militants of the FSLN [Sandinista National Liberation Front] are reevaluating their practice of struggling against sexism, and some of them are self-critical that they subordinated the struggle of women to the needs of the so-called greater societal good. What it means now is that abortion and the struggle for reproductive rights under the new non-revolutionary society are being set back generations, and the level of consciousness among women is not (at this point) strong enough to effectively challenge this development. I believe that to subordinate either women or gay people and our demands is a big mistake.

QUISP: What is the connection between the primarily white middle class gay rights movement and the struggles of other oppressed people? How do we envision a gay movement that encompasses other struggles?

LAURA: I believe that any struggle of "primarily white middle class" people has the danger of being irrelevant to real social change unless it allies itself with the struggles of oppressed people. This country has a great track record for buying off sectors that have privilege. Once that happens, not only do things stay the same, they get worse. But even more than that, I feel that we cannot be full human beings unless we fight for all the oppressed. Otherwise, our struggle is just as individualist and racist as the dominant society. In that case, we'll never win anything worth fighting for. I think the queer movement needs to talk to other movements and communities, in order to work out common strategies and figure out how to support one another. I think we need to talk to groups in the national liberation struggles in order to figure out how to set our agenda and strategy—like what demands can we raise in the fights about AIDS that can help other communities fighting AIDS? It's a struggle, not necessarily an easy process, but it's crucial. It's also true that our movement has already adopted lessons from other movements—often without even realizing or recognizing it. We've especially incorporated strategic concepts developed (at a high cost!) by the Black Liberation struggle from the Civil Rights movement to the Black Power and human rights struggle. It's no accident that Stonewall's leadership was Third World gay men and lesbians.[4] So I think it's important to recognize that whenever we pose the question of alliances and coalitions, we don't need to "encompass" other people, we need to ally with them, learn from, and struggle side by side with them. We need to support them. And we need to fight for them as well as for ourselves, because the second we accept divisions or ignore the urgency of fighting racism, we lose.

LINDA: I don't think that struggles against sexism or homophobia or racism can be delayed, because these are forms of discrimination/oppression that actively disempower individuals and groups of people who can be mobilized to actively partici-pate in the struggle. Racism, sexism, and heterosexism cannot be tolerated in our movement or in our alliances because we don't want to duplicate the oppression that we're fighting against. Of course the process of building these alliances is diffi-cult and long-term, because building trust and respect requires building relation-ships that are really different from those that exist in society in general. So I don't think the primarily white middle-class gay rights movement can, or should, "encompass" other struggles. White middle class gay men and women cannot set the agenda for other movements or for other communities. Rather, I think that this movement should actively support struggles against other forms of oppression as a way of making our own movement stronger, more revolutionary, less self-centered, and more supportive of the goal of liberation and self-determination for all oppressed people.

SUSAN: This is a big question and has many aspects to it. I can only offer a small answer, as I believe that prisoners who have no social practice in a movement because of being locked up have a warped or limited understanding of the real dynamics in the free world movements. The gay movement as it is currently consti-tuted has reemerged since I have been in prison so I have not been a part of its development. I don't think the gay movement can be relevant to other oppressed peoples and their struggles without an anti-imperialist analysis of the roots of gay oppression and then correspondingly a practice that implements that. In other words a movement that is led by white middle class men—even those oppressed because of their sexual identification/orientation—without ceding power (within the movement) to Third World women and men, and dealing with their agendas will never be anything but reform-oriented. To only struggle for gay rights without struggling for the rights (human and democratic) of all those in need, and specifi-cally those who are nationally oppressed sets up competing struggle rather than a cohesive radical opposition to the government.

QUISP: What was going on in your life that led you to participate in or support armed struggle?

LAURA: I began supporting armed struggle in the late 1960s, when I realized the government would keep on killing Third World people if left to its own devices. The murder of Fred Hampton (chairman of the Chicago BPP) by the Chicago pigs and FBI was a turning point, not only because it was an assassination, not only because the state tried to cover it up, but also because it made me understand that the U.S. would never agree to "give" oppressed nations their human rights. That's why the government had to kill Fred, and Malcolm X, and so many other leaders.

I'd hated the injustice of this society for years, but it was in the 1960s, when I supported the Vietnamese, Native American struggles, the Black struggle, Puerto Rico and saw those nations waging struggles for freedom that included armed strug-

gle—that I started to see that there could be a struggle to win. Once I began supporting Third World nations' right to use armed struggle to win self-determination,
it made sense to me that I should be willing to use many forms of struggle to fight,
too.

Mostly, I think that it's my vision of what a wonderful thing it would be to live
in a just, humane, creative world that motivates me to embrace armed struggle as
one part of what it takes to fight for a new society.

LINDA: When I first became a political activist, I was a pacifist. I had never experienced real violence in my own life, and naively hoped that the changes I envisioned
could come about non-violently. Then, I got beat over the head and teargassed by
cops guarding the Pentagon at my first major demonstration. I came "head-to-head"
with the fact that this system maintains its power through violence on every level—
from beating up protesters, to genocide against internally-colonized nations, to waging war against nationally-colonized nations, to waging war against the people of
Vietnam.

I became an activist in a time that was defined by the victories and development
of national liberation struggles around the world and inside the U.S. I was especially
inspired by the Vietnamese and by Black people struggling for civil rights and then
for Black Power/Black Liberation. Vietnamese women fighters and Black women in
the struggle were role models for me because they were dedicated to fighting until
victory was won. Their courage and dedication, their willingness to risk everything
for freedom, the fact that women were being empowered by the process of struggle—
all were exemplary.

So by supporting these national liberation struggles I came to support the right
of oppressed people to fight for liberation by any means necessary. Malcolm X, Che
Guevara, and Ho Chi Minh were important influences in my life and political
development. But I actually became determined to participate in armed struggle
because of the rage I felt after the FBI/police raids on Black Panther Party offices
and homes all over the U.S. and particularly the murder of Fred Hampton and Mark
Clark by Chicago police.

The intensity of this police terrorism against the Black community in so many
cities made me realize that whenever a political movement even begins to threaten
the stability of the status quo, the state will act in whatever ways it must to destroy
it. In order for a revolutionary movement and vision to prevail, therefore, it's necessary for us to defend ourselves and our comrades, and to build our own capacities
toward a day when we can seriously challenge the repressive power of the state, so
that state power can be taken out of the hands of those who use it to oppress, and,
instead, taken over by the people themselves. I know this sounds idealistic, yet it is
a struggle that has succeeded in many countries around the world.

I believed then—as I do now—that U.S. imperialism was the main enemy of the
people of the world, and I wanted to fight on the side of the oppressed to build a
better world for all. This was the era of Che Guevara's call for "two, three, many

Vietnams," and I recognized that the U.S. government depends on the "domestic tranquility" of its population to allow for imperialist interventions around the world. This is one reason the Black Liberation struggle was such a threat, and why white people fighting in solidarity with national liberation struggles were threatening as well. That's part of the reason that the repression of the internal liberation movements was so immediate and devastating and why there were such efforts to divide off white struggles from these struggles.

SUSAN: The war against the Black Liberation movement by the FBI/U.S. government was most influential for me in seeing the necessity for armed self-defense. The challenge placed on us who were in a position of solidarity with revolutionary nationalist Black organizations was to uphold self-determination and to fight for it. The other element that most personally propelled me into armed clandestine resistance was witnessing the genocide of the chemical war being waged in the South Bronx against Black and Puerto Rican people. As a doctor of acupuncture and community health worker I watched us fail to stop the plague.

QUISP: What do you do all day?

LAURA: My time is divided among: fighting for decent conditions and against the prison's denial of those things (a daily necessity!), working on my political and legal work, communicating with people via letters and phone calls, talking to other prisoners (and working with them to try to deal with legal issues, health issues, etc.), meeting with my codefendants, trying to find out how my comrade Alan is (he's engaged in a hard, life-and-death battle with cancer, shackled to a bed in the I.C.U. oncology unit at D.C. General Hospital [Since this interview took place, Alan has recovered and was released from prison in July 1992.]). I spend a lot of time talking to women about AIDS—by one estimate, 40–50% of the women in here are HIV positive, yet there is no program, no education, no counseling provided. Like my other comrades, I spend a lot of time doing informal counseling and education on this.

LINDA: Work and work out.

SUSAN: Because I am a doctor of acupuncture and a conscious person, I have become (in addition to a political prisoner) a peer advocate/AIDS counselor. It is not recognized by the jail but I spend seventy-five percent of my time counseling people—women who are HIV positive. The other time is spent doing my other work, and talking with others. We spend a lot of the day locked down in our cells. Because of the overcrowding and lack of programs, the administration keeps us locked down an enormous amount of time.

QUISP: How do you deal with your white privilege in jail?

LAURA: I struggle to be aware of it; I fight racism actively and organize for that fight; I try to make the resources that I have access to, available to others. Educating people about how to fight AIDS is another way, because that's information that the gay and lesbian movement has that women in the D.C. Jail lack—and it means that women are continuing to contract HIV every day. That is a crime.

LINDA: I try to use the resources and education I've had access to as a result of my white privilege to benefit all the prisoners I live with and to fight for our interests. This takes many forms, from struggling as a prisoner for the institution of AIDS education and counseling programs, to helping individual women with legal problems or abuses of their rights by the jail. When I was in jail in Louisiana, we were able to win a jailhouse lawyer's legal suit forcing the jail to give women glasses and false teeth (all jail dental care amounts to is pulling teeth, and few jails replace them). One of the conflicts I confront is between dealing with immediate needs and crises as an individual counselor/agitator/jailhouse lawyer, and always pushing the institution to provide the services and programs that prisoners should be entitled to as a basic human right—education, medical care, exercise, mental health and AIDS counseling.

SUSAN: Well! I struggle against racism in every way I can. I have learned patience, and how to be quiet, and how to really listen to who is talking, and what they are saying.

QUISP: What observations or advice do you have for lesbian/gay and AIDS activists as we start to experience police surveillance, harassment and abuse?

LAURA: Fight it. Don't back away. Develop clandestine ways of operating so that the state won't know everything that you're doing. Support one another so that when anyone is targeted for state attack, they can resist—that resistance will build us all. Don't ever give information—even if you think it's "safe" information—to the state. Don't let the state divide the movement by calling some groups "legitimate" and others not. Unity is our strength. Support other movements and people who are also targets of state attack. When the state calls someone a "terrorist," or "violent," or "crazy," or anything, think hard before ever believing it to be true. Resist. Resist. Resist.

LINDA: Be cool. Develop a clandestine consciousness. Value your work enough that you don't talk to the enemy about it (like over tapped phones). Don't underestimate the power and viciousness of the state, and don't expect white privilege to make you exempt from repression. Take the lessons of past repression against political movements seriously—not to demobilize you or make you afraid, but to safeguard and defend your work. Remember you're building for the future, not just for today, and keep struggling to broaden your vision. Remember that reforms are only temporary concessions, that they're neither permanent nor do they really solve fundamental problems.

SUSAN: Study other movements here and around the world and examine the state's methods in order to develop tactics that allow you to keep functioning. Very important, if one self-consciously is building a movement that knows the state will destroy it if the movement begins to pose a real or perceived threat.

QUISP: What is your position on go-go girls in women's bars?

LAURA: Take me to a bar and we'll have a scintillating discussion of this issue, OK?

LINDA: Take me to a bar and I'll let you know!

SUSAN: I think that anything that objectifies women as sexual objects (versus sexual beings) is anti-woman. Even in an all-woman context. Being lesbian is subversive because women loving women is a crime against the state, and against the bourgeois patriarchal morality of this society—but being subversive doesn't necessarily mean it's about liberation. If nothing else I have learned that liberation and the need for it begins in oneself. Objectification/sexual stereotypes/misogyny not only destroy us in the world, they corrode our own hearts. I am not interested in a society that promotes those things. Although I don't believe that they will be ended until we decide to end them—they cannot be overturned through the law of this state.

NOTES

This interview was conducted in early 1991 while Evans, Whitehorn, and Rosenberg were housed in a Washington, D.C., jail. It was first made available by QUISP in 1991.

Editor's note: QUISP (Queer women and men In Solidarity with Political Prisoners, 1991–1996) was a New York City collective of lesbians and gay men organizing community support for political prisoners in the United States. A QUISP leaflet stated, "we do this work because we believe that our liberation as queers is tied to the liberation of all oppressed peoples. QUISP believes that just as different oppressions—be they racism, classism, sexism, or homophobia—are intertwined, so too must our efforts for progressive social change be mutually supporting."

1. Editor's note: Jonas Savimbi was killed in February 2002. UNITA was a counterrevolutionary or contra paramilitary group funded by first the South African apartheid government and then by the U.S. government. It was associated with massive and horrific human rights violations. See Elaine Windrich, The Cold War Guerrilla: Jonas Savimbi, the U.S. Media, and the Angolan War (New York: Greenwood, 1992).

2. *Editor's note:* See Audre Lorde, "The Master's Tools Will Never Dismantle the Master's House," in "*Sister Outsider*": *Essays and Speeches* (Freedom, Calif.: The Crossing, 1984). Lorde's comments were initially directed at the patriarchal and racist politics of the 1979 Second Sex Conference in New York at which she made this speech. The comments are not specifically about violence, but about the way that the women's movement reproduces hegemonic and repressive structures in their own organizations and politics:

> Those of us who stand outside the circle of this society's definition of acceptable women; those of us who have been forged into the crucibles of difference—those of us who are poor, who are lesbians, who are black, who are older—know that *survival is not an academic skill*. It is learning how to stand alone, unpopular and sometimes reviled, and how to make common cause with those others identified as outside the structures in order to define and seek a world in which we can all flourish. It is learning how to take out differences and make them strengths. *For the master's tools will never dismantle the master's house.* They may allow us temporarily to beat him at his own game, but they will never enable us to bring about genuine change. And this fact is only threatening to those women who still define the master's house as their only source of support. ("*Sister Outsider*," 112)

3. *Editor's note:* RCC6 refers to the Resistance Conspiracy 6: Alan Berkman, Marilyn Buck, Susan Rosenberg, Linda Evans, Laura Whitehorn, and Tim Blunk, the six white anti-imperialists who fought in the Armed Resistance Unit, Red Guerilla Resistance; worked to free political prisoners; and worked in solidarity with Puerto Rican *independentistas* and Black Liberationists. They were convicted under federal criminal statutes for conspiring to change and alter government policy. See the documentary *Resistance Conspiracy* (San Francisco: Bay Area Committee to Support the Resistance Conspiracy Defendants [distributor], Oakland: Peralta Colleges Television [PCTV] Production Company, 1990). Videocassette.

4. *Editor's note:* The Stonewall Rebellion refers to an incident in June of 1969, in which the New York City police raided a popular gay bar in Greenwich Village. The mostly black and Latino "queens" inside responded to years of harassment and abuse from the police by fighting back in violent protest. The resistance that took place over a series of nights became known as the "Stonewall Riots." The rebellion is considered the beginning of a new militancy in the movement for gay liberation. Stonewall has been widely misinterpreted by a white hegemonic (gay) appropriation of the historical moment, erasing the fact that the Stonewall rebels were primarily working-class men of color.

Chapter Twenty

José Solís Jordan

José Solís Jordan was born in 1952 in San Juan, Puerto Rico. Growing up in a military family, he spent part of his youth in Long Beach, California, where his father was stationed on a naval base. Jordan was educated in both private and public junior and high schools in Puerto Rico when his father was transferred to a U.S. military base on the island. After receiving his undergraduate degree at Texas Christian University, Jordan returned to Puerto Rico to teach in the public school system.

In 1987 he received his doctorate degree in education at the University of Illinois at Champaign–Urbana. Jordan organized with the U.S.-based Committee in Solidarity with the People of El Salvador (CISPES), serving in 1989 as a translator for CISPES in El Salvador. From 1991 to 1995, Jordan taught at DePaul University and worked at the Puerto Rican Cultural Center in Chicago with his wife, Martha.[1] He then retuned to Puerto Rico with his wife and five children to teach at the University of Puerto Rico (UPR) at the Eugenio Maria de Hostos College of Education.

As a professor at UPR, Jordan became a member of La Asociación de Profesores Puertorriqueños Universitario (APPU) (the Puerto Rican Association of University Professors). The association addressed university problems and participated in various labor strikes.[2] Both in Chicago and in Puerto Rico, Jordan was politically involved in the Independence movement.

Jordan was first arrested after an FBI commando raid of his San Juan home on November 6, 1997. Despite lack of physical evidence, he was accused of being a participant in the December 10, 1992, bombing of a U.S. Army recruiting station in Chicago.[3] He was charged with a four-count indictment of conspiracy, possession of explosives, causing destruction to property of the United States, and attempted destruction of government property. Jordan was convicted by a federal jury on March 12, 1999. During the trial, the FBI relied almost exclusively on the testimony of Rafael Marrero, an FBI agent provocateur who worked at Chicago's Puerto Rican Cultural Center from 1987 to 1995. It is alleged that Marrero himself may have been a participant in the 1992 bombing.[4] On July 7, 1999, Jordan was sentenced to fifty-one months in prison and was incarcerated at the Federal Correctional Institution in Coleman, Florida. One of the *"Faltan 6"* (six remain) Puerto Rican political prisoners/prisoners of war incarcerated for their involvement in the struggle for Puerto Rican independence, Jordan served the remainder of his sentence in a correctional halfway house in Puerto Rico. He currently lives in Puerto Rico.

REFERENCES

Can't Jail the Spirit, 5th ed. Chicago: Committee to End the Marion Lockdown, 2002.

Carr, Raymond. *Puerto Rico: A Colonial Experiment*. New York: Vintage, 1984.

Jackson, Sandra, and José Solís Jordan, eds. *I've Got a Story to Tell: Identity and Place in the Academy*. New York: Peter Lang, 1999.

Jordan, José Solís. "Language as Possibility: Comments on Identity and Language: [A Review of] *Puerto Rico: Culture, Politics and Identity*, by Nancy Morris." *International Journal of the Sociology of Language*, special issue on "Languages of Former Colonial Powers and Former Colonies—The Case of Puerto Rico," guest editors Carlos M. Ramirez Gonzalez and Rome Torres. 3, no. 142 (2000): 157–73.

———. *Public School Reform in Puerto Rico: Sustaining Colonial Models of Development*. Westport, Conn.: Greenwood, 1994.

"José Solís Jordan." *Prolibertad Faltan6 Freedom Campaign*. www.prolibertad.org/Faltan6.htm (22 July 2002).

Rodriguez, Michael. "In His Own Words: Interview with José Solís Jordan." *Que Ondee Sola* (student publication of Northeastern Illinois University), January 1999. Reprinted in *The Critical Criminologist* (July 1999). sun.soci.niu.edu/~critcrim/CC/Solís/Solís-int.html (22 July 2002).

NOTES

Research and draft for this biography were provided by Hana Tauber.

1. "José Solís Jordan," *Can't Jail the Spirit*, 5th ed. (Chicago: Committee to End the Marion Lockdown, 2002).

2. Michael Rodriguez, "In His Own Words: Interview with José Solís Jordan," *Que Ondee Sola* (student publication of Northeastern Illinois University), January 1999, reprinted in *The Critical Criminologist*, July 1999, sun.soci.niu.edu/~critcrim/CC/Solís/Solís-int.html (22 July 2002).

3. "José Solís Jordan."

4. Rodriguez, "In His Own Words: Interview with José Solís Jordan."

This Is Enough!

September 2001

"¿Maestro, estas bien?" (Teacher, are you okay?) I heard, as if coming from a distance. Stopping from my regular meditative walk, I turned and realized that the question had been asked by a fellow prisoner working out at a pull-up bar on the prison yard. My attention was suddenly drawn to a small bird that had, for whatever reason, and who knows why, decided to sit atop the razor wire at the highest point of the fences. Looking at that incredible scene, I smiled and answered, "Si, muy bien, gracias" (Yes, fine, thank you). Later that day I was told that the question arose out of a concern for my well being, since the inmates had been watching me walk very slowly, an exercise rarely practiced. I remember telling them something like, "sometimes the objective is to walk or move very slowly, if not to be still." Quite naturally I guess, these guys associated moving slowly with being sad, troubled or depressed—that is, something negative. More significantly, many who find my outlook perplexing often question me. "You must like this place," I've been told. "I am here, and here I struggle, and this is good." This then is the point. As a Puerto Rican political prisoner incarceration is but the reaffirmation of the truth. I have been imprisoned because I insist on freedom, the freedom made possible only by the decolonization of Puerto Rico; a process that is our human right.

Our home had been invaded, our land. Dressed as commandos, the FBI arrested me. The house was pepper-sprayed and I was stripped naked in front of my family in our living room. Over twenty feds pointed their weapons at me. Handcuffed, I stood there surrounded by these agents of "justice" and for a fleeting moment contemplated the irony of being handcuffed. They were ordered to restrain me because I am free. The handcuffs only underscored this fact. Everything about the arrest and subsequent processes aimed at separating, decontextualizing and imposing the will of the feds. Completely oblivious to any sense of what an arrest is, I was quickly overcome by solitude. There it was, silence amidst the noise, floating about in a sea strange to me and somehow empowering, somehow so humiliating. Silence would become my friend, solitude my classroom.

I am an educator. As a teacher I've grown accustomed to the pressures of the profession: rush, deadlines, books, read, write, meet, grade, rush and move, move constantly. I would like to share with you a short story about my education as a Puerto Rican political prisoner, as a human committed to human freedom. But first, I feel compelled to contextualize this reality. It remains troubling to me the problematic treatment that so many scholars continue to exercise on the topic of Puerto Rico–U.S. relations, if the topic is even treated. Generally speaking, and this is unfortunate, rather than carefully studying Puerto Rico's colonial status, mainstream academe and critical scholars do themselves and their studies a disfavor and

281

all of us an injustice by essentially subscribing to the conventional view and official discourse regarding Puerto Rico.

HISTORY

On November 25, 1897, Spain granted Puerto Rico autonomy through the Autonomous Charter. Among the sections of the charter that highlighted Puerto Rico's autonomy, Article Two provided that: "[The charter] shall not be amended except by virtue of a special law and upon the petition of the insular parliament." Thus, the Treaty of Paris, which ceded Puerto Rico to the United States from Spain was a violation of International Law, an act of violence following the invasion of July 25, 1898, and a violation of the Thirteenth Amendment to the U.S. Constitution, as Puerto Rico became what it remains: a non-incorporated territory of the United States. This property (Puerto Rico and Puerto Ricans) belonging to the United States violates the Thirteenth Amendment prohibition against treating persons as chattel, subject to ownership by others as mere appendages to the land. In the words of William McKinley, President of the United States, "while we are at war and until its conclusion, we must keep all we can get. When the war is over we must keep what we want."[1] And so we lived under military rule for nearly two years. With the passage of the Foraker Act of 1900, government in Puerto Rico was appointed by the president of the United States.

Under the Foraker Act, Congress stated that the people of Puerto Rico were citizens of Puerto Rico. Puerto Rico would also have a House of Delegates made up of eleven members. Six would be presidential appointees and five elected. Decisions on legislative matters would be determined by a majority. Naturally, the governor held veto power. In 1917, under the second organic act, the Jones Act, Congress passed legislation to make Puerto Ricans citizens of the United States. Why was legislation necessary to confer citizenship upon inhabitants of a territory? Because Puerto Rico was (as it is) a non-incorporated territory of the United States, according to the U.S. Constitution, belonging to, but not a part of, the United States. Resistance to U.S. citizenship was widespread in Puerto Rico. Senator Arthur Yager expressed in 1914, "that we give them [i.e., Puerto Ricans] simply an opportunity to become citizens without any cost or delay—just offer it to them and let them have an opportunity to take it or leave it."[2] On April 1, 1917, President Woodrow Wilson declared, "We welcome the new citizens, not as a stranger but as one entering his father's house."[3] Reaction from Washington to the resistance presented our people with a catch-22. First, Congress reminded Puerto Rico's delegates that any quarrel over U.S. citizenship was not a domestic issue and so not to be addressed by the U.S. Congress, and any insistence upon the Congress to address the issue first required that the people be U.S. citizens. Secondly, any Puerto Rican not wanting U.S. citizenship could refuse it but, by doing so, could not hold public office and would be severely limited in terms of private progress. The Fourteenth Amendment to the U.S. Constitution affirms: "all persons born or naturalized *in the United States*, and subject to the jurisdiction thereof, are citizens of the United States" (emphasis added).

Puerto Ricans born in Puerto Rico after it became a United States possession were not U.S. citizens as in other territorial possessions for two fundamental reasons:

First, because by the Treaty of Paris, the political status of the inhabitants of the ceded territories was left to the determination of Congress, and Congress in the pursuance of that treaty made Puerto Ricans and the children born to them subsequently, "citizens of Puerto Rico." And secondly, because the Fourteenth Amendment is only coextensive throughout the United States, and the United States did not include unincorporated territories like Puerto Rico, as decided in *Downs v Bidwell* (1900 Supreme Court Decision: Puerto Rico belonged to the United States but was not a part of the United States). The collective nationalization of the inhabitants effected by the Jones Act of 1917 is conclusive evidence that those born subsequently to the transfer of sovereignty from Spain were never American citizens.[4]

And so U.S. citizenship was imposed on those that Congress had already recognized as citizens of Puerto Rico (under the Foraker Act, 1900).

Between 1900 and the establishment of what is referred to as the *Estado Libre Asociado* (Free Associated State) or Commonwealth of Puerto Rico in 1952, the people struggled for the right to self-determine and decolonize Puerto Rico. *Independentistas* were persecuted, imprisoned and killed. Setting the stage for a Puerto Rican elected governor in 1947, Washington and the aspiring gubernatorial candidate, Luis Marin, passed a law criminalizing the struggle for national liberation. The law was known as "*la Ley de la Mordazo*" (The Muzzle Law). Even speech and publication of pro-independence materials became felonious acts.

In its Report (1832) in 1952, the United States House of Representatives declared that:

It is important that the nature and general scope of 5.3336 be absolutely clear. The bill under consideration would not change Puerto Rico's fundamental political, social and economic relationship to the United States.[5]

Puerto Rico became in 1952 what it is today, what it was in 1900 and 1917, a nonincorporated territory, a colony with another name—The Commonwealth of Puerto Rico (El Estado Tibu Asociado de Puerto Rico). Representative Fred Crawford reaffirmed Congress' position that, "Puerto Rico can be a colonized possession and have a great deal to say about her own government under which the Puerto Ricans live." Congressman Javits drove the point home noting that, "the only thing we agree to now is that you should have a constitution within the organic act. . . . Congress controls the organic act."[6]

In his 1989 State of the Union Address, President George Bush urged Congress to "[t]ake the necessary steps to authorize a federally recognized process allowing the people of Puerto Rico, for the first time since the Treaty of Paris, to freely express their wishes regarding their future political status," a step in the process of self-determination which the Congress has yet to authorize. And again in 1991, Attorney General Richard Thornburg echoed the colonial reality by stating that, "the Congress of the United States holds full power over Puerto Rico, a relationship Puerto Ricans are incapable of altering."[7]

Speaking in terms of economics, the principal strategy of the industrialization project in Puerto Rico has been based on the attraction of capital through the incentive of high rates of profit. "One of the consequences of foreign capital is the external factor payments (non-distributed corporate profits, dividends and interests which exit the country) which are reflected in the extraordinary gap between the Gross Domestic Product (the value of Puerto Rico's production) and the Gross National Product (the payment of workers and entrepreneurs who reside in Puerto Rico)."[8] 1981 Nobel Prize Laureate in Economics James Tobin highlighted the problem by assuming that:

> The difference between the Gross Domestic Product and the Gross National Product and their respective growth rates are [sic] an additional reflection of Puerto Rico's increasing dependency on foreign resources in order to foster growth. From the point of view of Puerto Rico's residents, high levels and increasing growth rate of the Gross Domestic Product are of meager significance if they are not accompanied by high levels and relatively high growth rate of the Gross National Product.[9]

Today:

- 70% of domestic income of capital owners leaves Puerto Rico.
- In 1999, Gross Domestic Product amounted to $59.946 billion.
- Gross National Product represented $38.220 billion. The difference ($21.717 billion) represents the "exit" profit alluded to by Tobin.
- Net Federal Transfers amounted to $8.315 billion, most of which is represented by funds such as Social Security, Medicare and benefits and pensions, toward which the people of Puerto Rico contribute.
- Among the transfers not considered acquired benefits (entitlements) is the National Assistance Plan, representing $1.087 billion—extremely pale when compared to the profits that leave the island yearly.
- Over 12% of Puerto Rico territory is occupied by military bases.
- The Census for 2000 indicates that approximately 60% of the population lives under the poverty level.
- Over 1 million Puerto Ricans living in Puerto Rico are functionally illiterate.
- Federal law prohibits Puerto Rico from developing trade agreements with other countries and Puerto Rico is forced to buy U.S. products at prices that far exceed those in the U.S.

And so on. . . .

Today, the United States remains in violation of its constitution and numerous international laws regarding Puerto Rico's right to self-determination and freedom from colonial rule. These laws include: the United Nations General Assembly Resolution 1514 (xv); The International Covenant on Economic, Social and Cultural Rights (UNGA 2200A[xxi]); and many other internationally recognized conventions, resolutions and accords.[10] And still the U.S. Supreme Court rhetorically affirms the peremptory nature of international law as "part of our law." Former Chief Justice of Puerto Rico's Supreme Court, José Trias Monge, stated the situation clearly and precisely when he remarked that "any change in the terms of association have been degrading."[11]

On August 15, 1998, the United Nations Special Committee on the Situation with regard to the Implementation of the Declaration of Independence to Colonial Countries and Peoples issued its Special Committee decision concerning Puerto Rico under UN Res. 1514(xv) and decided to keep the question of Puerto Rico under UN review. In November 2000, an international panel of private jurists from five continents convened an International Tribunal on the U.S. violations of human rights in Puerto Rico and Vieques. The Tribunal found the United States guilty on the nine-count indictment. Meanwhile, the island municipality of Vieques continues to be bombed by the U.S. Navy; this, despite a referendum where approximately 70% of the population on Vieques voted for an immediate cease and leave alternative to the U.S. Navy. The people of Puerto Rico receive nothing from the military presence. On the other hand, the Navy draws $80 million from its NATO allies for allowing them to train in Vieques. The Navy has also responded to the people's efforts by offering money to the fishermen and a few jobs, home appliances, and several services to the population of Vieques. Most recently the Navy has bought air time on different radio stations with the hope of changing public opinion. A long and ugly history precedes the events since the Navy's bombing death of David Sanes on April 19, 1999; a long history of persecution, deaths, rape, and intimidation.

Presently, the United States Department of Justice, through the FBI, continues to release millions of pages of illegal files that the Bureau kept of Puerto Rican independentistas throughout the twentieth century. The files (*las carpetas*) reveal the Federal Bureau of Investigation (FBI)'s leading role in the fabrication of cases, disruption of legal activities, and infiltration of legal groups with the intent to disrupt and destroy them and, as such, undermine the independence movement. The FBI's counterintelligence program (COINTELPRO) continues in Puerto Rico. I and many others are clear that such was the case with my arrest and conviction.

"But the people of Puerto Rico never vote for independence," we so often hear. First, self-determination and sovereignty are not matters of authorization awaiting congressional blessing. And furthermore, the terror of colonial rule might well be expressed by [Marxist philosopher] Herbert Marcuse's words:

> This loss of freedom is not experienced as the work of some hostile and foreign force; some relinquish their liberty to self-imposed rationalization. The point is that the appa-

ratus, to which so many have adjusted, is presented as so overpowering that protest and liberation appear not only hopeless but irrational.[12]

Clearly, the challenge for all of us is a pedagogical project, one whose resolution requires our sincerest commitment to social justice, to caring. But caring is born of love and of hope, not hate. And furthermore, to really care I must return to that solitude, to the tearing-away imposed by my arrest, arraignment, trial, conviction and imprisonment. I became the object of a process that I observed with great estrangement—forced to face the pain of the baptismal fire that would strengthen me not by the breadth of words or utterances but by the depth and humility of being a stranger, to it all and to myself. And so I share the following reflections because the most revolutionary aspect of liberation is not the substitution of political arrangements, but rather the transformation of our own humanity and our capacity to see ourselves in the enemy and the contributions that such a transformation can make to a more just and humanized polity.

THE PASSAGE

We walked into a crowded room. The back wall was lined with tables full of refreshments and a variety of breads and cookies. As the people continued to enter, my wife, one of our lawyers and two of our closest friends and I made our way to the front of the conference room. Taking off my jacket, I looked about and noticed a room filled to capacity with many others lining the walls standing, waiting to hear what I had to say. Yet the same strange feeling that had forced itself upon me since my arrest grew exponentially throughout the trial. Here we were again, like so many other times before, capacity-filled rooms and auditoriums brimming with solidarity and yet I felt so alone. I was learning so much more than I could express. As we dialogued in that room the evening before the verdict I found myself reaching out, hoping to find refuge from my sense of solitude in the expressions and presence of others. Was I using them as a crutch against my understanding? As I spoke, the audience seemed further away and at the same time I also felt so much closer to them. There were hugs and words of support. Some cried as if anticipating a tragedy. Others smiled as they expressed warmth and hope. I reminded them that those of us who struggle for Puerto Rico's liberation have never won a trial.

I slept well that night. Yet, at one point I awoke and, turning to look at my wife who was sound asleep, I passed my hand over her face and hair. I spoke to her of my love for her, our children, family and people. Thanking her for her love, I reminded her that she too was my strength in so many ways.

The following morning was cold, Chicago cold, in March. DePaul University, where I had been a professor until 1995, granted the defense team a room at the DePaul Center some three blocks from the Federal Building. The room was furnished with a variety of comfortable sofas, chairs, tables and a couple desks. It was a quiet place, but by no means empty. All present awaited with a nervous silence, nervous smiles and a general sense of tempered anxiety. There were students, professors, a few journalists, religious leaders from the community and our legal team. I spent the day dialoguing with my wife, our lawyers, Jed and Linda, and the others. That sense that I was being pulled away kept haunting me. And yet I found myself trying to make others laugh. Maybe it was my attempt to shake off the impending solitude. Seeking refuge from myself, I sat next to my wife on one of the sofas and rested my head on her shoulder. Again, I felt so far and yet closer in some strange way; closer to everyone. At about 3:20 PM, someone entered the room and spoke, "They've reached a verdict."

My wife and I looked at one another. Linda and Jed looked at me and I remarked, "this is but another beginning." Jed put out his arm over my shoulder. The entire room emptied as we walked those extremely cold blocks to the Dirkson Federal Building. I remember taking deep breaths of cold air, fresh cold air, and absorbing as many sights as I could. These would be my last breaths of fresh air for a long time.

Entering the 21st floor of the building, we made our way into the courtroom. As with the trial, the room was completely filled. Many wore buttons and patches of the Puerto Rican flag. The feds had a large contingent of marshals and FBI agents present. I sat with my wife until the court was brought to order. Called to order, the judge entered. I looked at the people and signaled for them to relax and smile. One of the marshals noticed my gestures to the supporters and smiled to himself, nodding approvingly. I tipped my head to him as if to acknowledge.

Called for by the judge, the jury entered. That feeling embraced me, squeezing me inside out. Linda held my hand. Jed placed his hand on my shoulder. "Yes we have," answered the jury to the judge's question. "We find the defendant guilty as charged." The judge looked at me. We exchanged a look that spoke a thousand words: "I know that you know what happened here, but you are incarcerated by the rules even if applied unjustly," was my look. I wasn't angry. This wasn't the first time in our history. The judge recessed the court for about twenty minutes. I was ordered to remain in the courtroom. Embracing my wife, I tried to speak words of hope as she cried. Or was I doing this for me? Her pain scorched my heart. The faces of many grew teary-eyed. The press hurried about. One journalist said, "This is terrible. How could they convict with no real evidence? This is wrong." I looked at the journalist and responded, "Wrong? Colonialism is wrong. Don't write about me, learn from this and search for the right in the wrong that this government has imposed as a colonial ruler in my country." Looking at all those sad faces I smiled and, holding my wife's hand, I spoke to those present. "Do not cry for me nor for our people. This cannot be all that. Let the pain be a wake-up call. This is all but a reminder of our responsibility to educate and continue to forge our right to be free."

Remanded into the custody of the U.S. Marshals and the Federal Bureau of Prisons, I was swiftly and abruptly separated from everyone. Five or six marshals took me by the arms and surrounded me, leading me to another door at the side of the courtroom. Before entering I was ordered to give my wife all personal belongings (watch, necklace, money, ring). Swept away, we looked at each other in between the wall of marshals that cuffed me. Within three minutes I had been stripped naked and searched. Ordered to put on a jumpsuit, I was taken into a room some four by five feet and locked in. There I was. That feeling gestating, waiting and foreboding finally reared up its head. Steel surrounded me. I could hear no sounds other than my breathing and my own movement, other than my voice. It was cold. All they gave me was a jumpsuit and slippers. The handcuffs were tight, my arms numbed by the tension of having been handcuffed from behind. I felt like the pain would suffocate me. It was heart-wrenching. I couldn't move. There were no windows, no chairs. "Where is everyone?" I thought. Would this mean anything to anyone? Why should anyone care? My heart beat rapidly. My body was sweaty despite the cold room. For not subscribing to the U.S. government agency's plan, I was punished. Integrity, honor, commitment, dignity are all good values, but only when they serve those that wish to define these according to their interests.

Within a few hours I was escorted in a van to the Metropolitan Correctional Center (MCC-Chicago), a federal administrative detention center (maximum security). The trip between the federal building and the MCC was short and strange. There were two cars escorting the van and one in the back. The journey was marked by lights and sirens, as if announcing that someone dangerous was coming through.

Once at the MCC, I heard guards and others commenting on my conviction. The trial was of a rather high-profile nature. Again I was strip-searched and issued another orange jumpsuit. The attending officers looked at one another. One of them remarked, "So you're Solís Jordan. I've heard a lot about you. It's been all good." My only response was, "and so here I am." I was taken into a holding room with other prisoners. This was my first contact with other prisoners. I remember all of the generalizations and biases we are brought up with about prison and persons in prison. I looked at them cautiously. They were reluctant to respond by looking back. In fact, they avoided me. They gestured at one another as they looked at my hands. I had been handcuffed with a "blackbox." This is a restraining device used on those the government considers dangerous. So their looks of apprehension were, I was later told, more like concern for themselves in my presence. I thought, "Wow, this is crazy."

Suddenly, I was removed from the room and taken to another room. I was left alone in this room. The other prisoners could see me from across the hallway. Again I waited for hours. After that time, a few guards ordered me to strip and put on a green jumpsuit. Having changed and again handcuffed, I was escorted in an elevator to another floor. As I exited the elevator I felt the cold. It was dark. Everything was painted gray. The ceiling was low and pipes ran along its sides. The lighting was minimal. The only clear light was at the officer's station. There were three steel gates and a steel door that led to the cell block. All I could see were the ominous locking doors of raw, cold steel. The doors had narrow slits that passed for windows to the hallway. I saw no faces. I heard the cries of prisoners coming from what seemed like two cells. They yelled and cursed at one another violently. These were the expressions of outrage fallen into the depths of what seemed like a madness brought on by the isolation, the sensory deprivation. I was taken to a corner cell flanked by the two cells where the prisoners considered as lunatics by the guards lived. Later I would be told that my placement in that cell was deliberate. And so I entered my cell, an eight-by-eight-foot space of walls painted white, steel bed and toilet, penetrating lights left on for days and a cold that produced vapor when I exhaled. I thought to myself, "My God, just last night I was with so many people, talking, eating, sharing so much energy—and now. . . ."

My mind continued to rush. Within a few minutes of being in the cell a guard passed by and said, "Machetero, right? Or is it FALN?" The *Macheteros* are a clandestine armed organization and FALN (*Fuerzas Armadas de Liberación Nacionál*) were another. I nodded and responded "No, *puertorriqueño*." "Well, here you go, Mr. Puerto Rico," expressed the guard sarcastically as he looked in the cell through the slit in the door. Silence settled in. I looked around. The only signs of life were the scratch marks left by others who had been here before. The most legible was left next to the bed and read, "God help me, I'm losing it." Yet it had been blackened by paint not allowing even diffused natural light to enter. The only sounds I could hear were those of the "lunatics" yelling and making weird noises at one another, the blowing of the cold air coming in through the air conditioning vent, the guard's keys and my own heart and breathing. I was alone. Would that be enough?

The light bounced off the walls, piercing my eyes. The walls seemed to close in, suffocating my mind. Powerlessness played with me. I'd never been locked up or in anything. I always had the option to move about—not this time. Being locked up in a segregation unit, the "hole" as it is referred to, is shocking. I was in the cell twenty-three hours per day, every day. That thing, that feeling kept slapping me about. The aloneness, the solitude had been shaking me as if trying to assist me to anticipate for days, for months, what was to come. Still, I resisted and reached out, crying painfully for the ones I loved, for my people, for the right. After hours of mental games that rushed through me with maddening speed I thought, "Okay, they'll realize the injustice and call me out soon." But no. Why did I insist on this? After all, wasn't it I who told people about the history of persecution? It was my turn. No one here but me. I was alone. Was that enough?

I couldn't think. The "lunatics" spent their days and nights screaming like animals, making noises, cussing at one another, threatening all with death, and defecating and urinating in their cells. But this was my first night. "They're going to drive me crazy," I thought. No sooner did I think this than I discovered myself assuming a lotus position on the bed. I began to meditate. During my meditation I found myself struggling to block out the madness of the noises from those two. It seemed somehow worse when they would remain silent for a few minutes and then resume. The abruptness would test anyone's nerves. I fell slowly into a deep meditation. Rather than blocking the "lunatics" out, I absorbed their noise until it became part of the silence. After some time, I was distracted by a guard pounding on the door. He looked inside and forcefully asked, "Are you okay? You haven't moved for hours." Smiling at the guard, I said, "I can't go outside, so I'll go inside." Raising his eyebrows, the guard uttered passingly, "Whatever," and left. The aloneness had washed all over me during the meditation. It was like a baptism, a rite of passage, a leap into a radically new sense of time, space and movement.

I stood up to sip some water from the faucet. The floor was freezing. The cell smelled old, cold and wasted. I did some push-ups in an attempt to warm my body. Doing so, I realized that there were things I could do despite the limitations to counter the impositions. Turning over to do some abdominal exercises, I noticed a small strip of paper in the far corner of the floor under the bed. There, too, was a piece of pencil, at best two inches in length. This was it, my opportunity to write something, anything. What would it be? On the slip of paper I wrote the Serenity Prayer: "God grant me the serenity to accept the things I can't change, the courage to change the things I can, and the wisdom to know the difference." With a finger-tip of toothpaste I stuck the message to the wall. Reflecting upon it became a daily exercise. I was alone. Was this enough? Loneliness is one thing, solitude or being alone, another.

I couldn't change the cell, the prison itself, but I could [change myself]. The wisdom to know the difference between what we can and cannot change is nothing less than our capacity to struggle. That which drives us to accomplish anything is also the limit to what will be. And so I learned to listen to the silence, to touch and be touched by emptiness, to dialogue with myself. Little by little this made every subsequent encounter with another nothing less than unique.

How capable are we of dialogue when so often it is tempered by the cluttered existence of things, assumptions and movement with little time dedicated to really understanding how and why we forge tomorrows? Paulo Freire spoke abundantly of love and struggle. Dialogue, asserted Freire, is not a tactic, not a turn-taking mechanical back-and-forth, not a description. It is curiosity, struggle, anger, joy. Solitude then is not the absence of dialogue; it is self-reflection, self-critique, a dia-logue of one. Our unwillingness to reflect critically yet compassionately on the self, to step back, if you will, from the movement of time and space and our assumptions continues to limit our commitment. We skate about on blades of words and ideas whose cleverness establishes the rationalizations for our own stagnation. Do our anger, rage and indignation become excuses for our arrested state? I recalled [Anto-nio] Gramsci, [Paulo] Freire, Socrates, Albizu Campos and so many other educators who suffered imprisonment. What made them so great? Their capacity to love and understand the power of struggle as a most human expression of love.

When we are torn from our families, friends and people, our bodies, hearts and minds are shocked—profoundly so. The feedback, reaffirmations, the stimuli and sharing that move back and forth from the "I" to others is suddenly silenced. Here we enter into the "I." Is this enough? No, but it is necessary. We read often of how the political prisoner leaves prison stronger than s/he entered. How? Aloneness, solitude and reflection have washed us with an enriched sense of life, of struggle. This is not due to a loss of freedom but to the realization that the political prisoner is free—s/he has a freedom not contingent upon an imposed convention. Such a position strengthens the sovereignty of freedom to be forged by the sheer power of humanity's love for being more. The greatest contribution I can make as a Puerto Rican political prisoner, as a human being, is to struggle for more life. This, to me, begins with the I and its context, our fight to be free of colonial rule. The solitude, the tearing-away is at once also a reaffirmation of just how close we really are. Being alone has brought me back to being with myself and this *is* enough. ¡*Que viva Puerto Rico libre!*

NOTES

1. Ronald Fernandez et al., *The Disenchanted Island: Puerto Rico and the United States in the Twentieth Century* (Greenwood, Conn.: Praeger 1992), 1.

2. *The Disenchanted Island,* 55.

3. *The Disenchanted Island,* 55.

4. Jose Lopez Barralt, *The Policy of the United States towards Its Territories with Special Reference to Puerto Rico* (University of Puerto Rico Press, 1999), 235–36.

5. *The Disenchanted Island,* 180.

6. *The Disenchanted Island,* 180.

7. Richard Thornburg, "On promoting a referendum with regards to the political status of Puerto Rico," 102nd Congress, 1st Session. Washington, D.C.: Government Printing Office, United States Congressional Record (February 1991), 7.

8. José Catala Oliveras, "Sobre la economía de Puerto Rico," *El Nuevo Día* (October 21, 2000), 18.

9. James Tobin et al., *Welfare Programs: An Economic Appraisal* (A & I Press, 1976).

10. *Editor's note:* For full text of United Nations documents, see www.un.org/documents.

11. José Trias Monge, *Puerto Rico: The Trials of the Oldest Colony* (New Haven, Conn.: Yale University Press, 1997), 249.

12. Herbert Marcuse, quoted in Solís Jordan, *Public School Reform in Puerto Rico* (Westport, Conn.: Greenwood, 1994), 89.

Chapter Twenty-One

Elizam Escobar

Born on May 24, 1948, Elizam Escobar spent the first ten years of his life in Ponce, Puerto Rico, and the following seven years in Lomas Verdes, Bayamón, Puerto Rico. Escobar records that his first "initiation into politics was as a direct 'observer' in 1950, as a young child, during the Nationalist insurrection, where his uncle, Arturo Ortiz was killed."[1] Both his grand-uncle, Eliphaz Escobar, and uncle Ortiz were members of the Nationalist Party of Puerto Rico and were politically active in the anticolonial struggle.

In 1965, Escobar entered the University of Puerto Rico. Participating in the Federation of Proindependence University Students, he became involved in the Puerto Rican decolonization struggle. Under Juan Antonio Corretjer and George Fromm, Escobar studied Marxist revolutionary thought and then joined the Puerto Rican Socialist League.[2]

After arriving in New York City in 1970, he finished his philosophy and art studies at New York City College, where he worked as an art teacher in addition to teaching in various community programs. Participating in several socialist and communist organizations and active in the independence movement and the campaign to release Nationalist prisoners, Escobar soon joined the Puerto Rican clandestine movement.[3] Elizam Escobar describes the clandestine movement as "a symbolic force capable of invigorating the psychological aspect and self-esteem of a people or a struggle. . . . [It provided] the right to our self-determination and independence, to self-defense and to respond to the repression that existed in those years."[4]

On April 4, 1980, Escobar was arrested with ten other Nationalists in Evanston, Illinois. The eleven Puerto Ricans were tried in state and federal courts. Under state charges, Escobar was sentenced to eight years for seditious conspiracy to commit armed robbery and possession of an unregistered gun. These charges were also filed in the federal case, where the indictment alleged that the defendants "willfully and knowingly combined, conspired, confederated and agreed together with each other to oppose by force the authority of the government of the United States."[5] Defendants were also accused of being members of the FALN (*Fuerzas Armadas de Libera-*

ción Nacionál), an underground organization that engaged in armed actions against military, economic, and government sites, targeting largely in Chicago and New York symbols of U.S. domination over Puerto Rico. Twenty-eight of the bombings occurred in the Northern District of Illinois (none of which resulted in death or injury).

The *independentistas* argued that they were challenging a foreign, colonial power, that the United States had no jurisdiction and could not try them as "Americans," and thus the seditious conspiracy charges were invalid. Escobar and his codefendants declared themselves "combatants in an anti-colonial war of liberation against the U.S. government, which illegally occupies [Puerto Rico]."[6] They then invoked their prisoner of war (POW) status and international law: UN General Assembly Resolutions and the 1949 Geneva Conventions and 1977 protocols, which prohibit a colonial government from criminalizing anticolonial acts.[7] The U.S. government refused to acknowledge the *independentistas* as POWs. Although none of the *independentistas* had ever been convicted of a murder or other felony, because of their political beliefs, they were given unusually lengthy sentences and housed and isolated in high-security, special control units.

Escobar was sentenced to sixty-eight years in federal prison. None of the *independentistas* were convicted of any actual bombings, but they were found guilty for their participation in the FALN. After sentencing, Escobar was placed in the Federal Correctional Institution at El Reno, Oklahoma. In federal prison with restricted visitations, he could be visited by his mother only once a year; he was not allowed to be at the bedside of his dying father or attend his funeral in 1991.

On September 10, 1999, President Bill Clinton granted executive clemency to eleven of the *independentistas*, permitting Escobar to return home to Puerto Rico. The clemency, which did not free all *independentistas*,[8] set conditions that limit the political activities and associations of those released.

REFERENCES

"Elizam Escobar." In *Can't Jail the Spirit: Political Prisoners in the U.S., A Collection of Biographies*. 4th ed. Chicago: Committee to End the Marion Lockdown, 1998.

Escobar, Elizam. "The Heuristic Power of Art." In *The Subversive Imagination: Artists, Society, and Responsibility*, edited by Carol Becker. New York: Routledge, 1994.

"Faltan6 Freedom Campaign." *Prolibertad*, www.prolibertad.org/Faltan6.htm (23 June 2002).

"Puerto Rican Political Prisoners and Prisoners of War Released: ¡Que Viva Puerto Rico Libre!" www.prisonactivist.org/quesalgan/turningtide.html (9 July 2002), originally published in *Turning the Tide: Journal of Anti-Racist Action, Research & Education* 2, no. 3 (Fall 1999).

Susler, Jan. "Puerto Rican Political Prisoners." *Radical Philosophy Review* vol. 3, no. 1 (January 2000).

Torres, Andres, and Jose E. Velzquez, eds. *The Puerto Rican Movement: Voices from the Diaspora*. Philadelphia: Temple University Press, 1998.

NOTES

1. Carlos Gil, "An Interview with Elizam Escobar," in *The Puerto Rican Movement: Voices from the Diaspora*, ed. Andres Torres and Jose E. Velazquez (Philadelphia: Temple University Press, 1998), 232.

2. "Elizam Escobar," *Can't Jail the Spirit: Political Prisoners in the U.S.A., A Collection of Biographies*, 4th ed. (Chicago: Committee to End the Marion Lockdown, 1998), 122.

3. "An Interview with Elizam Escobar," 235. The Nationalist prisoners consisted of Lolita Lebron, Rafael Cancel Miranda, Andres Figueroa Cordero, Irvin Flores, and Oscar Collazo. All five Puerto Rican nationalists were granted executive clemency by President Jimmy Carter in 1978, and were released after over twenty-five years in prison for firing weapons in the House of Representatives and wounding several congressmen.

4. "An Interview with Elizam Escobar," 235.

5. Quoted in Jan Susler, "Puerto Rican Political Prisoners," *Radical Philosophy Review* 3, no. 1 (January 2000): 29.

6. "An Interview with Elizam Escobar," 237.

7. Jan Susler, "Today's Puerto Rican Political Prisoners/Prisoners of War," in *The Puerto Rican Movement: Voices from the Diaspora*, 147. Cites General Assembly Resolution 1514 (XV), December 12, 1960; General Assembly Resolution 2621 (XXV), October 12, 1970; General Assembly Resolution 3103, December 12, 1973; Geneva Conventions of 1949; and the Additional Protocols (I and II), June 8, 1977.

8. Among those still incarcerated are Juan Segarra Palmer (who received a shortened sentence through clemency); Antonio Camacho Negrón (who was returned to prison for refusing to obey parole restrictions); Oscar López-Rivera (serving a fifty-five-year sentence, he rejected Clinton's offer to spend another ten years prior to release); Carlos Alberto Torres (serving a seventy-eight-year sentence); José Solís Jordan (serving a fifty-one-month sentence); and Haydee Beltrán (sentenced to life in prison). See "Puerto Rican Political Prisoners and Prisoners of War Released: ¡Que Viva Puerto Rico Libre!" www.prisonactivist.org/quesalgan/turningtide.html (9 July 2002), originally published in *Turning the Tide: Journal of Anti-Racist Action, Research & Education* 12, no. 3 (Fall 1999); and "*Faltan6* Freedom Campaign," *Prolibertad*, www.prolibertad.org/Faltan6.htm (23 June 2002).

Art of Liberation: A Vision of Freedom

The *political* is found in the least likely of places, covered by multiple layers of ideological counterfeiting and acculturation. Our daily lives, our dreams, love, death, and even our bodies are all spheres of "invisible" yet intense political and human dramas that take place behind the "visible" political struggle. This inner struggle is, above all, more painful and more real. For it is from *inside* that we must decide our real needs, both material and spiritual. Art of liberation springs from this perspective, recognizing the power of the imagination's struggle. Throughout history, the imagination's struggle against prohibitions based on fear and ignorance has been one of the leading political processes that pushes forward the liberation of the human spirit by rescuing and creating new territories of freedom.

I have been active in the struggle for Puerto Rican national liberation since the 1960s. From the socialist-Marxist perspective, I have simultaneously engaged in political-direct[1] as well as art/cultural work in support of this struggle, but not always with the same intensity or understanding.

In my "first period" I separated "personal" work—my paintings—from more "public" works—political illustrations, propaganda, caricatures, etc. Both activities were done under the dictates of my ideological assumptions. Nevertheless, there were always elements that would completely or relatively escape the dictates of my "ideology." Thematic elements drawn from my particular experiences exposed me to conflicts between what was supposed to be and what actually was, creating tensions that were contained by generic images (political monsters, doubts repressed by ideology, etc.). Formal elements, devalued by socialist realism and other "realist" aesthetics also escaped.

The "second period" began when I moved from Puerto Rico to New York, and was defined by an almost total exclusion of painting due to the demands of my job (schoolteacher), my political-direct work, and my mixed feelings about art. I was under the influence of a politics of "art is useless unless it is for direct propaganda purposes." My work was limited almost exclusively to political caricatures for the party publications. (Not a bad thing.)

In my "third period," I made an almost about-face toward "personal" painting, but this time working as a "professional" artist for different cultural institutions, where I combined teaching art with learning other art techniques. At that point, I was seriously dealing with the fundamental question of the relative autonomy and the specificity of the theory and praxis of art (i.e., that art has its own "rules" within a space that is its own but always in relation to all other levels or spheres of "reality," so to speak), not out of an academic or abstract drive but as a result of an accumulation of experiences. Both my political and artistic commitment were more intense than ever.

In 1980, I was arrested, together with ten other Puerto Rican *independentistas*,

Desvelo, 1990, acrioleo on canvas, 72 × 43 inches.

and accused of seditious conspiracy and participation in the Puerto Rican armed clandestine movement for national liberation. Since then I have been in prison. Here, my "fourth period" is taking place, and it is from the perspective of these experiences that I consider the visionary role of the artist.

THE STRUCTURES OF SIMULATION

We live in societies divided into social classes, where there is no true consensus, only the fictitious and spurious consensus determined by the ruling classes. Electoral

Extended Vacation, 1994, acrioleo and gesso on collage
photocopies on wood, 16 × 17.75 inches.

processes are national epics manipulated in the name of the people to legitimize social control and coercion. To resolve these contradictions we must assume the class struggle in all its diverse forms and confront the questions of Power. Only then will the immense majority of excluded, oppressed, and exploited obtain the real power. But we cannot wait for the day when the majority will rule in order to bring forward the structures needed for building a free, just, egalitarian, and non-classist society. We must build within the ruins and the hostilities of present conditions by creating transitional alternatives now. We must build socioeconomic, political, and cultural structures that are controlled by those struggling for change and the communities they serve. These structures, "schools" for discussing all these problems, will put into practice the notion that only by confronting the reality of subjection can we begin to be free to create an art of liberation that frees people from the illusions perpetrated by dominant culture.

The contemporary State creates structures of simulation. These are indispensable both to cover the real nature of the system and to show tolerance and acceptance for dissidents. Furthermore, they not only create their own structures, but they obligate us to create our own.

For example, the ruling classes create the simulation of cultural democracy (the illusion of real political power, equal opportunity and the freedom of difference in order to make others believe that they have a real participation in the cultural space) through the mass culture and the media. They need "false enemies" to wage relatively inoffensive and limited "cultural wars" that end up strengthening the social body's health.[2] One example is what happened to the spontaneous street graffiti expression: from symbolic exchange it became another commodity with status exchange value. In Puerto Rico under colonialism, popular art is institutionalized and becomes a folkloric domestication of the people's unconscious. Some of the Left's culture of resistance has been depoliticized by obligating artists to make false choices between a sort of one-dimensional domesticated "nationalist art" and mass culture. This way, artists either turn their "criticism" against an abstract enemy or they wear themselves out by contributing an "original" aesthetic to the status quo (but always in the name of "Puerto Ricanness") because they fear the worst evil, that of U.S. statehood—to the benefit of the colonial bourgeois lackeys. Part of the Puerto Rican independence movement reproduces itself as a simulation model through this "cultural nationalism." At the same time, artists are domesticated by continuous government subsidies, status, fame, wealth, and by aspiring to national titles, while those who persist to the contrary, whose politics are to unveil the whole system of simulation are censored even by some orthodox Left publications who want to reduce the debates to their own political good, that is, they won't allow dissent within the dissent. Paradoxically, art (as the power of imagination), the only "true" simulation, is the one that can lead us to the *understanding* (not necessarily to the resolution) of that other "false" simulation.

THE CULTURE OF FEAR

But in order to liberate art from the nets of political power, we, the artists, must first liberate ourselves from the nets of the *culture of fear*, and the inferiority/superiority complex we have in our dealings at the political-direct level. If art is to become a force for social change it must take its strength from the *politics of art*, art's own way of affecting both the world and the political-direct. It must take strength from that specific manner in which our praxis expresses the aspirations of the people, the political collective unconscious, the contradictions, etc., through a symbolic language. But the *politics of art* will happen only if the power of the imagination is able to create a symbolic relationship between those who participate, the artwork, and the concrete world; and then always understanding the work of art's sovereignty (or relative autonomy) in relation to concrete reality.

What is important is not the didactic pretension that we possess the solutions, but the idiosyncratic ways in which works of art can bring out the real aspects of the human condition in particular and specific contexts or experiences. Art is, from this perspective, an encounter where we have the possibility for a symbolic, political, and real exchange. Since our forms are also used to deliberately appeal to people for political-direct goals, it is logical that at some point these strategies become dominant and in conflict with the internal problems (the how) of art. If we can understand how the political affects and shapes everything else, and the difference between the specific practices of art and the practices of the political-direct, then the artist would be clearer on how to decide his/her strategies, sources, themes, aesthetics, etc. When it comes to the theory and praxis of art, the *political* is beyond any "political (direct) issues."

Most U.S. "Political Art," as I have come to understand it, wants to present political-direct issues through images, in a clear and communicative form, irrespective of the medium, the style, or the aesthetic selection. It presupposes that one can predict the kind of political effect a work of art is going to have. Thus the important thing is the message. This emphasis on the message is akin to Marshall McLuhan's naive optimism "the medium is the message," and finds its extreme in the inversion of McLuhan's dictum: "The message is the message." Both are founded in the arbitrariness of the sign, which artificially separates and reunites everything in terms of a signifier (in this case, the medium) and a signified (here, the message). The political and the symbolic are de-politicized by the imposition of a code that comes directly from ideology, since as Jean Baudrillard argues, "every attempt to surpass the political economy of the sign that takes its support from one of its constituent elements is condemned to reproduce its arbitrary character."[3]

In this way the participants are excluded from creating meanings other than those already transmitted by the message since once the signal is sent either you accept it or reject it. There is no need to search for more. In this respect the art of the message shares common ground with the *formal theory of communication*[4] which goes like this: transmitter (encoder)—message—receiver (decoder). One speaks, the other doesn't. The message is assumed to contain information that is legible and univocal, based on a pre-established and rationalized code composed of signs. Two terms are artificially reunited by an objectified content called message. The formula has a formal coherence that assures it as the only *possible* schema for communication, since a code names everything in terms of itself and anything else that is not "designed" or "adapted" to the agency of the code cannot be utilized since it won't work in this schema. The problem then is that this structure denies the ambivalence of exchange; the reciprocity or antagonism between two distinct interlocutors. As soon as ambivalence shows up the structure collapses, since there is no code for ambivalence, and without code no more encoder, no more decoder.

I am not saying that U.S. "Political Art" is equal to this over-obsession with "communication," but that it is constricted to the code if its intentions are mainly to present a message. Thus, anything that is not in the sign form is ambivalent and it is from ambivalence (i.e. the impossibility of distinguishing respective separated terms and to positivize them as such) that any symbolic exchange (allusions through images, discourse, objects, etc.) can emerge. On the other hand, this impasse is, of course, disturbing, since we cannot absolutely do away with the signific code.

The ironic dilemma is that we have to make use of this code though we realize that it reduces and abstracts the irreducible experience of that which we call "liberation" (or "freedom," "desires," "needs," etc.). It is the all-too-familiar situation where words (like "liberation," "political," "freedom of expression") take command over the real concrete experience and are used to legitimize and justify a practice or a state of things. There is a brutal difference between "freedom" as exchange-sign-value or slogan of ideologies and abstractions, and the real freedom of experience— one that is as necessary as it is terrible. Even under extreme repression, individual freedom is unavoidable as we must keep on exercising our decisions and responsibilities. Here again art comes to the rescue, because it has the inventive power and wit to deride, deceive, and betray censorship as well as self-censorship.

But how one is going to affect others is another matter, since it is almost impossible to know how an artwork will be taken. The effect is always diverse, contingent, and unpredictable. Whether this ambivalence is richer than a clear-cut message is for others to decide. But the important thing is that an artist must reestablish an element of confidence through his/her intentions of being as honest as possible and as consistent in his/her views as convictions allow. In this sense a "solitary voice" is as strong as a collective one.

Works of art are provocations, but in order for an artist to be provocative she/he first has to have true vocation, that is, true dedication to her/his art and to those who have been reduced to invisibility. It is from there that art cannot only obtain relevancy but also can transcend its immediate references.

The political aspect of art is to confront all of reality, without ideological permissions and through its own means. In order to discover our real needs we must be incredulous about what we are told and why we believe it. We must re-find the internal relationship between human desires and aspirations and human necessity, but in a new way. We must put into question any philosophical system or form of knowledge that claims to be the only and absolute truth. To that Marxist thought of freedom ("freedom is the knowledge [or recognition] of necessity") I add a concept of art: *art is the necessity of freedom.*

ART, PRISON, AND LIBERATION

Twenty-five centuries ago, when Socrates was incarcerated, he wrote his first and only poems.[5] Ever after, the experience has been repeated. In prison, many non-artists, men and women of action and thought who never saw art or poetry as important or "useful," have engaged in some sort of creative expression. Art has come through prison. But also through art, prison has come to the outside; many poets, writers, and painters have had some essential experiences in prisons or other places of internment, and many others have become writers or artists in prison. Certainly, art usually comes to the rescue of those who have to confront these conditions at one point in their lives, people who otherwise may never have done much or anything for the defense or estimation of art. Art demands certain introspection, solitude, and abandonment; and certain confrontation with the self and death; that is, themes that are usually repugnant to "revolutionaries" and "practical" people unless it has to do with heroism or the glorification of a personality. Therefore, it is no surprise that adversity and forced solitude are able to liberate that "obscure" region of the imagination.

In prison life, there is—consciously or not—a constant and extreme interaction between the pleasure principle and the reality principle (for example, the realization that in politics as in love one must learn how to wait), much sublimination/desublimation, daydreaming, hope/cynicism, disillusionment, anger, unreality, skepticism, repression, censorship, and hypocrisy. All this shapes one's life and art. We are penetrated as much by the means of communication as people on the outside; sometimes more, because of our encloistering and lack of direct outside contact. This combination of suppression and diversion keeps prisoners as apathetic consumers and participants in a vicious circle. The human condition, in a state of extreme control and intensity, distorted to the most complete absurdity: either life is only a simulacrum (the art of the living death) or only through simulation are you able to survive.

There are exceptions, but the final balance is dehumanization, a waste of human lives. Cheap slave labor, and the continuation of criminal activity through other means and under different circumstances, are what characterize the "rehabilitation shop" of a society that is itself in need of radical transformation. The decadence of this society is displayed in its prisons through a spectacle of extreme collective madness. To "liberate" this experience through art is a responsibility to others.

Prison has reconfirmed to me the great importance of art in our lives because the deep reflection and the intense involvement that art requires help us to better understand the real necessities and the true meanings of freedom, for the individual as well as the collective. And to fight for that truth, to defend that truth, art also becomes a weapon. A weapon not only because one can create meaning for one's own existence or inspire others to continue the struggle. But simply because one can understand better the intrinsic relationship between the visions coming through the praxis of art and those unveiled aspects of the too-much-rationalized and arbitrary aspects of our ideologies, as well as our daily mechanical rituals and common nonsense. My own experience of repression expressed through art can relate to other general human experiences of repression and exclusion better than, let's say, if I start to think through my "ideological eyes." Art must spring from real life.

If art becomes theoretical discourse, *that* is also a necessary weapon. To theorize art directly from the praxis of art is a necessity in opposition to those who would like to keep art as inoffensive "aesthetics" or as mere echoes of the political-direct. And since some people would like to reduce art to a slogan of metaphysical propor-

tions, one must always make the distinction between the art of propaganda, publicity, or design; and art as an act of liberation. The fundamental distinction is that
an art of liberation can neither be a model nor a specific aesthetic or style. It is a
concept and an attitude with no specific formulations, only that it must be open to
any strategy that can help liberate art (and through art, people) from the dictatorship of the logic, politics, and metaphysics of the sign.

ART OF LIBERATION

To me, art is the best argument for talking about freedom and about necessity when
one does not separate the body from the spirit. In my experience I have learned
more about politics through art than through politics. And by *art* here I mean all
the arts and their discourses—and all the ways in which the symbolic and the power
of the imagination influence the political-direct and help us to better understand
social reality.

I do not express this with blind enthusiasm. I have come to suspect all those who
depend on and are moved only by enthusiasm. So when I say that I believe in the
fundamental role of art in life—to provoke, to provide a critical outlook, a paradoxical reassurance of our common humanity—I am not implying that this is a universal, shared judgment. Nor am I saying that art should conquer the world. It is
enough for me to be conquered by art and to be able to let it go wherever it must
go. So my bet on art is my bet on life. It is my bet on the possibility of linkage
between the political struggle and the struggle for survival in a hostile environment.
I am not referring merely to prison per se, but to all those environments created by
the prison of social systems, in the name of the people and freedom, as well as by the
prison of "communication." Political awareness makes us confront all that reality. It
makes us both assault the status quo and critically inspect ourselves.

Art is an extension of life, and if you have artists whose politics are insubornable,
committed, and uncompromised, then they become as strengthening and inspiring
to others, artists and non-artists, as art is to life.

NOTES

Originally published in *Reimaging America: The Arts of Social Change*, ed. Mark O'Brien and
Craig Little (Philadelphia: New Society Publishers, 1990), 86–94.

1. The *political* is ubiquitous in today's world, but its more pure form is when you engage
directly in the struggles for change and power. . . .

2. See Roger Bartra, *Las redes imaginarias del poder político* (Mexico: Ediciones Era, 1981).

3. Jean Baudrillard, *For a Critique of the Political Economy of the Sign* (St. Louis: Telos,
1981), 160.

Editor's note: Marshall McLuhan, "The Medium Is the Message," in *Media Studies*, ed. Paul
Marris et al. (Edinburgh: Edinburgh University, 1996), 30–34.

4. Based on Roman Jacobsen and criticized by Baudrillard.

5. *Editor's note:* Socrates' *The Crito* contains his prison writings.

Chapter Twenty-Two

Standing Deer

Standing Deer (Robert Hugh Wilson) was born in Oklahoma in 1923. The son of an Oneida mother from Wisconsin and Choctaw father from southwestern Oklahoma, he learned to speak both Choctaw and Oneida, the languages spoken by his paternal and maternal grandmothers, respectively, before he spoke English. However, within the first years of his life, his parents forbade him and his two siblings from speaking any of their native languages and discussing their grandparents or the clans that were their heritage. By the age of six, Standing Deer, a light-skinned young boy living in a white neighborhood, attending white schools in Oklahoma City, learned to disassociate himself and his two siblings from other Native Americans around him and to think of himself as "white" and "American," not "Indian." When any of the students in his school called him an Indian, he fought them—following his father's instructions—until they agreed to call him American. Yet, he maintained, he did not completely internalize the shame and self-hatred of his parents. Between the ages of twelve and seventeen he ran away from home several times, often to live with his father's and his mother's families and other Native Americans. But he no longer remembered the Oneida and Choctaw languages and customs of his very early childhood and so remained an outsider.

As a young adult, Wilson was arrested several times for a number of minor offenses and received his first prison sentence in 1963: ten years for interstate trafficking of counterfeit money. After his release in 1970, he was sentenced to another twenty-five years in the state penitentiary in Oklahoma for armed robbery and larceny involving the theft of an automobile. During that sentence, he spent a year in solitary confinement for his involvement in a prison riot on July 27, 1973.[1] He escaped on April 29, 1975, when he hijacked a bus transporting him to another prison and remained underground until police apprehended him in Chicago on April 6, 1976. At that time, Robert Wilson was a notorious and skilled bank robber, and his prison records reflect that prison and state officials considered him dangerous (he routinely assaulted officers who tried to apprehend him).[2]

After his arrest in Chicago, Wilson faced indictments on seven felony charges in the western and midwestern United States, including a June 3, 1975, bank robbery in Oklahoma City that resulted in a near-fatal shooting of a police officer. Wilson faced up to seven life sentences for interstate transportation of stolen jewelry and bank robberies. Along with an accomplice, Steven Berry, he was sent to the United States Penitentiary super-maximum-security prison in Marion, Illinois. While in the Marion prison, Wilson suffered from degenerative disc disease, high blood pressure, and diabetes. In March of 1978, he was in the prison hospital under treatment for his chronic back problems when, according to Wilson, Dr. J. Plank at the hospital approached him to help the chief correctional officer, Max Carey, monitor Leonard Peltier. A Lakota and member of the American Indian Movement (AIM) also imprisoned at Marion, Peltier was then and remains now one of the most prominent political prisoners in the United States.[3] Wilson refused, and Plank returned him to solitary confinement. On May 5, the increasing degeneration of his back culminated in Wilson falling in the shower and being unable to force himself upright. Within days, Carey visited him, offering medical treatment in exchange for his cooperation against Peltier.

On May 17, 1978, according to Wilson's account, Carey entered his hospital room with a well-dressed white man who claimed that he could obtain medical treatment and parole for Wilson if he would help "neutralize" Leonard Peltier.[4] Further discussion elicited the intent behind Peltier's "neutralization": Wilson would befriend Peltier through the prison's Native American cultural group, convince Peltier that he had the means and materials to help him escape from prison, then prison officials would kill Leonard Peltier during the escape attempt. Wilson would be provided with zip guns, wire cutters, a hacksaw, materials to make dummies, and any other components needed to prove that he could help Peltier escape.

That day proved to be a turning point in the life of Robert Hugh Wilson, who would soon reclaim the name of "Standing Deer" that his grandfather gave him during childhood. Wilson agreed to his role in the plan. Oklahoma authorities dropped the warrants that they held on him and on June 1, they cancelled the pending trial. After his discharge from the hospital, Wilson had his first chance to meet Leonard Peltier, whom he had not previously supported, on July 4, 1978.

In *Coming Home*, an excerpt from a public message that he wrote in 1994, Standing Deer relayed the significance of meeting Peltier: "[That] transformed my life, brought me home to my People, and put me dead in the middle of the political struggle for the survival of my People."[5] He describes the events of that and the following day as a spiritual and political cleansing and transformation. As he approached Peltier that day, he could sense the love, respect, and commitment Peltier radiated and recognized his scars as piercings and flesh offerings from the Sun Dance (a sacred Lakota ceremony outlawed by U.S. institutions such as the Bureau of Indian Affairs and the Bureau of Prisons). Wilson confessed his role in the government plot to assassinate Peltier. The next day, Leonard Peltier and another Lakota man escorted Wilson to an empty room in Marion's law library. The other man produced a rope and bandanna that he used to bind and blindfold Peltier in a chair before he left the room. According to Wilson, Peltier instructed him to barricade the door with a bookcase, then verbally directed him to a fifteen-inch knife hidden in a bookcase. Wilson recalls that as he picked up the knife:

> The knife turned into a snake in my hand, and as I stared paralyzed it became the face of the blond, blue-eyed stranger [the unnamed agent who accompanied Carey] who wanted Leonard dead. As I looked into the blue eyes, I saw the face of the man who murdered my grandfathers and grandmothers. I was terrified, but when I looked at Leonard he was smiling, and I could hear his smile and it sounded like a gentle waterfall. I could no longer see through my tears, but I heard the waterfall say, "Do whatever it is you have to do, my Brother." And I fell to the floor and cut his bonds and removed his blindfold and he had tears in his eyes that looked like a rainbow.[6]

The events in the library marked an epiphany for Wilson. He pretended to continue with the assassination plans and joined the prison's Native American culture group. His oratorical and organizational skills quickly led to his promotion to chairperson and spokesperson for the group. Standing Deer became an active and outspoken advocate for prisoners and political prisoners, in particular for their religious, physical, medical, and intellectual and educational rights. Seeking Native American religious rights, medical access for chronically ill patients, and an end to forced labor for elderly inmates, Standing Deer continuously sent letters of protest to prison officials, and supporters and families of prisoners, to challenge what he termed "the dungeon" of "America's gulag."[7] Released in September 2001, he lived with his wife in Houston, Texas. Standing Deer was murdered in his home on January 21, 2003.

REFERENCES

Churchill, Ward, and Jim Vander Wall. *Agents of Repression: The FBI's Secret Wars against the Black Panther Party and the American Indian Movement.* Rev. ed. Boston: South End Press, 2002.

Matthiessen, Peter. *In the Spirit of Crazy Horse.* New York: Viking, 1980.

Standing Deer, Robert. "Coming Home." 19 November 1994. www.sonic.net/~doretk/archivearch...erican/coming%20homestanding%20deer.html (18 March 2002).

———. "A Message to the People from Standing Deer." *IA Center.* 18 June 2000. www.iacenter.org/stdeer1.html (4 April 2002).

———. "Prisons, Poverty and Power." In *Cages of Steel: The Politics of Imprisonment in the United States,* edited by Ward Churchill and Jim Vander Wall. Washington, D.C.: Maisonneuve Press, 1992.

———. "Standing Deer: A Message to the People." 18 September 1999. www.angelfire.com/biz/backtotheblanket/standingd.html (18 March 2002).

———. "Step into the Nightmare." *Native Web,* 28 September 1998. www.nativeweb.org/pages/legal/sdnightmare.html (17 March 2002).

———. "Take Heed—Trouble Coming." *Huntsville Item,* 6 January 1998.

———. "What Is in Your Heart They Cannot Take." February 1998. www.sonic.net/~doretk/ Issues/98-04%20%20spr/whatsin.htmlHyperlink

NOTES

Research and draft for this biography were provided by Yvette Koch.

1. The riot caused $21 million in damages and resulted in the prison burning down. For a detailed list of Standing Deer's prison record, see Peter Matthiessen, *In the Spirit of Crazy Horse* (New York: Viking, 1980), 380–88 and 500–3.

2. "Medical Record of Federal Prisoner in Transit: Wilson, Robert H., No. 01499-164, from MCC, Chicago, IL to USP, Marion, IL, 29 October 1976," quoted in Ward Churchill and Jim Vander Wall, *Agents of Repression: The FBI's Secret Wars against the Black Panther Party and the American Indian Movement* (Boston: South End Press, 1990), 354.

3. See the Leonard Peltier biography in this anthology.

4. *Agents of Repression*; *In the Spirit of Crazy Horse*; and Standing Deer, "Coming Home," 19 September 1994. www.sonic.net/~doretk/archivearch...erican/coming%20homestanding %20deer.html (18 March 2002).

5. "Coming Home."

6. "Coming Home."

7. For more writings by Standing Deer, see "What Is in Your Heart They Cannot Take," *Sonic Net*. February 1998. www.sonic.net/~doretk/Issues/98-04%20%20spr/whatsin.html (16 March 2002); *Can't Jail the Spirit: Political Prisoners in the U.S.*, 3rd ed. (Chicago: Committee to End the Marion Lockdown, 1997); and "Prisons, Poverty and Power" in *Cages of Steel: The Politics of Imprisonment in the United States*, ed. Ward Churchill and Jim Vander Wall (Washington, D.C.: Maisonneuve Press, 1992).

Violence and the State (*Abridged*)

The violence thing is what really has my head spinning. If violence is "the imposing of a set of conditions on another party without regard to the other's interest, or without sensitivity to their situation" then by that definition, I have been the victim of state-imposed violence all my life and not just the twelve years I have recently spent in prison. . . . In a way, I feel like my education is just beginning because so sheltered have I been that these ideas on violence have not been available in any writings I've been able to get past the censors in these maximum security pigsties I've lived in all these years. Let me say again I haven't read Ward Churchill's paper "Pacifism as Pathology" and I would very much like to.[1] I'm not opposed to violence, but the support for violent action of any kind has always been absent in positions I have read while condemnation has been overwhelming.

I live in this prison where all my information comes out of the mind-destroying, capitalist-promoting, thought-stealing TV, and the brain-washing, propaganda-spewing daily papers. If you could sample the *Tulsa World*, *The Daily Oklahoman* and the *McAlester News-Capital* for thirty days, plus be bombarded with the constant blathering about how [President Ronald] Reagan is a subversive who loves niggers and has packed the U.S. Supreme Court with Communists. So far to the right are these people that it is exhausting just keeping myself reasonably sure what my own beliefs are. I'm enclosing a couple of letters to the editor columns to accent what I mean about the political climate in Oklahoma (as if you didn't know). The guards are another 360° to the right of these newspaper views.

I read with fascination turning to amazement the three paragraphs Mike Ryan devoted to Native Nations on page sixteen.[2] I, of course, agree that Native Nations exist, that the Dine Nation has a large land base rich in natural resources, that the Dine are poverty-stricken, ill-educated, without jobs, have an outrageously high infant mortality rate, and all the rest of it. And, of course, I agree that this situation must be changed, but I had no idea that American Indians are in a position to cripple North American imperialism. I would have thought that if the Native Nations appeared to be in a position to deprive the United States of crucial resources, the Indians would be stepped on like so many bugs. Neither would they let us do it through their courts since their laws are carefully designed to prevent just such a happening from ever taking place. If there was a violent movement formed, it would consist of about twenty percent FBI agents and undercover Indians; there would probably be no more than five percent of the total Indian population involved in the liberation struggle, and they would be branded the lunatic fringe. Many of our own people would turn against us after Jane Pauley and Bryant Gumble explained to them that we were Communists or worse. Since we are so easily identified by our skin color and appearance, they would, if they felt it necessary, bring into play the ultimate discourager as the prosecutor at [Nelson] Mandela's trial said:

"If any threat to white rule were to arise, the shooting of 5,000 natives by machine gun would provide quiet for a long time." And it would. Mostly because that would be just about the number of us involved. Then it would not be necessary for Euroamerican radicals to implement their position as to what they would do to support us, for we would no longer exist.

Just because American Indians can be fit into [Joseph] Stalin's conceptual scheme defining a nation doesn't make us any more unified than the nation of the dominant culture that oppresses us.[3] But the State's ability to command discipline and obedience from the worker ants who would be called upon to dispense their violence is so total, and the weapons of destruction available to them are so awesome that unity becomes a moot point for the State. But unity is indispensable to our side, and we have none.

Being around the Indian brothers here in Oklahoma has been an experience. Outside of Ben Carnes and Harry Hall I haven't met a single one who knows anything about the struggle in general or [the American Indian Movement] AIM in particular. Most of the brothers are racists hating whites and Blacks almost equally with a slight edge going to whites. Many of them believe AIM has caused a lot of trouble for our people. If they have any religion it is Christian. Many believe long hair is worn by trouble-makers. They are nearly all anxious to learn what I have to teach them about our struggle, but it is hard because they have been taught to assimilate. Getting along with the white folks is their first priority, and they are timid about expressing their new-found political consciousness to other brothers for fear of ridicule. The "Indian Leaders" in Oklahoma think folks like me and Ben and Harry should be put to death for stirring up "trouble" in the minds of the other Indians. I'm not speaking hyperbole. David Hilligoss knows a lot about how the "Indian Leaders" think about us down here at the prison because Dave has tried in vain to organize some sort of support for us among the Oklahoma Indians.[4] There is none. I can't even get Indians as verifiers on my application for exemption I want to file to keep my hair from being forcibly cut.

I sit in my cage and listen to my yuppie/buppie news programs on TV and the country seems to be rushing to the right. Then I read my *Guardian* and *Worker's World* and find a world frothing at the mouth for socialist change. I wake up each day in an intellectual vacuum, and I have no way to test reality. I still have sense enough to know the Republicrats offer no solutions with their big, serious presidential election. But isolated as I am, I can't decide if the talk about violence is serious or if it is theoretical and will remain forever so. I know you can't organize a violent response to oppression unless you do it in such tiny cliques that it would almost surely be ineffectual. Because of the secrecy required (in this day and time when children are trained to turn their mothers over to the police for smoking marijuana, and where block wardens are being organized in some big cities to act as "Snitch Central," where members of the community can report the suspicious activities of their neighbors) they would have to remain too remote to develop the "from the masses, to the masses" relationship out of which could germinate the revolutionary politics necessary for support of violent action. I feel like I'm missing something. I love the idea of violent response to State violence, but I am so afraid that the funerals would mostly be ours and I can't see what it would achieve. I want to read Churchill's paper. Maybe then it will make more sense to me.

If it seems I don't know what I'm talking about it's because I don't. I feel like I'm in a dark room looking at things going on in a room with bright lights but I'm separated from the light-filled room by a sheet partition. I can see all of you as shadows, but can't quite make out what is happening in your room. I wonder if Ward and Mike are looking through their own sheet out onto the sun-filled world and seeing a little more definition than I. I have been around people—when I was in Marion Prison—who knew so much about radical politics that it was easy to get so caught up in the redolence of revolution that I'd forget that in real life on the outside, revolutionaries were actually quite scarce.

People who think as we do are rare and I don't like it. If only there were more of us. You've heard about the National Geographic Society study that was done by the Gallup organization in May? Forty-five percent of Americans are unaware that apartheid is the government policy in South Africa; forty-seven percent are unaware that Israel is the site of conflict between Arabs and Jews; fifty percent are unaware that Nicaragua is the country in which the Sandinistas and contras are in conflict. One American in seven cannot identify the U.S. on a map of the world!?! My next door neighbor thinks Boston, Massachusetts, is in Texas (somewhere down around Houston). I'm not kidding.

Before ya'll think I mean to be the purveyor of doom and gloom, please remember that the thought of violence makes me happier than two dead dogs lying in the sun, but I just believe "the time is not right." Conditions are *more* than bad enough, but I would like to sit in on a strategy and tactics session and hear just how such a response can be organized and implemented without the police neutralizing our group before we get to first base. I know most of the students and intellectuals who took Huey P. Newton's advice on attacking the enemy in their communities are either dead, in jail or have become militant Republicans. They will let you talk about violence so long as your propaganda and agitation appear to be abstract and idealistic. They will even let you print intellectual discourses about it. It's just doing it that they won't let you do.

NOTES

Originally published in *Radical Therapy* 13, nos. 3 & 4 (1988).

1. *Editor's note:* Ward Churchill's essay is fully titled "Pacifism as Pathology: Notes on an American Pseudopraxis." It appears in the larger volume by Ward Churchill and Mike Ryan, *Pacifism as Pathology: Reflections on the Role of Armed Struggle in North America* (Winnipeg: Arbeiter Ring, 1998). Churchill first wrote the essay in 1986, arguing for the necessity of violence in strategic revolutionary organizing. While pacifism promises that nonviolence can

transcend the racism and imperialism of state power through purity of purpose, argues Churchill, the universal application of pacifism is counterrevolutionary and defends or reinforces the power apparatuses that it opposes. According to the authors, violence is a necessity for state transformation just as it is a daily reality in the lives of Third World and U.S. minorities who experience the brunt of racialized state violence.

2. *Editor's note:* The author refers to the second of two essays that comprise *Pacifism as Pathology.*

3. *Editor's note:* According to Joseph Stalin, "a nation is a historically constituted, stable community of people formed on the basis of a common language, territory, economic life and psychological make-up manifested in a common culture." Josef Stalin, *Marxism and the National and Colonial Question* (New York: International Publishers, 1935).

4. *Editor's note:* David Hilligoss, Ph.D., is a speaker on tribal rights, professor emeritus of Native American Studies, University of Illinois, and Native News Service correspondent and producer.

Chapter Twenty-Three

Leonard Peltier

A citizen of the Anishinabe/Lakota Nation, Leonard Peltier was born on the Turtle Mountain reservation in North Dakota in 1944. During his youth, Peltier's community experienced extreme poverty largely due to federal neglect through the Bureau of Indian Affairs (BIA). Peltier describes a failed attempt to steal heating oil for his house, his first of many run-ins with the law, as an example of the measures that he and community members had to resort to in order to live under harsh conditions. Of his early experiences with non-Native children, shopkeepers, BIA officials/officers, and the police, he comments, "I'm seven or eight by now and beginning to understand the meaning of hate and racism. It seemed as if all white people hated us, and I was beginning to hate just as much."[1]

Raised by his Sioux grandmother who only spoke Ojibwa, Peltier did not learn English until he was forced to attend a BIA-run boarding school. For most Native American youths at the time, the only opportunity for education on the reservation was in racist, government-sponsored boarding schools. Largely designed to assimilate Native children, these boarding schools denied students the right to speak in their native language or practice traditional customs and proved a leading cause in the dissolution or loss of Native traditions and culture.[2]

Leonard Peltier left school at the age of fourteen, moving to Denver, Colorado, to find work. There, he met Dennis Banks, cofounder of the American Indian Movement (AIM). Banks gave political instruction to Peltier, who became his bodyguard. Soon, Peltier, with other young Native Americans, strategized actions to restore value for Native culture and attain economic assistance for poverty-stricken reservations.[3]

Peltier served in the "Trail of Broken Treaties," AIM's attempt to force the government to fulfill neglected treaties, by occupying the Bureau of Indian Affairs offices in Washington, D.C., in November of 1972. The occupation ended with a verbal agreement between the Nixon administration and AIM members in which the administration promised to fulfill the "Twenty Points" of AIM's grievances and not prosecute any of the AIM members. The demands were never met. Instead, the

Federal Bureau of Investigation (FBI) began its long campaign to destroy AIM through intimidation, arrests, imprisonment, and violence.[4]

Following the Trail of Broken Treaties, Peltier was charged with the attempted murder of an off-duty police officer in Milwaukee. After five months in prison, he was released on bail and fled the state to avoid legal proceedings. While conclusions about Peltier's role in this violent exchange with the Milwaukee police vary, for some, the allegations against Peltier are an example of police harassment and prosecutorial malfeasance stemming from the FBI COINTELPRO and government attempts to imprison or "neutralize" members of AIM.[5]

A fugitive, Peltier joined other AIM activists on the Pine Ridge reservation in North Dakota in the spring of 1973. There tribal authorities, under the direction of tribal president Dick Wilson and the GOONs (Guardians of the Oglala Nation), had terrorized traditional elders and progressive Native Americans and transformed Pine Ridge into a state of siege where police abuse was rampant. The GOONS initiated violence against members of AIM and other traditional Native Americans. AIM had seized the town of Wounded Knee, symbolic site of the 1890 massacre of hundreds of Native Americans, to draw national attention to injustice and repression on the reservation. In early May 1973, satisfied by the government's commitment to discuss past treaties, recognize traditional governments, and investigate police brutality by Dick Wilson's GOONs, AIM left Wounded Knee, and in the two years that followed, the U.S. government proceeded to arrest or imprison over five hundred AIM members. The government and Dick Wilson were not held accountable for any injuries, deaths, or malfeasance despite the under- or uninvestigated numbers of assaults and murders occurring on the Pine Ridge reservation.[6]

In this context, two years later, an FBI shootout at Pine Ridge occurred while Peltier, along with AIM members Bob Robideau and Dino Butler, were protecting citizens on the reservation from unlawful police attacks. Two agents were killed, and three Native American men were charged with the killings. While Peltier's codefendants were acquitted on grounds of self-defense, Peltier, who was tried separately the following year, was sentenced to two life sentences. Upset by the acquittal of the other two defendants, the FBI had revamped their case for Peltier. He had been faced with a changed venue to Fargo, North Dakota, a city known at the time for its animosity toward Native Americans; a new conservative judge; and newly obtained witness testimonies and incriminating evidence.[7] To incite prejudice against Peltier, the FBI publicly assigned agents to "protect" the judge and jury. The state refused a public trial for "security reasons."[8]

Convicted, Peltier, incarcerated at Leavenworth, has been imprisoned for decades, although the evidence of his guilt is questionable. In 1985, Prosecutor Lynn Crooks retracted his earlier condemnation of Peltier as a "cold-blooded murderer" and admitted that "the government [did not] really know who shot those agents.'"[9] Author Peter Matthiessen observes: "Whatever the nature and degree of his participation at Oglala, the ruthless persecution of Leonard Peltier has less to do with his own actions than with the underlying issues of history, racism and economics, in particular Indian sovereignty claims and growing opposition to massive energy development on treaty lands and the dwindling reservations."[10]

REFERENCES

Anderson, Scott. "The Martyrdom of Leonard Peltier." *Outside Magazine*. July 1995. www.outsidemag.com.

Associated Press. "Indian Is Found Guilty of First-Degree Murder in Death of 2 F.B.I. Men." *New York Times*, 19 April 1977.

Churchill, Ward, and Jim Vander Wall. *The COINTELPRO Papers: Documents from the FBI's Secret Wars against Domestic Dissent*. Boston: South End Press, 2002.

Incident at Oglala. Video. Robert Redford, producer.

Matthiessen, Peter. *In the Spirit of Crazy Horse*. New York: Penguin, 1992.

Peltier, Leonard. *Prison Writings: My Life Is My Sun Dance*. New York: St. Martin's, 1999.

Weyler, Rex. *Blood of the Land*. Philadelphia: New Society Publishers, 1992.

NOTES

Research and draft for this biography were provided by Elizabeth Kaufman.

1. Peter Matthiessen, *In the Spirit of Crazy Horse* (New York: Penguin Books, 1992), 44.
2. Peter Matthiessen, *In the Spirit of Crazy Horse*, 46.
3. Scott Anderson, "The Martyrdom of Leonard Peltier," *Outside Magazine*, July 1995.
4. Ward Churchill and Jim Vander Wall, *The COINTELPRO Papers: Documents from the FBI's Secret Wars against Dissent in the United States* (Boston: South End Press, 1990), 234.
5. *COINTELPRO Papers*, 235.
6. Rex Weyler, *Blood of the Land* (Philadelphia: New Society Publishers, 1992), 96.
7. *COINTELPRO Papers*, 294.
8. (Associated Press). "Indian Is Found Guilty of First Degree Murder in Death of 2 F.B.I. Men," *New York Times*, 19 April 1977, 22.
9. *COINTELPRO Papers*, 298.
10. *In the Spirit of Crazy Horse*, xx.

Inipi: Sweat Lodge

I lie here in my bed this Saturday afternoon, my head propped up on the hard little pillow, my chewed pencil stub poised above the yellow legal pad in my lap, and I redream today's *inipi*, or sweat-lodge ceremony, not wanting to let it go. The *inipi* makes each Saturday morning holy here in otherwise unholy Leavenworth. When I return to my cell after that inward journey in the sweat lodge, I try to relive each moment, reimmersing myself in those higher feelings not only for the pure spiritual pleasure of it but also to search among them for anything of special significance, any specific instructions to me from the Great Mystery. Things come to you in the sweat that you don't even realize at the time, that only later—sometimes years later—you suddenly realize were part of your own instructions, what we call Original Instructions.

I was taught by the Elders that there are three kinds of Original Instructions. There are the Original Instructions for all of humankind, sort of like a Ten Commandments that's true for all human beings. Those kinds of instructions come only through the highest individuals, like Moses or Jesus or Muhammad or White Buffalo Calf Woman. Next there are the Original Instructions for each people, each nation, each tribe. Those come through great spirit-warriors like Crazy Horse or Sitting Bull or Geronimo or Gandhi. Then, third, there are the Original Instructions for each one of us as individuals, for the path our own individual spirit is supposed to follow. This last kind of Original Instructions are most likely to come to you during the *inipi* or other sacred ceremonies.

As I sit here, my whole body feels aglow, warm with inner vibrations. In my mind's eye, I relive all the events leading up to and coming after today's *inipi* ceremony. I can't really take you into the central moments of the sweat with me. What happens in there is intensely personal. You never celebrate, or even speak of, the most important things that happen to you, the deepest and most spiritual things. Those are between you and Wakan Tanka and no one else. To put those into words is to freeze them in space and time, and they should never be frozen that way because they're continually unfolding, changing with and adapting to each passing moment. You can only approach such matters with words, not describe or capture them, just as you can never define or capture the Great Mystery itself with words. Words take you only to the threshold of meaning. Meaning itself is something you have to feel, to experience for yourself. So consider this description simply an approach, an attempt to bring you to the threshold of some of the meanings, the higher meanings, as I see them, of what I experience in the sweat.

Many people are terrified of sweats—and not without some reason. It can get so hot in there when they pour the water on the red glowing stones that, if you're not used to it, you literally reach the end of your tether, of your self-control. In that scalding, flesh-poaching steam, you feel there's absolutely nothing you can do but

314

cry out *Mitakuye Oyasin*—"All my relations!"—and be permitted to exit through the sweat-lodge door, which is swung open so you can leave. That option is always available to you. You're never forced to stay in the *inipi*.

And yet, with rare exceptions, you don't do it. You resist the temptation. You suck in your gut and tough it out. You dig your nails into the bare soil of the floor. Sitting there naked in the superheated darkness, your bare knees only inches from the molten rocks in the central pit, you come right against the cutting edge of your own fear, your own pain. But the fear of pain is much worse than the pain itself. That's what you quickly come to realize. And that's a lesson you'll need to learn if you're going to survive in this world, so you may as well learn it well. And yet, in that fear, when you face it eye to eye, there's an *awareness*. . . .

If nothing else, it begins with an awareness of the fear itself. And then, somehow, you pass right through fear, right through that pain. You enter a realm both within and beyond fear and pain. So long as you feel pain, it means you're thinking of yourself. Only when you stop thinking of yourself can you actually get past that pain and that fear. You've got to forget yourself to find yourself. You yourself are the entryway. Your own mind, suddenly clear of all thoughts, all fear, is the door. And when you open that door and pass through into that other realm. . . .

But no, please forgive me, I have to stop here. Beyond this point it becomes utterly private, incommunicable. To put it into words would destroy it.

I'm permitted to speak or write only of the before and the after, of the simple actions that precede and follow that holiest of moments. Yet each of those simple actions is holy in its own way, too, from the moment at 6:30 when my cell door suddenly lumbers open with a metallic hiss and hum and grind and slam and my Saturday morning, my most sacred time of the week, begins.

I'm already up for half an hour or more—preparing my thoughts, my mind, and my heart, for the *inipi*. I try to keep my thoughts together, not let them wander too much. I take out my sacred pipe, slowly and methodically cleaning and polishing the unassembled red pipestone bowl and the long stem as a kind of contemplative spiritual practice. I don't put the two pieces together until just before the actual ceremony. Putting the two parts of the pipe together is like putting an electric plug into a socket—it creates a connection and releases powers that only a proper ceremony can contain. White Buffalo Calf Woman taught us how to use the original Pipe. [The pipe that] she brought us still exists among the Lakota people, guarded over by Chief Arvol Looking Horse, the nineteenth-generation keeper of the sacred white buffalo calf Pipe. To us, that original Pipe is as sacred as the original Cross would be to a Christian. Arvol has come to visit us here at Leavenworth, giving us spiritual counsel and even more personal sense of connection with that Pipe.

So, just cleaning and polishing my pipe—a descendant of that wonderful original—and sharing some of its power, helps focus my mind and pushes away all dark thoughts. I'm proud to have been chosen as a pipe carrier. That sacred pipe, when I smoke it during the ceremony, takes my prayers of thanks right up to the Creator.

Wakan Tanka hears us. The Great Spirit listens to every word of every prayer—yes, even to the prayers of these castaway children here in Leavenworth.

After rolling my pipe, still in two parts, back into its bundle, I prepare the contents of my medicine bag. Exactly what's in there only I need to know, though there's nothing that would surprise you. The usual stuff for the ceremony, but nonetheless sacred and personal to me. I also gather in a separate bundle two bags of noodles I've bought at the prison commissary; they'll go into the pot of boiling water the cook keeps going on the fire outside the sweat lodge. We each bring something like that, if we can—a couple of sausages, a bottle of chili peppers, a six-pack of soda pop, some potato chips, whatever. These are for the communal sharing held after the ceremony.

I'm grateful not to be working my usual eight hours at the furniture factory today, as I do during the week. Though Saturday is the most common visiting day at Leavenworth, I've asked family and friends not to schedule visits in the morning or early afternoon, the hours of the sweat. I also skip breakfast this morning, focusing my whole being on the coming ceremony.

Shortly after 8:00 AM, the prison chaplain's voice comes over the loudspeakers: "Native American sweat ceremony will be held today," he announces. That's good news. You're never quite sure when you wake up on Saturday morning if the sweat will actually be held. The only reason we don't have a sweat is if there's a lockdown, or a heavy fog, or some especially stormy weather that prevents the guards up in the guntowers from keeping an eye on us down in the yard. Otherwise, we go no matter what the weather is like. We've been out there on below-zero winter days and in pouring rain. Nothing stops us if we can help it. It amazes me how we learn to call a rainstorm "bad." There's nothing more beautiful than a storm—something you rarely get to experience in here other than vaguely hearing the thunder shuddering through the thick stone walls as you lie in your cell without even a window to the world outside. There are times I'd give anything just to go out walking in a storm, soaking up the rain and thunder and the lightning in the flesh, feeling a oneness with the Great Mystery.

Being out in storms was something I always loved as a boy. All that thunder and lightning spoke to me. I used to go out walking in it. They say you can hear Crazy Horse's voice in the thunder if you listen hard. But that, too, has been taken from us in here. Even the thunder and the lightning they take away. Not much they let us have.

Even the *inipi* itself they allow only because of years and years of struggle in the courts, which finally ruled that Native Americans in prison have at least limited religious rights, such as practicing the *inipi* and carrying a pipe and a medicine bundle. Those rights are given—sometimes grudgingly—here in Leavenworth, but at least they're given. State prisons can be worse than federal prisons in that regard. Just recently a Creek-Seminole inmate named Glen Sweet was to be executed at a state prison, not far from here in Missouri. After all his appeals were exhausted and the hour for his execution approached, he asked to have one last *inipi*, one final cleansing in the prison sweat lodge, just before his execution by lethal injection. Not much to ask, you'd think. But, no. His request was refused, and he died without any ceremony. Imagine if he were a Catholic and had been denied last rites! I learned all this from our own spiritual advisor, Henry Wahwassuck, who walked Glen Sweet to the execution chamber and watched him die.

"He was an Indian," Henry told me. "He died brave, like an Indian dies. He'll have his *inipi* ceremony in the Sky World. They can't take it away from him up there!"

Now I wait for the call to go down to the sweat lodge.

One of the bros calls down the corridor, "Hey, weather's clear. Temperature's about twenty out there!"

Good. I like it when it's cold. Being in the scalding heat inside of the sweat lodge with all that pure freezing cold on the outside somehow makes the sweat ceremony seem even more intense.

A little after 7:30 AM, I gather my pipe and bundles, head out of my cell down the narrow corridor to the stairwell and make my way down the stairs to the prison chaplain's office door, where we gather around until we get the final OK to have the sweat—or as the hacks (guards) like to call it, the "Pow-Wow." I pass through two metal detectors before I'm finally out through the complex of corridors and outbuildings into the icy open air of the yard. Outside there's one more metal detector check.

With the other bros I stand there for quite a while in front of the locked gate to the tall wire fence they've built around the sweat lodge. Wearing just sweatpants and T-shirt and the like, we're all shivering in the bracing air as we wait for the guard to unlock the gate. But the cold air feels good. And it's pure, unlike the heavy worn-out, breathed-out air in the cellblock. I fill my lungs with the coldness, enjoying every second of it. We stand there exchanging pleasantries, but there's not much joshing around on this sacred occasion. We're all focusing on the inward journey we're about to take. Finally, the chaplain unlocks the gate and we file in, maybe sixteen or eighteen of us.

The guard counts us for the third or fourth time, and says, "Okay, you're in. Back later." He locks us in and walks away. We may be locked inside a twelve-foot-high steel fence inside a maximum-security prison directly up against the north wall flanked by two towering gun towers, but—suddenly—*we're free!*

Now we each make our preparations. The drum keepers set up the drum outside the lodge. The fire keeper starts the big fire outside the lodge, the fire that will heat all the sacred stones for the ceremony to come. Each of us sets a pinch or two of tobacco, along with our prayers, onto the fire. The cook gets the big pot of water boiling on another fire off to the side. I hand him the two bags of noodles I've brought. Beside him he gathers a growing pile of packaged foodstuffs, a few fresh vegetables and some soft drinks. We set up the little stone altar and dress it with sage and sweetgrass and other ceremonial items. Those of us who are pipe carriers assemble our pipes for the ceremony ahead, setting them down for the time being

Leonard Peltier

at the altar as an offering. We also set out our eagle feathers with a prayer of offering. Then we stand around and chat good-naturedly, maybe sip some hot coffee, all of us feeling good. It's pretty much a social hour until about 10:30 AM or so, when the loudspeakers ring out, "The count is clear!" meaning everybody's been accounted for at the last head count.

By now it's nearly 11:00 a.m. and we await the arrival from the outside world of our spiritual advisor, Henry, whom I've known since we were kids together at the Wahpeton BIA school.[1] He also had the high honor of spending five years within these walls himself back in the 1970s. Henry was one of those brave souls against whom the government built a case at that time—as they did against so many others who had done nothing but defend their people.

Henry's our sweat leader for today. He's a friend to all of us, a wonderfully spiritual guy—and one tough-nosed dude, let me tell you. When it comes to the *inipi*, he sees to it that everything's done just right. Every detail has to be followed just so. Henry himself brought in most of the materials for the building of the sweat lodge—the saplings that create the skeletal structure of the domed lodge, and the rocks—small and large stones of fire-resistant gray-black lava—that we use in the fire. The lodge's covering we've pieced together from torn blankets and miscellaneous pieces of canvas we managed to scrounge up here in Leavenworth. Maybe five feet high and nearly fifteen feet across, it's sort of make-shift looking, I suppose, but to us it's as impressive looking, and certainly as holy, as any cathedral.

Now the singers set up the drum and start beating out a low, steady rhythm. They begin one of the sacred songs, a pipe song, the first of many songs to be sung this day, and we finally start filling our pipes for the ceremony ahead. The big bass boom of the drum catches the attention of the guards up in the gun towers on either side. We can see the shadowed silhouettes of their heads bobbing around up there, staring down at us. I guess they're used to looking down at our strange doings. Must lighten up an otherwise boring Saturday morning for them. I wonder if they get a whiff of the perfumed smoke from the sage and sweetgrass and cleansing cedar. I pray they do.

Now Henry finally arrives—they don't let him in till the last possible moment, it seems—and the chaplain locks him into the sweat compound with us. Henry has a big hearty hello and a handshake and a bear hug for just about everyone. But his smiles quickly turn to seriousness. He checks the place out to make sure everything's ready for the ceremony. When he sees that all is in order down to the last tiny detail, he finally announces: "Everything's in its place. It's time!"

Those are his exact words every time. That's the signal for us to enter the sweat lodge.

By now we've stripped down bare naked, wrapped only in a torn strip of old army blanket—which we've had to use lately since they confiscated our ceremonial towels. We line up outside the door to the *inipi*, carrying our pipes and gourd rattles and our eagle feathers. Someone once asked Henry why we had to be naked and he said, "Did you ever see a baby born wearing a diaper or underpants?" Often the door of the sweat lodge is compared to the opening into the womb of Mother Earth. I also like to think of it as a doorway *into* yourself and *through* yourself and then right *out* of yourself. Your *self*'s the first thing you've got to leave behind when you enter the *inipi*.

We enter through the pulled-back door flap, turning immediately to the left and moving clockwise around the interior of the lodge, each of us assuming our places on the bare, well-smoothed dirt floor. Whoever's been chosen that day to pour the water on the red-hot rocks to create the steam enters first, moving around the circular lodge and taking his seat beside Henry, who's already in his place, sitting just to the right of the still-open door, preparing his ceremonial paraphernalia. It's still cool inside the lodge; the central firepit in the center is empty. The red-hot stones will be handed in later by the fire keeper from the fire outside, each glowing stone brought reverently inside on deer-antler carriers. The first seven are brought in one by one—one each for the four sacred directions, Mother Earth, the People, and Wakan Tanka. More rocks will be brought in later, depending on how hot Henry wants it to get. But even before the stones are brought in, the body heat of some twenty men quickly warms it up to a cozy temperature in there.

Outside stands the doorkeeper, who will close and open the door four times, or four "rounds" as we call them, during the two-to-three hour ceremony. Next we pray and "offer thought," as Henry calls it, trying to bring our collective minds together as one mind. We pass the sage around the circle; everybody takes a little pinch and chews it or maybe puts it into their hair. And then the eagle feathers are passed around, so we can all share their energy. The flap is still open, and the first seven rocks are brought in on the antlers and placed in the central pit at our knees. We offer cedar on the stones, to cleanse and purify the air, driving out any bad thoughts. Then Henry asks for the water, and a bucket is brought in and placed in the center of the doorway inside the lodge. Cedar is offered onto the glowing stones themselves, hissing sharply as it fills the air with its lovely smell. Then Henry sprinkles the cedar onto the stones, and blesses the water four times.

Now the pourer takes Henry's buffalo-horn scoop, fills it with water, and makes the first pour onto the rocks. By now the door's closed and . . . But, no, that's as far as I can take you here. The rest, Henry tells me, cannot be told. It can be experienced, but not told.

I can only say that four times the door is opened and closed, four times the water is poured from the buffalo horn onto the molten rocks, four times the superheated steam explodes and envelops us . . . but, *no more!* "Don't divulge what happens, none of the specifics that happen to you in there!" Henry insists.

And I honor that. I hope you will, too. Already I've probably said too much, but Henry will go over this and see that what should be unspoken remains unspoken. This precaution is for your sake as much as mine. To speak of what happens to me in the *inipi* would be like giving *you* the medicine intended for *me*. It would be pointless, even harmful—to you as well as to me.

Enough said. *Mitakuye Oyasin.*

After the fourth round, and our final prayers, the door to the *inipi* is opened for the final time and we file out the way we came in. The twenty-degree air hits me like a powerful slap, almost knocking me backward. Yet it feels wonderful. Off to one side there's a jerryrigged shower with unheated water that I enjoy shivering under for a few seconds, washing off the sweat and slapping wildly at myself. It's unbelievably invigorating after the scalding-hot sweat bath. My flesh seems to come alive. I could swear I'm glowing, I feel so good. I *have* been reborn!

We make a circle outside and light our pipes, and "offer thought" again. It's all very intimate, very moving. After burning some more sage and sweetgrass, we empty out our pipes, then dress and have our communal sharing of all the foodstuffs the cook has fixed up. By now everyone's bright-eyed, smiling, laughing, talking a blue streak. There's a really powerful camaraderie. It's a happy and a holy moment. We hate for it to end. But soon the chaplain appears at the gate, and a guard barks, "Time's up. Gotta get ready for four o'clock head count!" That instantly dampens the magic, and moments later we're on our way back through those three metal detectors, back into the cellblock, back into the ordinary world. Back to Leavenworth after seven hours of blessed freedom. And those guards in their gun towers never even realized we'd escaped!

NOTES

Originally published in Leonard Peltier, *Prison Writings* (New York: St. Martin's, 1999), 183–98.

   1. *Editor's note:* In 1953, when Peltier was nine years old, the Bureau of Indian Affairs (BIA) took Peltier, his sister, and his cousin away from their grandmother. They were brought to the Wahpeton Indian School in North Dakota. As at many BIA schools, the environment was highly abusive; students were beaten if they were not considered "clean" upon inspection. Peltier left the school as soon as he could. See Peter Matthiessen, *In the Spirit of Crazy Horse* (New York: Penguin, 1980), 45.

Epilogue

Incommunicado: Dispatches from a Political Prisoner

Marilyn Buck

September 11, 2001

before
morning-slow
I move
Julan hollers
    come come see
    the world trade center's
    exploding

she's not serious
no one would make that up
  would they?
    maybe
live on TV
  video mantra
    replay: plane crash
    replay: collapse
    slow motion, dying morning

no, not a made-for-TV movie
not a disaster film
not Hollywood special effects
  one tower falls
  the other follows

do chickens come home to roost?
enormity crashes
    dazed   disbelief
        (chickens won't roost here again
            pigeons either)

I, a political prisoner, can
conceive why
but comprehension is not complicity
    I look around me
    I know nothing
    I know too much
there is no answer in death
        nor in dying
I know
    soon others will die
    dark smoke spreads
    cinders of wrath rise
    the eagle's talons flex
    hungry for revenge

    (eyes locked on the shocking scene
    a Muslim sister whispers
        they will blame the Muslims)

I know
    many will feed the eagle
    the Palestinians?
        (Palestinians are always suspect)

Muslims?   Arabs?
        many will die red upon the land

I can't comprehend
men who commit suicide
taking civilians with them
        (a u.s. postal worker
        Columbine high school boys
        a man at McDonald's
            all-American suicide killers)

civilians
used as warheads
    I shudder and walk away
    from death
        to my cell

Bich Kim runs in
   if there's a world war three
   they will shoot all the prisoners, won't they?

I shake my head
I don't think so
   but you, political prisoners
   like you, won't they?
I hope not
     (question marks
     the corners of my mouth:
       what do I know
       about the fine-print)

I turn to sweep the floor
     find rhythms of the ordinary

The Order: 9:00 AM PDT

a tap
   I turn
a guard
   come with me

I won't return today

I stand before the captain
   we must lock you up
     for your own safety
(not for my safety)
   you're intelligent you know why
I speculate, no
not for my safety
   you must be locked up
   just for your safety

I am
   stripped naked
   ID card confiscated
   everything taken
I need my glasses!
   keep the glasses

I keep a neutral face
   handcuffed behind the back
   clad in bile yellow for isolation
      and flip-flops

I keep outrage
   wrapped within my fists
I swallow anger
   metal clangs swallow sound
the concrete cocoon swallows me

The "SHU": Special Housing Unit

"there was an old woman
she lived in a shoe"
what did she do?

9/11   *no prisoner may speak to you*
        you may not speak to any prisoner
9/12   overheard voices
      there are terrorists here
        who are the terrorists?
    silence, everyone behind her door listens
9/14   a legal call
    small relief: it's political—Washington—
      not something i did
9/17   no more calls
    no visits
    no mail
      until further notice

    incommunicado
    i hang from a winding string
      winding in this cocoon
    i breathe deep
      the air isn't good here

    (from outside the walls Susan yells
      you are not alone)
    i breathe deeper

Sunday i get a radio: KPFA lifeline
   Sikhs dead, detainees disappeared
   political prisoners buried deeper
    incommunicado

i remember another September 11: Chile '73
   more than 3,000 dead
   tortured assassinated disappeared
    a CIA-supported coup
    (the WTC bombers not-yet-born)
   many people there still mourn
let us mourn all the dead
and the soon-to-die

i worry about the prisoners
isolation sucks at the spirit
i am furious: inferred association
held hostage in place of men
   with u.s. weapons and CIA training
    an infernal joke
the puppet masters laugh

i laugh to stay sane
before i explode in irony's flames

we are hostages
   to blood-thirsty oil men
   ready to splatter deserts
    with daisy-cutters
their collateral damage
   dead mothers and children
   dead mother earth
    dead daisies

(hasn't this happened before?
   u.s. cavalry and smallpox blankets
   special forces and blanket bombing)

(Susan is back
   she taps on the wall: *you are not alone*)

i walk around the edges
   how many walk on edges?
    what edges do the Palestinians walk?

cold radiates whitewashed
    walls press against my edges
       suspend animation
       no butterflies to break out
       no silken thread to weave sweet dreams

    panic rises in my throat
       thick white choking cold
so cold
       i swing hope on a thread
a transparent sliver it crashes
against the cinderblocks
    i drop
frozen chrysalis
cold into a coffin box

Night

i lay down on suspect blankets
a Cyclops light pins me
    onto the metal cot
       an altar for vengeful gods
    metal restraints for hands and feet
       "just in case"

the suicide cell has ghosts
    desperate women
    lain here chained four-pointed
    to command composure
    sacrificed to voyeur visions
       through the glass starkly
       through a burqa window

i don't want to think of i
    i meditate
i think of other politicals
    behind wires and walls
i remember the assaulted
    the accidental
    the collaterally damaged
    killed, corrected, coerced

i remember: the u.s. funds the fundamentalists
    Muslims   Christians   Zionists
    self-righteous missiles
    of mayhem and retribution

i remember Afghani women held hostage
    inside indigo cocoons
    cells smaller than a confessional box

      my veil is this cell
      i will put on no other
      except the veil of sleep

the light, damn the light
    the Cyclops spies
i toss between the tomb-thick walls
    how long will this go on?
    will my bones break
      into ice shards or will they desiccate
      stranded in this cell

at last i doze
till dawn the Cyclops watches
clanging keys, slamming metal traps
    shift change
    daylight creeps inside
i rise: i must seek cycles
inside
    without clocks or mirrors
    without all but i

The Weekend

a glacier, daylight advances
    imperceptibly
a plank of light teeters
    on the edge of board-faced windows
travels obliquely across
    then it's gone
warmth fades fast

the food trap opens
   cold eggs the color of our clothes
   plunk—weekend brunch
i swallow in silence

silence flees before sudden cacophony
two women beat plastic bowls on metal doors
   we want rec we want rec
   the sun is out we want out
my head is wrapped in metallic clanger
   bang bang bang
i stay silent
i bite my lip

hours pass: shift change 2:00
   the sun drops fast behind the wall
finally: *who wants recreation?*
   I do
     me too
       let me out first
voices reach through the metal doors
food traps clank
handcuffs click
one by one women are led
   to wire cages
   joy rings louder than the chains

i wait
no guard comes
i break silence
   you didn't ask me
disembodied denial echoes through the walls
   you can't go with the others
   wait
   not my decision
i will miss the sundrops

"Perchance to Dream"

night comes
i fall exhausted into sleep
i dream of Dresden Hanoi Baghdad

whistles scream
walls fall apart
   in waves
Dali deserts
   watches tick
      waterdrip

dream shift:
   swords of steel glint against the sky
   a swarm and puff
   dark blood drops
   bituminous birds bank
   spread-eagled free fall
   ashes ashes they all fall
      down dark flashes
   cherry splashes on concrete
   Babel towers collapse in crying heaps
   a curtain rises gray
   covers gladiators draped across the stage

i wake cold-throated
what time is it?
my limbs locked
beneath a concrete rockslide
is this my tomb falling on me?

my chest is piled rock-heavy
   bodies rise from the shallows of my breath
graze my eyes and flee
     across the desert scape
        shadow prints dissipate
am i awake?

the Cyclops stabs my eye
   i must be awake
i wrap a scratchy towel
around my face
i escape electric night
   into sightlessness

a ghost voice wails
   what time is it?

a deep male boom
    1:24, go to sleep
     no, turn on the radio, talk to me
no! no! please no, my eyes blink
inside their blind
    little Brueghel men dance
    wooden-shoe notes
    ruthless on my sleep
sound streams woman's babble
pools beneath the door
i hunker under the winding sheet

does she stop talking
or do i descend?
i don't remember

    shift change
      shift change
guards come and go
officials pass by peering
    into our crypt-cages
    taking notes, verifying

Monday, September 24

the captain appears
we may release you today after 2:00
2:00 comes and goes
the shift changes
i wait and wonder: will other politicals be released today
    i wait
hope is the moment's thief
    don't wait!

at last: *Buck roll out*
i leap a jack-in-the-box
          ready
        ready
the metal key clangs just before the 4:00 count
i gasp relief
and hurry through before the gates slam
shut and i am left below

Eurydice whom Orpheus glimpsed
    a moment too soon
i step out
a four o'clock unfolding, fuchsia in the shading light
back into the routine prisoner's plight

Appendix

Internet Sources

American Gulag: News and Resources on Prisoners, Prisons and Prison Abolition. www.infoshop.org/gulag/.

Anarchist Black Cross Network. www.anarchistblackcross.org.

Black Radical Congress. (n.d.) "BRC-NEWS." www.blackradicalcongress.org/comm/voices/lists.html.

Federal Bureau of Investigation's COINTELPRO, counterintelligence program. www.cointel.org.

The Freedom Archives (1999–) [website] www.freedomarchives.org.

The Jericho Movement (1998–) [website] www.thejerichomovement.com (New York, New York: The Jericho Movement).

The Jericho Movement, San Francisco Bay Area Chapter (1998–) [website]. www.prisonactivist.org/jericho_sfbay. (San Francisco and Oakland: The Jericho Movement).

Laura Whitehorn. prisonactivist.org/pps + pows/laurawhitehorn.html. www.kersplebedeb.com/mystuff/profiles/whitehorn.html.

Linda Evans. prisonactivist.org/pps + pows/linda.html.

National Boricua Human Rights Network. www.geocities.com/chiboriken/index.html.

Nuclear Resisters. www.nonviolence.org/nukeresister/insideandout.html.

Prison Activist Resource Center. (1982–). "prisonact-list." www.prisonactivist.org (Oakland, Calif.: Prison Activist Resource Center).

RM of Jericho. (2002, February 15). "Torture in Guantánamo? Senator Condones, Protestors Condemn." Friday, February 15, 2002 at 11:24 PM at sf.indymedia.org/news/2002/02/116357.php.

United Nations. (1948). Universal Declaration of Human Rights. www.un.org/Overview/rights.html. www.kersplebedeb.com/mystuff/powpp.html.

POLITICAL PRISONER(S) WEB SITES

Mumia Abu-Jamal

International Concerned Family and Friends of Mumia Abu-Jamal.
  www.mumia.org.
Pacifica Radio. [Mumia Abu-Jamal's radio commentaries].
  www.savepacifica.net/strike/news/audio/mumia.
Free Mumia NYC. www.freemumia.com.

Sundiata Acoli

Acoli, Sundiata, and the Sundiata Acoli Freedom Campaign. (1997–).
  afrikan.i-dentity.com/sundiata.
Acoli, Sundiata. (1992). www.prisonactivist.org/pubs/brief-hist-naps.html.

Angola Three (Herman Wallace, Robert King Wilkerson, Albert Woodfox)

National Coalition to Free the Angola 3. (1997–). prisonactivist.org/angola.

Marilyn Buck

PARC, with Marilyn Buck. (1998–). "Marilyn Buck."
  www.prisonactivist.org/pps + pows/marilynbuck.

Independentistas

www.prolibertad.org.

Mondo we Langa and Ed Poindexter

www.nebraskansforpeace.org

New York Three (Herman Bell, Jalil Muntaqim, Nuh Washington)

Bell, Herman, and PARC. (1996–). prisonactivist.org/pps + pows/bell.html.
Bell, Herman, and Jericho Movement. (2001). "Victory Gardens Project–New Season Begins." www.thejerichomovement.com/victorygardens.html.
Muntaqim, Jalil, and PARC. (2002). "Jalil Abdul Muntaqim: Black Liberation Army Political Prisoner." prisonactivist.org/pps + pows/jalilmuntaqim.
Washington, Nuh, and PARC. "Nuh Washington." (2000).
  prisonactivist.org/pps + pows/nuh-washington.

Leonard Peltier

Leonard Peltier Defense Committee. www.freepeltier.org.

Plowshares

www.swords-to-plowshares.org/.

Assata Shakur

Afro-Cuba Web. (n.d.) "Assata Shakur." afrocubaweb.com/assata.htm.

Mutulu Shakur

www.prisonactivist.org/ppstpow.

Bibliography

GENERAL BIBLIOGRAPHY

Alisberg, Nancy. "GUILD & NCBL Focus on U.S. Political Prisoners." *Guild Notes* (November/December 1990).

All Power to the People! The Black Panther Party and Beyond. Directed by Lee Lew-Lee. New York: Filmmakers Library, 1996. Videocassette.

Amnesty International USA. *Allegations of Mistreatment in Marion Prison, Illinois, U.S.A.* May 1987 (Doc. #AMR 51/26/87).

Anderson, Sam, and Tony Medina, eds. *In Defense of Mumia.* New York: Writer's and Reader's Publishers, 1996.

Ayers, Bill. *Fugitive Days: A Memoir.* Boston: Beacon, 2001.

Badillo, Herman, and Milton Haynes. *A Bill of No Rights: Attica and the American Prison System.* New York: Outerbridge & Lazard/Dutton, 1972.

Bennett, James R. *Political Prisoners and Trials: A Worldwide Annotated Bibliography, 1900 through 1993.* Jefferson, N.C.: McFarland & Company, 1995.

Berry, Mary Frances. *Black Resistance/White Law: A History of Constitutional Racism in America.* New York: Appleton-Century-Crofts, 1971.

Black Prison Movements USA. Trenton, N.J.: Africa World Press, 1995.

Blackston, Nelson. *COINTELPRO: The FBI's Secret War on Political Freedom.* New York: Vintage, 1976.

Blunk, Tim, and Ray Luc Levasseur, eds. *Hauling Up the Morning/Izana la Mañana.* Trenton, N.J.: Red Sea Press, 1990.

Boyle, Robert. "Tribunal Urges Freedom for U.S. Political Prisoners." *Guild Notes* (Winter 1991).

Brotherton, David, and Luis Barrios. *Between Black and Gold: The Street Politics of the Almighty Latin King and Queen Nation.* New York: Columbia University Press, 2003.

Brown, David J., and Robert Merrill, eds. *Violent Persuasions: The Politics and Imagery of Terrorism.* Seattle: Bay Press, 1993.

Buck, Marilyn, David Gilbert, and Laura Whitehorn. *Enemies of the State.* Brooklyn: Resistance in Brooklyn (RnB), 1999, 2nd printing.

Buhle, Mari Jo, Paul Buhle, and Dan Georgakas, eds. *Encyclopedia of the American Left.* Chicago: Illini Books, 1992.

Burns, Haywood. "Racism and American Law." In *Law against People*, edited by Robert Lefcourt. New York: Bintae Books, 1971.

Burton-Rose, Daniel, Dan Pens, and Paul Wright, eds. *The Celling of America: An Inside Look at the U.S. Prison Industry*. Monroe, Maine: Common Courage Press, 1998.

Bussing, Sabine. *Of Captive Queens and Holy Panthers: Prison Fiction and Male Homoerotic Experience*. Frankfurt and Main: Peter Lang, 1990.

Can't Jail the Spirit, 5th edition. Chicago: Committee to End the Marion Lockdown, 2002.

Chomsky, Noam. *The Culture of Terrorism*. Boston: South End Press, 1988.

"Church Committee" Report on COINTELPRO, U.S. Senate, 94th Congress, 1975, 1976. www.icdc.com/~pawwolf/cointelpro/cointelpro.htm

Churchill, Ward, and Jim Vander Wall. *Agents of Repression: The FBI's Secret Wars against the Black Panther Party and the American Indian Movement*. Boston: South End Press, 2002.

———. *The COINTELPRO Papers: Documents from the FBI's Secret Wars against Domestic Dissent in the United States*. Boston: South End Press, 2002.

Churchill, Ward, with Mike Ryan. *Pacifism as Pathology*. Winnipeg: Arbeiter Ring, 1998.

Clark, Richard X. *The Brothers of Attica*. Edited by Leonard Levitt. New York: Links Books, 1973.

Cleaver, Eldridge. *Soul on Ice*. New York: McGraw-Hill, 1968.

Cleaver, Kathleen, and George Katsiaficas, eds. *Liberation, Imagination, and the Black Panther Party*. New York: Routledge, 2001.

Davidson, Howard, ed. *The Journal of Prisoners on Prisons*.www.jpp.org.

Davis, Angela, and Bettina Aptheker, eds. *If They Come in the Morning; Voices of Resistance*. New York: Third Press, 1971.

Day, Susie. "Political Prisoners: Guilty until Proven Innocent." *Sojourner: The Women's Forum*, February 1989.

Deutsch, Michael E., and Jan Susler. "Political Prisoners in the United States: The Hidden Reality." *Social Justice* 18, no. 3.

Eakin, Paul John. "Malcolm X and the Limits of Autobiography." *Criticism* 18, no. 3 (Summer 1976): 230–42.

Escobar, Edward J. "The Dialectics of Repression: The Los Angeles Police Department and the Chicano Movement, 1968–1971." *Journal of American History* (March 1993): 1483–1514.

Esposito, Barbara, and Lee Wood. *Prison Slavery*. Edited by Kathryn Bardsledy. Washington, D.C.: Committee to Abolish Prison Slavery, 1982.

Fanon, Frantz. *The Wretched of the Earth*. New York: Grove Press, 1968.

Foucault, Michel. *Discipline and Punish: The Birth of the Prison*. Translated by Alan Sheridan. New York: Vintage Books, 1979.

Franklin, H. Bruce. *Prison Literature in America: The Victim as Criminal and Artist*. New York: Oxford University Press, 1989.

Garrow, David. *The FBI and Martin Luther King, Jr.: From "Solo" to Memphis*. New York: Norton, 1981.

Gelbspan, Ross. *Break-ins, Death Threats and the FBI: The Covert War against the Central America Movement*. Boston: South End Press, 1991.

Goldstein, Robert Justin. "An American Gulag?: Summary Arrest and Emergency Detention of Political Dissidents in the United States." *Columbia Human Rights Law Review* 10 (1978).

Goodell, Charles. *Political Prisoners in America*. New York: Random House, 1973.

Gramsci, Antonio. *Selections from The Prison Notebooks*. Edited and translated by Quintin Hoare and Geoffrey Nowell Smith. New York: International Publishers, 1985.

Gross, Samuel R., and Robert Mauro. *Death & Discrimination: Racial Disparities in Capital Sentencing*. Boston: Northeastern University Press, 1989.

Halperin, Morton H., et al. *The Lawless State: The Crimes of the U.S. Intelligence Agencies*. New York: Penguin, 1976.

Harlow, Barbara. *Barred: Women, Writing and Political Detention*. Hanover, N.H.: Wesleyan University Press, 1992.

Healey, Dorothy, and Maurice Isserman. *Dorothy Healey Remembers: A Life in the American Communist Party*. New York: Oxford University Press, 1990.

International Indian Treaty Council. "Violations of American Human Rights by the United States: Wounded Knee, 1973." In *Illusions of Justice: Human Rights Violations in the United States*, by Lennox S. Hinds. Iowa City: University of Iowa, 1979.

Jackson, George. *Blood in My Eye*. Baltimore: Black Classic Press, 1990.

———. *Soledad Brother: The Prison Letters of George Jackson*. Chicago: Lawrence Hill Books, 1994.

Jaimes, M. A. "The Trial of the 'Columbus Day Four.'" *Lies of Our Times* (September 1992).

James, Joy, ed. *The Angela Y. Davis Reader*. Malden, Mass.: Blackwell, 1998.

———. *Resisting State Violence*. Minneapolis: University of Minnesota Press, 1996.

———, ed. *States of Confinement: Policing, Detention and Prisons*. New York: St. Martin's, 2002, revised paperback edition.

Johnson, Troy, et al., eds. *American Indian Activism: Alcatraz to the Longest Walk*. Urbana: University of Illinois Press, 1997.

Jones, Charles E., ed. *The Black Panther Party [Reconsidered]*. Baltimore: Black Classic Press, 1998.

Kempton, Murray. *The Briar Patch: The Trial of the Panther 21*. New York: Da Capo Press, 1997.

Kohn, Stephen M. *American Political Prisoners: Prosecutions under the Espionage and Sedition Acts*. Westport, Conn.: Praeger, 1994.

Lederer, Bob. "U.S. Political Prisoners Face Media Silence." *EXTRA!* (September 1992).

Levy, Howard, et al. *Going to Jail: The Political Prisoner*. New York: Grove Press, 1971.

Marable, Manning, and Leith Mullings, eds. *Let Nobody Turn Us Around: Voices of Resistance, Reform, and Renewal*. Lanham, Md.: Rowman & Littlefield, 2000.

May, John P. ed., and Khalid R. Pitts, associate ed. *Building Violence: How America's Rush to Incarcerate Creates More Violence*. Thousand Oaks, Calif.: Sage, 2000.

Meyer, Matt. "Freedom Now." *The NonViolent Activist* (November–December 1993).

Miller, Jerome G. *Search and Destroy: African American Males in the Criminal Justice System*. Cambridge University Press, 1996.

Minor, W. William. "Political Crime, Political Justice, and Political Prisoners." *Criminology* 12 (February 1975).

Myerson, Michael. *Nothing Could Be Finer*. New York: International Publishers, 1978.

Nathanson, Nathaniel L. "Freedom of Association and the Quest for Internal Security: Conspiracy from Dennis to Dr. Spock." *Northwestern University Law Review* 65, no. 2 (May–June).

Nelson, Jack, and Ronald J. Ostrow. *The FBI and the Berrigans: The Making of a Conspiracy*. New York: Coward, McCann & Geoghegan, Inc., 1972.

Oates, Stephen B. *Let the Trumpet Sound: The Life of Martin Luther King, Jr.* New York: Harper & Row, 1982.

The Official Report of the New York State Special Commission on Attica. New York: Bantam, 1972.

O'Hare, Kate Richards, sometime Federal Prisoner Number 21669. *In Prison.* Seattle: University of Washington Press, 1976 (original 1923).

Oppenheimer, Martin. *The Urban Guerrilla.* Chicago: Quadrangle Books, 1969.

O'Reilly, Kenneth. "The FBI and the Politics of the Riots, 1964–1968." *Journal of American History* 75, no. 1 (June 1988).

Parenti, Christian. "Assata Shakur Speaks from Exile: An Interview." *Z Magazine* (March 1998): 27–32.

———. *Lockdown America.* London: Verso, 1999.

Peltier, Leonard. *Prison Writings: My Life Is My Sundance.* Edited by Harvey Arden. New York: St. Martin's, 1999.

"Political Prisoners in the United States." Washington, D.C.: Center for Constitutional Rights, September 1988.

Political Prisoners: Racism and the Politics of Imprisonment. Washington, D.C.: U.S. Department of Justice, National Minority Advisory Council on Criminal Justice, August 1980.

Rosenblatt, Elihu, ed. *Criminal Injustice: Confronting the Prison Crisis.* Boston: South End Press, 1996.

Sabo, Donn, Terry A. Kupers, and Willie London, eds. *Prison Masculinities.* Philadelphia: Temple University Press, 2001.

Scheffler, Judith A., ed. *Wall Tappings: An International Anthology of Women's Prison Writings, 200 A.D. to the Present.* New York: Feminist Press, 2002.

Seager, Moe. "America's Secret: Political Prisoners." *Z Magazine* (1991).

Staples, William G. *The Culture of Surveillance: Discipline and Social Control in the United States.* New York: St. Martin's, 1997.

Swede, Shirley. "Who Is Jean Gump?" *Z Magazine* (October 1989).

Theoharis, Athan. *The FBI: An Annotated Bibliography and Research Guide.* New York: Garland, 1994.

Thiers, Naomi. "Designed to Intimidate." *Sojourners* (May 1991).

Thompson, Becky W. *A Promise and a Way of Life: White Antiracist Activism.* Minneapolis: University of Minnesota Press, 2001.

Tolbert, Emory J. "Federal Surveillance of Marcus Garvey and the U.N.I.A." *Journal of Ethnic Studies* (Winter 1987): 14.

United Nations. *Standard Minimum Rules for the Treatment of Prisoners.* New York, 1984.

U.S. Commission on Civil Rights. *The Navajo Nation: An American Colony.* Washington, D.C.: U.S. Government Printing Office, September 1975.

"U.S. Political Prisoners?" *Newsweek* 92 (31 July 1978).

U.S. Senate. *Final Report of the Select Committee to Study Government Operations with Respect to Intelligence Activities.* Washington, D.C.: U.S. Government Printing Office, 1976.

Wicker, Tom. *A Time to Die: The Attica Prison Revolt.* New York: Quadrangle/NYTimes Books, 1975.

Williams, Daniel R. *Executing Justice: An Inside Account of the Case of Mumia Abu-Jamal.* New York: St. Martin's, 2001.

Witt, Shirley Hill. "The Brave-Hearted Women: The Struggle at Wounded Knee." *The Civil*

Rights Digest 8, no. 4. Washington, D.C.: U.S. Government Printing Office (Summer 1976).

Zimroth, Peter L. *Perversions of Justice: The Prosecution and Acquittal of the Panther 21*. New York: Viking, 1974.

Zinn, Howard. *A People's History of the United States*. New York: Harper & Row, 1980.

SELECT BIBLIOGRAPHIES FOR CONTRIBUTORS

Mumia Abu-Jamal (Wesley Cook)

Abu-Jamal, Mumia. *All Things Censored*. New York: Seven Stories Press, 2000.

———. *Death Blossoms: Reflections from a Prisoner of Conscience*. Farmington, Pa.: Plough Publishing House, 1997.

———. *Live from Death Row*. New York: Avon, 1996.

Bisson, Terry. *On a Move: The Story of Mumia Abu-Jamal*. Farmington, Pa.: Litmus Books, 2000.

Ledbetter, James. "Silence of the Damned: Why America Won't Listen to Mumia Abu-Jamal." *The Village Voice*, 6 September 1994, 26–28.

Miller, Arthur. *Fair or Foul: The Case of Mumia Abu-Jamal*. Produced by Andy Halper and directed by Jeffery Nachbar. 45 min. Courtroom Television Network, 1996. Videocassette.

Mumia: A Case for Reasonable Doubt? Produced and directed by John Edginton. 72 min. Fox Lorber, 1997, 1996. Videocassette.

Rimer, Sara. "Death Sentence Overturned in 1981 Killing of Officer." *New York Times*, 19 December 2001.

"The Story of the MOVE Organization, from 20 Years on the MOVE." *Prison Activist Resource Center*. www.prisonactivist.org/pps+pows/move-story.html.

"USA: A Life in the Balance: The Case of Mumia Abu-Jamal." *Amnesty International*. www.amnestyusa.org/abolish/reports/mumia/content.html.

Weinglass, Leonard. *Race for Justice: Mumia Abu-Jamal's Fight against the Death Penalty*. Monroe, Maine: Common Courage Press, 1995.

Williams, Daniel R. "The Ordeal of Mumia Abu-Jamal." In *States of Confinement*, edited by Joy James. New York: St. Martin's, 2000.

Sundiata Acoli (Clark Squire)

Acoli, Sundiata. "A Brief History of the Black Panther Party and Its Place in the Black Liberation Movement." *Sundiata Acoli Freedom Campaign* (2 April 1985). afrikan.i-dentity.com/sundiata/.

———. "Hands Off Assata!" Statement of Sundiata Acoli for October 5, 1998, Demonstration against H.C.R. 254. *Sundiata Acoli Freedom Campaign*. afrikan.i-dentity.com/sundiata/.

———. "Unique Problems Associated with the Legal Defense of Political Prisoners and Prisoners of War." *Southern University Law Review*. Baton Rouge, La.: Southern University Law Center, 1996.

Foner, Philip S., ed. *The Black Panthers Speak*. Philadelphia: Lippincott, 1970.

Hanley, Robert. "At 2 Brink's Trials, Accusations and New Motions." *New York Times*, 23 August 1983, Late City Final Edition.

Kaufman, Michael T. "Seized Woman Called Black Militants' 'Soul'," New York Times, 3 May 1973.

Lubasch, Arnold H. "Convicted Killer Defends 'Revolutionary' Acts at U.S. Brink's Trial." New York Times, 16 August 1983, Late City Final Edition.

Sullivan, Joseph F. "Gunfight Suspect Caught in New Jersey." New York Times, 4 May 1973.

———. "Panther, Trooper Slain in Shoot-Out." New York Times, 3 May 1973.

"Sundiata Acoli." Can't Jail the Spirit: Political Prisoners in the U.S. A Collection of Biographies. 4th ed. Chicago: Committee to End the Marion Lockdown, 1998.

"Sundiata Acoli: New Afrikan Liberation Fighter." Revolutionary Worker #941, 25 January 1998. rwor.org/a/v19/940-49/941/acoli.htm.

Daniel Berrigan

Baron, Virginia. "Pushy Priests." Nonviolent Activist. September–October 1997. www.warresisters.org/nva0997-6.htm (18 March 2002)

Berrigan, Daniel. America Is Hard to Find: Notes from the Underground and Letters from Danbury Prison. New York: Doubleday, 1972.

———. "Daniel Berrigan: War in Heaven, Peace on Earth." Spirituality Today 40, no. 1 (Spring 1988). www.spiritualitytoday.org/spir2day/884013berrigan.html (18 March 2002).

———. Lights on in the House of the Dead: A Prison Diary. New York: Doubleday, 1974.

———. Prison Poems. Greensboro, N.C.: Unicorn, 1973.

———. To Dwell in Peace: An Autobiography. San Francisco: Harper & Row, 1987.

———. The Trial of the Catonsville Nine. Boston: Beacon, 1970.

———, and Robert Coles. The Geography of Faith: Underground Conversations on Religious, Political and Social Change. 30th Anniversary Edition. Woodstock, Vt.: Skylight Paths, 2001.

———, and Lee Lockwood. Daniel Berrigan: Absurd Convictions, Modest Hopes: Conversations after Prison with Lee Lockwood. New York: Random House, 1972.

Berrigan, Philip, with Fred A. Wilcox. Fighting the Lamb's War: Skirmishes with the American Empire: The Autobiography of Philip Berrigan. Monroe, Maine: Common Courage, 1996.

Billitteri, Thomas J. "Still Waging Peace." St Petersburg Times, 21 January 1991.

Casey, William Van Etten, and Philip Nobile, eds. The Berrigans. New York: Praeger, 1971.

Fox, Alan. "A Conversation between Daniel Berrigan and Alan Fox." Rattle. www.rattle.com/rattle11/poetry/interview.html (18 March 2002).

Gallagher, Michael. Laws of Heaven: Catholic Activists Today. New York: Ticknor & Fields, 1992.

Jacobs, Harold, ed. Weatherman. Berkeley, Calif.: Ramparts Press, 1970.

Lerner, Jonathan. "I Was a Terrorist." Washington Post, 24 February 2002.

Pennsylvania, Commonwealth v Rev. Daniel Berrigan. PA Super. Ct. 1984.

Pennsylvania, Commonwealth v Rev. Daniel Berrigan. PA Super. Ct. 1987.

Polner, Mary, and Jim O'Grady. Disarmed and Dangerous: The Radical Lives and Times of Daniel and Philip Berrigan. New York: Basic, 1997.

Raines, John C., ed. Conspiracy: The Implications of the Harrisburg Trial for the Democratic Tradition. New York: Harper & Row, 1974.

Stringfellow, William, and Anthony Towne. Suspect Tenderness: The Ethics of the Berrigan Witness. New York: Holt, Rinehart & Winston, 1971.

Wallis, Jim. "Steadfast with a Smile: A Conversation with Daniel Berrigan." *Sojourners Magazine*, November–December 1995. home.onestop.net/wilderness/berrigan2.htm (18 March 2002).

Dhoruba Bin Wahad (Richard Moore)

Anderson, Cerisse. "Retrial Ordered in Murder Case After 20 Years." *New York Law Journal* (23 December 1992): 1.

Bin Wahad, Dhoruba. "Beggars on Horseback." Unpublished essay.

———. "COINTELPRO and the Destruction of Black Leaders and Organizations." *Bulletin in Defense of Marxism* (May 1993): 22–26.

———. Interview with Bill Weinberg. "Dhoruba Bin Wahad: Veteran Black Panther and 19-year Political Prisoner." *Shadow* 36. 6 March 2002. shadow.mediafilter.org/mff/s36/s36.dbw.html.

———. "Speaking Truth to Power: Political Prisoners in the United States." In *Criminal Injustice: Confronting the Prison Crisis*, edited by Elihu Rosenblatt. Boston: South End Press, 1996.

Boyd, Herb. "Ex-Panther's Lawsuit Settled." *Black World Today*, 9 December 2000. 6 March 2002. www.twbt.com.

Cohen, Patricia. "One Man's Lifetime Struggle." *New York Times*, 13 December 1993, city ed., 47.

Fletcher, Jim, Tanaquil Jones, and Sylvere Lotringer, eds. *Still Black, Still Strong: Survivors of the U.S. War against Black Revolutionaries*. New York: Semiotext(e), 1993.

Framing the Panthers in Black and White. Directed by Annie Goldstein and Chris Bratton. Chicago: Video Databank, 1990. Videocassette.

Fraser, Gerald C. "F.B.I. Files Reveal Moves against Black Panthers." *New York Times*, 19 October 1980, late ed., A1.

Heath, G. Louis, ed. *Off the Pigs!: The History and Literature of the Black Panther Party*. Metuchen, N.J.: Scarecrow Press, 1976.

Newton, Huey. *War against the Panthers: a Study of Repression in America*. New York: Harlem River Press, 1996.

People of the State of New York v Dhoruba Bin Wahad, Formerly Richard Moore. Lexis 1232. NY Sup. Ct., 8 February 1990.

People of the State of New York v Joan Bird and Afeni Shakur. Lexis 1791. NY Sup. Ct., 4 March 1971.

Richard Moore v New York State Board of Parole. Lexis 11746. NY Sup. Ct., 14 November 1990.

Sullivan, Ronald. "Court Erupts as Judge Frees Panther." *New York Times*, 23 March 1990, late ed., B1.

Wolf, Paul, ed. "COINTELPRO: The Untold American Story, Part III." *Freedom: Channel 4*. 1 September 2001. www.mumia.org/afrikan.net/html/article.php (7 March 2002).

Rita Bo Brown (Rita Darlene Brown)

Brown, Bo. "White North American Political Prisoners." In *Criminal Injustice: Confronting the Prison Crisis*, edited by Elihu Rosenblatt. Boston: South End Press, 1996.

————, et al. "Reflections on Critical Resistance." *Social Justice: A Journal of Crime, Conflict and World Order* 27, no. 3 (Fall 2000).

Burton-Rose, Daniel. "Guerrillas in Our Midst: Where Do Armed Revolutionaries in the US Go after They Lay Down Their Arms?" *Lip Magazine.* 15 February 1999. www.lipmagazine. org/articles/featrose_9.htm.

"Member of Revolutionary Group Arrested by the F.B.I. in Seattle." *New York Times*, 6 November 1977, 34 col. 6.

Out of Control Lesbian Committee to Support Women Political Prisoners. *Prison Activist Resource Center.* www.prisonactivist.org/ooc/.

"The Radical George Jackson Brigade . . ." *The Associated Press*, 2 November 1977, PM cycle.

Rita Darlene Brown v Kenneth R. Neagle. United States District Court for the Southern District of West Virginia, Beckley Division, 486 F. Supp. 364; December 10, 1979.

United States of America v Rita Darlene Brown. United States Court of Appeals, Ninth Circuit, 602 F.2d 909, August 22, 1979.

Winn, Scott. "Seattle Welcomes Back Radical Queer Activists from the 1970s: An Interview with Lesbian Activist Bo (Rita D. Brown)." *Seattle Gay News Online.* www.sgn.org/ Archives/sgn.8.13.99/bo-sgn.htm.

————. "Talkin' about a Revolution: An Interview with Prison Rights Activist Bo Brown." *Real Change.* www.realchangenews.org/pastarticles/interviews/fea.bo.html.

"Woman Admits Bank Robbery." *New York Times*, 12 January 1978, section 2, p. 4, col. 4.

Marilyn Buck

Baraldini, Sylvia, Marilyn Buck, Susan Rosenberg, and Laura Whitehorn. "Women's Control Unit." In *Criminal Injustice: Confronting the Prison Crisis*, edited by Elihu Rosenblatt. Boston: South End, 1996.

Buck, Marilyn. "On Self-Censorship." Berkeley, Calif.: Parentheses Writing Series, Small Press Distribution, 1995.

————. "On the Burning of African American Churches." *Prison News Service* 55 (Summer/ Fall 1996).

————. "Prisons, Social Control, and Political Prisoners." *Social Justice* 27, no. 3: 200.

————. *Rescue the Word: Poems.* San Francisco: Friends of Marilyn Buck, 2001.

————. "Thoughts on the Surrender of Kathy Power." *Downtown*, New York, 1993. www. etext.org/Politics/Arm.The.Sp...oners/marilyn-buck.interview.december-93 (17 March 2002).

————, and Laura Whitehorn. "Legal Issues for Women in Federal Prisons: FCI Dublin California." *The Legal Journal* 10, no. 11 (Winter 1996).

————. "Interview with Resistance in Brooklyn." In *Enemies of the State: A Frank Discussion of Past Political Movements, Victories and Errors, and the Current Political Climate for Revolutionary Struggle within the U.S.A.* Toronto: Resistance in Brooklyn and Arm the Spirit, 2001.

Can't Jail the Spirit: Political Prisoners in the U.S. 5th ed. Chicago: Committee to End the Marion Lockdown, 2002.

"Marilyn Buck Page." *Prison Activist Resource Center.* www.prisonactivist.org/pps + pows/ marilynbuck/ (27 February 2002).

Pagán, Dylcia, Alicia Rodríguez, Ida Luz Rodríguez, Carmen Valentín, Marilyn Buck, Linda

Evans, and Laura Whitehorn. "Statement from Women Political Prisoners on the Take-over of the KPFA." *Prison Activist Resource Center.* www.prisonactivist.org/pps+pows/pps4kpfa.html (17 March 2002).

Resistance Conspiracy. San Francisco: Bay Area Committee to Support the Resistance Conspiracy Defendants [distributor], Oakland: Peralta Colleges Television (PCTV) Production Company, 1990. Videocassette.

Shakur, Mutulu, Marilyn Buck, Geronimo Pratt, Albert Washington, Sekou Odinga, Cecilio Chui Ferguson El, Susan Rosenberg, and David Gilbert. "Prisoners of War: The Legal Standing of Members of National Liberation Movements." In *Cages of Steel: The Politics of Imprisonment in the United States*, edited by Ward Churchill and J. J. Vander Wall, 152–73. Washington, D.C.: Maisonneuve, 1992.

Safiya Bukhari-Alston (Bernice Jones)

Bukhari, Safiya. "Coming of Age." *Notes From a New Afrikan P.O.W. Journal, Book 7.* Spear & Shield Publications.

Bukhari-Alston, Safiya. "The Death Penalty is a Politically Repressive Tool." In *The Machinery of Death: A Shocking Indictment of Capital Punishment in the United States*. Amnesty International USA, 1995.

———. "Interview with Safiya Bukhari-Alston." New York City, 27 September 1992. *Arm the Spirit.* 8 March 1995. burn.ucsd.edu/archives/ats-l/1995.Mar/0017.html.

———. "On the Question of Sexism within the Black Panther Party." *The Black Panther*, Fall/Winter 1993, I(2). 4 www.hartford-wp.com/archives/45a/014.html.

Matthews, Tracye A. "No One Ever Asks What a Man's Role in the Revolution Is: Gender and the Politics of the Black Panther Party." *The Black Panther Party [Reconsidered]*, edited by Charles Jones. Baltimore: Black Classic Press, 1998.

Montgomery, Paul L. "4 Seized near Manhole in Alleged Plot to Free Black Army Friends in Tombs." *New York Times*, 28 December 1973, 36 col. 1.

"Police Break Gang Plot!" *Tri-State Defender* 22, no. 52 (5 January 1974): 2.

Safiya Asya Bukhari, a/k/a Bernice Jones v. Virginia Correctional Center for Women. No. 75-1809, United States Court of Appeals for the Fourth Circuit, 530 F.2d 967; 1975 U.S. App. LEXIS 11791. Submitted October 28, 1975; November 24, 1975.

"3 in an Alleged Plot to Free 6 at Tombs Released by Judge." *New York Times*, 24 January 1974, 41 col. 4.

United States of America v. Bernice Jones, a/k/a Safiya Asya Bukhari, a/k/a/ Beverly Dunlap. United States Court of Appeals for the Fourth Circuit, 529 F.2d 518; 1976 U.S. App. LEXIS 12725. Submitted December 30, 1975; February 23, 1976.

Angela Y. Davis

Aptheker, Bettina. *The Morning Breaks: The Trial of Angela Davis.* New York: International Publishers, 1975.

Davis, Angela Y. *Angela Davis: An Autobiography.* New York: Random House, 1974.

———. *Violence against Women and the Ongoing Challenge to Racism.* Latham, N.Y.: Kitchen Table, 1985.

———. *Women, Race & Class.* New York: Vintage, 1983.

————, and Bettina Aptheker, eds. *If They Come in the Morning: Voices of Resistance*. New York: Third Press, 1971.

James, Joy, ed. *The Angela Y. Davis Reader*. Malden, Mass.: Blackwell, 1998.

————. *Shadowboxing: Representations of Black Feminist Politics*. New York: St. Martin's, 1999.

Perkins, Margo V. *Autobiography as Activism: Three Black Women of the Sixties*. Jackson: University Press of Mississippi, 2000.

Lorenzo Komboa Ervin (Lorenzo Edward Ervin)

Abdullah, Ali Khallid. "Black Liberation and Anarchism." *Anarchist Black Cross*. www. anarchistblackcross.org/content/essays/articles/race/blib.html (14 March 2002).

Abron, JoNina M. *Protest*. www.protest.net/view.cgi?view = 1933 (14 March 2002).

————. "State's High Court Nixes Chattanooga 8 Case over Arrest." *Tri-State Defender*, 21 March 2001, A1.

Committee to Defend the Chattanooga 3. "Lorenzo Returned to Court and Has Been Assigned a New Prosecutor and Judge." *Infoshop*, 1999. www.infoshop.org/komboa_ervin. html (14 March 2002).

Ervin, Lorenzo Komboa. *Anarchism and the Black Revolution*. Philadelphia: Mid-Atlantic Anarchist Publishing Collective, 1993.

————. "Behind the Walls of Prison." In *Race Traitor*, edited by Noel Ignatiev and John Garvey, 59–66. New York: Routledge, 1996.

————. "A Call for Amnesty for Black Political Prisoners and POWs." *Black Autonomy*. www.afrikan.net/black.autonomy/farc43.html (14 March 2002).

————. "Interview with Lorenzo Komboa Ervin: The Need for Black Autonomy." *Organise!* burn.ucsd.edu/%7Eacf/org/issue46/lorenzo.html (14 March 2002).

————. "The Racist Frame-Up of the Chattanooga Three Continues." *Indymedia* 2001. www.indymedia.org/news/2001/01/1315.php (14 March 2002).

"Hijacker of Plane to Cuba Gets First Life Sentence for Offense." *New York Times*, 7 July 1970, 58.

"Hijacking Suspect Seized at Kennedy." *New York Times*, 25 September 1969, 21.

"Jet with 68 Hijacked to Cuba; 'Big Bore,' One Passenger Says." *New York Times*, 26 February 1969, 94.

Lorenzo Edward Ervin, Jr. v Billy Ray Lanier. No. 74 C 1681, United States District Court for the Eastern District Of New York, 404 F. Supp. 15; 1975 U.S. Dist. LEXIS 15135 (November 24, 1975).

United States of America v Lorenzo Edward Ervin, Jr. No. 30442 Summary Calendar, United States Courts of Appeals for the Fifth Circuit, 436 F.2d 1331; 1971 U.S. App. LEXIS 12329 (January 18, 1971).

Elizam Escobar

Associated Press. "Clinton Gives Clemency to Activists." 11 August 1999.

————. "11 Puerto Rican Political Prisoners Welcomed Home." 11 September 1999.

————. "Family, Memories Greet Ex-Prisoner." 13 September 1999.

————. "Nationalist Freed/Big Welcome Expected in Puerto Rico." 11 September 1999.

Editorial Desk. "Leniency and Silence." *New York Times*, 9 September 1999.

"Elizam Escobar." In *Can't Jail the Spirit: Political Prisoners in the U.S. A Collection of Biographies*. 4th ed. Chicago: Committee to End the Marion Lockdown, 1998.

"Freed FALN Members Will Rally." *Daily News*, 14 September 1999.

The Human Rights Committee. "Statement by the Human Rights Committee. Response to FBI." *Prison Activist Resource Center*. www.prisonactivist.org/quesalgan.HRCrespondeto FBI.html.

"Inmate: Offer Won't Be Accepted." *Los Angeles Times*, 3 September 1999.

Johnston, David. "Federal Agencies Opposed Leniency for 16 Militants: Report Offered Options, President Was Aware of Views When He Offered Clemency to Jailed Puerto Ricans." *New York Times*, 27 August 1999.

Napoli, Lisa. "The Legal Recognition of the National Identity of a Colonized People: The Case of Puerto Rico." *Boston College Third World Law Journal* (Spring 1998).

People against Racist Terror. "Puerto Rican Political Prisoners and Prisoners of War Released: Que Viva Puerto Rico Libre!" *Turning the Tide: Journal of Anti-Racist Action, Research and Education* 12, no. 3, Fall 1999. prisonactivist.org/quesalgan/turningtide.html.

Ramos, Efrén Rivera. *The Legal Construction of Identity: The Judicial and Social Legacy of American Colonialism in Puerto Rico*. Washington, D.C.: American Psychological Association, 2001.

Remes, Michael. "Bill on Clemency Offered; The Granting of Clemency to Puerto Rican Nationalists Prompts Congressional Republicans to Introduce Legislation Requiring Victims to Be Notified in Such Cases." *The Hartford Courant*, 9 February 2000.

Santiago, Roberto. "Poet of Puerto Rican Independence Still Marches for Freedom." *New York Daily News* (New York), 21 August 1999.

Seelye, Katharine Q. "Director of F.B.I. Opposed Clemency for Puerto Ricans." *New York Times*, 22 September 1999.

Squitieri, Tom. "House Rebukes Clinton on Clemency for FALN Members. Senate Is Scheduled to Vote Its Own Resolution." *USA Today*, 10 September 1999.

Statement from the Puerto Rican Political Prisoners. "United States House Resources Committee Hearings on Proposed Legislation Concerning the Status of Puerto Rico." Submitted April 19, 1997. *Prison Activist Resource Center*. www.prisonactivist.org/quesalgan/RCS.html.

Susler, Jan. "Puerto Rican Political Prisoners." *Radical Philosophy Review* 3, no. 1 (2000).

———. "Today's Puerto Rican Political Prisoners/Prisoners of War." In *The Puerto Rican Movement: Voices from the Diaspora*. Edited by Andrés Torres and José E. Velazquez. Philadelphia: Temple University Press, 1998.

Linda Evans, Susan Rosenberg, and Laura Whitehorn

Anderson, S. E., and Tony Medina, eds. *In Defense of Mumia*. New York: Writers and Readers Publishing, 1996.

Conspiracy of Voices: Poetry, Writings, and Art by the Women of the Resistance Conspiracy Case. Washington, D.C.: Emergency Committee to Defend the Human and Legal Rights of Political Prisoners, Madison, 1990.

CovertAction Information Bulletin #31, Winter 1989 (articles on Resistance Conspiracy case and Lexington High Security Unit).

Day, Susie. "Lesbian Political Prisoners." *Chicago Outweek*, November 5, 1989.

———. "Political Prisoners: Guilty until Proven Innocent." *Sojourner: The Women's Forum*, February 1989.

———. "Resistance Conspiracy Trial." *Z Magazine*, September 1989.

Goldberg, Eve, and Linda Evans. *The Prison Industrial Complex and the Global Economy*. San Francisco: Agit Press, 1998.

OUT: The Making of a Revolutionary. Third World Newsreel, 2000, videocassette.

Resistance Conspiracy. Bay Area Committee to Support the Resistance Conspiracy Defendents, 1990, videocassette.

Rosenblatt, Elihu. *Criminal Injustice*. Boston: South End Press, 1996.

Taifa, Nkechi, Kathleen Neal Cleaver, Michael Tarif Warren, Bruce Ellison, Geronimo ji Jaga, and Laura Whitehorn. *Human Rights in the U.S.: The Unfinished Story of Political Prisoners/Victims of COINTELPRO*. Atlanta: Human Rights Research Fund, 2001.

Through the Wire, produced by Nina Rosenblum, narrated by Susan Sarandon, 1990, videocassette.

Emma Goldman

Falk, Candace Serena. *Love, Anarchy, and Emma Goldman*. New Brunswick, N.J.: Rutgers University Press: 1984.

Goldman, Emma. *Anarchism and Other Essays*. New York: Mother Earth Publishing Association, 1911.

———. *Living My Life*. New York: Knopf, 1931.

———. *My Disillusionment in Russia*. Garden City, N.Y.: Doubleday, Page & Company, 1923.

———. *The Traffic in Women and Other Essays on Feminism*. New York: Times Change Press, 1970.

Shulman, Alix. *To the Barricades: The Anarchist Life of Emma Goldman*. New York: Thomas Y. Crowell, 1971.

Wexler, Alice. *Emma Goldman: An Intimate Life*. New York: Pantheon, 1984.

George Jackson

Armstrong, Gregory. *"The Dragon Has Come."* New York: Harper and Row, 1974.

———. Preface. *Blood in My Eye*. Baltimore: Black Classic Press, 1990.

Boyers, Jill Witherspoon. "George Jackson." In *Adam of Ifé: Black Women in Praise of Black Men: Poems*, edited by Naomi Long Madgett, 136–37. Detroit: Lotus Press, 1993.

Cummins, Eric. *The Rise and Fall of California's Radical Prison Movement*. Stanford, Calif.: Stanford University Press, 1994.

Durden-Smith, Jo. *Who Killed George Jackson?* New York: Knopf, 1976.

Eyes on the Prize II: A Nation of Law? Directed by Sheila Curran Bernard et al. PBS Home Video, 1990. Videocassette.

Genet, Jean. Appendix. "Introduction to the First Edition." *Soledad Brother: The Prison Letters of George Jackson,* by George Jackson. Chicago: Lawrence Hill Books, 1994.

"George Jackson: One-Third of His Life in Prison." *Washington Post*, 22 August 1971, A3.

"George Jackson Was New Breed of Convict." *Chicago Tribune*, 22 August 1971, 2.

Grady-Willis, Winston A. "The Black Panther Party: State Repression and Political Prisoners." In *The Black Panther Party [Reconsidered]*, edited by Charles E. Jones, 363–90. Baltimore: Black Classic Press, 1998.

Henderson, Earl Anthony. "Shadow of a Clue." In *Liberation, Imagination, and the Black Panther Party*, edited by Kathleen Cleaver and George Katsiaficas, 197–207. New York: Routledge, 2001.

Isserman, Maurice. "Where Have All the Convict Heroes Gone, Long Time Passing?" Review of *The Rise and Fall of California's Radical Prison Movement*, by Eric Cummins. *Radical History Review* 64 (1996): 113–17.

Jackson, George. *Blood in My Eye.* Baltimore: Black Classic Press, 1990.

———. *Soledad Brother: The Prison Letters of George Jackson.* Chicago: Lawrence Hill Books, 1994.

———. "A Talk with George Jackson." Interview with Jessica Mitford. *New York Times*, 13 June 1971, sec. 7, 30.

Jackson, Jonathan Jr. Introduction. *Soledad Brother: The Prison Letters of George Jackson*, by George Jackson. Chicago: Lawrence Hill Books, 1994.

Leapman, Michael. "Leader of Soledad Brothers Shot Dead 'in Prison Escape.'" *London Times*, 23 August 1971, A1 +.

Lewis, Melvin E. "Once I Was a Panther." In *The Black Panther Party [Reconsidered]*, edited by Charles E. Jones, 109–14. Baltimore: Black Classic Press, 1998.

Liberatore, Paul. *The Road to Hell: The True Story of George Jackson, Stephen Bingham, and the San Quentin Massacre.* New York: Atlantic Monthly Press, 1996.

Mann, Eric. *Comrade George: An Investigation into the Life, Political Thought, and Assassination of George Jackson.* New York: Harper & Row, 1974.

Newton, Huey P. Afterword. *Blood in My Eye*, by George Jackson. Baltimore: Black Classic Press, 1990.

Prisons on Fire: George Jackson, Attica & Black Liberation. Produced by Anita Johnson and Claude Marks. Freedom Archives. Oakland, Calif.: AK Press, 2002. Compact disc.

"San Quentin Escape Bid! 3 Guards, 3 Convicts Die." *Chicago Tribune*, 22 August 1971: 1 +.

Shakur, Sanyika. "Flowing in File: The George Jackson Phenomenon." *Wazo Weusi (Think Black): A Journal of Black Thought* 2, no. 2 (1995). www.efn.org/~chinosol/shakur (6 March 2002).

Singh, Nikhil Pal. "The Black Panthers and the 'Undeveloped Country' of the Left." In *The Black Panther Party [Reconsidered]*, edited by Charles E. Jones, 57–105. Baltimore: Black Classic Press, 1998.

"Soledad Brother Jackson, 5 Others Slain in San Quentin Escape Attempt." *Washington Post*, 22 August 1971, A1 +.

Soledad Brothers: George Jackson, 1941–1971, John Cluchette, 1943–, Fleeta Drumgo, 1945–. San Francisco: Soledad Brothers Legal Committee, 1971.

"3 Guards, 4 Convicts Killed as San Quentin Break Fails." *Boston Globe*, 22 August 1971, 1.

"3 Guards, 3 Prisoners, Soledad Brother Slain." *Atlanta Constitution*, 22 August 1971, A1.

Touré, Askia M. *A Song in Blood and Tears: A People's Poem.* San Francisco: Marcus Books, 1972.

Umoja, Akinyele Omowale. "Repression Breeds Resistance: The Black Liberation Army and the Radical Legacy of the Black Panther Party." In *Liberation, Imagination, and the Black Panther Party*, edited by Kathleen Cleaver and George Katsiaficas, 3–19. New York: Routledge, 2001.

Yee, Min S. *The Melancholy History of Soledad Prison: In which a Utopian Scheme Turns Bedlam*. New York: Harper's Magazine Press, 1973.

José Solís Jordan

Can't Jail the Spirit, 5th ed. Chicago: Committee to End the Marion Lockdown, 2002.

Carr, Raymond. *Puerto Rico: A Colonial Experiment*. New York: Vintage, 1984.

Catala Oliveras, José. "Sobre la economía de Puerto Rico." *El Nuevo Día*, October 21, 2000, 18.

Jackson, Sandra, and José Solís Jordan, eds. *I've Got a Story to Tell: Identity and Place in the Academy*. New York: Peter Lang, 1999.

Jordan, José Solís. "Language as Possibility: Comments on Identity and Language: [A Review of] *Puerto Rico: Culture, Politics and Identity*, by Nancy Morris." *International Journal of the Sociology of Language*, special issue on "Languages of Former Colonial Powers and Former Colonies—The Case of Puerto Rico," guest editors Carlos M. Ramirez Gonzalez and Rome Torres. 3, no. 142 (2000): 157–73.

———. *Public School Reform in Puerto Rico: Sustaining Colonial Models of Development*. Westport, Conn.: Greenwood, 1994.

"José Solís Jordan." *Prolibertad Faltan6 Freedom Campaign*. www.prolibertad.org/Faltan6.htm (22 July 2002).

Rodriguez, Michael. "In His Own Words: Interview with José Solís Jordan." *Que Ondee Sola* (student publication of Northeastern Illinois University), January 1999. Reprinted in *The Critical Criminologist* (July 1999). sun.soci.niu.edu/~critcrim/CC/Solís/Solís-int.html (22 July 2002).

Thornburg, Richard. "On promoting a referendum with regards to the political status of Puerto Rico." 102nd Congress, 1st Session. Washington, D.C.: Government Printing Office, United States Congressional Record, February 1991, 7.

Martin Luther King, Jr.

Ansbro, John J. *Martin Luther King, Jr.: The Making of a Mind*. Maryknoll, N.Y.: Orbis, 1982.

Branch, Taylor. *Parting the Waters: America in the King Years, 1954–1963*. Touchstone Books, 1989.

Cone, James. *Martin and Malcolm*. New York: Orbis, 1991.

Dyson, Michael Eric. *I May Not Get There with You: The True Martin Luther King, Jr*. New York: Free Press, 2000.

Garrow, David. *Bearing the Cross: Martin Luther King, Jr. and the Southern Christian Leadership Conference*. New York: William Morrow, 1999.

Hailey, Foster. "Dr. King Arrested at Birmingham." *New York Times*, 13 April 1963, late ed., A1.

King, Martin Luther, Jr. *The Autobiography of Martin Luther King, Jr*. Edited by Clayborne Carson. New York: Time Warner, 1998.

———. *Where Do We Go from Here: Chaos or Community?* Boston: Beacon, 1967.

———. *Why We Can't Wait*. New York: New American Library, 1964.

Lewis, David L. *King, A Critical Biography*. New York: Praeger, 1970.

Lincoln, C. Eric. *Martin Luther King, Jr.: A Profile*. New York: Hill and Wang, 1970.

McKnight, Gerald D. *The Last Crusade: Martin Luther King, Jr., the FBI, and the Poor People's Campaign.* Boulder, Colo.: Westview, 1998.

Miller, Keith D. *Voice of Deliverance: The Language of Martin Luther King and Its Sources.* New York: Free Press, 1992.

Schulke, Flip, and Penelope Ortner McPhee. *King Remembered.* New York: Norton, 1986.

Raymond Luc Levasseur

Anderson, Lisa. "US CO: 'Supermax' Prisons Typify U.S. Attitudes on Crime." *Chicago Tribune*, 2 August 1998. www.mapinc.org/drugnews/v98.n648.a02.html (18 March 2002).

Barrenador, Gusano. "On the Political Offense." *Social Anarchism* 22 (1996). library.nothingness.org/articles/SA/en/display/277 (18 March 2002).

Fink, Elizabeth. "Two-Year Sedition Trial Ends in Defense Victory." *Guild Notes* (January/February 1990).

Hundley, Kris. "Behind the Revolutionaries; The Ohio 7 Tell Their Stories: Part I." *Valley Advocate* (Springfield, Mass.), 24 August 1987. www.valleyadvocate.com/25th/archives/ohio_seven.html (18 March 2002).

———. "The Ohio 7 Tell Their Stories: Part II." *Valley Advocate* (Springfield, Mass.), 31 August 1987. www.valleyadvocate.com/25th/archives/ohio_seven.html (18 March 2002).

Levasseur, Raymond Luc. "Armed & Dangerous." *Letters from Exile.* home.earthlink.net/~neoludd/armed.htm (18 March 2002).

———. "Comrade George." *Inside Ktes.* WORT, Madison. 16 August 1990. home.earthlink.net/~neoludd/comgeo.htm (18 March 2002).

———. "Dear Betty." *Letters from Exile.* March 1990. home.earthlink.net/~neoludd/betty.htm (18 March 2002).

———. "For Nuh Washington." *Letters from Exile.* April 2000. home.earthlink.net/~neoludd/nuh2.htm (18 March 2002).

———. "John Brown 2000." *Letters from Exile.* 2000. home.earthlink.net/~neoludd/brown.htm (18 March 2002).

———. "Letter from 'America's Gulag.'" *Sunday Times* [London], 23 May 1993, Features.

———. "Malcolm." *Letters from Exile.* May 1993. home.earthlink.net/~neoludd/malcolm.htm (18 March 2002).

———. "Raymond Luc Levasseur." In *Can't Jail the Spirit*, 5th ed., 182–83. Chicago: Committee to End the Marion Lockdown, 2002.

———. "The Trial Statement of Ray Luc Levasseur." *Letters from Exile.* January 1989. (Opening Statement, 10 January 1989: Springfield, Mass.)/home.earthlink.net/~neoludd/statement.htm (18 March 2002).

———. *Until All Are Free: The Trial Statement of Ray Luc Levasseur* (Pamphlet). London: Attack International, 1989.

In re: Levasseur et al. 815 F.2d 691. U.S. App. 1987.

Levasseur v Magnusson et al. 774 F.2d 1149. U.S. App. 1985.

Levasseur v State of Tennessee. 464 S.W.2d 315. TN Crim. App. 1970.

"Mistrial for Radicals." *Newsday*, 30 November 1989, home ed., 16.

Myers, Ken. "In the Matter of a Haircut: A Test of Will—and Power." *The National Law Journal*, 10 December 1984, 13.

"The Nation." *Los Angeles Times*, 30 April 1986, 2.

Teitell, Beth. "Life on the Lam; For Fugitives, There's No Happily Ever After in a Life Underground." *Boston Herald*, 22 August 1995, 33.

"U.S. Drops '86 Sedition, Bombing, Case." *St. Louis Post-Dispatch*, 3 December 1989, 12D.

U.S. v Levasseur. 609 F. Supp. 849. U.S. Dist. 1985.

U.S. v Levasseur et al. 618 F. Supp. 1390. U.S. Dist. 1985.

U.S. v Levasseur et al. 619 F. Supp. 775. U.S. Dist. 1985.

U.S. v Levasseur et al. 620 F. Supp. 624. U.S. Dist. 1985.

U.S. v Levasseur et al. 635 F. Supp. 251. U.S. Dist.1986.

U.S. v Levasseur et al. 816 F.2d 37. U.S. App. 1987.

U.S. v Levasseur et al. 826 F.2d 158. U.S. App. 1987.

U.S. v Levasseur et al. 699 F. Supp. 965. U.S. Dist. 1988.

U.S. v Levasseur et al. 846 F.2d 786. U.S. App. 1988.

U.S. v Levasseur et al. Crim. A. No. 86-18—Y. U.S. Dist. 1988.

U.S. v Levasseur et al. 699 F. Supp. 995. U.S. Dist. 1988.

U.S. v Levasseur et al. 704 F. Supp. 1158. U.S. Dist. 1989.

Malcolm X (Malcolm Little)

Abu-Jamal, Mumia. "Musings on Malcolm." *All Things Censored*. Edited by Noelle Hanrahan. New York: Seven Stories, 2000. Compact disc.

Appiah, Kwame Anthony, and Henry Louis Gates, Jr., eds. *Africana: Encyclopedia of African and African-American Experience*. New York: Civitas, 1999.

Breitman, George. *The Last Year of Malcolm X: The Evolution of a Revolutionary*. New York: Schocken, 1967.

Collins, Patricia Hill. "Learning to Think for Ourselves: Malcolm X's Black Nationalism Reconsidered." In *Malcolm X: In Our Own Image*, edited by Joe Wood. New York: St. Martin's, 1992.

Davis, Angela Y. "Meditations on the Legacy of Malcolm X," and "Prisons, Repression, and Resistance." In *The Angela Y. Davis Reader*, edited by Joy James. Malden, Mass.: Blackwell, 1998.

Davis, Thulani, and Howard Chapnick. *Malcolm X: The Great Photographs*. New York: Stewart, Tabori, & Chang, 1993.

Dyson, Michael Eric. "Inventing and Interpreting Malcolm X." In *The Seductions of Biography*, edited by Mary Rhiel and Davis Suchoff. New York: Routledge, 1999.

———. *Making Malcolm: The Myth and Meaning of Malcolm X*. New York: Oxford University Press, 1996.

Malcolm X. *The Autobiography of Malcolm X*. New York: Ballantine, 1964.

———. *By Any Means Necessary*. Edited by George Breitman. New York: Pathfinders Press, 1970.

———. "To Mississippi Youth." In *Malcolm X Speaks: Selected Speeches and Statements*, edited by George Breitman. New York: Grove Weidenfeld, 1990.

"Malcolm X." Editorial. *New York Times*, 22 February 1965, L20.

"Malcolm X Grassroots Movement." *Malcolm X Grassroots Movement Page*. 6 March 2002. www.malcolmxgrassroots.com.

Yakubu, Owosu Yaki. "The Meaning of Malcolm X for the Imprisoned Afrikans in the United States." In *Teaching Malcolm X*, edited by Theresa Perry. New York: Routledge, 1996.

Jalil Abdul Muntaqim (Anthony Bottom)

Agard-Jones, Vanessa. "Urgent Action: Jalil Muntaqim Needs Our Help!" December 2000. www.prisonactivist.org/pipermail/prisonact-list/2000-December.txt.

Bell, Herman. "New York Three Update." June 1997. prisonactivist.org/pps + pows/ny3_ update.html.

Bloom, Steve. *Against the Current*. "'Amnesty and Freedom for All Political Prisoners': The Jericho '98 March." (1998). www.igc.org/solidarity/atc/bloom73.html.

Can't Jail the Spirit: Political Prisoners in the U.S. 4th ed. Chicago: Committee to End the Marion Lockdown, March 1998; 5th ed., 2002.

Fried, Joseph. "2 Policemen Slain by Shots in Back, 2 Men Sought." *New York Times*, 21 May 1971, 1.

Kaufman, Michael T. "Slaying of One of the Last Black Liberation Army Leaders Still at Large Ended a 7-Month Manhunt." *New York Times*, 16 November 1973, 10.

Muntaqim, Jalil Abdul. "The Cold War of the 90's." *Prison Activist Resource Center*. prison activist.org/pubs/jalil-cold-war-90s.html. Reprinted from Prison News Service, Issue #52, September–October 1995.

———. "Criminalization of Poverty in Capitalist America." *Prison Activist Resource Center*. www.prisonactivist.org/pubs/jalil-crim-pov.html. Reprinted in Chinosole, ed., *Schooling the Generations in the Politics of Prison*. Berkeley, Calif.: New Earth Publications, 1996.

———. "On the Black Liberation Army." *Arm the Spirit* (18 September 1979).

———. "Statement for the September 21, 1996 founding rally of the know INJUSTICE Coalition." Dolores Park, San Francisco, 1996. *Prison Activist Resource Center*. prisonactivist.org/pps + pows/jbottom.html.

New York State Task Force on Political Prisoners. "Clemency Petition."

Revolutionary Worker #951. "Report from Jericho '98." Washington, D.C. 5 April 1998. rwor.org/a/v19/950-59/951/jerico.htm.

Schweizer, Errol. "Free the Land! The Victory Gardens Project." *Commonsense Ecology* (May 2001).

Van Gelder, Lawrence. "Weapons Found Smuggled to 3 Sentenced in Murder." *New York Times*, 13 May 1975.

Michele Naar-Obed

Naar-Obed, Michele. *Maternal Convictions: A Mother Beats a Missile into a Plowshare*. Maple, Wisc.: Laurentian Shield Resources for Nonviolence, 1998.

Obuszewski, Max. *Press Release—Protest Mistreatment of Plowshares by Baltimore Probation*. 12 April 1999. csf.colorado.edu/forums/peace/apr99/0029.html.

Rivera, John. "Jonah House Supporters Protest Probation Terms; 2 with Criminal Records Not Allowed to Live There." *The Baltimore Sun*, 14 April 1999.

Huey P. Newton

Black Panthers. *Up against the Wall*. London: Ellipsis, 2000. Compact disc.

Courtright, John. "Rhetoric of the Gun: An Analysis of the Rhetorical Modifications of the Black Panther Party." *The Journal of Black Studies* 4, no. 3 (March 1974): 249–67.

Erikson, Erik H., and Huey P. Newton. *In Search of Common Ground: Conversations with Erik H. Erikson and Huey P. Newton*. New York: Norton, 1973.

Foner, Philip. *The Black Panthers Speak*. Philadelphia: Lippincott, 1970.

Henderson, Errol Anthony. "The Lumpenproletariat as Vanguard?: The Black Panther Party, Social Transformation, and Pearson's Analysis of Huey Newton." *The Journal of Black Studies* 28, no. 2 (November 1997): 171–79.

Jones, Charles, ed. *The Black Panther Party [Reconsidered]*. Baltimore: Black Classic Press, 1998.

Marine, Gene. *The Black Panthers: Eldridge Cleaver, Huey Newton, Bobby Seale, A Compelling Study of the Angry Young Revolutionaries Who Have Shaken a Black Fist at White America*. New York: Signet, 1969.

Newton, Huey P. *Revolutionary Suicide*. New York: Harcourt and Brace, 1973.

———. *To Die for the People*. New York: Random House, 1972.

Panther! Directed by Mario Van Peebles. 1995. Videocassette.

Pearson, Hugh. *The Shadow of the Panthers: Huey Newton and the Price of Black Power in America*. Cambridge, Mass.: Perseus Publishing, 1994.

Smith, Jennifer. *An International History of the Black Panther Party*. New York: Garland Publishing, 1999.

Winston, Henry. "The Crisis of the Black Panther Party." In *Strategy for a Black Agenda: A Critique of New Theories of Liberation in the United States and Africa*. New York: International Publishers, 1973.

Leonard Peltier

Abu-Jamal, Mumia. "Peltier's Life: A Sun Dance (A review of Peltier's book, *Prison Writings: My Life Is My Sun Dance*)." 11 November 1999. www.iacenter.org/sundance.htm.

Anderson, Scott. "The Martyrdom of Leonard Peltier." *Outside Magazine*, July 1995. www.outsidemag.com.

Associated Press. "Indian Is Found Guilty of First-Degree Murder in Death of 2 F.B.I. Men." *New York Times*, 19 April 1977.

Incident at Oglala. Directed by Michael Apted. Carolco International and Spanish Fork Motion Picture Company, 1991.

Johnson, Troy. *American Indian Activism*. Chicago: University of Illinois Press, 1997.

Matthiessen, Peter. *In the Spirit of Crazy Horse*. New York: Penguin, 1992.

Messerschmidt, Jim. *The Trial of Leonard Peltier*. Boston: South End Press, 1983.

Peltier, Leonard. "Leonard Peltier on Withheld FBI Documents in the Timothy McVeigh Case." www.iacenter.org/lp_fbimcveigh.htm.

———. *Prison Writings: My Life Is My Sun Dance*. New York: St. Martin's, 1999.

———. "Statement from Leonard Peltier in Response to 'Forum' Article Titled: Forum Receives Letters Indicating Bomb Threats." 15 July 2001. www.iacenter.org/lp_forum.htm.

Weyler, Rex. *Blood of the Land*. Philadelphia: New Society Publishers, 1992.

Assata Shakur (JoAnne Chesimard)

"Assata Shakur: The Continuity of Struggle." *Souls* 1, no. 2 (Spring 1999).

Bin Wahad, Dhoruba, Mumia Abu-Jamal, and Assata Shakur. *Still Black, Still Strong: Survi-*

vors of the U.S. War against Black Revolutionaries. Edited by Jim Fletcher, Tanaquil Jones, and Sylvère Lotringer. New York: Semiotext(e), 1993.

Hinds, Lennox S. Foreword. Assata: An Autobiography. Chicago: Lawrence Hill Books, 1987.

Mealy, Rosemari. "Assata Shakur: The Life of a Revolutionary." CovertAction Quarterly 65 (Fall 1998).

Parenti, Christian. "Assata Shakur Speaks from Exile: Post-modern Maroon in the Ultimate Palenque." Z Magazine 11, no. 3 (March 1998).

Perkins, Margo V. Autobiography as Activism: Three Black Women of the Sixties. Jackson: University Press of Mississippi, 2000.

Ratner, Michael. "Immoral Bounty for Assata." CovertAction Quarterly 65 (Fall 1998).

Shakur, Assata. Assata: An Autobiography. Chicago: Lawrence Hill Books, 1987.

———— (as told to Ida E. Lewis). "Assata Shakur: Profiled and on the Run." The New Crisis 107, issue 6 (November/December 2000).

Williams, Evelyn. Inadmissible Evidence: The Story of the African-American Trial Lawyer Who Defended the Black Liberation Army. Brooklyn: Lawrence Hill, 1993.

Mutulu Shakur (Jeral Wayne William)

Bandele, Tarikh Tehuti. "Prisoners Continue to Languish." The Michigan Citizen 23, no. 27 (27 May 2001–2 June 2001): A9.

————. "Opinions & Views: Prisoners Continue to Languish." The Michigan Citizen 23, no. 28 (3 June 2001–9 June 2001): A9.

"Dr. Mutulu Shakur." Prison Activist Resource Center. www.prisonactivist.org/pps + pows/mutulu-st.html.

Gado, Mark. "Ambush: The Brink's Robbery of 1981." Crime Libraries Online. www.crimelibrary.com/terrorists/brinks/index.htm.

"In US-Brink's Trial, New Afrika Wins." New Afrikan: Organ of the Provisional Government of the Republic of New Afrika 9, no. 3 (December 1983): 3.

"Inside the Brink's Story: A War of National Liberation Disclosed." New Afrikan: Organ of the Provisional Government of the Republic of New Afrika 9, no. 3 (December 1983): 6.

Kilaam, Malik, and Mutulu Shakur. "Freedom Fighter—Mutulu Shakur." nationtime.com/nationtime/012001mutulu.ram.

"Memorandum Opinion." Shakur v Federal Bureau of Prisons, et al. U.S. District Court for the District of Columbia. Civil Action No. 96-646. February 3, 1998. Available online, Lexis Nexis.

"Memorandum Opinion and Order." Mutulu Shakur and Marilyn Buck v United States of America. U.S. District Court for the Southern District of New York. 97-CV-2908. January 13, 1999. Available online, Lexis Nexis.

Odinga, Sekou, Hanif Shabazz Bey, Mutulu Shakur, Kojo, Jalil Muntaqim, Jihad Mumit, Sundiata Acoli, and Geronimo ji-Jaga. "Statement in Support of Consolidation from New Afrikan POWs and Political Prisoners in Lewisburg, Penn., New York, and California Prisons: Toward the Objective of Building a National Liberation Front." Jericho Movement (27 March 1998): 3.

Shakur, Mutulu. "Another Crime Bill?" www.efn.org/~ironplow/mutulush.

————. "Letter to Biggie's Family." www.pacup.com/tuth/special/mutulubig.html.

————. "Mutulu Shakur: New African Political Prisoner." In Can't Jail the Spirit: Political

Prisoners in the U.S., 4th ed. Chicago: Committee to End the Marion Lockdown, March 1998.

———. "To My Son." www.tupacnet.org/life/letter.htm.

Standing Deer (Robert Hugh Wilson)

Fortier, Barbara. "Standing Deer's Health Update as of November 17, 1999." 17 November 1999. www.iacenter.org/sdmed.html.

Matthiessen, Peter. *In the Spirit of Crazy Horse.* New York: Viking, 1980.

"Peltier Files Lawsuit; Claims Mistreatment at Federal Center." *U.P.I.*, 6 February 1985.

People of the State of Illinois v Robert Wilson. Lexis 2224. Appellate Ct. of Ill., 21 April 1976.

Standing Deer, Anna. "Standing Deer Released from Prison after Almost 25 Years!" *Spirit of Freedom.* 27 February 2002. www.spiritoffreedom.org.uk/content/court.html (16 March 2002).

Standing Deer, Robert. "Coming Home." 19 November 1994. www.sonic.net/~doretk/archivearch...erican/coming%20homestanding%20deer.html (18 March 2002).

———. "A Message to the People from Standing Deer." *IA Center.* 18 June 2000. www.iacenter.org/stdeer1.html (4 April 2002).

———. "Standing Deer: A Message to the People." 18 September 1999. www.angelfire.com/biz/backtotheblanket/standingd.html (18 March 2002).

———. "Step into the Nightmare." *Native Web.* 28 September 1998. www.nativeweb.org/pages/legal/sdnightmare.html (17 March 2002).

———. "Take Heed—Trouble Coming." *Huntsville Item*, 6 January 1998.

———. "What Is in Your Heart They Cannot Take." February 1998. www.sonic.net/~doretk/Issues/98-04%20%20spr/whatsin.html (16 March 2002).

Wexler, Rey. *Blood of the Land: The Government and Corporate Wars against First Nations.* Philadelphia: New Society Publishers, 1992.

Index

Permissions

Contributors to this volume, as well as *The Black Scholar*, *Radical Therapy*, and Writers House, granted free access to reprint their respective essays; Pathfinder Press provided its essay for a reduced fee.

Chapter 1: *Letter from Birmingham Jail*, by Martin Luther King, Jr. is reprinted by arrangement with the Estate of Dr. Martin Luther King, Jr. c/o Writers House as agent for the proprietor. Copyright 1963 Martin Luther King, Jr., renewed by Coretta Scott King.

Chapter 2: *The Ballot or the Bullet (Abridged)*, by Malcolm X. Copyright © 1965, 1989 by the estate of Betty Shabazz and Pathfinder Press. Reprinted by permission of Pathfinder Press.

Chapter 4: *Prison, Where Is Thy Victory?* by Huey P. Newton, copyright © by Stronghold Consolidated Productions. Used by permission of Random House, Inc.

Chapter 6: *COINTELPRO and the Destruction of Black Leaders and Organizations (Abridged)*, by Dhoruba Bin Wahad, is reprinted by permission of the author.

Chapter 7: *On the Black Liberation Army (Abridged)*, by Jalil Abdul Muntaqim is reprinted by permission of the author.

Chapter 8: *July 4th Address (Abridged)*, by Assata Shakur, is reprinted by permission of *The Black Scholar*.

Chapter 9: *Coming of Age: A Black Revolutionary*, by Safiya Bukhari-Alston, appears by permission of the author.

Chapter 10: *An Updated History of the New Afrikan Prison Struggle (Abridged)*, by Sundiata Acoli, appears by permission of the author.

Chapter 11: *Anarchism and the Black Revolution (Abridged)*, by Lorenzo Komboa Ervin, appears by permission of the author.

Chapter 12: *Intellectuals and the Gallows*, by Mumia Abu-Jamal, is reprinted by permission of the author.

Chapter 13: *Genocide against the Black Nation in the U.S. Penal System (Abridged)*, by Mutulu Shakur, Anthony X. Bradshaw, Malik Dinguswa, Terry Long, Mark Cook, Adolfo Matos, and James Haskins, appears by permission of Mutulu Shakur.

Chapter 14: *The Struggle for Status under International Law*, by Marilyn Buck, appears by permission of the author.

Chapter 15: *White North American Political Prisoners*, by Rita Bo Brown, appears by permission of the author.

Chapter 16: *On Trial (Abridged)*, by Raymond Luc Levasseur, is reprinted by permission of the author.

Chapter 17: *Letter to the Weathermen*, by Daniel Berrigan, appears by permission of the author.

Chapter 18: *Maternal Convictions: A Mother Beats a Missile into a Plowshare (Abridged)*, by Michele Naar-Obed, is reprinted by permission of the author.

Chapter 19: *Dykes and Fags Want to Know: Interview with Lesbian Political Prisoners*, by Linda Evans, Susan Rosenberg, and Laura Whitehorn—QUISP. Printed with permission of the political prisoners interviewed and with their gratitude to the queer activists who supported them.

Chapter 20: *This Is Enough!* by José Solís Jordan, appears by permission of the author.

Chapter 21: *Art of Liberation: A Vision of Freedom*, by Elizam Escobar, is reprinted by permission of the author and New Society Publishers.

Chapter 22: *Violence and the State (Abridged)*, by Standing Deer (Robert Hugh Wilson), appears by permission of *Radical Therapy*.

Chapter 23: *Inipi: Sweat Lodge*, by Leonard Peltier is reprinted by permission of the author and St. Martin's Press.

Epilogue: *Incommunicado: Dispatches from a Political Prisoner*, by Marilyn Buck, appears by permission of the author.

About the Editor

Joy James is professor at Brown University. She is the author of *Transcending the Talented Tenth: Black Leaders and American Intellectuals*; *Resisting State Violence: Radicalism, Gender and Race in U.S. Culture*; and *Shadowboxing: Representations of Black Feminist Politics*. Her edited works include *States of Confinement: Policing, Detention and Prisons*; *The Angela Y. Davis Reader*; *The Black Feminist Reader*; and the forthcoming *Abolitionists*. She is currently working with Laura Whitehorn on a critique of political incarceration in the United States.